THE ROMANIANS,

1774–1866

KEITH HITCHINS

CLARENDON PRESS · OXFORD
1996

Oxford University Press, Walton Street, Oxford OX2 6DP

Oxford New York
Athens Auckland Bangkok Bombay
Calcutta Cape Town Dar es Salaam Delhi
Florence Hong Kong Istanbul Karachi
Kuala Lumpur Madras Madrid Melbourne
Mexico City Nairobi Paris Singapore
Taipei Tokyo Toronto
and associated companies in
Berlin Ibadan

Oxford is a trade mark of Oxford University Press

Published in the United States
by Oxford University Press Inc., New York

British Library Cataloguing in Publication Data
Data available

Library of Congress Cataloging in Publication Data
Hitchins, Keith, 1931–
The Romanians, 1774–1866 / Keith Hitchins.
p. cm.
Includes bibliographical references and index.
1. Romania—History—1711–1821. 2. Romania—History—1821–1859.
3. Romania—History—1859–1866. I. Title.
DR241.H575 1996 949.8'01—dc20 95–38279
ISBN 0–19–820591–0

1 3 5 7 9 10 8 6 4 2

Typeset by Best-set Typesetter Ltd., Hong Kong
Printed in Great Britain
on acid-free paper by
Biddles Ltd., Guildford & King's Lyrn

THE ROMANIANS,

1774–1866

FOR

Renée and Dan
Eric and Yvette

PREFACE

THIS book describes a distinct period in the history of modern Romania, one of transition from long-established agrarian economic and social structures and medieval political forms to a society moulded by urban and industrial values and held together by allegiance to the nation-state. Signs of such an evolution were evident in the last quarter of the eighteenth century. Although modest and fragmentary at the beginning, the forces that were to bring about change steadily gained momentum, especially from the 1830s on. It was then that the two principalities of Moldavia and Wallachia, the core of modern Romania, were largely freed of Ottoman Turkish suzerainty and were drawn into the international political and economic order dominated by Western Europe. By the mid-1860s the institutional foundations and the new mental climate that would carry the process of nation-building into the twentieth century were largely in place.

Political events serve as the framework for this study of the early phases of nation-building. They begin with an account of men and institutions in Moldavia and Wallachia in the later eighteenth century and the early decades of the nineteenth, continue with an analysis of administrative reorganization between the 1820s and 1840s, and end with the extensive reforms of Prince Alexandru Cuza in the 1860s. It is against this background that broad trends in economic and social development and dramatic shifts of mentality are measured: the undermining of the suzerain–vassal relationship with the Ottoman Empire and the assertion of the right to self-determination; the cultivation of the idea of the ethnic nation as the foundation of community; the emergence of new ways of producing goods and doing business; and the relentless advance of Western political forms, economic models, and cultural achievements.

I am glad to have the opportunity here to remember persons who have helped to bring this book to print. Many colleagues and friends in Romania have helped me to gain an understanding of their country's history, past and present. I would like to express my gratitude to Pompiliu Teodor, Cornelia Bodea, Mihai C. Demetrescu, Ioan Beju, Mircea Păcurariu, Aurel Jivi, and Lucian Boia. The extent of my debt to others is suggested in the footnotes and the Bibliographical Essay. Sir William Deakin made many valuable comments on an early draft of the manuscript, and Maurice Pearton gave the text a thorough reading. At Oxford University Press Anthony Morris has provided constant encouragement. Colleagues in the Department of History at the University of Illinois and students in my classes have created a stimulating atmosphere in which to work. I would also like to record my debt to four historians, now dead, who expanded my understanding of history and sustained my study of it: Joseph Doty, Union College, Schenectady, New York; Andrei Oțetea, University of Bucharest; David Prodan, University of Cluj; and Robert Lee Wolff, Harvard University.

K.H.

CONTENTS

LIST OF MAPS

Note: Maps based on map No. 75, The Romanian Lands from the Eighteenth Century until 1859, in the *Atlas istoric*, Bucharest: Editura Didactică şi Pedagogică, 1971.

ABBREVIATIONS

BRV Ioan Bianu and Nerva Hodoş, *Bibliografia românească veche,1508–1830*, 4 vols. (Bucharest, 1910–44).

FM *Foaia pentru minte, inimă şi literatură.*

Hurmuzaki, *Documente* Eudoxiu de Hurmuzaki, *Documente privitoare la istoria Românilor*, 44 vols. (Bucharest, 1876–1942), and *Documente privind istoria României*, NS, 4 vols. (Bucharest, 1962–74).

Introduction

To begin a history of modern Romania in 1774 may at first glance seem odd. No epic battle and no sudden break with the past occurred in that year. Yet, in however undramatic a fashion, it marked the onset of fundamental changes in the international status and the internal political and social structure of the principalities of Moldavia and Wallachia. In 1774 Russia and the Ottoman Empire ended six years of war by signing the Treaty of Kuchuk Kainardji, which contained among its articles one granting the Russian ambassador in Constantinople the right to make 'representations' to the sultan to protect the two principalities from violations of their autonomy. In the following decades this provision offered a pretext for systematic Russian intervention in the affairs of both Moldavia and Wallachia, which slowly eroded and ultimately destroyed Ottoman suzerainty. The year 1774 also marked the accession of Alexandru Ipsilanti as Prince of Wallachia. For nearly eight years he initiated enlightened reforms in all areas of public life, thereby encouraging a general, if still modest, transformation of political and social life which continued under his successors. The decade of the 1770s taken as a whole also witnessed a significant change in the way educated Romanians thought about themselves and their relationship to Europe. This shift in mentality was symbolized by the publication in 1779 by a Romanian monk in Transylvania of a small book of prayers, *Carte de rogacioni*. It was printed in Latin rather than the traditional Cyrillic alphabet and thus stood as a declaration of the Romanians' ethnic distinctiveness and an affirmation of their bond with Europe.

The Romanians had occupied a singular place among the peoples of South-eastern Europe ever since the founding of Moldavia and Wallachia in the fourteenth century. They were, to be sure, Orthodox and, along with the Serbs, Bulgarians, and Greeks, they belonged to the Byzantine religious and cultural world. Like the South Slavs, too, they owed ecclesiastical allegiance to the Greek patriarch of Constantinople and until the seventeenth century they used Slavonic as the official language of the church and of the prince's chancellery. Until well into the eighteenth century they also shared an ecclesiastical high culture and an agrarian economic and social order common to the region as a whole. But at the same time the Romanians were different from their neighbours. They looked to the West as well as to the East, for they spoke a language derived from Latin, and they claimed descent from the Romans.

In fundamental ways the Romanians stood apart from the South Slavs and Greeks as they developed between the fifteenth and eighteenth centuries. During this long period of Ottoman domination in South-eastern Europe they succeeded in preserving their political autonomy and with it their traditional social and economic structures. As a result, the *boiers* (nobles) maintained their place as the ruling élite, and the great estates which they controlled and were worked by a large, dependent peasantry, remained the foundation of agriculture. The situation south of the Danube was strikingly different. Here the Turkish conquest of the Bulgarian and Serbian kingdoms in the fourteenth and fifteenth centuries had resulted in the destruction of native élites and the incorporation of almost the entire region into the Ottoman Empire as provinces administered by a host of Turkish civil and military officials. The community life of the South Slavs was thus largely reduced to the level of the village and the parish church. In the seventeenth century Moldavia and Wallachia continued their separate path of development, maintaining and even enhancing their autonomy. Although princes acknowledged the sultan's suzerainty and fulfilled the military and financial obligations of vassalage, they carried on direct relations with foreign countries, a blatant violation of their status, and gave unstinting support to Orthodox holy places and clergy in Ottoman-held territory. Yet, the overall effect of three centuries of Ottoman predominance was to strengthen the Romanians' links to the East. In foreign relations and trade, not to mention spiritual life and culture, they were drawn to Constantinople.

In the eighteenth century the principalities entered a period of crisis. Their autonomy became increasingly precarious as Ottoman authorities, alarmed by Austria's and Russia's relentless pressure on the empire's northern frontiers, intervened at will in their affairs. The sultan appointed and dismissed princes as it suited him, imposed unprecedented taxes, and drained the countries of their agricultural wealth through requisitions and forced sales. It was at this low point in their fortunes in the 1770s that patriotic Romanian *boiers* and intellectuals turned to Orthodox Russia to avert the catastrophe that had overtaken their neighbours south of the Danube.

The course of events between the 1770s and the 1860s reveals one central fact about the evolution of the principalities—their steady integration into Europe. 'Integration', not 'Westernization', is the proper word, since their reception of European models and experience was an act of adaptation rather than of imitation. The process assumed tangible form in the 1830s, when a new intellectual and political élite coalesced. Educated in the West and deeply troubled by the disparities they observed between Western material advances and intellectual dynamism, on the one hand, and the seemingly intractable backwardness at home, on the other, they set out to stir men's minds and reform institutions. In the decades that followed they relentlessly pursued their agenda at the expense of the Romanians' Orthodox, Eastern heritage. While they adopted an urban, commercial outlook on life, the religious and folk traditions of earlier centuries continued to animate the peasantry and others in the rural world. Here was a separation that was to have profound consequences, not the least of which was a widening of the material and spiritual gulf between the city and the village and between the élite and the mass of the population.

The salient characteristic of internal political development in the principalities between the 1770s and the 1860s was the gradual rationalization of government. Reformers among the princes and the élite engaged in a sustained effort to codify the law, to introduce a separation of powers between the executive, legislative, and judicial branches, to bring order to public finances, and to create a well-trained, professional bureaucracy. The general consequences of all these measures were undoubtedly greater efficiency and predictability of administration, but the concentration of power in the hands of the prince and the central organs of government deprived local officials of authority and discouraged local participation and initiative in public affairs. None the less, at the centre—in Bucharest, the capital of Wallachia, and in Iaşi, the capital of Moldavia—political activity became better organized as individuals, linked by principles as well as by class, formed groups and eventually parties to achieve their ends.

Marked changes also occurred in the structure of society. The great *boiers*, the leading economic and political force of the old regime, whose status depended upon the control of land, saw their monopoly of power undermined as the economy of the principalities became diversified and the opportunities to acquire wealth and social position multiplied. Their most formidable competition came from the emerging native middle class. Composed of small groups of wealthy merchants and businessmen and members of the liberal professions, notably lawyers, it was well on its way to becoming the chief bearer of the entrepreneurial spirit in both the economy and politics. Social differentiation also intensified within the mass of the peasantry, who constituted the overwhelming majority of the population. Caused primarily by the penetration of capitalism into the countryside, it increased the number of well-off peasants, but the bulk of the peasantry remained at the bottom of the social scale, able only to eke out a bare existence. Somewhat apart from traditional class structures stood a small number of intellectuals, many of them the sons of *boiers*, who looked to Western Europe to provide models of political and economic development. Together with the middle class and a few *boiers* they formed the new élite that gradually assumed direction of the country's fortunes.

This élite was the bearer of a new conception of community, which decisively affected the development of modern Romania. In the past the Orthodox commonwealth of Greeks, Slavs, and Romanians, the legacy of Byzantium, had provided the moral framework for individual and public endeavours. But in the later decades of the eighteenth century a handful of Romanian intellectuals had begun to define community from a different perspective. Terms such as 'fatherland' and 'nation', both used in an ethnic sense, appeared with increasing frequency in discussions about how to organize politically and how to ensure the general good. By the 1830s the idea of the ethnic nation had come to absorb the energies of the élite as they assumed the task, almost as a sacred mission, to bring about the union and independence of Moldavia and Wallachia. They also sought a new spiritual foundation upon which to build the united Romania and chose the brand of secularism nourished by enlightened and liberal thought in Western Europe as their guide. They thus fostered a system of ethics independent of religious teachings and based upon the supposedly natural attributes of human beings, and they systematically reduced the role of the Orthodox Church in public affairs to the performance of its strictly religious functions.

The rhythm of change in the economy lagged behind that of political institutions and mentalities. Agriculture, in particular, displayed a stubborn resistance to innovation. Its organization and methods of production were essentially the same as in previous centuries: peasants continued to supply the labour, tools and draft animals, and the majority of them remained economically dependent on the masters of the large estates. Industry, too, was bound by the past: the bulk of goods continued to be made in small artisan shops, and the guild system remained the overseer of production and distribution. But change there was, none the less, as capitalist forms and procedures made gradual inroads on tradition. Agriculture was affected by the steady advance of private property and the relentless breakdown of the communal village and by the mounting demands of the international market for Romanian agricultural products, especially grain. In the cities artisans and their guilds were under siege from imports of foreign consumer goods and from the local 'manufactory', the forerunner of the modern factory. More difficult to measure, but no less crucial to economic progress, was a change of attitude towards investment and profit, as a new spirit of enterprise emerged at least as early as the 1830s.

Underlying internal developments in the principalities was the change in their international status brought about through competition among the great powers to gain predominance in the region, on the one hand, and the determination of the Romanian political and intellectual élite to pursue independence, on the other. The intervention of the powers in the affairs of the principalities had profound effects on their evolution, since it loosened their ties to both the Ottoman state and the Orthodox cultural world and accelerated their integration into Europe. The Romanian élite was thus confronted by a crisis of identity and challenged by new models of development. Their growing consciousness of the dichotomy between East and West and the choices they made are the substance of Romanian history between the 1770s and the 1860s.

1
Moldavia and Wallachia, 1774–1821

OTTOMAN suzerainty was the overwhelming fact of political and economic life for the Romanian principalities during the period bounded by the Treaty of Kuchuk Kainardji of 1774 and the beginning of the Greek War for Independence in 1821. The sultan determined the succession of princes and decisively influenced their policies, and his demands for foodstuffs and other supplies at once strained and spurred the productive capacity of Moldavia and Wallachia. Nevertheless, this was a dynamic half-century for the principalities, and vassalage, however onerous, could neither stop the evolution of institutions nor stifle the spread of ideas. The rationalization of government, the concentration of power in the hands of the prince and the expansion of the bureaucracy, the codification of laws, and the secularization of public life, all hallmarks of modern society, moved forward inexorably. Nor was Ottoman suzerainty itself immune to change. Certain enlightened princes and reforming nobles took advantage of growing Russian and Western European interest in the principalities to try to cast off Ottoman predominance and replace it with autonomy and, eventually, independence.

THE OTTOMAN CONNECTION

Political relations between the Ottoman Empire and Moldavia and Wallachia had their beginnings in the final decade of the fourteenth century. Hardly had the principalities taken form in the first half of that century when their very existence was threatened by rising Ottoman military power south of the Danube. Ottoman armies had overwhelmed the Serbian feudal nobility on Kossovo Field in 1389 and had completed the conquest of Bulgaria with the seizure of its capital, Trnovo, in 1393. As a result, all that stood between them and the Romanian principalities was the Danube, which had traditionally served as an avenue into the interior of the peninsula rather than as a barrier to hostile armies.

The first political contacts between Wallachia and the Ottomans cannot be dated precisely, but the first payment of the tribute (*haradj*) may have been made as early as 1394, an event which suggests that the Turks were eager to follow up their successes in Bulgaria without delay. Another payment of the tribute was made in 1417, following a military expedition into Wallachia by Sultan Mehmed I (1413–21).[1] These payments do not appear to have reduced Wallachia to vassal status. Rather, as Prince Mircea the Old (1386–1418) claimed, they signified

---

[1] M. Maxim, 'Din istoria relaţiilor româno-otomane—"capitulaţiile" ', *Anale de istorie*, 28/6 (1982), 45–8.

arrangements between equals, since in return for the tribute the sultan agreed to prevent Ottoman forces from crossing the Danube for plunder and slaves.[2] Yet, Wallachia was henceforth subject to unremitting Ottoman pressure. Following a series of new military campaigns after the death of Mircea the sultans imposed increasingly heavy burdens on the principality. In 1432, for example, as the price of peace, Prince Alexandru Aldea (1431–6) was forced to pay an annual tribute and to render military service at the sultan's pleasure. Similar arrangements, rather like armistices, were concluded in 1444 and 1451. Finally, in 1462 Mehmed II (1451–81) drove Prince Vlad Ţepeş (1456–62) from the throne as punishment for 'rebellion' and installed the more pliant Radu cel Frumos (1462–73) in his place. That the sultan could dispose so freely of the succession suggests how severely Wallachia's independence had been compromised, and many historians have thus taken 1462 as the beginning of Wallachia's formal vassalage to the Ottoman Empire.[3] In any case, these events marked the end of large-scale military confrontations between the two parties. Henceforth, Wallachian princes regarded payment of the tribute as an unavoidable obligation and resorted to negotiation rather than arms to protect their country's administrative autonomy.

Moldavia's submission to the Ottoman state followed a similar pattern, but it came later, partly at least because of her greater distance from Ottoman centres of power. The first important engagement between Moldavian and Ottoman armies occurred in 1420, when the latter unsuccessfully attacked Cetatea Albă (Akkerman), a Moldavian port on the estuary of the Dniester River. Afterwards, Moldavian princes maintained generally peaceful relations with the sultan through money payments. The Turks referred to these as gifts (peşkeş), not haradj, and they do not seem to have compromised Moldavian independence. Moldavia began to pay the tribute in 1456 in response to an ultimatum from Mehmed II to Prince Petru Aron (1451–2, 1454–7). None the less, Moldavian rulers, in particular the gifted Ştefan cel Mare (1457–1504), avoided vassalage by alternating negotiation with armed resistance. But under Ştefan's successors Moldavia's situation became increasingly precarious. Independence came to an end in 1538, when Sultan Suleiman I (1520–66) drove Prince Petru Rareş (1527–38, 1541–6) from the throne. He replaced him with Ştefan Lăcustă (1538–40), who did homage to the sultan as his suzerain, thereby acknowledging the vassal status of his country.[4]

Relations between the principalities and the Ottoman Empire came to be regulated by various treaties, known as ahdnames or sulhnames, which were later known, inaccurately, as capitulations, and by supplementary writs of appointment (berats), issued by sultans to princes upon their accession to the throne. In

---

[2] G. I. Constantin, 'Le Traité entre le Sultan Baiazet Ier et la Valachie', Der Islam, 59/2 (1982), 254–84; M. Maxim, 'Cu privire la înţelegerile de pace româno-otomane din timpul domniei lui Mircea cel Mare', in I. Pătroiu (ed.), Marele Mircea Voievod (Bucharest, 1987), 365–96.

[3] N. Stoicescu, Vlad Ţepeş (Bucharest, 1976), 120–4.

[4] L. Şimanschi (ed.), Petru Rareş (Bucharest, 1978), 136–74.

accordance with Islamic law, the Ottomans regarded the Romanian principalities as lying between conquered territories, which were subject to direct Muslim rule, and areas outside the boundaries of Islam, which were hostile to the Muslim state and with which there could be only temporary peace. Moldavia and Wallachia were thus *ahd* (treaty) territories and lay in the intermediate zone of peace (*dar al-sulh*), since they had not been occupied by Ottoman armies and had not been incorporated into the Ottoman state.[5] Instead, the princes and *boiers* (nobles) were allowed, in theory at least, to manage as before the internal affairs of their respective countries without interference from Turkish military and civil officials. Under this arrangement the *boiers* preserved their traditional privilege of electing the prince, but now the sultan assumed the right to confirm their choice and to invest the new prince with the insignia of office. The tangible signs of submission were payment of an annual tribute and participation in Ottoman military campaigns when summoned. Another consequence of vassalage was the cessation of direct diplomatic relations with foreign countries. Henceforth, the princes were forbidden to have contacts with European states except through Constantinople.

The relationship between the two parties was far from one-sided, at least at the beginning. The sultan assumed formal obligations of his own towards the principalities. As their suzerain he took responsibility for their defence against foreign attack, but refrained from garrisoning Ottoman troops in either principality, except for a small personal guard for each prince. He instructed Ottoman officials along the Danube to enforce strictly the prohibition against Muslims' acquiring land or settling permanently in the principalities. That prohibition was extended to all Ottoman merchants and officials, who were allowed to travel north of the Danube only on official business and with the consent of the prince or his representatives.

The princes and *boiers* in the sixteenth and seventeenth centuries insisted that these restrictions be rigidly enforced in order to prevent a massive influx of Turks and other Muslims north of the Danube and thus preserve a semblance of autonomy and the Christian character of their countries. But they were only partially successful. Ottoman military and commercial bridgeheads, the so-called *raya*s, were established in Wallachia on the north banks of the Danube at Giurgiu and Turnu as early as 1417 and at Brăila in 1542, and in Moldavia at Hotin on the northern border with Poland in 1723.

All the *raya*s were organized in the same fashion, but Brăila was the largest and economically the most important. The bridgehead consisted of a fortress, which the Turks built immediately after they occupied the city in 1539, together with the *raya* properly speaking, that is, the territory around the city which

[5] Ş. Gorovei, 'Moldova în "Casa păcii" pe marginea izvoarelor privind primul secol de relaţii moldo-otomane', *Anuarul Institutului de Istorie şi Arheologie*, 17 (1980), 629–77; M. Maxim, 'Cu privire la statutul de *'Ahd* al ţărilor române faţă de Poartă: Consideraţii pe marginea unor izvoare otomane', *Revista de istorie*, 39/6 (1986), 523–34.

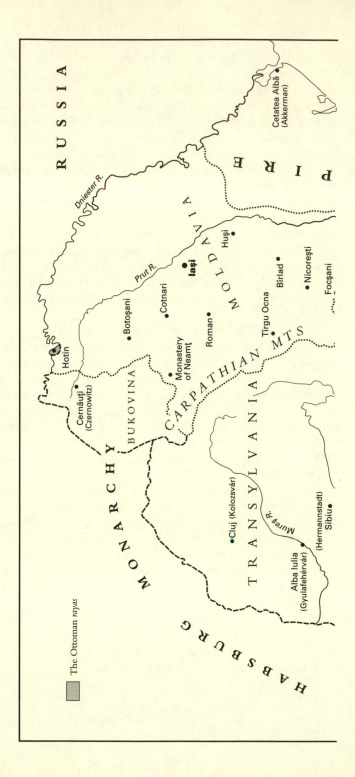

The Ottoman *rayas*

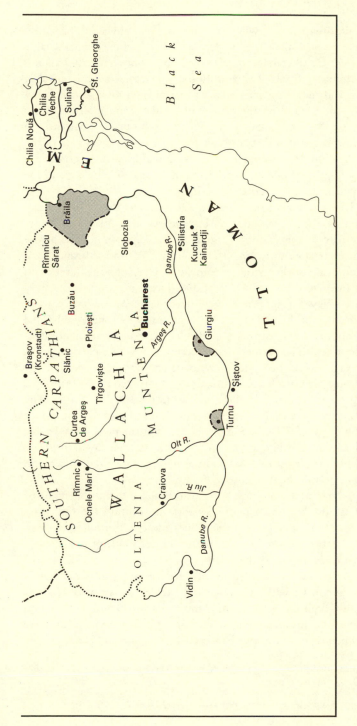

MAP 1. Moldavia, Wallachia, and Transylvania, 1775–1811

encompassed some fifty-five villages, whose inhabitants were obliged to provision the fortress and perform various labour services. The *raya* also contained large properties which were distributed as fiefs (*hasses*) to members of the sultan's family and high Ottoman officials. The administrator (*nazir*), who had jurisdiction over both civil and military affairs, was a pasha of high rank, usually with three *tuğs* (horsetails) on his standard (the princes of Moldavia and Wallachia were entitled to only two). Muslim judges (*kadis*) rendered justice to Muslims in disputes among themselves and with Christians. Along with the governor of the *sanjak* (county; subdivision of a province) of Silistra, within whose jurisdiction Brăila fell, all these officials exercised a significant influence in Wallachia, and the princes strove to remain on good terms with them.[6]

The first formal treaty (*ahdname*) between the Ottomans and the principalities was concluded with Wallachia probably during the reign of Vlad I (1394–7; recognized in only part of the country) and with Moldavia sometime before 1456. These and later treaties were, in effect, alliances of unequals and were extended indefinitely and usually without formality. The last formal renewals seem to have been made in the second half of the sixteenth century.[7] The links which they reinforced between the parties were never static. In the latter part of the sixteenth and throughout the seventeenth century the equilibrium established by the early treaties broke down as princes and sultans pursued goals incompatible with a genuine truce. The former strove continuously to free themselves from Ottoman tutelage, while the latter left no device untried to reduce the principalities to complete subservience. Although Ottoman control during this period gradually tightened, structurally the relationship remained the same. The sultans continued to exercise their powers by indirect means through the prince and native institutions, a method which allowed the Romanians a considerable degree of internal autonomy. The princes thus retained their own, if small, armies, exercised traditional legislative and judicial powers, and even engaged in diplomatic exchanges with foreign countries.

The threat of incorporation into the Ottoman Empire all but disappeared during this period. By the beginning of the seventeenth century the Ottomans had given up the idea of occupying the principalities and transforming them into *pashaliks* (provinces), as they had done with the territories south of the Danube and with two-thirds of Hungary to the north. The causes appear to lie in the changing strategic and economic calculations of Ottoman officials. When Ottoman armies first made contact with Wallachia and Moldavia they were engaged in major campaigns through the Serbian lands and along the Danube valley into Central Europe. The principalities were of little strategic importance for these operations. Later, when these campaigns had been successfully completed, Otto-

    [6] R. I. Perianu, 'Raiaua Brăilei: Noi contribuţiuni', *Revista istorică română*, 15/3 (1945), 287–333.
    [7] For a wide-ranging discussion of autonomy, see M. Maxim, 'Le Statut des pays roumains envers la Porte ottomane aux xvie–xviiie siècles', *Revue roumaine d'histoire*, 24/1–2 (1985), 29–50.

man suzerainty over Moldavia and Wallachia was not seriously challenged by other European powers until the end of the seventeenth century. Consequently, neither the protection of supply lines to Hungary nor an exposed frontier status required a military occupation of the principalities.[8] Moreover, by the time Ottoman conquests in South-eastern and Central Europe had run their course a working relationship between the sultan and the Romanian princes based on the *ahdname*s had taken form and had proved a boon to the Ottoman treasury. Countless economic benefits persuaded the sultans and their bureaucracy not to tamper with existing arrangements. Instead, they intensified the fiscal and agricultural exploitation of the principalities as far more profitable than a military occupation and the division of the arable land into *timar*s (fiefs). Existing economic relations, which tapped the enormous natural resources of the principalities, brought such substantial benefits to all concerned, not least to merchants and bankers, whose influence in Constantinople was on the rise, that successive sultans rejected all proposals to reduce Moldavia and Wallachia to the status of provinces under Turkish governors. The willingness of the Moldavians and Wallachians to negotiate also facilitated a peaceful accommodation with the Ottomans. They were prepared to fight, and did on numerous occasions, but their princes seem to have grasped the political and strategic realities of their situation. They thought it wise to parley before their independence had been irrevocably compromised.

None the less, the seventeenth century witnessed the inexorable decay of Moldavian and Wallachian autonomy. Although strong princes like Matei Basarab (1632–54) and Şerban Cantacuzino (1678–88) of Wallachia and Vasile Lupu (1634–53) of Moldavia reasserted their prerogatives in foreign and military affairs, such revivals proved short-lived. By the end of the century the sultan had come to regard the prince simply as a high Ottoman functionary, and, as a consequence, the princely throne had become notoriously insecure. The sultan removed princes almost at will and with startling frequency in order to strengthen his hold over incumbents and to increase the financial benefits he derived from a change of ruler. In Moldavia between 1612 and 1711 the average reign lasted two and a half years, and in Wallachia during roughly the same period four and a half years. Yet, the prince's authority in domestic affairs was little diminished by his vassal status. If he was capable and had secured the favour of the sultan and his advisers, he could conduct himself as an absolute ruler at home.

The political subservience of the principalities was accompanied by mounting fiscal and economic burdens. As tributary states they had to assume numerous formal obligations to their suzerain besides payment of the tribute. Among them were extraordinary contributions to the Ottoman treasury to support military

[8] P. P. Panaitescu, *Interpretări româneşti: Studii de istorie economică şi socială* (Bucharest, 1947), 149–59.

campaigns, military service itself, the recruitment of labourers for various tasks such as the repair of fortresses along the Danube, and, of increasing importance as time passed, the delivery of provisions (*zahire*) to the Ottoman army and to Contantinople.

An even more onerous burden and a more pernicious influence on public life than these state-to-state obligations was the endless stream of gifts required to placate the sultan, his family, and countless officials high and low. Some were made at specified times, as on the accession to the throne of a new sultan, when munificence was the measure of the prince's personal loyalty. Then there were the payments, in effect bribes, which candidates for the thrones of both principalities made to the sultan and others to gain their goodwill. As early as the second half of the sixteenth century the princely throne had become the object of spirited bidding, and the sums offered by those in the running often reached enormous proportions, as much as seven times the annual tribute. By this time it had become customary for every negotiation or agreement to be accompanied by gifts, their size depending upon the rank and influence of the recipient.

As loyal vassals, the princes were expected to make available animals and foodstuffs to their suzerain whenever he requested them. The delivery of supplies probably began in the fifteenth century and became a regular feature of Romanian–Ottoman relations in the sixteenth century. The Ottomans transformed their commercial relations with the principalities into a virtual monopoly in the second half of that century.[9] The dependence of Constantinople and the army on foodstuffs and other supplies from the principalities led Sultan Suleiman I and his successors to restrict the export of cattle, sheep, wheat and other grains, honey, and timber from the principalities to other countries until Ottoman needs had been satisfied. They obliged the princes to oversee the collection and shipment of these supplies and to assist Ottoman merchants in obtaining the necessary quantities at the lowest possible prices. Both principalities were periodically flooded by Ottoman and other merchants from the Eastern Mediterranean, who enjoyed a distinct advantage over native merchants. All these practices ensured the economic vassalage of the principalities, which was to last until the early decades of the nineteenth century and was to drain them of much of their wealth.

In the eighteenth century Ottoman political control over the principalities tightened, and economic exploitation intensified. In the first decades of that century the Ottoman court lost confidence in the native princes. The immediate cause was the alliance between Dimitrie Cantemir (1710–11) of Moldavia and Peter the Great of Russia and the secret dealings with Austria and other powers by Constantin Brâncoveanu (1688–1714) of Wallachia. The sultan removed both from their thrones, and to replace them he turned to a group that had served the

[9] M. Maxim, 'Regimul economic al dominaţiei otomane în Moldova şi Ţara Românească în a două jumătate a secolului al XVI-lea', *Revista de istorie*, 32/9 (1979), 1731–65.

empire loyally for over a century—the wealthy Greek families of the Phanar district of Constantinople. Because of their commercial skills, wealth, and knowledge of Europe and of European languages, these Phanariot families and numerous other Greek or Hellenized families had rendered invaluable services to the Ottoman court and, as a consequence, had acquired immense influence in high places, especially in the office for foreign affairs. Here, they occupied such key positions as grand dragomans, or chief interpreters (and, in effect chief advisers), in dealings with the great powers of Europe.[10]

The Phanariots were thus logical candidates for the thrones of Moldavia and Wallachia. Their loyalty had become all the more indispensable because the principalities were now on the frontiers of the empire and were the objects of increasing Austrian and Russian interest. The sultans expected the Phanariot princes to oppose foreign encroachments and further the political and economic integration of the principalities into the empire.

This partnership laid the foundations of the so-called Phanariot regime, the specific form which Ottoman domination of the principalities assumed in the eighteenth century.[11] It increased the prince's dependence upon the goodwill of the sultan, and the modest freedom of action he had retained in foreign affairs all but disappeared. Even the formality of an election was discontinued after 1730, the last known instance when the *boiers* were allowed a voice in choosing their prince. The national army disintegrated and was reduced to ceremonial functions and guard duty for the prince. The princes were allowed to maintain contact with foreign countries, but not for their own benefit. Rather, they served as agents and gatherers of information for their suzerain.

Ottoman fiscal and economic demands upon the principalities in the eighteenth century were practically boundless. Their amounts reflected the general crisis that had overtaken the empire. To the tribute and gifts were added the expenses of the competition for the princely thrones. To stay in the running and win the prize the successful candidate incurred enormous debts, which he did not hesitate to pass on to the taxpayers of his new realm. Although these debts were supposed to be private, as soon as the new prince arrived in his capital he raised taxes or resorted to other stratagems to pay off creditors and discourage rivals for his throne. The Ottoman court and bureaucracy took full advantage of the situation. To make a good business better they changed princes with dizzying frequency, often moving them from one principality to the other and back again. The traffic became most intense in the middle of the century: Wallachia had no fewer than eighteen princes between 1730 and 1768, and Moldavia seventeen

---

[10] On the career of an outstanding representative of the group, see N. Camariano, *Alexandre Mavrocordato, le Grand Drogman: Son activité diplomatique (1673–1709)* (Thessaloniki, 1970).

[11] On the character of the Phanariot regime, see Ş. Lemny, 'La Critique du régime phanariote: Clichés mentaux et perspectives historiographiques', in A. Zub (ed.), *Culture and Society* (Iaşi, 1985), 17–30; C. Papacostea-Danielopolu, 'État actuel des recherches sur "l'époque phanariote"', *Revue des études sud-est européennes*, 24/3 (1986), 227–34.

between 1733 and 1769. During this period Constantin Mavrocordat was prince of Wallachia six times and of Moldavia four times.

The deliveries of supplies to Constantinople and the fortresses along the Danube became veritable requisitions. The change in the Ottoman attitude towards provisioning was manifest in a decree of 1755 of Sultan Osman III (1754–7), who required each principality to send 11,000 tons of wheat annually to Constantinople at a price set by Ottoman officials. The dependence of the capital and the army upon foodstuffs from the principalities led to a tightening of Ottoman commercial restrictions. As early as 1729 Sultan Ahmed III (1703–30) had forbidden Prince Nicolae Mavrocordat of Wallachia to sell wheat grown along the Danube to the Austrians on the grounds that such sales might reduce the grain reserves of the capital. Throughout the eighteenth century Ottoman authorities insisted that the needs of the empire came first, and, accordingly, they took drastic action whenever supplies grew short, as in 1761 and 1764, when the sultan temporarily suspended exports of grain and animals to other countries.[12]

As the autonomy of the principalities steadily deteriorated prohibitions against the settlement of Muslims and limitations on their activities were violated with impunity. Turks and other Ottoman subjects acquired land in the vicinity of the *raya*s and settled on it; Turkish merchants bought large quantities of grain and animals from peasants on their own account at prices well below the market average; and the large number of Ottoman officials travelling through the principalities required the local population to pay for their food, lodging, and transportation (the so-called right of *conac și olac*). Efforts by the princes and *boier*s to persuade the Ottoman court to curtail these abuses were generally fruitless, in part because the central government could not enforce its own decrees on officials along the Danube frontier and in the *raya*s. The principalities thus bore the consequences of the general breakdown of Ottoman administration in South-eastern Europe.

THE MORE THINGS CHANGE

The Treaty of Kuchuk Kainardji, which ended the Russo-Turkish War of 1768–74, promised significant changes in the relations between the principalities and their suzerain. Although the treaty was concerned mainly with other matters, it contained at least one provision, which, if carried out, would curtail the powers exercised by Ottoman officials over the principalities. Article 16 gave the Russian ambassador in Constantinople the right to make representations on behalf of the principalities 'when circumstances required', and obliged the Ottoman government to give such interventions a sympathetic hearing.[13] In the next half-century,

---

[12] M. M. Alexandrescu-Dersca, 'A propos d'un firman du sultan Mustafa III', *Balcania*, 7/2 (1944), 363–91.

[13] On the significance of Article 16, see E. I. Druzhinina, *Kiuchuk-Kainardzhiiskii mir* (Moscow, 1955), 295–300.

in fact, Russian diplomats, exercising their new prerogative, helped to lay the foundations of a new legal status for the principalities. In part because of such pressure, the sultan was obliged to define more precisely the ties which bound the principalities to the empire, and in the process he grudgingly recognized the long-ignored principle of autonomy.

A few months after the conclusion of peace in 1774, in response to Russian demands, the sultan issued rescripts (*hatti-sherifs*) to the princes of Moldavia and Wallachia which imposed drastic limits on Ottoman political suzerainty and economic privileges. They recognized in principle the autonomy which the *ahdnames* had guaranteed several centuries earlier and thus curtailed the power of the Ottoman bureaucracy to intervene in the internal affairs of the principalities. They forbade the sultan to depose princes without sufficient cause and removed legal cases involving Christians and Muslims along the frontier and in the *raya*s from the jurisdiction of Muslim judges, designating instead the prince's privy council as the court of first instance and the *kadi* courts of Giurgiu (for Wallachia) and Brăila (for Moldavia) as courts of appeal. The rescripts also restricted the entrance of Ottoman civil and military personnel and merchants into the principalities to those who were on official business and had obtained the necessary permission from Wallachian and Moldavian authorities. Finally, they forbade Turks to settle permanently in the principalities, to own landed property there, or to engage in agriculture or cattle raising, and they required all lands taken from monasteries and individual Christians near the *raya*s to be returned without delay.[14]

Most of these injunctions remained on paper. The Ottoman government simply ignored the provisions of the Treaty of Kuchuk Kainardji and the *hatti-sherifs* of 1774. It continued to interfere as before in the internal affairs of the principalities and raised its economic demands still higher, until new wars and treaties with Russia temporarily brought a measure of relief.

In a sense, the Ottoman government had no choice but to persist in its economic exploitation of the principalities. In the last quarter of the eighteenth and the early decades of the nineteenth century Constantinople and the Danube fortresses were so dependent upon them for foodstuffs that Moldavia and Wallachia were repeatedly referred to in official correspondence as the 'granaries of the empire'. The quantities demanded were often staggering. For example, between December 1786 and April 1788, as a new war with Russia seemed imminent, Ottoman military commanders ordered from Moldavia 219,833 Constantinople *kile* of wheat (1 Constantinople *kile* = approximately 26 kg.), or 5,715,000 kg., 265,267 *kile* of barley (6,796,000 kg.), 119,631 *kile* of flour (2,937,000 kg.), and, in the first nine months of 1787, 117,000 sheep.[15] It is by no means certain that all these demands were met, but for his zeal in trying to

[14] M. M. Alexandrescu-Dersca, 'Rolul hatişerifurilor de privilegii în limitarea obligaţiilor către Poarta (1774–1802)', *Studii: Revistă de istorie*, 11/6 (1958), 101–19; M. A. Mehmed (ed.), *Documente turceşti privind istoria României*, i. *1455–1774* (Bucharest, 1976), 319–28.

[15] M. A. Mehmed (ed.), *Documente turceşti*, ii. *1774–1791* (Bucharest, 1983), 155–302.

satisfy them Prince Alexandru Ipsilanti drew high praise from the sultan himself. As usual, the burden fell almost exclusively upon the peasantry. Besides agricultural produce, the Ottomans demanded lumber for the repair of fortresses along the Danube and the border with Russia and for the construction of bridges and ships, and ordered the princes to mobilize skilled artisans and labourers to perform these tasks. The exact quantities of lumber and the numbers of workers, sometimes as many as 2,000 at a time, were left to the discretion of local military commanders. These officials took little account of conditions in the principalities when drawing up their lists of requisitions. As a result, by the time the Russo-Turkish War of 1787–92 had ended, both sides acknowledged the desperate economic situation of the principalities and in the Treaty of Iaşi (1792) granted them relief from provisioning for two years. But the Ottoman government ignored the stipulation. It immediately ordered new deliveries of foodstuffs for Constantinople, and in 1792 Wallachia provided 265,554 *kile* of wheat and barley, an enormous quantity at a time when the peasants of Oltenia were making flour from acorns and eating moss from trees. Nor did the great famine of 1794–6 in the principalities cause the Ottoman government to moderate its demands. In the next two decades it continued to rely upon large quantities of Wallachian and Moldavian animals and grain, especially sheep and wheat. Other products were also in demand. In 1819, for example, substantial amounts of *caşcaval* (sheep's cheese; 230,400 kg.), *seu topit* (animal fat; 2,280,960 kg.), *grăsime* (tallow; 136,960 kg.), and *miere* (honey; 72,960 kg.) were acquired in Wallachia for the provisioning of Constantinople.[16]

The allocation and collection of all these provisions proceeded in time-honoured fashion. The total quantity of the provisions was divided by districts (*judeţe*) and subdivided by villages. The district prefects (*ispravnici*), aided by *boiers* and clergy, took overall charge of the operation. The actual collection was the occasion for numerous abuses: quantities greater than those demanded by the Turks were taken (the difference was appropriated by local *boiers* and officials); payment was made by receipt rather than in cash (the receipt might never be redeemed); or the items were simply taken by force. Ottoman merchants often shared in this organized pillage. The only recourse left to the peasant producer was revolt, a powerful weapon which impressed the bureaucracy, since prolonged violence would disrupt collection and delivery, reduce profits, and strain relations with Constantinople. Although Ottoman authorities assumed formal responsibility for payment of the provisions, in fact, they often required their delivery without payment. Even when producers were compensated, they sometimes ended up paying for their own grain and animals, since the prince might impose new taxes to cover his own expenses as middleman, as Nicolae Caragea of Wallachia did in 1783.

A landmark in economic relations between the principalities and their suzerain

[16] M. Guboglu, *Catalogul documentelor turceşti*, i (Bucharest, 1960), 261–73.

was the *hatti-sherif* issued by Sultan Selim III (1789–1807) in 1802 under Russian pressure. For the first time the Ottoman government took into account the capacity of the principalities to supply the required goods and acknowledged the right of the prince to negotiate quantities and prices with Ottoman officials.[17] In a sense, these concessions were a response to changes taking place in the market on the lower Danube caused by increasing international interest in Romanian agricultural products. Competition required a modification of the old price-fixing mechanism, and the sultan thus allowed the give and take of merchants in Brăila to influence the prices of goods.

The principal entrepôt for the *zahire* in the eighteenth and early nineteenth century was Brăila, the most important Wallachian port on the Danube. Here wheat, barley, lumber, and many other products from every part of the principality were warehoused until they could be shipped to Constantinople and other Ottoman ports. So important had the grain trade through Brăila become that much of it was conducted in a new unit of measure—the *chilă* (*kile*) of Brăila, which was roughly 307 kg. The price of grain at Brăila was determined by a variety of circumstances, notably the abundance of the crop and the prevailing political situation (war or peace and the urgency of Ottoman needs).[18] The price offered by Ottoman officials and merchants was invariably lower than the value of the grain on the international market, but it could not fall so low as to discourage the producer from raising sufficient quantities. Nor was it in the interest of the prince to acquiesce in the wholesale spoliation of the peasants, for such treatment would undermine their capacity to pay state taxes. The new mechanisms for establishing prices assured continued deliveries of supplies to Constantinople until the eve of the Wallachian and Greek uprisings of 1821.

State-to-state obligations and the competition for the princely thrones continued to drain both principalities of substantial wealth. Following the Treaty of Kuchuk Kainardji the sultan had set the amount of the tribute for Wallachia at 619 *pungi* (*pungă*, sack) and for Moldavia at 135 *pungi*. By 1812 these sums had risen to 1,000 and 500 *pungi* respectively. The *rikabiyye* (an annual tax paid to the sultan to cover the expenses of his retinue) paid by Wallachia increased from 80 to 500 *pungi* and by Moldavia from 50 to 300 *pungi*. Princes continued to spend immense sums of money to obtain and keep their thrones. Alexandru Mavrocordat is reputed to have bought the throne of Moldavia in 1782 for the enormous sum of one million piastres. In the final decade of the century the efforts of princes to maintain themselves on the throne of Moldavia took at least half the principality's annual income of four million piastres. Failure to pay the required sums often meant exile and the confiscation of the prince's private fortune.

[17] M. A. Mehmed (ed.), *Documente turcești*, iii. *1791–1812* (Bucharest, 1986), 167–77; T. Ionescu, 'Hatișeriful de 1802 și începutul luptei pentru asigurarea pieții interne a principatelor dunăene', *Studii și articole de istorie*, i (Bucharest, 1956), 37–78.
[18] C. C. Giurescu, *Istoricul orașului Brăila* (Bucharest, 1968), 97–115.

The cumulative effect of Ottoman domination—specifically, whether it was primarily responsible for the economic underdevelopment of the principalities—has long been a subject of controversy, but an accurate assessment must await further research in Ottoman archives. Although the evidence for certain periods suggests an affirmative response to the question, recent studies have shown that Ottoman restraints on Moldavian and Wallachian trade never amounted to a monopoly, but were, in fact, the exercise of the right of pre-emption over certain goods.[19] Still other studies, on the seventeenth century, have shown how the principalities regularly directed much of their commerce to the markets of Central Europe, how their prosperity depended upon the demands of consumers and the fluctuation of prices in that quarter, and how the Ottoman Empire itself served as an indispensable market for the goods of the principalities.[20]

What is clear is that neither the treaties between Russia and the Ottoman Empire nor the *hatti-sherifs* issued periodically by the sultan brought tangible changes in the political subordination of the principalities to the Ottoman Empire or diminished their economic obligations. But at the same time, new forces, the harbingers of change, were already making themselves felt. A reform party among both Moldavian and Wallachian *boiers* pressed unceasingly for autonomy and internal political reform, and the great powers began to discern a 'Romanian problem' within the broader Eastern Question.

THE STATE AND ITS BUSINESS

The political, legal, and fiscal institutions of the principalities in the final half-century of Ottoman domination had not yet assumed modern forms. Executive and judicial functions remained intertwined; civil and church law overlapped; and annual budgets and a precise accounting of state income and expenditures still lay in the future. None the less, several important innovations in public administration were already manifest: the codification of law had been undertaken and the principle of separation of powers proclaimed as ways of rationalizing the judicial system; the concentration of political power in the hands of the prince and of an expanding central bureaucracy was proceeding relentlessly at the expense of the provincial *boiers* and local governments; and secularizing currents among the educated were undermining the influence of religion and the role of the clergy in civil institutions.

The weight of Ottoman political and economic domination affected the development of public administration in important, if not always easily discernible, ways. Institutions, geared to satisfying the myriad fiscal and economic demands of the suzerain state, evolved as circumstances demanded. Unrelenting

---

[19] Id., *Probleme controversate în istoriografia română* (Bucharest, 1977), 111–22.

[20] B. Murgescu, 'Impactul conjuncturii europene asupra comerțului românesc în a două jumătate a secolului al XVII-lea', *Revista de istorie*, 41/5 (1988), 514–24, and 41/6, 587–96.

and arbitrary Ottoman intervention in the internal political affairs of the principalities—the frequent depositions of princes are only the most striking example—disrupted the continuity of administration and, by creating a climate of fear and uncertainty, helped to discourage government by firm rules and rational procedures.

The political system in place during the period can best be described as an oligarchy. Power was exercised by the prince and the great *boiers*. The prince retained considerable authority under Ottoman suzerainty, even as the autonomy of the country deteriorated in the eighteenth century. The initiative in defining and carrying out public policy was his, but he could not manage the internal affairs of the country or satisfy the demands of his suzerain without the support of the leading *boiers*. Despite continuous tension between them, they were one in their commitment to preserving the existing social and economic order.

A striking feature of political development was the failure of representative institutions to become a forceful presence. The causes were many. The *boiers*, who had every reason to limit princely authority, lacked cohesion. They were divided by rank and wealth and competed among themselves for their prince's favour and were thus rarely able to mount an effective opposition to his policies. The absence of a strong native middle class, with a stake in rational, limited government, also explains the absence of strong representative bodies and the preponderance of the executive. But Ottoman domination was the key to the problem. The sultan and his bureaucracy supported the office of the prince, even if his person was expendable, because he was their man in the principality who had the responsibility for carrying out their policies and ensuring the smooth delivery of money and supplies. The *boiers*, on the other hand, were fractious and insubordinate and a constant source of disquiet for Ottoman authorities. Their intractability could occasionally be useful in keeping a wilful prince in line, but the Ottoman court had no interest in institutionalizing opposition to him.

The key figure in the government of the principalities was the prince.[21] His political and judicial powers were nearly absolute, and his voice in fiscal and economic policy usually decisive. He controlled all the levers of central and provincial administration, and its personnel was directly or indirectly responsible to him. He was the supreme judge, who heard cases from any jurisdiction, civil or criminal, secular or ecclesiastical, and he served as a court of final appeal. He could pronounce sentences harsher or milder than those prescribed by law and could pardon or commute sentences as he wished. The management of the economy was in his hands, a responsibility that derived mainly from his role as the procurer of all manner of goods and taxes for his suzerain and from his power of initiative in taxation and other fiscal matters. It was also he who negotiated

---

[21] *Istoria dreptului românesc*, i, pt. 2 (Bucharest, 1984), 95–100. For a contemporary exposition of the powers of the prince in judicial matters, see excerpts from manuals of law drawn up by Michael Fotino in 1765 and 1766 in V. A. Georgescu and E. Popescu-Mihuţ, *Organizarea de stat a Ţării Româneşti, 1765–1782* (Bucharest, 1989), 93–6, 106–8, 114–17.

with Ottoman merchants and officials the prices to be paid for the *zahire*. But his involvement in the economy did not end there. He had the power to set the maximum prices of goods sold on the local market and to intervene almost at will in the affairs of merchant and artisan guilds. Few constitutional restraints impeded the exercise of these considerable powers.

Over time, none the less, various forces had combined to curtail the absolutism to which all the princes aspired. The most important limitation came from outside the principalities. The right assumed by the Ottoman sultan to select and remove the prince was perhaps the most formidable single check on princely authority. The sultan treated the prince as an Ottoman functionary, and in the Ottoman bureaucratic hierarchy he ranked below the important viziers. Yet, the Greeks of the Phanar coveted the thrones of the principalities as the culmination of their public careers, even though the manner in which they realized their ambitions imposed severe constraints upon their freedom of action. In order to preserve their thrones they had to ingratiate themselves with a host of Ottoman officials. The loans and other favours the princes received obliged them to distribute public offices and to adopt fiscal measures that were often contrary to their best interests, not to mention the welfare of the country they had come to govern. In any case, the princes were subject to dismissal at any time by the sultan, no matter what limitations the treaties imposed by Russia specified. In 1786, for example, Mihai Suţu of Wallachia and Alexandru Mavrocordat of Moldavia were summarily removed on suspicion of disloyalty. The precariousness of the princeship may be gauged from the fact that between 1791 and 1802 there were six princes in Wallachia and five in Moldavia.

The tenure of princes was continually at issue between Russian and Ottoman officials in the first two decades of the nineteenth century. In the *hatti-sherif* of 1802, which provided for an orderly succession, Sultan Selim III agreed to a seven-year term for the prince and promised that an incumbent would not be removed earlier except for serious cause verified by both the Russian and Ottoman courts. Despite this solemn undertaking, only one prince after 1802— Scarlat Callimachi of Moldavia (1812–19)—completed his term.

An important step towards ensuring political stability was taken by the leading contenders for the princely thrones themselves. The Phanariot families and their clienteles had become alarmed by the rising financial outlays required to stay in the competition. In 1818, for example, the wife of Prince Alexandru Suţu of Wallachia (1818–21) is reported to have offered a sum equal to twice the country's annual budget to assure the accession of her son. Unsuccessful candidates naturally incurred enormous financial losses, but even the winners arrived in Iaşi or Bucharest so burdened by debts that they had too little time during a short reign to satisfy their creditors and put something aside for their 'retirement'. The leading families had sought desperately for some time to bring order to the process. At last they gained a sympathetic hearing at the Ottoman court, where officials had concluded that it was not always wise to award the throne to the highest bidder. Influenced perhaps by the flight to Austria of Prince Ioan Caragea of Wallachia in 1818, Sultan Mahmud II (1808–39) issued new instructions concerning the appointment of princes which reduced the number of Phanariot families from whom they could be chosen to four: the families of Scarlat Callimachi, Alexandru Suţu, Mihai Suţu, and Dimitrie Moruzi. They, in turn, agreed to contribute to the maintenance of the other fifty Phanariot families in Constantinople, a considerable financial burden which, in fact, came to be borne by the inhabitants of the principalities. Thus, out of the annual budget of Wallachia for 1820 of about six million piastres, one million went to support those Phanariots who had been excluded from the competition for the throne.

The princes' freedom of action was also limited by the Russian ambassador in Constantinople and the consuls in Bucharest and Iaşi. Examples of their interference abound, from protests against the imposition of new taxes on the *boiers* and clergy to the encouragement of *boiers* to bring complaints against a reigning prince to the attention of Ottoman officials in Constantinople.[22] The consuls had primary responsibility to ensure that princes respected the treaties between Russia and the Ottoman Empire. In 1792, for example, the consul in Iaşi, in accordance with instructions from St Petersburg, persuaded Prince Alexandru Moruzi not to collect new taxes, action that would have violated the Treaty of Iaşi.[23]

Despite the mode of their selection, the instability of tenure, and other inconveniences, a number of talented figures ascended the thrones of both Moldavia and Wallachia in the last half-century of Phanariot rule. They exhibited complex patterns of virtues and vices. Nicolae Mavrogheni (Wallachia, 1786–90), unlike most of his colleagues, a Greek of humble origins, was the most gifted military commander among the Phanariot princes and had numerous successes in the Russo-Turkish War in 1788–90. He was generous in support of the Orthodox Church and spared the mass of the population from arbitrary taxation, but he earned the abiding enmity of the *boiers* by making them bear unaccustomed heavy fiscal burdens. Constantin Ipsilanti (Wallachia, 1802–6), a Phanariot, was an able administrator who nurtured ambitious plans for a union of the principalities and the creation of a kingdom of Dacia to be ruled by hereditary princes of the Ipsilanti family. Ioan Caragea (Wallachia, 1812–18), a Phanariot, combined a cultivated intellect with inordinate greed. He raised taxes continually and was ingenious at discovering new ones such as *birul femeilor rele* (tax on evil women) as he sought to amass a personal fortune, but he introduced a new code of laws, promoted education, and translated eight of Goldoni's comedies from Italian into Greek. Scarlat Callimachi (Moldavia, 1812–19), a gentle, cultured man, supported innovations in education and initiated a new codification of civil law.

The outstanding figure among the princes of the period was undoubtedly Alexandru Ipsilanti (prince of Wallachia, 1774–82, 1796–7, and of Moldavia,

---

[22] The extent of the problem is suggested in the introd. to Hurmuzaki, *Documente*, NS i. *Rapoarte consulare ruse, 1770–1796* (Bucharest, 1962), 5–59.　　[23] Ibid. 496–9.

1786–8).[24] He merits the epithet enlightened despot, for he sought to introduce into the principalities many of the ideas that were transforming Europe. A Greek from one of the most prominent Phanar families, he was well educated and as grand dragoman had already demonstrated his skills as an administrator. He attempted to bring about a complete overhaul of Wallachia's governmental machinery, reform the judicial system, reinvigorate higher education, and establish relations with his Ottoman suzerain on a rational, legal foundation. If much of what he did lacked permanence, the cause lay mainly with others and the circumstances of the time.

The only social class capable of challenging the power of the prince from within the country had traditionally been the great *boiers*. But by the middle of the eighteenth century their position had seriously deteriorated. The fundamental structures of the nobiliary regime of the seventeenth century had either disappeared or had been drastically modified. The right to choose the prince had been pre-empted by the sultan, and the old assembly of the estates (*adunarea de stări*), which, in the seventeenth century had been an independent body representative of *boier* interests, had given way to a general council (*sfatul de obște*) composed of great *boiers* appointed by the prince.

Although the role of the great *boiers* in political affairs had thus waned, they continued to represent the main social, economic, and political power in the country.[25] The Phanariot princes and their entourages came and went, but the *boiers*, whose wealth and position in society were rooted in the land, remained a permanent force. United, they could exert strong pressure on even the most authoritarian prince, for without at least their tacit support he could not hope to fulfil his obligations to the sultan.

The great landowning families—the Cantacuzinos, the Sturdzas, and the Văcărescus—continued to compose the prince's council (*sfatul domnesc*), an advisory body of considerable influence, and along with the prince's favourites they filled the highest offices in the land. The prince often relied upon them for both material and moral support. He borrowed money from them in order to satisfy the extraordinary demands of the sultan and consulted them regularly on state expenditures, practices which gave them a measure of control over public finances. The interests of the prince and *boiers*, in fact, often coincided. They stood as one against fundamental changes in the economic and social structure of the country and almost always cooperated in passing on new fiscal burdens to the peasantry.

There was, nevertheless, always an inherent tension between the prince and the *boiers*. The former was engaged, consciously or not, in centralizing the

[24] M. D. Vlad, 'Iluminism și modernism în politica reformatoare a domnitorului Alexandru Ipsilanti', *Revista de istorie*, 40/10 (1987), 997–1016.

[25] A perceptive contemporary description of the *boiers* was written in 1822 by L. Kreuchely, the Prussian consul in Iași and later Bucharest, for the Prussian ambassador in Constantinople: 'Explication des boyars valaques', in Hurmuzaki, *Documente*, x (Bucharest, 1897), 495–548.

functions of government, a tendency manifest in his codification of law, his control of the judicial system, and his growing intervention in the relations between landlords and dependent peasants. Every measure he took diminished in some degree the power and influence of the *boiers*. They, in turn, clung tenaciously to their remaining privileges and sought to blunt the powers of the prince. They used the Ottoman and Russian courts to combat 'despotic' princes by raising frequent protests against violations of 'ancient rights and customs', especially in regard to taxation. They also conspired against the princes, as in 1782 when a group of Moldavian *boiers* swore a secret oath to fight for the rights and privileges of the '*boier* state', an act which led to the execution of their leaders; they petitioned for the return of old privileges, as in 1790, when Wallachian *boiers* urged the commander of Austria's occupation army to reinstate serfdom, whose abolition in the middle of the eighteenth century they attributed to tyrannical rulers; and they went so far as to call in question the very institution of the princeship, as in 1802, when a group of Moldavian *boiers* devised a plan to establish an 'aristo-democratic republic'. Sometimes, as a last resort, they would flee the country, usually to Austrian territory, as in 1802, when from their refuge in Braşov (Kronstadt) they addressed memorials to the emperors of Austria and Russia complaining against the deplorable state into which Wallachia had sunk.[26]

All these acts of defiance were rarely effective. They could occasionally be dangerous for the prince, since one of his chief responsibilities to the sultan was to maintain peace and order. Disturbances that might interrupt the flow of supplies or give Russia a pretext for intervention brought immediate demands from Constantinople for explanations. Yet, the opposition of the *boiers* remained sporadic, for they lacked an institutional base that would give their efforts cohesion and continuity.

A potentially serious challenge to the prince's authority came from two deliberative bodies which had retained at least a semblance of their earlier representative character.[27] The more important of these was the prince's council, which, besides advisory functions, carried out special judicial responsibilities. That section of the council which served as a court was technically known as the *divan domnesc*, a term that came to be applied to the entire council (henceforth, divan will be used in this latter sense). After 1774 frequent military occupations and resulting vacancies on the throne enhanced the divan's importance. At times it exercised broad powers, but it was always subordinate to the occupying power. In any case, these episodes were too brief and the *boiers* too undisciplined to permit the divan to become an independent institution with political power of its own.

[26] V. Georgescu, *Mémoires et projets de réforme dans les Principautés Roumaines, 1769–1830* (Bucharest, 1970), 43–4, 45–6.

[27] V. A. Georgescu and P. Strihan, *Judecata domnească în Ţara Românească şi Moldova (1611–1831)*, pt. 1. *Organizarea judecătorească*, vol. ii. *1740–1831* (Bucharest, 1981), 63–76, 96–100.

The members of the divan were appointed by the prince from among *boiers* of the first and second rank. Tradition, buttressed by *firmans* (decrees) from the sultan, acknowledged the right of the prince to choose whomever he wished from among native or Greek *boiers*. But a wise prince took into account the social position, political influence, and length of state service of his appointees. Such considerations help to explain why the prince often encountered opposition in a body he himself had chosen. Although the personnel of the divan was constantly changing, a small nucleus of great *boiers* retained their places on it along with high administrative offices from one reign to the next or reappeared frequently in these positions. Thus, the internal affairs of the country were run by the prince with the assistance of a small cluster of noble families, who formed an aristocratic caste or oligarchy which dominated political, economic, and cultural life well into the 1820s.

The second important body representing *boier* opinion was the general council. It was the remnant of the old general assembly of the estates, now reduced in size to those persons specifically invited by the prince to attend. As in the seventeenth century, no legal statute regulated its structure or defined its powers. Neither the Treaty of Kuchuk Kainardji nor the numerous codifications of law undertaken by various princes between 1765 and 1818 mentioned it, even though it was, at least in theory, a fundamental political institution alongside the prince and the divan. As the embodiment of the traditional autonomy of the country, the general council had the potential to alter the balance between the prince and the *boiers* and to become a truly representative body. Naturally, both the prince and the sultan preferred to leave it in an amorphous state.

Only the prince, or someone designated by him, could convoke the general council. As few as twelve or as many as 140 persons might gather at a time, but their number rarely exceeded thirty-six. No public matter—secular or ecclesiastical, economic or political, from the election of metropolitans and bishops and the codification of law to taxes and central and local administration—was beyond its competence. The council was no docile instrument of the prince. Debates were often animated, especially about taxes, and sometimes the *boiers* ended their work by denouncing the prince to Constantinople. But it was the prince who always set the agenda and retained the power of decision, and as long as the Ottoman court was satisfied with his performance, he prevailed over any opposition.

The prince also owed his predominance in domestic affairs to the growing and increasingly complex bureaucracy over which he presided at both the central and local level. He himself was mainly responsible for a steady centralization of authority—the transfer of powers and initiative from local organs of government and the provincial *boiers* to institutions headquartered in Bucharest and Iaşi and administered by high *boier* functionaries responsible solely to him.

The administrative organization of both principalities suggests why the bureaucracy was expanding. Wallachia was divided into seventeen *judeţe* (districts), which in turn were grouped into three large geographical units: five *judeţe* to the west of the Olt River constituted historical Oltenia, which, although retaining little of its former autonomy, continued to be administered by a Ban (governor), who resided in Bucharest; the twelve remaining *judeţe* on the left bank of the Olt in the seventeenth century formed Ţara de Sus (the upper country) and, further to the east, Ţara de Jos (the lower country), each administered by a Mare Vornic (minister of justice) and a Mare Logofăt (grand chancellor). Each *judeţ* was administered by two *ispravnici* (prefects), one Greek and one Wallachian, who combined executive, judicial, and fiscal functions, despite efforts by the princes to introduce a separation of powers. Every *judeţ* was subdivided into *plăşi* (in the mountains they were called *plaiuri*) and were administered by officials (*zapcii* and *vătafii*) appointed by the Mare Vornic. Like the prefects, they had executive, judicial, and fiscal authority. At each of these administrative levels the number of officials multiplied steadily in the eighteenth century. New positions were created and the personnel of old ones doubled or tripled mainly to satisfy the pressure from the *boiers* for office and the prince's need for money. The administrative system and the trend towards centralization in Moldavia were essentially the same as in Wallachia.

The sale of offices was endemic. As soon as a new prince arrived he put high offices up for auction. The purchasers of these, mainly *boiers* and members of the prince's entourage, in turn, sold district offices, and the *ispravnici* and *vătafi* local posts. Everyone was naturally eager to recoup what he had spent on his own office and to come away with a profit. The most sought-after position was that of Mare Vistier (high treasurer), who was the key figure in the country's fiscal system. It sold for as much as 300,000 piastres in 1820, a huge sum, but it assured the incumbent of at least 500,000 piastres income because it was he who appointed the *ispravnici*. The sale of offices had a ruinous effect upon administrative morality and efficiency. Many persons who obtained positions lacked both training and aptitude. At the *judeţ* level, for example, appointments as *ispravnici* usually went to the sons of *boiers*, whose only qualification for this key place in local administration was the wealth and power of their families. Once installed, they took their incomes from the monies that were destined for the public treasury—taxes and fines—supplemented by gifts and other sources which were known collectively as *havaieturi* (fees, favours). The practice was accepted as normal because officials did not receive regular salaries. Thus, office-holders considered their posts an investment and used their powers to enrich themselves at the expense of the inhabitants under their jurisdiction. They performed their tasks primarily with the expectation of personal gain, not out of a sense of duty.

An official who stood apart from the bureaucratic hierarchy, but whose role was, none the less, crucial to the smooth working of the administrative system was the divan-effendi, the prince's Turkish secretary.[28] Mentioned in documents as early as the second half of the sixteenth century, he served then and in the

---

[28] P. Strihan, 'Divan-Effendi în Ţara Românească şi Moldova în secolele XVII–XIX', *Studii: Revistă de istorie*, 21/5 (1968), 881–96.

eighteenth century as a protocol officer when Ottoman dignitaries visited Bucharest and Iaşi, and was responsible for translating communications to and from Ottoman officials at all levels. Not the least of his tasks was to keep an eye on the prince and report to Constantinople on his activities and degree of loyalty. He regularly took part in the sessions of the divan. Among his functions there was the reading in Turkish of *firmans* issued by the sultan, an act of great symbolic meaning, since it made manifest throughout the entire administration the presence and authority of the Ottoman state. In the eighteenth and early nineteenth century the divan-effendi assumed important judicial powers. He became responsible for judging or arbitrating cases between the local population and Ottoman subjects. The princes themselves probably encouraged this activity as a means of curtailing the interference of the *kadis* along the Danube in the judicial affairs of their countries.

Indispensable also to the smooth operation of the princely administration was the *capuchehaie* (Turkish: *kapikâhaya*; lieutenant, representative).[29] He was the intermediary between the prince and Ottoman officials and the banking and commercial world of Constantinople. Through him the prince paid the tribute, placed gifts with the powerful to gain their favour, transmitted political information, denounced his enemies, and justified himself. The *capuchehaie* thus had to be someone with an intimate knowledge of the workings of the Ottoman court and bureaucracy and who was well regarded by them, someone who had friends, whose word counted for something. In early times a native *boier* had occupied the post, but with the rise to prominence in the Ottoman polity of Greeks the *capuchehaie* in the eighteenth century was invariably a Greek or someone thoroughly Hellenized.

The prince lacked one important instrument of public policy—a standing army. Its dissolution had gone so far that by the middle of the eighteenth century he had at his disposal only a token force for guard duty and the maintenance of public order. Attempts in the second half of the century to re-establish a national army were only temporarily successful. The wars between Russia and Turkey offered favourable opportunities. During the campaigns of 1768–74 as many as 4,000 volunteers in each principality, the majority peasants, joined the Russian armies. But they were quickly disbanded when the war ended because neither the Russians nor the Ottomans saw any advantage to themselves in maintaining a Moldavian and Wallachian standing army. The army of 10,000 assembled by Prince Nicolae Mavrogheni of Wallachia to fight alongside the Turks against the Austrians in 1788–90 suffered a similar fate.

Since a native standing army was out of the question, the princes had recourse to local, irregular forces. In Wallachia, for example, in the first decade of the

---

[29] A. H. Golimas, *Despre capuchehăile Moldovei şi poruncile Porţii către Moldova până la 1829* (Iaşi, 1943), 1–72. On their activities, see the reports they sent to the prince in A. Camariano-Cioran, *Reprezentanţa diplomatică a Moldovei la Constantinopol (30 august 1741–decembrie 1742)* (Bucharest, 1985).

nineteenth century they expanded the role of the pandours (*panduri*) of Oltenia. Organized in the first half of the eighteenth century from among free peasants as frontier guards and a kind of gendarmerie, the pandours combined various military activities with traditional agricultural pursuits in return for exemption from certain taxes. In the early nineteenth century they served as a territorial militia which could be activated in time of war or internal unrest.[30] Prince Constantin Ipsilanti expanded their numbers rapidly, for he had decided to break with his Ottoman suzerain and wanted a large military force of his own in addition to Russian aid to assure independence. The pandours took part in the Russian campaign in Oltenia in 1807 in support of the Serbian uprising to the east, but an armistice between Russia and Turkey ended the need for a large Wallachian army and led to a reduction in the number of pandours. Yet, the idea of a standing army remained uppermost in the minds of anti-Turkish *boiers* and Russian generals. In 1812 the commander of Russian forces in the principalities submitted detailed plans for permanent armies to the Wallachian and Moldavian divans, but before they could act, Russia made peace and withdrew. Several more decades were to pass before a modern regular army came into being.

A striking feature of the judicial system of the principalities in the eighteenth century and the early decades of the nineteenth was the multiplicity of legal codes and customs. First of all, there was written law, which consisted of various Byzantine codes of civil and canon law and the interpretations and supplementary regulations promulgated by Moldavian and Wallachian princes. In the nineteenth century Western European codes, mainly French and Austrian, came into use. Customary law, for the most part unwritten and highly diversified by locality, still retained its vitality, despite the steady encroachments of written codes. Written and customary law had developed independently of one another, and until the latter half of the eighteenth century no attempt had been made to combine them into a single, national code.

Byzantine law (*ius receptum*), generally known in Romanian as the *pravilă*, was the foundation of Romanian jurisprudence in the eighteenth century.[31] Its authority is evident in the decisions rendered by judicial bodies and in the continual references to Byzantine sources in all the codification projects undertaken between 1765 and 1818. The *pravilă* was the standard by which the reliability of all the new codes was measured.

The most widely used Byzantine legal texts in the eighteenth century were the *Basilicae*, called in Romanian *Basilicale* or *Cărţi împărăteşti* (imperial books).

[30] On the *panduri*, see *Istoria militară a poporului român*, iv (Bucharest, 1987), 96–102.

[31] On the general problem of the reception of Byzantine law in the Romanian principalities, see V. A. Georgescu, *Bizanţul şi instituţiile româneşti pînă la mijlocul secolului al XVIII-lea* (Bucharest, 1980), 87–120, and E. Popescu-Mihuţ, 'Remarques sur la place des textes de droit criminel byzantin dans la pratique judiciaire roumaine du XVIIIᵉ siècle', in *Études byzantines et post-byzantines* (Bucharest, 1991), 180–92. See also G. Cronţ, 'Byzantine Juridical Influences in the Rumanian Feudal Society: Byzantine Sources of the Rumanian Feudal Law', *Revue des études sud-est européennes*, 2/3–4 (1964), 359–83.

Another important source of legal decisions was the *Hexabiblos*, a compilation containing material on civil and criminal law and procedure put together in 1345 by Constantine Harmenopoulos, which began to circulate in the principalities in the eighteenth century. Other collections of laws based upon Byzantine sources and used in earlier centuries continued to influence Romanian jurisprudence in the eighteenth century: the *Syntagma* of Matthew Vlastares, an alphabetical repertory of canon law composed in 1335, which was translated into Slavic but not into Romanian, and a number of nomocanons, collections of Byzantine imperial law and the canons of ecumenical church councils. Noteworthy among the latter were the nomocanon of Malaxos (1561–2), the Romanian translation of which became the *Pravilă aleasă* (Iaşi, 1632); the nomocanon of Daniil Panoneanul, which formed the basis of *Îndreptarea legii* (Tîrgovişte, 1652), an expanded nomocanon containing the entire Wallachian *pravilă*; and the nomocanon of Iacob of Janina (1645), which was translated as *Cîrja arhierilor* (the bishop's crozier) in Iaşi in 1754.

During the century of Phanariot rule many of the Byzantine codes used in the courts were available only in Greek. Some, like Harmenopoulos's *Hexabiblos* went through a number of printings in the eighteenth century (all outside the principalities), while other codes circulated in manuscript. But Greek could not become the standard language of the judicial system because the majority of those who dispensed justice could not read it. Beginning in the latter decades of the eighteenth century Romanian steadily gained ground against Greek. Several enlightened princes recognized the trend by ordering Romanian translations of important texts. Alexandru Ipsilanti of Wallachia initiated the translation of the penal sections of the *Basilicale*, and Alexandru Moruzi of Moldavia ordered a complete translation of the *Hexabiblos*.

Existing side by side with the Byzantine *pravile* and often supplementing them was customary law (*obiceiul pămîntului*), which had developed out of the economic and social conditions prevailing before the founding of the Romanian principalities in the fourteenth century.[32] Customary law had never been confirmed by the ruler or a high tribunal; it had never been codified or studied by scholars or taught in academies of higher learning; and there was no private or official edition. Yet, it remained a crucial support of the social and economic structure of the principalities until at least the first decades of the nineteenth century. Paradoxically, so long as Byzantine codes held sway, its place was secure. Since many institutions and practices were not covered by the *pravile* and since there was no comprehensive codification of Moldavian and Wallachian law, the only recourse for jurists was to invoke the traditional norms of their respective regions. Such fundamental social questions as the right claimed by the *boiers* to direct the affairs of the country, the reciprocal obligations of landlords and

---

[32] On the rise and decline of customary law, see V. Hanga, *Les Institutions du droit coutumier roumain* (Bucharest, 1988), 44–158.

dependent peasants, the control of land by free peasants, and the solidarity of the village commune towards outsiders were more often than not decided on the basis of customary law. Although the *pravile* were used especially in cases involving *boiers* and monasteries, in which large amounts of property or other complicated matters were at issue, plaintiffs and defendants often requested that the proceedings be conducted and the decision rendered in accordance with custom.

The importance of customary law is evident in attempts at the end of the eighteenth century to compile collections of regional legal traditions. In 1782 in Moldavia information about local legal norms and procedures was gathered in response to inquiries from the Austrian governor of Bukovina about landholding in the principality, and in 1797 Prince Alexandru Ipsilanti of Wallachia established a department of customs (*logofeția de obiceiuri*), which had responsibility for collecting the 'norms of private law' along with information about the history and geography of the country. Further collecting, however, does not seem to have taken place in either principality, nor was there any attempt to codify materials already in hand, probably because of the steady encroachment of written law upon the domain of custom.

In spite of a certain vitality, custom slowly gave way to the *pravilă* and princely legislation. Norms established long ago in the old village commune where a patriarchal social system and a natural economy predominated could not resolve the problems of an increasingly complex society. They could not, for example, serve the needs of a prince and bureaucracy engaged in centralizing public institutions. Only occasionally in the second half of the eighteenth century did unwritten tradition prevail over written codes, as in 1797 when the divan of Wallachia stipulated that custom be followed in matters relating to dowries, even though it was admittedly contrary to the *pravilă*. Besides its inadaptability to the changing needs of society, customary law had the further disadvantage of being essentially local and thus inapplicable on a national scale.

The princes recognized the shortcomings of multiple legal systems and in the 1760s and 1770s took the first steps towards their unification and a general reform of judicial norms and procedures. Their immediate aim was to bring the *pravilă* up to date and to eliminate obsolete laws. In previous centuries the precepts of Byzantine imperial and canon law had been accepted as binding, and, consequently, no sanction or even any discussion of their validity had been thought necessary. But in the second half of the eighteenth century it became increasingly apparent to the princes how little suited Byzantine codes were to the needs of contemporary Moldavian and Wallachian society, and, consequently, they tried to harmonize tradition and necessity through new legislation and the codification of law. In effect, they undertook to create a national law code. The initiative necessarily belonged to them because their right to legislate and, thus, to modify existing law was generally recognized.

The princes exercised their broad legislative powers in various ways. Their most important activity was the drawing-up and promulgation of *hrisoave*, normative acts which dealt with specific social and economic questions and confirmed or modified an existing regulation or established new norms. The promulgation of a *hrisov* was usually preceded by a report drawn up by the members of the divan at the prince's request. His approval gave their report the force of law, and the special enacting legislation in the form of a *hrisov* was often dispensed with. If the matter in question was of exceptional importance, the prince might convoke the general council, but he was not obliged to follow its advice. Many *hrisoave* dealt with the fiscal and judicial organization of the country and civil matters concerning inheritance, adoption, and gypsies. Another type of princely legislation, which regulated the status of various social groups, especially dependent peasants, and was promulgated in the same way as the *hrisoave*, was the *aşezămînt* (law, foundation). The prince also regularly issued instructions in the form of circular letters to district officials establishing new administrative and judicial rules or amending old ones. Often they contained a number of articles, or *ponturi*, and had the full force of law, but they were often intended to prepare the ground for the more formal enactment of a *hrisov* or *aşezămînt*. Among important *ponturi* were those issued by Prince Mihai Suţu in 1795 concerning the judicial powers of the district prefects.

The decisions of the princes in specific court cases also formed an important body of law and reveal the full extent of his judicial powers. All courts were subordinate to him. Although they were empowered to investigate the substance of cases, they did not render judgements. Rather, their function was to collect the evidence, especially the testimony of the litigants, and to make recommendations, but the final disposition of the case rested with the prince. As a result, his workload was enormous, since the majority of plaintiffs, even in the most insignificant matters, addressed themselves directly to him rather than to the judicial authorities of their respective districts. The power to render final judgements, which had the same force as a law code or other judicial act, became one of the prince's most valuable instruments in adapting both the *pravilă* and custom to the changing needs of society and the state.

Of fundamental importance for the development of law and of public institutions in general were the codifications undertaken in the last half of the eighteenth century. Such enterprises were in accord with the spirit of the times and bore witness to the transition of Romanian society from medieval to modern forms.

The first attempt at codification was made by Prince Ştefan Racoviţa of Wallachia (1764–5). He commissioned Mihail Fotino, a *boier* who had recently come to Wallachia from his native Chios, to bring Byzantine imperial and canon law (*ius receptum*), princely law (*ius novum*), and local custom together into a single code in the form of a manual to serve the practical needs of judges. Fotino, one of the most learned legal scholars of his day, completed his first manual of laws in 1765 and a revised edition in 1766, both in Greek. They took the form of an expanded nomocanon, one book consisting of imperial secular law (constitutional, fiscal, criminal, agricultural, and maritime), and the other of canon law, Fotino drew mainly upon the *Basilicale*, a practice which would be followed by all later codifiers until the introduction of Western European codes in the 1830s. He also consulted Wallachian sources, but customary law occupied only a small place in this scholarly synthesis.[33] Although these manuals were never officially sanctioned, the numerous manuscript copies suggest that they were widely used.

Alexandru Ipsilanti of Wallachia undertook the most comprehensive programme of codification and judicial reform attempted in the last half-century of Phanariot rule.[34] He began his reorganization of justice in 1775 at the top. His *Hrisov cu ponturi* dealt with the high courts and made precise the duties of the divan, which now formally assumed the attributes of a supreme court. It also created new departments, each concerned with a specific category of cases—criminal, commercial, and civil. His *Carte domnească* (princely charter) of the same year dealt with principle. Most important was the stipulation that the judiciary should be separate from the executive, and for the first time it provided for the appointment of an official in each *judeţ* whose functions would be exclusively judicial. The *ispravnic*, who had traditionally acted as the chief judge of his district, retained his considerable administrative and police powers, but, henceforth, he was forbidden to hear cases or levy fines. Ipsilanti's aim was to enhance the efficiency and honesty of the judicial system and to make it a more responsive instrument of his own policies, but he had little success in substituting the new principle of the separation of powers for tradition.

Ipsilanti's judicial reforms culminated in the promulgation of a new law code in 1780, the *Pravilnicească condică* (register of law). Based on the *Basilicale* and customary law and published in both Greek and Romanian, it was not a complete code, but rather dealt with the organization of the courts, judicial procedure, and selected questions of civil law. Its provisions reflected both the prince's commitment to general social reform and his recognition of its limits. On the one hand, he reaffirmed the curtailment of the judicial powers of the *ispravnici*, but, on the other, he sanctioned the claims to property and labour services made by the *boiers* on their dependent peasants.

Numerous codifications in both principalities followed Ipsilanti's initiative. In Wallachia a new comprehensive law code became necessary because judges continued to apply a variety of legal norms, a practice which often led to confusion and contradictory rulings. Shortly after his accession to the throne in 1812 Prince Ioan Caragea appointed two jurists to draw up a new code. They based their work mainly on Byzantine law, Ipsilanti's *Pravilniceasca condică*, and *obiceiul pămîntului*, but they also drew upon Western sources, notably the French Civil Code of 1804, in matters relating to contracts and inheritance, borrowings

[33] V. A. Georgescu, 'Un manuscrit parisien du "nomikon procheiron" (Bucarest, 1766) de Michel Fotino (Photeinopoulos)', *Revue des études sud-est européennes*, 8/2 (1970), 329–64.
[34] See Ipsilanti's own instructions in *Pravilniceasca condică 1780* (Bucharest, 1957), 161–8; V. A. Georgescu and E. Popescu, *Legislaţia agrară a Ţării Româneşti, 1775–1782* (Bucharest, 1970), 58–62.

which suggest the evolution of Wallachian society towards more modern economic and social forms. A general council, convoked by Caragea in 1818 and composed of the higher clergy, *boiers* who held important state offices, and other *boiers*, recommended approval of the code. Published in Greek and Romanian, it was applied immediately and remained in force until 1865, when a new civil code was introduced. The foremost contribution of *Legiuirea Caragea* to the administration of law was its arrangement of the material systematically by subject, a significant innovation in the development of written law in Wallachia. The code also affected many areas of social life, especially landlord–peasant relations, for it reinforced the prerogatives of the *boiers* over the land at the expense of those who worked it.

The codification of law proceeded with equal intensity in Moldavia, where princes sought to bring greater uniformity to the administration of justice and to respond to urgent social problems. In 1785 Alexandru Mavrocordat promulgated *Sobornicescul Hrisov* (the Council Code), which dealt with the disposition of land and the status of gypsy slaves. It confirmed the ancient right of pre-emption enjoyed by relatives or members of the village commune when land changed hands and was intended to prevent the destruction of the free peasant villages by powerful *boiers*. It also forbade the division of gypsy families and clarified the status of Moldavians who married gypsies. In 1814 Andronache Donici, a high court judge, elaborated a manual of civil law, which was based on the *Basilicale* and custom. Although never formally sanctioned by the prince, it was widely used by judges until 1865 because it offered a handy and systematic summary of applied judicial norms. Scarlat Callimachi promulgated a comprehensive code in 1817 which was based on traditional sources, but now for the first time on a large scale its authors drew upon Western codes.[35] Their main source was the Austrian civil code of 1811, which they adapted to Moldavian conditions, especially for economic matters. Since the *Cod Calimach* was published in Greek and was not translated into Romanian until 1838, judges continued to use Byzantine codes, customary law, and Donici's manual. But the evolution of Moldavian society had made the compilation of an indigenous criminal code imperative. In 1820 Prince Mihai Suţu promulgated a code of penal procedure in Romanian, which combined the prescriptions of Byzantine and customary law with articles taken from the Austrian penal code of 1803 (it had been translated into Romanian in 1807 for use in Bukovina) and remained in force until 1865, when a new criminal code was drawn up.

The two most pressing official financial responsibilities of princes between the Treaty of Kuchuk Kainardji and the end of Phanariot rule in 1821 were to satisfy the demands of the sultan and to balance the budget. State expenditures in both principalities increased dramatically during the period. By the fiscal year 1818–19

---

[35] A. Rădulescu, 'Izvoarele Codului Calimach', in id., *Pagini din istoria dreptului românesc* (Bucharest, 1970), 133–54.

in Wallachia the amount had reached the enormous sum of 5,910,000 *lei*, and in Moldavia, 1,443,000 *lei*. An additional 1,000,000 *lei* were secretly paid by Wallachia (and a proportional amount by Moldavia) to a host of Turkish officials. In each principality roughly 35 per cent of all regular expenditures for that year went to the Turks and 25 per cent to the prince, while 40 per cent was reserved to the country (*ţara*). A breakdown of the latter category for Moldavia shows that the largest amount, approximately half, went for the support of functionaries, followed by substantial expenditures on the postal service.[36] These figures reflect the steady growth of the state bureaucracy. Little appears to have been spent on social services; such matters as poor relief, orphans, and even education were not yet thought of as public responsibilities.

State income kept pace with expenditures only by means of heavy and often arbitrary taxation of the general populace. The annual income of Wallachia rose from 3,550,000 *talers* to 6,000,000 between 1782 and 1818, while that of Moldavia declined from 2,840,000 *talers* in 1785 to 1,450,000 in 1818, mainly owing to the loss of Bessarabia to Russia in 1812. Because of loose bookkeeping procedures and the lack of formal annual budgets, it is not always possible to distinguish the income and expenditures of the state treasury from those of the prince. Public monies and the personal fortune of the prince were still treated as one and the same, although efforts were under way to separate them. The princes themselves favoured such a change in order to avoid the destruction of their personal fortunes by the insatiable demands of the Ottoman bureaucracy.

The main source of income for the state treasury was the *bir*, a tax on every head of household payable in instalments. Along with other taxes assessed on the heads of households, such as the *menziluri* to support the postal system and *banii zaherelei*, money to pay for provisions for the sultan, the *bir* brought into the state and princely treasuries between 60 and 70 per cent of their annual incomes. The other 30 to 40 per cent came from regular tithes on pigs and beehives (*dijmărit*; *deseatina* in Moldavia), sheep (*oierit*; *goştina* in Moldavia), and wine (*vinărici*; *vădrărit* in Moldavia), known collectively as *huzmeturi* in Wallachia and *rusumaturi* in Moldavia. The income of the prince of Wallachia from these tithes was over one million *lei* in the 1814–15 fiscal year. Of this sum, the tithe on wine accounted for roughly 42 per cent, the *oierit* 37 per cent, and the *dijmărit* 21 per cent. The prince also drew income from numerous excise duties, such as those on goods sold at fairs, and he had the exclusive right to the proceeds from mining, mainly of salt. He collected tariff duties on goods entering and transiting the country, but he had no control over the rates, which were set by Ottoman authorities in negotiations with foreign powers. He could also raise the *huzmeturi* almost at will, sometimes to meet state obligations and sometimes for his own benefit. For example, in Wallachia in 1815 Ioan Caragea increased the *vinărici*, *dijmărit*, and

---

[36] Georgescu, *Mémoires et projets*, 71–80: Report of Iordache Rosetti-Rosnovanu to the Russian ambassador in Constantinople, 1818.

oierit drastically in order to satisfy Ottoman demands for labourers and wagons, and in 1819 Alexandru Suţu tripled these sums in order to pay off the debts he had incurred in his campaign to win the throne. If all else failed, the prince had recourse to loans, especially from monasteries and high churchmen, sums which he often never repaid.

The main tax, the *bir*, was paid almost exclusively by the peasantry. In 1775 Prince Alexandru Ipsilanti established it as a fixed levy payable in four regular instalments (*sămi*; *sferturi* in Moldavia). It was assessed on each head of household until 1783, when a new fiscal unit, the *ludă*, was introduced.[37] The *ludă* was composed of a certain number of taxpayers (*birnici*), which varied according to circumstances. A single family that was well off might form a *ludă* by itself, but more often the poor were grouped together with several prosperous neighbours. After the turn of the century, as the amount of the *bir* increased, there might be as many as a dozen families in a *ludă*. In Wallachia in 1804 there were roughly 40,000 *lude*, a number that fell to 19,500 by 1820. But the princes, as inventive as ever in fiscal matters, simply increased the total amount of the tax. The consequences of this policy were reflected in the rise in the sum each *ludă* was expected to pay: 16 *talers* in 1775, 80 in 1804, and 212 in 1818. Even if due account is taken of the increase in the number of contributors in each *ludă* and the depreciation of silver money during the period, the burden on the average taxpayer grew substantially. Decisions about the number of *lude* per district, which categories of taxpayers should be included in each, and how the tax should be collected were made by central treasury officers in consultation with local officials. The same system may have functioned in Moldavia also, but here, it seems, village elders had the deciding voice in apportioning the tax among the rural inhabitants. Certain other fiscal categories, such as the merchant and artisan guilds, were also subject to the *bir* and were organized into fiscal units, called *cruci* (crosses), but they paid less than the peasants.

The great advantage to the state of the allocation of its most important tax by *lude* and *cruci* was collective responsibility for its payment. Such insurance was essential in the countryside, where flight was the chief weapon used by the peasants to elude both state taxes and the exactions of private landlords. If a family fled or for some other reason could not meet its obligations, the other taxpayers in the *ludă* were forced to make up the difference. Thus, the burden of preventing the flight of the rural population to escape taxes, a major economic and social problem of the period, was shifted from the state bureaucracy to the village.

Unlike the *bir*, which was always collected by the fiscal agents of the prince, other taxes such as the tariff duties and the *oierit* were leased to great *boiers* and wealthy merchants. The *otcupci*, as these tax-farmers were known, found the

---

[37] S. Columbeanu, 'Sistemul de impunere pe lude din Ţara Românească (1800–1830)', *Studii: Revistă de istorie*, 21/3 (1968), 469–79.

practice extremely lucrative because they could engage in an extensive subleasing of taxes on a district and even town level. Both the taxpayer and the state treasury suffered. The former was often forced to pay more than legally required, since taxation had in effect become a private business in which the entrepreneur sought to increase his profits by every means possible. The treasury's revenues were diminished for the same reason.

By creating the *ludă* and by introducing other reforms, Alexandru Ipsilanti and several of his successors had hoped to make the country's financial system more rational, but inevitably they ran up against two major obstacles: the total or partial exemption from taxation of the *boiers* and the monasteries, the possessors of the greatest wealth, and the fiscal privileges enjoyed by many other categories of the population. The princes had, of course, to deal continuously with the immense, and often arbitrary, financial demands of the Ottoman bureaucracy, which made long-term planning and sound management impossible.

The tax burden was thus borne disproportionately by the poor. Perhaps half the population of each principality was excused for one reason or another from paying the *bir*. Social position was decisive. Besides the *boiers* and higher clergy, certain categories of former officials and of relatives of *boiers* in state service paid little or nothing. Only in extraordinary circumstances did the mighty join the ranks of taxpayers, as in 1798 when the church in Wallachia contributed 131,000 *talers* to the *zahire*, and in 1804 when the privileged orders had to pay the *dijmărit* and the *vinărici*. Besides *boiers* and higher clergy, an almost infinite number of privileged groups enjoyed some degree of exemption from the *bir*. According to the Wallachian census of 1819, there were 194,000 families which belonged to the 'third estate' and were, consequently, liable to taxation, but of these, 76,000 were privileged, that is, removed from the ranks of the *birnici* and exempted partially or completely from all taxes.[38] The most numerous of these were the *scutelnici* (protected), of whom there were 20,610 in 1819, and the *posluşnici* (servants) (20,558). They had come into existence in the 1740s after the abolition of serfdom as a means of compensating landlords for the loss of peasant labour. In return for performing various labour and other services for them the *scutelnici* and *posluşnici* were exempted from paying state taxes. Still other categories managed to escape the full weight of taxation. The *neamuri* (*mazili* in Moldavia), the relatives of *boiers* who did not have positions in state service and who formed a kind of provincial gentry, paid a personal tax and were thus not included in the allocation of taxes by *ludă*. Finally, the *ruptaşi*, mainly foreigners, paid a tax on their wealth on the basis of individual arrangements with the treasury.

The fiscal system was thus constrained by tradition. It had been designed

---

[38] N. Grigoraş, 'Privilegile fiscale în Moldova, 1741–1821', *Anuarul Institutului de Istorie şi Arheologie*, 14 (1977), 41–53, and 18 (1981), 183–200; I. Constantinescu, 'Aspecte ale destrămarii feudalismului în Ţara Românească şi Moldova la sfîrşitul secolului al xviii-lea şi începutul secolului al xix-lea', *Studii şi materiale de istorie medie*, 9 (1978), 9–42.

primarily to satisfy the immediate needs of the prince, his suzerain, and the *boiers*. But at the end of the eighteenth century its antiquated structures impeded economic development and social progress, partly because the princes and *boiers* were not masters in their own house and could not change it, but also because too few of them thought in terms of nation and of their responsibilities to it.

THE ORTHODOX CHURCH

The Orthodox Church in Moldavia and Wallachia at the end of the eighteenth century was a national church: the overwhelming mass of the inhabitants belonged to it; it had been intimately connected with the political fortunes of the principalities since their formation in the fourteenth century; and it had impressed its theology on both high culture and literature and popular beliefs and customs. The church's role in economic life was also substantial, for monasteries collectively were the largest landholders in both principalities, and their productivity vitally affected the ability of the country to meet its obligations to the Ottoman state. For the population at large the church provided a variety of services for which the state had not yet taken responsibility—health, education, poor relief, and the recording of vital statistics. In public administration the clergy sat alongside the *boiers* in the highest councils of state and dispensed justice in civil as well as ecclesiastical cases.

While the church thus served as a national institution, it was at the same time an integral part of the Eastern Orthodox world. Romanian contacts with the South Slavic churches went back at least to the tenth century, and canonical links with the patriarchate of Constantinople had been inaugurated in the fifteenth century. By the eighteenth century Greek influence in the Moldavian and Wallachian churches had become pervasive, thanks in large measure to the influence of the Phanariot princes and their families. The patriarch of Constantinople still exercised the right to approve the election of the metropolitans of Moldavia and Wallachia (or Ungrovlachia in ecclesiastical terms) and was the final authority in questions of doctrine and ritual, but in all other matters the Romanian churches were independent. Direct ecclesiastical contacts with the other Eastern patriarchates—Alexandria, Antioch, and Jerusalem—were far less intense than they had been in the seventeenth century, but the financial support which all the Orthodox churches of the East traditionally drew from the principalities increased in the eighteenth century. In particular, the 'dedicated monasteries', part of whose income was reserved for good works in the East, contributed enormous sums to the defence of Orthodoxy in the Ottoman Empire. As a result, the two Romanian churches enjoyed a special place within Eastern Orthodoxy, and their metropolitans were entitled to follow immediately after the patriarch of Constantinople at meetings of the patriarchal synod.

Relations between the Romanian churches and the Russian Orthodox

Church dated from the sixteenth century and, while friendly, they had never been as close as those between the Romanians and the Greek world. These contacts entered a new phase after the Treaty of Kuchuk Kainardji. Although they became more intense in the period 1774–1812 than they had ever been before, the experience did little to promote better relations between the two church hierarchies. Attempts by Catherine II and Alexander I to impose their political will on the principalities were accompanied by the heavy-handed interference of the Holy Synod in St Petersburg in the governance of the two Romanian metropolitanates.

Two examples stand out. During the Russo-Turkish War of 1787–92 Russian occupation authorities placed the Romanian churches in the hands of prelates sympathetic to Russian political aims in South-eastern Europe. In Moldavia after the death of Metropolitan Leon Gheuca in 1788 the Russian military commander, with the approval of Catherine II and the Holy Synod, brought Archbishop Amvrosii of Ekaterinoslav to Iaşi as administrator of the metropolitanate. His deputy was Gavriil Bănulescu-Bodoni, a Romanian born in Transylvania who had served in the Russian church in various capacities. When the Russian army withdrew from Moldavia in 1792 under the terms of the Treaty of Iaşi, it left behind Bănulescu-Bodoni, whom Russian occupation authorities had installed as metropolitan. He was arrested by the new prince at the behest of the sultan and sent to Constantinople, from where he was soon repatriated to Russia.

The two Romanian churches fell under Russian control again during the Russo-Turkish War of 1806–12. This time the relationship appeared permanent because the tsar had plans to annex the principalities and subordinate their churches to the Holy Synod. An imperial decree in 1808 appointed Bănulescu-Bodoni, who had retired as metropolitan of Kiev in 1803, exarch of Moldavia and Wallachia.[39] The Holy Synod quickly followed with instructions to the new prelate to seek its guidance in all administrative and spiritual matters. These acts signified nothing less than the annexation of the Romanian churches and the severing of their links to the patriarchate of Constantinople.

The two Romanian metropolitans firmly resisted these uncanonical proceedings. Veniamin Costache of Moldavia resigned immediately after Bănulescu-Bodoni's appointment as exarch and withdrew to the monastery of Neamţ. In Wallachia Dositei Filitti refused to recognize Bănulescu-Bodoni and was, as a result, summarily removed by the Russian Holy Synod in 1809. His replacement was a Greek, Ignatie, the metropolitan of Arta in Epirus, who was installed without regard for the traditional forms of election. His inability to speak Romanian and his unfamiliarity with local custom added to his unpopularity.[40]

[39] E. C. Suttner, 'Metropolit Gabriel Bănulescu-Bodoni', *Ostkirchliche Studien*, 22/4 (1973), 281–301; A. Stadnitskii, *Gavriil Banulesko-Bodoni, Ekzarkh Moldo-Vlakhiiskii (1808–12 gg.) i Mitropolit Kishinevskii (1813–21 gg.)* (Kishinev, 1894), 86–90.

[40] E. G. Prōtopsaltēs, *Ignatios Mitropolitēs Oungrovlachias (1766–1828)*, i (Athens, 1959), 73–82.

He and Bănulescu-Bodoni were, none the less, supported by Russian authorities because they belonged to that large body of Orthodox prelates in South-eastern Europe who loyally served Russian interests as a means of freeing their own churches from Ottoman domination. But neither had any interest in the burgeoning national movements of the South Slavs and Romanians. Bănulescu-Bodoni was a talented administrator who had ambitious plans for church reform in the principalities, but he was obliged to leave when Russian troops withdrew after the signing of the Treaty of Bucharest in 1812. He was immediately appointed metropolitan of a new exarchate formed between the Prut and Dniester Rivers (Bessarabia). At about the same time Ignatie left Bucharest for Vienna, where he became active in the Greek political and cultural revival.

The metropolitanate of Ungrovlachia, with its suffragan bishoprics of Rîmnic, Buzău, and Argeş (after 1793), and the metropolitanate of Moldavia and its suffragan bishoprics at Roman and Huşi possessed extensive and complex administrations. The clergy enjoyed considerable autonomy in managing church affairs, but laymen, especially the prince and the great *boiers*, played crucial roles in fiscal and personnel matters and in broad questions of policy. The supreme legislative authority of the church was vested in the general assembly (*adunarea obştească*), or *Sobor*, which dealt with the most important matters of church government such as the drafting of new laws and the judging of members of the higher clergy and *boiers* of the first rank charged with some grave offence. Besides the metropolitan, who presided, the bishops, and the egumens of the largest monasteries, the prince and councillors of the divan were members by right. The general assembly met infrequently, in part because the princely divan, on which the metropolitans and bishops sat, also concerned itself with a variety of ecclesiastical matters. The metropolitan synod, which was composed of leading churchmen, dealt with the more routine problems of church government. It, too, was rarely convoked because many questions which fell within its purview were settled directly between the prince and the metropolitan. A consistory, whose functions were primarily judicial, was used by the clergy to blunt the interference of the prince and his officials in matrimonial cases and the judging of priests, a practice that had become common in the eighteenth century. At the local level the protopope, an archpriest who had supervisory powers over a number of parishes, played a key role in church administration. He was the vital link between the metropolitan and the bishops, on the one hand, and the parish clergy, on the other. It was he who collected the ecclesiastical taxes, carried out the investigation of priests accused of wrongdoing, served as a judge of the first instance in certain, minor cases, and had primary responsibility for the instruction of the parish clergy in the performance of their pastoral duties.

The prince and the *boiers* had a decisive voice in choosing the metropolitans and bishops by virtue of their control of the divan and the general council. The process of electing the metropolitan of Ungrovlachia began when the prince summoned the divan to nominate a candidate. Sometimes the divan might propose as many as three candidates, from among whom the prince would choose one. The prince then summoned the general council, which was composed of high churchmen, egumens of important monasteries, and *boiers*, to approve his choice. They rarely disappointed him. In 1793, for example, Alexandru Moruzi's sponsorship of Dositei Filitti in the divan, where the decisive vote usually came, was sufficient to ensure his accession to the metropolitan throne. The canonical election, carried out by the higher clergy alone, followed the action of the general council. The whole procedure had evolved over many centuries, and the election of the metropolitan by an assembly of churchmen and *boiers* continued in this way until the 1830s. The participation of the prince and other laymen seemed natural to all concerned because the election of high churchmen was an event of general public, not simply ecclesiastical, concern.

The parish clergy, although excluded from higher ecclesiastical bodies, also played a crucial role in public affairs at the local level, but the majority were ill-prepared for their multiple spiritual and administrative responsibilities.[41] As a group they had only a partial understanding of Holy Scriptures, and many could not perform the liturgy or administer the sacraments properly. The lack of seminaries was the main cause of their imperfect training. Several schools for priests were established in the last quarter of the eighteenth century at the metropolitanates, the bishops' sees, and a few monasteries, where candidates received an elementary introduction to their priestly duties. Here and there in a larger village or town an enterprising priest might open a modest school to provide the would-be priest with the rudiments necessary for conducting the service. But the majority of priests did not attend these schools. Instead, they were recruited from among young men, usually the sons of priests, called *grămătici*, who assisted the priest in carrying out his duties and thus, through practice, learned the church service and the other responsibilities of their calling. The 'curriculum' they thus followed usually included reading exercises in the *ceaslov* (a book containing prayers for different times of the day) and the *psaltire* (psalter), church singing, and, occasionally, a little arithmetic. The language they used was always Romanian. In the eighteenth century Greek did not replace Romanian in the village church and was usually heard only if the priest uttered a *vozglas* (a phrase sung at the end of a prayer) in Greek, an act that was taken as a sign of great erudition by his flock. Once the village priest had taught his pupils all he could he sent them to be ordained. Sometimes after ordination they remained for a time at the metropolitanate or bishop's see for additional instruction.

Princes often took the initiative in improving the training of priests because they performed indispensable public services. While the higher clergy concerned itself with administration, doctrine, and the publication and translation of church

---

[41] Dumitru Furtună, *Preoțimea românească în secolul al XVIII-lea* (Vălenii de Munte, 1915), 23–36, 154–62.

books, and participated in the affairs of state, the parish priests were the ones who had direct, daily contact with the mass of believers. As models of good behaviour they had immediate responsibility for maintaining satisfactory moral standards and combating superstition among their flocks and preaching obedience to the reigning prince. They also helped to preserve public order in times of crisis, as when war came or the plague struck. In the general absence of other means of communication both the state and the church depended upon the priest to transmit vital information and instructions to the populace. Yet, despite the key role of the priest, fundamental changes in clerical training came only after the turn of the century.

Monasteries remained essential economic and social institutions in the eighteenth century. They controlled great expanses of arable and forest lands, and their income amounted to almost one-third of the total state revenues in both Moldavia and Wallachia. As in the past they performed important social and cultural functions. They maintained the first modern hospitals in the principalities, operated schools for neighbouring communities, trained monks and nuns, supported the translation of theological works from Greek and Russian into Romanian, and engaged in the copying of manuscripts in Romanian, an indispensable service in a period of limited printing facilities.[42]

The eighteenth century witnessed a general renewal of monastic life after a decline in the second half of the seventeenth century. Administration, finances, and discipline were strengthened by new legislation promulgated by the princes. The whole effort at reform reveals the power of the prince and of state institutions to direct church affairs. In Moldavia Prince Constantin Mavrocordat initiated the reforms in 1733 with a *hrisov* modifying the procedure for electing the heads of monasteries. It allowed the metropolitan and an assembly of clergy to continue to name the *egumen*, but reserved to the prince the right to invest him with his staff. Mavrocordat's *aşezămînt* of 1741 promoted stability in the administration of monasteries by permitting the removal of an *egumen* only after a thorough investigation and with the consent of the prince. It also required all monks to live in the monastery and forbade them to engage in commerce and other non-religious activities. Similar reforms were also being introduced in Wallachia. Here Alexandru Ipsilanti was concerned mainly with the fiscal disarray of the monasteries, which had adversely affected the general financial health of the country. Like his counterparts in Moldavia, he did not hesitate to use his powers to change internal ecclesiastical administration, as in the *hrisov* of 1777, which severely limited the authority of *egumen*s to contract loans. The fiscal and moral well-being of monasteries remained princely concerns well into the nineteenth century.

The dedicated monasteries created intractable problems for the princes and the

---

[42] In the absence of a general study, see the following for a detailed account of income and expenditures of a single monastery: D. Agache, 'Veniturile şi cheltuielile mănăstirii Sf. Spiridon din Iaşi între anii 1771 şi 1823', *Anuarul Institutului de Istorie şi Arheologie*, 15 (1978), 335–51.

Romanian church hierarchy.[43] The practice of dedicating monasteries had begun in the sixteenth century when the founders of monasteries provided for regular financial contributions to sister institutions outside the principalities. As Greek influence in the principalities grew in the seventeenth century, a number of monasteries were, in effect, taken over by Greek monks, who often ignored the bequests of their founders and used the income as they wished. The consequences of such acts grew more serious in the eighteenth century as the number of dedicated monasteries increased. Removed almost completely from native ecclesiastical and political jurisdiction, they sent abroad large amounts of money, which princes and metropolitans were eager to use for their own projects.

Efforts by several princes in the latter eighteenth century to modify the status of the dedicated monasteries encountered fierce opposition from all the Eastern patriarchs, who went so far as to seek from successive princes recognition of the monasteries as the inalienable property of the holy places of Eastern Christendom. These prelates enjoyed the full support of Russian officials, who counted upon the loyalty of the Orthodox clergy throughout the Near East to further Russia's aims in the Ottoman Empire. Because of these international complications, a solution to the problem of the dedicated monasteries did not come until the middle of the nineteenth century. From another perspective, the controversy over these institutions was but one aspect of the burgeoning process by which the Romanian principalities asserted their individuality within the Eastern Orthodox world.

As the administration of the monasteries suggests, the interests and activities of church and state were closely intertwined. Experience grounded in the Byzantine tradition, rather than specific legislation, had determined their relationship over the centuries. The cooperation of the higher clergy and the *boiers* on the same governmental and church bodies reinforced this tradition and was, moreover, a natural consequence of their similar social origins, education, and outlook on life.

The higher clergy did not regard the state as an entity separate from the church and did not challenge the prince and the *boiers* to a contest for supremacy. Nor did they formulate a political and social policy separate from that of the state. Instead, they recognized that church and state had complementary missions to fulfil. They provided the state with moral and spiritual support in return for material aid to the church and respect for its religious autonomy.

The nature of church–state cooperation is exemplified in the activities of the higher clergy on the divan and other public bodies. Here the prestige of ecclesiastical office entitled them to precedence over the *boiers*. The metropolitan occupied first place after the prince on the divan and in general gatherings of the nobility, and he was president by right of the divan. If the prince presided, the metropolitan spoke first in the deliberations. But if the metropolitan judged

[43] A. D. Xenopol, *Istoria Românilor din Dacia Traiană*, vi (3rd edn., Bucharest, n.d.), 24–32; I. F. Stănculescu, 'Reforme, rînduieli și stări bisericești în epoca fanariotă', *Biserica Ortodoxă Română*, 81/5–6 (1963), 540–4.

a case by himself, he made a report (*anafora*) to the prince, presenting the facts and recommending a solution. The prince reserved to himself the right of final decision, but he rarely withheld approval of the metropolitan's recommendation. At times of grave national crisis, when, for example, the throne was vacant, the metropolitan assumed political leadership of the country. In 1806 Metropolitan Veniamin Costache of Moldavia was *caimacam*, or temporary head of government, and in 1808 in Wallachia Metropolitan Dositei Filitti and the bishops of Buzău and Argeş were leading membes of the provisional government during the Russian occupation. At other times, the higher clergy spoke on behalf of the whole nation, as in 1802, when Dositei Filitti addressed memoranda to the emperors of Austria and Russia imploring their help in stopping the ravages of Turkish irregulars in Oltenia. High churchmen were often entrusted with delicate diplomatic missions, as in 1772, when the metropolitan of Wallachia headed his country's delegation at the peace negotiations between Russia and Turkey at Focşani. None of these churchmen, however, aspired to the permanent exercise of political authority. Once the crisis had passed or they had completed their mission, they returned to their ecclesiastical duties.

Another vital area of church–state cooperation was the administration of justice, even though a secularization of judicial institutions and procedures had been under way since the middle of the eighteenth century. Nevertheless, in Wallachia, despite the reforming zeal of Alexandru Ipsilanti and others, the church retained its own courts, and metropolitans and bishops continued to sit alongside the great *boiers* on the highest tribunals of the land.[44] The competence of church courts was not limited to strictly spiritual matters or to cases involving only the clergy. They had primary responsibility also for deciding cases of marriage, divorce, and inheritance. Metropolitans and bishops regularly authenticated legal documents such as dowry agreements and wills, and were often entrusted with the safe keeping of important papers, especially contracts for the sale of land. The clergy had thus made themselves indispensable to the judicial system and would remain so until fundamental structural changes began to be introduced in the 1830s. Alexandru Ipsilanti himself recognized their unique qualifications when in 1781 in a letter to the metropolitan he praised their intimate knowledge of *obiceiul pămîntului*, the *pravilă*, and the legislation of princes.

Despite their close cooperation, the relationship between church and state was not that of equals. In the latter half of the eighteenth century princes often treated the church and its clergy in a cavalier manner. They had a decisive voice in the selection of the highest ecclesiastics, taxed the clergy when it suited their purpose, and judged by themselves cases affecting the clergy. Occasionally, they

---

[44] A. Constantinescu, 'Contribuţii ale bisericii în justiţia Ţării Româneşti sub Alexandru Ipsilanti', *Biserica Ortodoxă Română*, 97/1–2 (1979), 165–78.

even instructed the clergy in matters of ritual, as Mihai Suțu did in a decree of 1785 concerning baptism. The clergy did not take these violations of its rights lightly. Disputes with the prince over taxation were especially acrimonious. In 1794 the Moldavian clergy led by Metropolitan Iacov Stamati rose up against Mihai Suțu's demand that they contribute grain to the *zahire*, protesting that they had never before been subjected to such a tax, and in 1798 Metropolitan Dositei Filitti publicly opposed new taxes announced by Prince Constantin Hangerli. Although the prelates might thus challenge the prince on specific issues, they did not question his right to rule or seek to create institutional limits to princely power.

THE ROMANIAN QUESTION

After the Treaty of Kuchuk Kainardji the political and economic development of Moldavia and Wallachia became increasingly tied to the growing interest of the major European powers in South-eastern Europe. Russia, which in the eighteenth century had replaced Poland on the eastern frontiers of Moldavia, was intent upon superseding the Ottoman Empire as the dominant power in the region and viewed control of the principalities as crucial to the success of this enterprise. Austria, which had extended her frontiers to western Moldavia and northern Wallachia as a result of successful wars against the Turks at the end of the seventeenth century and had briefly (1718–39) occupied Oltenia, nurtured projects for both economic and political expansion beyond the Carpathians. French interest in the principalities intensified at the beginning of the nineteenth century, when Napoleon perceived their usefulness as pawns in the great-power rivalries in the Near East. Great Britain also treated the principalities from the broad perspective of shifting international alliances and her own economic and strategic goals in the Eastern Mediterranean. All four powers were ready to dispose of the principalities as suited their purposes as they searched for solutions to the Eastern Question. Yet the rivalries and combinations of the powers, however threatening they might be to the existence of the principalities at a given moment, none the less gradually removed them from the exclusive jurisdiction of the Ottoman Empire and made them an object of international concern and, eventually, of international guarantees. In time the fate of the principalities, though never divorced from grander issues, became a distinct problem of European diplomacy.

The powers together advanced various schemes in the 1770s to use the principalities to compensate one another for gains and losses of territory elsewhere. Typical was Frederick the Great's proposal during the latter stages of the Russo-Turkish War of 1768–74 that Prussia and Austria also benefit from the hostilities. To settle conflicting territorial claims he suggested that Russia be compensated for any losses with a province of Poland, that Prussia and Austria also help themselves to Polish territory along their frontiers as compensation for Russia's gains, and that Poland be consoled with the acquisition of Moldavia and Wallachia. The project foundered because the principals could not agree on the precise division of the spoils.

The powers also occasionally found uses for the principalities as buffer states. Catherine II of Russia was willing, at least in 1770, to recognize the perpetual neutrality of the principalities as a means of checking the conflicting ambitions of the other major powers. Joseph II of Austria in 1771 even considered re-establishing them as independent states free from both Ottoman suzerainty and Russian occupation.[45] Nothing came of either idea, because of opposition from the sultan and lingering expectations of territorial gain by the powers themselves. A variation on the idea of Romanian independence was included in Catherine's so-called Greek Project of the 1770s and 1780s. This bold plan for the elimination of the Turks from Europe called for the cession of the western half of the Balkans to Austria and, in the east, the revival of the Byzantine Empire composed of Greece, the Aegean Islands, and the Slavic areas south of the Danube with Catherine's grandson as emperor; Moldavia and Wallachia, serving as a neutral zone between the three powers, would be united to form a kingdom of Dacia under a prince acceptable to Russia and Austria. Joseph at first approved the idea, but then drew back out of fear of unforeseen complications.

Russia was the most aggressive of the powers in pursuing her special interests in Moldavia and Wallachia. Between 1768 and 1812 she fought three wars with the Ottoman Empire and at the end of each weakened Ottoman suzerainty and expanded her own influence over the principalities. Outright annexation was rarely absent from the calculations of Russian statesmen. As early as 1770 the imperial council approved the incorporation of both Moldavia and Wallachia into the Empire as a legitimate war aim, but often the principalities were simply used to further Russia's territorial ambitions elsewhere.

The Treaty of Kuchuk Kainardji provided the legal sanction for Russia's intervention in the affairs of the principalities, giving her an initial advantage over Austria and other European rivals. When the Ottomans ignored the provisions of the treaty and the *hatti-sherifs* of 1774 Russia pressed her case so forcefully that a new war appeared imminent. Through the mediation of France, which sought friendly relations with both Russia and the Ottoman Empire, all the matters in dispute were papered over in the Convention of Ainali Kavak of 1779. The principal aim of Ottoman negotiators was to regain full suzerainty over the principalities by annulling the offending portions of the Treaty of Kuchuk Kainardji and abrogating the *hatti-sherifs*. They argued that there was no legal basis for the concessions they had granted the principalities because Sultan Mehmed IV (1648–87) had never offered them a privileged status through capitulations, as the Romanian delegates at Focşani in 1772 and later claimed.

---

[45] T. G. Djuvara, *Cent projets de partage de la Turquie* (Paris, 1914), 278–305.

The Russian government knew that the texts of these capitulations were forgeries, but its diplomats argued disingenuously that the inhabitants of the principalities should be treated in accordance with their own notion of what period had been most advantageous to them. This view prevailed in the final text of the convention. It provided that all the provisions of the *hatti-sherifs* of 1774 be strictly enforced, a stipulation which made the decrees international agreements no longer subject to annulment on the sole authority of the sultan.[46]

Of utmost importance also for the future of the principalities was Ottoman acquiescence in the appointment in Bucharest and Iaşi of Russian consuls, who quickly became the chief representatives of Russian interests in the principalities. The first Russian consul took up his post in Bucharest in 1782 and was followed by a vice-consul in Iaşi in 1784 and a commerical agent in Galaţi in 1796 to supervise Russian trade on the lower Danube. The main function of the consuls, who were directly responsible to the Russian ambassador in Constantinople, was political—to transmit advice and admonitions from their superiors to the prince and the *boiers* and to gather information on conditions in the principalities which could justify Russian intervention in their affairs. The consuls did not hesitate to negotiate with the prince and his divan on all sorts of matters, an activity which violated both the spirit and the letter of treaties between Russia and Turkey. Repeated protests from the Ottoman government brought forth assurances from the Russian ambassador that the consuls would deal only with him, not the princes or *boiers*, and that he in turn would inform Ottoman authorities of conditions in the principalities requiring action, but, in fact, the consuls carried on as before and acquired a decisive voice in the internal affairs of the principalities.

Russia's policy towards Moldavia and Wallachia appeared contradictory at times because it was dictated by the pursuit of broader objectives in the Ottoman Empire. On the one hand, Russian officials and diplomats sought the support of the Phanariots and other Greek lay and ecclesiastical leaders in Constantinople by promising them a dominant role in South-eastern Europe after Russia had expelled the Turks. But, on the other hand, they encouraged the peoples of the region to pursue their own national aspirations by rising up against Ottoman rule, a goal which ran counter to Phanariot ambitions to preserve the unity of the historical Greek cultural world. In the principalities themselves Russian officials tried to stiffen the resistance of the Phanariot princes to Ottoman political encroachments and economic demands and at the same time urged the *boiers* to defend the privileges of their class against both the Turks and the princes. By playing off these elements against one another, the Russians hoped to reserve the power of decision to themselves.

The Convention of Ainali Kavak proved to be only a truce. The matters at issue between Russia and the Ottoman Empire were wide-ranging and irrecon-

---

[46] Hurmuzaki, *Documente*, NS i. 14–19.

cilable—the Crimea, the Black Sea, and the Caucasus, besides the Balkans—and both sides continued to prepare for the next military showdown. The *sened* (note) issued by the sultan in 1783 extended the truce in the principalities by confirming the provisions of earlier agreements with Russia, but it left fundamental differences unresolved.

Austria was Russia's chief rival for economic and political advantages in the principalities. She had already manifested her intentions by annexing Bukovina, the northern portion of Moldavia, in 1775. The appointment of the first Austrian consul in Bucharest in 1783 and the granting of the right of free navigation on the lower Danube and in the Black Sea by the Turks in 1784 brought intensified interest in the principalities and made Russian preponderance there unacceptable. Austria sought in particular to use the Danube as the main route for her exports to the East and as a wedge challenging Russia's attempts to dominate the principalities and the territories to the south. In the pursuit of these goals in the final decades of the eighteenth century Austrian authorities supported the establishment of navigation companies, the exploration of the Danube, and, especially, the deepening of the Olt River in order to open a direct water route between Transylvania and Russian and Ottoman ports on the Black Sea.[47]

When war broke out between Russia and Turkey again in 1787 Austria joined the conflict in order to protect her new interests. The causes of the war were many, but disputes over Russia's expanding role in the principalities and the Ottoman demand for the withdrawal of the Russian consuls from Bucharest and Iaşi had contributed substantially to the deterioration of relations.

Austria declared war on Turkey in February 1788. In Moldavia Austrian armies won successes in the north, occupying Iaşi jointly with the Russians on 3 September and capturing the fortress of Hotin on the 19th, but their advance southwards was blunted by the combined forces of Prince Nicolae Mavrogheni of Wallachia and the Turks. Since Austrian armies were stretched thin along a battle line running between Hotin and the Adriatic, they undertook only minor action on the Wallachian front until the fall of 1789, when they finally crossed the Carpathians. Commanded by the Prince of Coburg, they won a decisive battle over the combined Wallachian and Ottoman armies near Rîmnic Sarat on 22 September and took Craiova on 8 November and Bucharest on the 10th.

It is evident from the way Coburg set about organizing the administration of Wallachia that military occupation was intended simply as a prelude to annexation. He formed a new governing council composed of leading *boiers* and higher clergy and required them to swear allegiance to Joseph II. But Coburg's mission was abruptly ended by the decision of Joseph's brother and successor, Leopold II, to cut Austria's losses in the Turkish war and make peace, because of the dangerous situation in the West caused by the French Revolution. By the Treaty

---

[47] N. Docan, 'Exploraţiuni austriace pe Dunăre la sfîrşitul veacului al XVIII-lea', *Analele Academiei Române*, Memoriile Secţiunii Istorice, 2nd ser. 36 (1913–14), 541–709; G. Netta, *Expansiunea economică a Austriei şi explorările ei orientale* (Bucharest, 1931), 36–132; Hurmuzaki, *Documente*, xix/1 (Bucharest, 1922), 680–5.

of Şiştovo (4 August 1791) Austria received small bits of territory in the Banat, but was obliged to evacuate the principalities.

Russia's aims in the principalities gradually changed as the war ran its course and other powers threatened to become involved. The main concerns of Russian policy-makers were, in any case, elsewhere: expansion in the Caucasus towards Persia and the acquisition of the ports of Ochakov and Akkerman on the Black Sea. As for the principalities, Catherine II at first continued to favour their union into an 'independent' state called Dacia under Russian patronage, and in February 1788 she urged the Moldavians and Wallachians to form militias to assist her armies, calling attention to their common Orthodox faith.[48] Yet, by the end of that year, having achieved her major objectives and concerned about Poland and the possibility of European intervention in the Balkans, Catherine was ready to make peace and to evacuate the principalities. When the Ottomans initially rejected peace overtures, Russian officials considered a permanent occupation of both Moldavia and Wallachia, but then the Turks, defeated on all fronts, and the Russians, facing the threat of war with Britain and Prussia, finally came to terms. The Treaty of Iaşi (9 January 1792) provided for the withdrawal of Russian armies from the principalities and recognized Ottoman suzerainty over them. But it left the Russian consuls in place and allowed Russia to annex the territory between the Bug and the Dniester Rivers, thus bringing Russia for the first time to the borders of Moldavia. The treaty also repeated all the guarantees of autonomy made to the principalities since 1774 and was followed by new statements of principle by the sultan regulating the payment of the tribute and the provisioning of Constantinople and limiting the entrance of Ottoman subjects into the principalities. Russia's position as the dominant power in the principalities had thus been immeasurably strengthened.

Other powers, particularly France, showed a growing interest in Moldavia and Wallachia as the century came to an end. Before this time French policy-makers had all but ignored the principalities as they focused their attention on the major issues at stake in the Near East. The tenure of Vergennes as foreign minister (1774–87) was marked by efforts to maintain friendly relations with both Russia and the Ottoman Empire. He sought to detach Russia from Britain and Prussia and bring her closer to Austria, the ally of France since 1756, and yet he wished to prevent the breakup of the Ottoman Empire, which, he was certain, would benefit only Britain. It was owing to his good offices, moreover, that the differences between Russia and Turkey had been temporarily smoothed over in the Convention of Ainali Kavak. His successor, Choiseul, was less successful in harmonizing conflicting interests in the Near East as the worsening economic and political situation at home diminished French influence in Ottoman affairs.

During the turbulent decade before Napoleon became first consul in 1799 the principalities continued to count for little in the calculations of French leaders. At

[48] G. S. Grosul, *Dunaiskie kniazhestva v politike Rossii, 1774–1806* (Kishinev, 1975), 91–9.

the height of the Revolution they paid little attention to the Near East in general, but in 1794 the Committee of Public Safety resumed an active policy in Eastern Europe as a means of counteracting hostile coalitions and of aiding Poland. The committee showed a special interest in the Romanian principalities as a convenient base from which to launch a Polish insurrection against France's continental enemies. French agents joined Polish *émigrés* in Moldavia and Wallachia in recruiting men and gathering supplies, but support among the local population for the venture proved lukewarm. In 1797 the Directory, which had come to power in Paris two years earlier, dropped the project, in part because it viewed Russia as a potential ally. Yet it also sought to remain on friendly terms with the Ottoman Empire in order to further French commercial interests and in the same year succeeded in establishing the first French consulates in Bucharest and Iaşi.[49] But no sooner had they begun to function than they were abruptly closed, casualties of Napoleon's Egyptian campaign. The Treaty of Amiens (27 March 1802), which brought a truce between Britain and France, also restored peace between the latter and the Ottoman Empire. The political settlement was followed shortly by a new commercial agreement, which allowed French merchant ships to navigate freely in the Black Sea and restored old privileges, which had granted French merchants favourable tariffs.

The reopening of French consulates in Bucharest and Iaşi in 1803 marked the beginning of a decade of intense French interest in the principalities. The prospects of increased trade in the Black Sea encouraged both French officials and businessmen to view Moldavia and Wallachia as sources of raw materials and especially as lucrative markets for French goods. They also figured prominently in Napoleon's many schemes for a reordering of the political map of Southeastern Europe as he shuffled them back and forth between prospective allies.

The rivalry between France and Russia to a great extent determined the political history of the principalities between 1803 and 1812.[50] It was a perilous time for them. As the great powers tried to settle differences among themselves they were constantly threatened by outright annexation or coveted as compensation for territorial exchanges elsewhere in Europe. Their claims to autonomy were largely ignored, as their princes were disposed of to suit the interests of the powers, as foreign military administrations were imposed upon them, and as the two metropolitanates became appendages of the Russian church.

Napoleon's treatment of Moldavia and Wallachia as he pursued his broader European ambitions was characteristic. Up to 1802, convinced that the territorial division of the Ottoman Empire was inevitable, he expressed sympathy for the aspirations of its subject Christians. Moldavian *boiers* took such pronouncements to heart and in 1802 presented him with a proposal to establish an independent

---

[49] Hurmuzaki, *Documente*, suppl. 1, pt. 2 (Bucharest, 1885), 100–30, 171–6, and pt. 3 (Bucharest, 1889), 396–402, 454–68.

[50] S. Columbeanu, 'Contribuţii privind situaţia internaţională a Ţărilor Române între anii 1806–1812', *Revista de istorie*, 29/5 (1976), 657–76.

'aristocratic republic'.[51] But their ideas made no impression in Paris because the realities of the great-power rivalry in the Near East had now persuaded Napoleon that a breakup of the Ottoman Empire would be of greatest benefit to his arch-enemy Britain. He thus came around to the idea that the empire could serve his purposes best if it remained intact as an impediment to both British and Russian expansion. He now bent all his efforts towards its preservation and sought to discourage movements for national self-determination. Changing course, he denounced the Serbian uprising of 1804 as an attack on a legitimate sovereign and recognized full Ottoman suzerainty over the Romanian principalities.

Napoleon was by now convinced that Russia was the chief threat to the integrity of the Ottoman Empire and, hence, to France's own position in the Eastern Mediterranean. His representatives in Constantinople sent back a stream of warnings about how insidious the influence of the Russian ambassador at the Ottoman court was and how effectively he used the competition among the Phanariots for the thrones of Moldavia and Wallachia and other high offices to obtain appointments favourable to Russia and to turn government policies to her advantage. The rivalry between the two powers in South-eastern Europe intensified after France acquired control of Dalmatia and other South Slav territories from Austria as a result of the Treaty of Pressburg (26 December 1805). Continued military successes in Central Europe, coupled with aggressive diplomacy, brought unprecedented French influence at Constantinople. French diplomats were successful in having members of the imperial divan favourable to Russia replaced by partisans of France, and Napoleon's own warnings to Sultan Selim III about the Russophilia and the dubious loyalty of Constantin Ipsilanti of Wallachia and Alexandru Moruzi of Moldavia brought about their dismissal in 1806. Tsar Alexander responded in kind. His forceful reminder to Selim that the removal of the princes violated earlier agreements and could have baleful consequences for continued good relations between their two countries brought their return a few months later. But the tsar had no intention of leaving Russia's position in the principalities to chance. He decided to use force. Citing Russia's treaty obligations to maintain order in the principalities, especially in Wallachia, which had been repeatedly attacked by Turkish troops and mercenaries from south of the Danube, he ordered his army to cross the Dniester on 22 November 1806. Meeting only moderate resistance, Russian troops entered Bucharest on 25 December.

A dramatic change now occurred in Napoleon's relations with Alexander, which boded ill for the future of the principalities. The French victory over the Russians at Friedland on 14 June 1807 led to negotiations between them on fundamental questions of European peace and order. Napoleon was eager to gain Alexander's support against Britain at a time when the overthrow of Selim III (29

---

[51] E. Vîrtosu, *Napoleon Bonaparte și proiectul unei 'Republici aristo-democraticești' în Moldova, la 1802* (2nd edn., Bucharest, 1947), 3–29.

May 1807) had caused him to revise again his estimate of the viability of the Ottoman Empire. The destruction of Selim's reform programme and the ascendancy of the conservatives in Constantinople convinced him that the empire could not long survive and disposed him to work out a division of the spoils with Alexander. At Tilsit in July they came to a general understanding. Alexander agreed to declare war on Britain and join the continental system, if Britain rejected Russian mediation of her war with France. In return, Napoleon, in a burst of generosity, agreed to the Russian annexation of all Ottoman territories in Europe except Rumelia and Constantinople.

The Romanian principalities were a side issue at Tilsit. Napoleon and Alexander regarded them as provinces of the Ottoman Empire subject to the same treatment as its other territories, not as autonomous states under Ottoman suzerainty. Article 22 of the treaty provided for the withdrawal of Russian armies, but stipulated that Turkish troops would not be allowed to return to their fortresses until the final peace treaty between Russia and Turkey had been ratified. Although Russian and Turkish negotiators signed a convention at Slobozia on 24 August 1807 calling for the evacuation of the principalities by both sides within thirty-five days, Alexander could not bring himself to give up his advanced positions on the Danube. In early November 1807 he requested Napoleon's formal approval to annex the principalities, citing his services to the French cause and the inability of the Turks to maintain order there. Why, he asked, refuse Russia provinces which circumstances would eventually bestow upon her anyway.[52] At the moment Napoleon could think of no better use for them. Besides, Russian greed could serve as a pretext for his own retention of Silesia and other Prussian territories.

Continued negotiations between France and Russia resulted in the Treaty of Erfurt (12 October 1808), which brought into being Napoleon's long-sought alliance with Alexander. It also appeared to settle the fate of the principalities. Napoleon recognized their annexation by Russia and accepted as a condition of any peace between France and Britain the latter's approval of Russia's actions. For his part, Alexander agreed to keep these provisions secret and to negotiate a peaceful cession of Moldavia and Wallachia with the sultan. In this way Napoleon sought to keep the Turks from 'running into the arms of the English', if they discovered prematurely how the principalities had been disposed of.

In the following years, as Napoleon's difficulties with Russia grew, he came to regret the concessions he had made at Erfurt.[53] He worried that he had compromised the independence of the Ottoman Empire and that the collapse could change completely the state of things. He now looked for ways to prevent Russia from establishing herself on the right bank of the Danube and began to woo Austria.

[52] D. A. Sturdza, *et al.*, *Acte și documente relative la istoria renașterei României*, i (Bucharest, 1900), 661–73.

[53] G. Lebel, *La France et les Principautés Danubiennes* (Paris, 1955), 155–66.

Absorbed in the struggle against Napoleon, Austria could do no more than watch with growing anxiety the increase of Russian power in South-eastern Europe. The Treaty of Erfurt had been especially painful because Austria had territorial pretensions of her own in the principalities and was, in any case, eager to share in the division of the Ottoman Empire. Her recovery after the Battle of Wagram (5–6 July 1809) and the growing strains in the Franco-Russian alliance raised her value as an ally. As Napoleon and Alexander competed for her favour the principalities became choice bait. The tsar wanted Austria's support in the struggle with Napoleon, which he thought inevitable, and offered to cede parts of Moldavia and Wallachia and all of Serbia to her in return for military assistance.[54] But Metternich, who had become foreign minister in October 1809, remained non-committal, for he knew that Austria had a more formidable and dangerous suitor in Napoleon. The latter, meanwhile, kept assuring Alexander of his steadfast friendship and of his lack of interest in the principalities. But in 1811 he promised to return them to the sultan, if he would join the war against Russia, and then later in the same year, calling the Danube an 'Austrian river', Napoleon offered the principalities, and Serbia to boot, to Austria as payment for an army of 50,000 men for the Russian campaign.

Yet another power showed an interest in the principalities. As a consequence, at least in part, of Russian pressure on the Ottoman Empire, Britain became more attentive to events generally in South-eastern Europe at the end of the eighteenth century. The Levant Company, though in decline, saw advantages in acquiring such Romanian raw materials as lumber and grain and sought markets for cloth and other manufactured goods. The company's persistence finally brought a concession from the sultan in 1802 granting British merchant ships the right to free navigation in the Black Sea and on the lower Danube. The British government, however, regarded the principalities in the 1790s mainly as a barrier to further Russian penetration of the Ottoman Empire and, thus, like the other powers, treated them at first as pawns of its own diplomatic manœuvring. Political, rather than economic, concerns led to the establishment of the first British consulate in the principalities in 1803. Its purpose was to serve as an advanced post from which to observe the activities of French agents and to counteract the growing influence of Russia and Austria in the Balkans.[55]

British trade with the principalities remained modest. Not even such a talented representative of the Levant Company as William Wilkinson, who also served as consul in Bucharest between 1813 and 1816, could overcome the control of Moldavian and Wallachian commerce exercised by the Ottomans or stir greater interest among British merchants. The number of ships flying the British flag in the Black Sea and the Danube increased significantly only after the Ionian Islands

---

[54] On Alexander's offer and the reaction of Austrian officials, see H. Heppner, Österreich und die Donaufürstentümer, 1774–1812 (Graz, 1984), 146–51.

[55] P. Simionescu and R. Valentin, 'Documents inédits concernant la création du consulat britannique à Bucarest (1803)', Revue roumaine d'histoire, 8/2 (1969), 241–62.

came under British protection in 1815, when many Greek merchants, representing British interests, established themselves in Galați and Brăila.[56]

In the autumn of 1811 a decisive political change occurred on the lower Danube. Tsar Alexander, who was anxious to free his armies for the showdown with Napoleon, signed an armistice with the Ottomans on 28 October. Further negotiations led to the signing of the Treaty of Bucharest on 28 May 1812. Confronted by Napoleon's anti-Russian coalition and certain that an attack was imminent, Alexander had gradually reduced his territorial demands on the principalities to that part of Moldavia that lay between the Dniester and Prut, the territory that came to be known as Bessarabia. He also agreed to evacuate both principalities three months after the ratification of the treaty, and indeed the last Russian troops departed in October 1812. The principalities came once again under Ottoman suzerainty, and new Phanariot princes were dispatched from Constantinople.

The defeat of Napoleon and the establishment of a new European order at the Congress of Vienna had little immediate effect on the principalities. The Ottoman Empire was not represented at the congress, and the powers implicitly recognized the Treaty of Bucharest as having regulated matters in South-eastern Europe. Yet, the Treaty of Vienna (9 June 1815) contained clauses which could not but affect the future development of the principalities. One of these proclaimed the freedom of navigation and commerce on the major rivers of Europe, including the Danube, from the point where they became navigable to their mouths. Together with Russia's new status as a riverain state and the increased presence of European shipping in the Black Sea, this stipulation promised to open the principalities further to international commerce and to bring them more directly to the attention of European diplomacy.

After the Congress of Vienna Russia regained the predominance she had had in Moldavia and Wallachia before 1812. Her ambassador in Constantinople and her consuls in Bucharest and Iași resumed forceful intervention in their internal affairs and sought to make their political élites supporters of Russian aims in South-eastern Europe. The task of Russian diplomats was made easy by the immense prestige their country enjoyed among both Phanariot princes and native *boiers*, because of her victory over Napoleon and the leading role she had played at the peace conference. Moreover, the Romanians were certain that their liberation from Ottoman domination would be carried out by Russia rather than Austria or the Western powers and eagerly offered their cooperation. They regularly supplied Russian diplomats with information on Ottoman abuses and drew up countless memoranda detailing their own aspirations, which they justified with ample legal and historical arguments. The princes, in particular, took advantage of the situation to expand their role in foreign affairs by corresponding

[56] P. Cernovodeanu, *Relațiile comerciale româno-engleze în contextul politicii orientale a Marii Britanii (1803–1878)* (Cluj-Napoca, 1986), 36–9.

directly with the Russian ministry of foreign affairs, a blatant violation of their vassal status.

The main Russian objective was to wrest permanent control of the principalities from the Turks, but the tsar preferred negotiation to war in order not to upset the international alliance system which he had promoted at the Congress of Vienna. Russian diplomats, therefore, insisted upon respect for the autonomy of the principalities, a tactic which they knew would weaken Ottoman suzerainty and enhance Russia's popularity among the *boiers*. Yet, the Russians did not always pursue these ends with perfect consistency. Alexander's desire for a peaceful accommodation with the sultan ran counter to the views of his representatives in Constantinople. Grigorii Stroganov, who became ambassador in 1816, favoured a hard line in dealing with the Turks. He was certain that offers of friendship and compromise would fail because the Turks would never allow Russia to exercise permanent influence over their Christian subjects. Nor did he think that Russia should sacrifice her vital interests in the region for the sake of an uncertain alliance with the West Europeans.[57]

In the principalities Russian officials found it advantageous to play the prince and the *boiers* off against one another. Stroganov from Constantinople and Alexander Pini, the consul in Bucharest, used the insatiable fiscal demands of the prince as a convenient ploy for invoking Russian protection of the population, both privileged and unprivileged. But they were careful not to alienate the prince completely. Rather, they sought to strengthen the divan, where the great *boiers* and the higher clergy sat, as a counterweight to the prince by giving it an expanded and more independent role in administering the country, especially in financial matters. Thus, when Prince Alexandru Suţu of Wallachia sought to increase his civil list in 1819, Stroganov instructed Pini not to allow the matter to come before the divan unless the *boiers* and clergy supported it.

The tsar received support in his efforts to reach a peaceful accommodation with the sultan from Metternich, who was anxious to prevent the outbreak of revolution in the Balkans. Metternich wanted particularly to remove the causes of conflict between Russia and Turkey because, in his view, they bore primary responsibility for the maintenance of order in the region. Through the correspondence of Friedrich von Gentz, his confidant, with Prince Alexandru Suţu of Wallachia he urged the sultan to make concessions to Russia on boundary questions in the Caucasus as a 'necessary sacrifice' to preserve stability in the Near East.[58]

Negotiations between Russia and Turkey, which had resumed in earnest in June 1820, finally led to a general agreement on a whole range of outstanding issues on 3 April 1821. With regard to Moldavia and Wallachia, the two parties repeated the principles first enunciated in the Treaty of Kuchuk Kainardji and

---

[57] I. S. Dostian, *Rossiia i balkanskii vopros* (Moscow, 1972), 145–51.

[58] I. C. Filitti, 'Corespondenţa domnilor şi boierilor români cu Metternich şi cu Gentz între 1812–1828', *Analele Academiei Române*, Memoriile Secţiunii Istorice, 2nd ser. 36 (1913–14), 973–1025.

reaffirmed most recently in the Treaty of Bucharest. Now the two powers went further. They specified that the divans should have a role in the drawing-up of future financial agreements regulating the taxes and supplies due the Ottoman suzerain, that payment of all deliveries of supplies be made at current market prices, and that freedom of commerce with foreign countries be guaranteed.[59] Although the outbreak of the Greek Revolution prevented implementation of the new agreement, the administrative reorganization of the principalities, to which the two parties agreed in principle, prepared the way for fundamental constitutional changes during the Russian occupation of 1829–34.

AUTONOMY

The principalities survived the vagaries of great-power rivalries in part at least because the powers themselves could never agree for long on a division of territory or a delineation of spheres of influence. Yet, survival would not have been possible without the strong historical consciousness nurtured by the leading classes of Romanian society. The merit of defending the political existence of the principalities belongs chiefly to representatives of the great and middle *boiers*. They were keenly aware of the differences in legal status between Moldavians and Wallachians, whose connection with the Ottoman state was contractual and provided for mutual rights and obligations, on the one hand, and, on the other, the Greeks, who had lost their political distinctiveness and whose country 'was called Turkey, not Greece'.[60] As the principal bearers of historical consciousness the *boiers* led the effort to convince the Russian, the Austrian, and even the Ottoman court that the principalities had never renounced their autonomy and that it was in the best interest of all concerned to respect it.

The *boiers* were heartened by the changing political circumstances in South-eastern Europe. The Ottoman Empire no longer seemed as formidable as it once had, and they, too, accepted the idea of its inexorable decline. Anonymous pamphlets circulating in Bucharest suggesting the possibility of a territorial division of European Turkey which would benefit the principalities gave forceful expression to their new attitude.

The *boiers*' demand for autonomy was rooted in history and tradition. Their memory of independence, which had been handed down by one generation after another of chroniclers, was manifest at the preliminary peace negotiations between Russia and Turkey at Focşani in 1772. Delegations of *boiers* and higher clergy from both principalities asked Russian officials to return their countries to their 'original relationship' with the Ottoman Empire and to eliminate all the 'additions' such as the exorbitant tribute and the myriad gifts, the deliveries of

---

[59] Hurmuzaki, *Documente*, xviii (Bucharest, 1916), 485–93.
[60] V. Georgescu, *Ideile politice şi iluminismul în Principatele Române, 1750–1831* (Bucharest, 1972), 138.

supplies, and the general subservience which they had suffered under the Phanariots. When the Russian plenipotentiary, Count Alexei Orlov, asked what that original relationship had been, the Romanians presented him with documents showing that the principalities had preserved their autonomy ever since their earliest encounter with the Ottomans in return for a fixed sum. The originals of these documents, however, were no longer to be found, but the Romanians, drawing upon the tradition that such documents (the *ahdnames*) had once existed, made up their own texts.[61] Orlov accepted them at face value, even though he knew them to be false, and two years later the Treaty of Kuchuk Kainardji recognized the old privileges of the principalities as dating from the reign of Sultan Mehmed IV.

The *boiers'* defence of autonomy after the Treaty of Kuchuk Kainardji took various forms. They dispatched petitions to the great powers, in the first instance, to Russia. They repeatedly called upon Catherine II and her diplomats to aid them against the common enemy and to save their countries from incorporation into the Ottoman Empire, a catastrophe, the *boier* Ioan Cantacuzino lamented in 1790, that would be worse than the Lisbon earthquake. The *boiers* also asserted the legal autonomy of the principalities at every favourable opportunity in order to prevent Ottoman officials from exercising their powers north of the Danube and thereby creating precedents for permanent interference in the affairs of the principalities. In the eighteenth century the *kadis* of Brăila, Giurgiu, and Turnu, in particular, had persisted in asserting jurisdiction over cases involving Muslims and Christians outside the *rayas*. In 1774 Moldavian *boiers* and clergy addressed the first of numerous petitions to the sultan in which they demanded that the decisions of their prince in all civil and penal cases not be subject to review by any authority outside the country, that natives of Moldavia and Wallachia not be allowed to appeal cases to any authority other than the prince, and that *kadis* be forbidden to hear cases in the two principalities. Although satisfaction was slow in coming, the *boiers* had none the less reasserted the rights of the prince as the supreme judge and the ultimate source of justice and legislation, a principle which served as the bulwark of political autonomy in subsequent decades. A characteristic expression of their intentions was Ioan Cantacuzino's petition of 1790, which demanded that the Danube be re-established as the border between Wallachia and the Ottoman Empire through the abolition of the *rayas*, that the *boiers'* right to elect the prince in accordance with 'ancient laws' be restored, and that all the fiscal and economic obligations of the principality towards the Ottoman state be combined in the tribute, a single fixed sum payable every two years.[62]

All these legal and historical arguments on behalf of autonomy carried little

---

[61] N. Iorga, *Genealogia Cantacuzinilor* (Bucharest, 1902), 492–508; M. Kogălniceanu, *Cronicele României sau letopisețele Moldaviei și Valahiei*, iii (2nd edn., Bucharest, 1874), 450–62.

[62] N. Iorga, 'Viața unui Mitropolit de altă dată: Filaret al ii-lea', *Convorbiri literare*, 35 (1901), 1125–31.

weight at the Ottoman court, even though the sultan had implicitly recognized the autonomy of the principalities on numerous occasions. As early as the middle of the eighteenth century he had Prince Matei Ghica of Moldavia (1753–6) issue a *firman* forbidding the pashas of Hotin and Bender to render decisions in legal cases in the principality or to summon the litigants to their courts. The office of *capuchehaie*, the representative of the prince in Constantinople, was an open recognition of autonomy. In 1775 the sultan enhanced the *capuchehaie*'s position as a diplomatic envoy by granting him certain immunities and the right to travel on horseback, a privilege reserved to foreign ambassadors. Of fundamental importance in advancing the *boiers*' cause was Selim III's *Kanun-i Cedid* (New Law) of 1792, a charter which was to govern Ottoman relations with the principalities until the Treaty of Bucharest in 1812.[63] By specifying the economic and fiscal obligations of the principalities and by restricting the movement of Ottoman officials and merchants north of the Danube, the sultan tacitly accepted the principle of autonomy, even though he often disregarded it in practice.

As the economic and strategic importance of the principalities grew in the latter eighteenth and early nineteenth centuries Ottoman observance of even the forms of autonomy diminished. The sultan remained impervious to the arguments of historical right advanced by the *boiers* and would not renounce his suzerain rights over them. He clung to a principle that had been restated generation after generation in the formula: 'Moldavia and Wallachia are my inherited property.' Nor would any sultan hear of lifetime tenures for the princes, the election of princes by the *boiers*, the return of the *rayas*, freedom of commerce, diplomatic representation in Europe, or the creation of a national army. Russian intervention was not without effect, but despite successes on the battlefield and intense diplomatic pressure, which brought Ottoman concessions on other fronts, the sultan would not yield in the principalities because they had become the empire's first line of defence in Europe and remained the granaries of Constantinople. Ottoman officials made no secret of their feeling that the cession of Moldavia and Wallachia meant the beginning of the end for the empire in Europe.

Between 1800 and 1812 the *boiers* tried to coordinate their campaign for autonomy with the policies of Russia, France, and Austria towards the Ottoman Empire. They still saw in Russia their main hope of liberation and still to some extent thought of the coming struggle in terms of Orthodox Christendom versus Islam. But their admiration for Russia was no longer as spontaneous and uncritical as it had been in the early years of Catherine II's reign. As their fear of the Turks diminished and as they experienced at first hand Russian military occupation and consular intervention in their affairs they became increasingly wary of exchanging Ottoman suzerainty for Russian autocracy. The *boiers*' sentiments

---

[63] M. A. Mehmet, 'O nouă reglementare a raporturilor Moldovei și Țării Românești față de Poarta la 1792', *Studii: Revistă de istorie*, 20/4 (1967), 691–707.

towards France also waxed and waned as Napoleon seemed inclined or not to further their cause. In any case, the so-called French party remained small, and massive Francophilia was still several decades away. Austria had no genuine supporters among the *boiers*; only as a last resort did they seek refuge across the mountains in Transylvania or send appeals to Vienna.

By the end of the Phanariot era the *boiers* of both principalities had committed themselves to the re-establishment of independence. Iordache Rosetti-Rosnovanu, a great *boier* and high treasurer of Moldavia, put their case succinctly in a memorandum to the Russian ambassador in Constantinople in 1818.[64] He proposed to limit all the obligations of the principality towards the Ottoman state to an annual 'gift'. But he insisted that Moldavia be governed as an independent state and no longer be forced to endure Ottoman interference in her economic and political affairs. A realist, he admitted that Moldavians could not achieve this goal by themselves and recommended that their country seek the 'protection' of Russia. This was the formula that would effectively end Ottoman domination of the principalities within a decade.

---

[64] Georgescu, *Mémoires et projecs*, 69–71.

2

Society and the Economy, 1774–1829

THE economic and social outlines of modern Romania in the latter decades of the eighteenth century and the beginning of the nineteenth were still blurred. Traditional structures appeared intact: agriculture continued to dominate the economy, and in both organization and technology it preserved the legacy of the past; the artisan crafts supplied the majority of consumers with the processed goods they needed in their daily lives and relied on the venerable guild system to regulate production and distribution; commerce deviated in neither direction nor volume from familiar patterns; social structures seemed fixed in time, as the *boiers* maintained their predominance and the majority of peasants, the chief bearers of society's burdens, languished in want and neglect. Yet, this image of immobility is misleading. Beneath the surface broad currents of change were gathering momentum: the population was growing, a phenomenon that was to affect material life and social organization in fundamental ways; within the various social classes differentiation and new alignments were taking place that would lead to the triumph of the bourgeoisie and the eclipse of the *boiers*; and subtle changes in mentality, especially in such matters as property and entrepreneurship would spur the adoption of new economic models.

POPULATION AND SOCIAL STRUCTURE

The paucity of data makes it difficult to follow with certainty the population changes that occurred in Moldavia and Wallachia between the 1770s and the 1820s. Statistics were not regularly or systematically kept. Censuses were occasionally taken for purposes of allocating taxes, but they registered villages and families rather than individuals. The figures they present are, none the less, clear on one point: the population of both principalities was increasing.

Estimates of total population vary considerably from source to source. For Wallachia they range between 600,000 and 1,350,000 in 1774, 915,000 and 1,767,000 in 1812–15, and 1,200,000 and 1,795,000 in 1819–20. The lower figures are probably closer to the actual situation. The population of Moldavia is estimated to have been 320,000 in 1772, 528,000 in 1803, and 1,115,000 in 1826. The latter figure is undoubtedly too high. These increases were occurring mainly in the rural areas, while the number of urban dwellers remained comparatively small. The rural population of Moldavia in 1803 was 479,850 (representing 90.9 per cent of the total), the urban 48,050 (9.1 per cent); in 1832 the figures were, respectively, 1,062,927 (89.1 per cent) and 129,413 (10.9 per cent).[1] Population density in Moldavia increased from 7.7 persons per km² in 1774 to 11.8 in 1803. Similar trends are also discernible in Wallachia.

It is difficult to account precisely for these population changes. Birth and death rates are unknown, although we must assume that the latter was high, because of the rudimentary nature of hygiene and sanitation in both villages and towns, the absence of professional health services for the mass of the population, and, especially, poor diet. Population growth was retarded also by the numerous wars fought on Romanian soil between 1768 and 1812. They disrupted normal agricultural activities and social life, for the movement of armies to and fro was accompanied by civil disorder, the destruction of crops, requisitioning and looting, and the spread of disease. Many villages were simply abandoned as their inhabitants fled to places less exposed to troop movements or sought refuge in another country. Besides war, the increasingly onerous fiscal and economic exactions of the prince, the *boiers*, and Ottoman officials, which were borne mainly by the peasantry, kept many rural inhabitants on the road. Flight was a common phenomenon in the eighteenth century, reaching its height during the Russo-Turkish War of 1768–74.[2] In those years, for example, 91 out of 791 localities in Oltenia were abandoned, and the account books of the metropolitanate of Ungrovlachia for 1772–4 recorded no revenue collections at all because 'the land was without men'. Many villages were similarly deserted during the war of 1787–92.[3] In 1804 and 1805 heavy taxation caused a massive exodus of population from Wallachia to south of the Danube. The effects of flight were usually temporary, for many of those who left their villages returned when conditions improved. At the same time a constant flow of population was taking place in the opposite direction, into the principalities, especially of Romanians from Transylvania and, after the turn of the century, of Jews from Galicia and Bukovina, which made up for some of the losses caused by emigration.[4]

A significant increase of population was evident after 1812. At first gradual, it accelerated between 1830 and 1860. The causes were many. The Treaty of Bucharest in 1812 ushered in a period of relative peace, and the removal of the last of the Phanariot princes in 1821 and new and stringent limitations on Ottoman political interference and economic exploitation brought a measure of

---

[1] E. Negruţi, 'Situaţia demografică a Moldovei în secolul xix-lea', *Revista de istorie*, 34/2 (1981), 243–57; ead., *Satul moldovenesc în prima jumătate a secolului al xix-lea: Contribuţii demografice* (Iaşi, 1984), 13–27; P. G. Dmitriev, *Narodonaselenie Moldavii (Po materialam perepisei 1772–1773, 1774 i 1803 gg.)* (Kishinev, 1973), 56–91.

[2] G. Iscru, 'Fuga ţăranilor—forma principală de luptă împotriva exploatării în veacul al xviii-lea în Ţara Românească', *Studii: Revistă de istorie*, 18/1 (1965), 125–46.

[3] S. Columbeanu, *Grandes exploitations domaniales en Valachie au xviiiᵉ siècle* (Bucharest, 1974), 38–47.

[4] Ş. Meteş, *Emigrări româneşti din Transilvania în secolele xiii–xx* (2nd edn., Bucharest, 1977), 148–73. On the immigration of Jews into Moldavia, see Verax (R. Rosetti), *La Roumanie et les Juifs* (Bucharest, 1903), 1–11, and the introd. to *Izvoare şi mărturii referitoare la evreii din România*, vol. ii, pt. 2 (Bucharest, 1990), pp. xxix–lxxv.

social stability and stirred expectations of progress among leading elements of both the rural and urban population. A change of mood is clearly discernible, but an improvement in the material conditions of existence, which might have reduced the death rate, is less easy to identify. The incidence and severity of the plague and other diseases decreased, in part, perhaps, because of the enhanced effectiveness of the quarantine along the Danube. Yet, the quality and availability of medical care for the mass of the population remained unchanged. Famines were less frequent and less extensive probably because the production of grains and other crops was on the increase, thereby making food more abundant. But it is doubtful that the diet of the majority of the population improved to any significant degree.

Society in the two principalities was organized on the basis of estates, but the pattern lacked the rigidity and clarity of similar structures in Central and Western Europe.[5] The juridical status of each estate had not been regulated systematically, but rather depended upon an accumulation of custom and sporadic legislation over many centuries. None the less, in the eighteenth century the several estates assumed more or less distinct contours. Princely *hrisoave*, especially the reforms of Constantin Mavrocordat in both principalities in the 1740s, solidified the juridical status of the *boiers* and clergy. Other legislation refined the organizational structure of the guilds, enhancing the standing of large merchants and master artisans as an urban élite.

The four principal estates—*boiers*, clergy, urban middle class, and peasantry— were set apart from one another by political, economic, and social privileges and, in some degree, disabilities, and by the often-enunciated principle that each individual should remain within the boundaries of his own estate. Social exclusiveness was expressed through marriage, which remained an association of equal ranks or orders. Discrimination between estates was expressed through titles, clothing and residence, the particular use of the native language, and attitudes towards certain foreign languages and cultures, notably Greek and French. The great *boiers* formed an aristocratic caste, sharply distinguished from *boiers* of the second and third rank. All *boiers*, in turn, were set apart from the *neamuri* and *mazili*, who were the descendants of *boiers* of the first and second ranks respectively, who did not perform state service. In the church a wide gulf of education and standard of living differentiated the higher clergy from the parish priests. In the towns merchants and artisans were far from homogeneous groups either socially or ethnically, and divisions within the ranks of both were often sharp. In the countryside the free peasant was at least marginally better off than his dependent neighbour, but dependency itself displayed myriad variations. The estates system was further complicated by the existence of numerous privileged groups outside the nobility and clergy such as the *poslușnici* and *scutelnici*, whose social position cannot be precisely defined.

[5] V. A. Georgescu, 'Les Assemblées d'états en Valachie et en Moldavie de 1750 à 1831/1832', *Revue roumaine d'histoire*, 11/1 (1972), 27–33.

The *boiers* were the main economic and political force in the country, although they were the least numerous social class.[6] In 1806, for example, there were 593 *boiers* (of all ranks) holding office in the bureaucracy in Wallachia. Even after the brisk selling of titles by the Phanariot princes in the last twenty years of their rule, when the size of the *boier* class grew appreciably, in 1832 there were still fewer than five *boier* families in every one thousand families in Wallachia.

Although the institution of the nobility was as old as the principalities themselves, no effort had been made before the reign of Constantin Mavrocordat in the middle of the eighteenth century to stipulate the conditions for membership of the *boier* class. The general rule until then had been that the possession of land was the primary criterion for *boier* status. At the beginning of the eighteenth century the historian and later prince of Moldavia, Dimitrie Cantemir, suggested in *Descriptio Moldaviae* that the control of land was the primary sign of nobility among the Romanians.[7] The size of the *boier*'s estate usually determined where he stood in the social hierarchy and whether he would be classed among the greater or lesser *boiers*. The large estate, moreover, suggests the existence of a hereditary *boier* class, and, in practice, nobility does seem to have been passed on from father to son.

Constantin Mavrocordat undertook to codify the position of the *boiers* in order to increase their dependence upon the prince and to strengthen their support of the existing political and social system. To accomplish the first goal he made state service (*dregătoria*) the sole criterion of membership in the nobility, and to ensure the loyalty of the *boiers* he guaranteed them exemption from taxes. He also formally divided the *boiers* into two categories—the great *boiers*, who held the nineteen most important state offices, and all the rest, who occupied lesser positions. In 1775 Alexandru Ipsilanti modified the order of *boier* ranks in response to the growing size of the bureaucracy. He divided the old first class into three, relegating the lesser *boiers* and gentry (*boiernaşi*) to classes four and five, but the criterion of state service for membership in the nobility remained in place. The requirement of state service for recognition of *boier* status clearly violated custom, but practical circumstances gradually reconciled tradition and innovation. The term *boier* now meant official, but the official in question was, with few exceptions, also the master of a landed estate. During the second half of the eighteenth century, therefore, state service established one's place in the *boier* hierarchy, but the control of land continued to determine membership itself in the boier class.

The *boiers* were obviously far from being the monolithic institution outsiders held them to be. There was continuous tension between the old *boiers*, who owed their position to inheritance and landholding, and newcomers, who en-

[6] D. Berindei and I. Gavrilă, 'Mutaţii în sînul clasei dominante din Ţara Românească în perioada de destrămare a orînduirii feudale', *Revista de istorie*, 34/11 (1981), 2029–46.

[7] D. Cantemir, *Descriptio Moldaviae* (Bucharest, 1973), 299. But in another place he indicates that it was service to the prince that conferred nobility: ibid. 281–7.

joyed *boier* rank through office-holding or purchase. The provincial *boiers* envied the great *boiers* and others who served in the capital, where they had first call on the favours dispensed by the prince. Then, there were ethnic differences. Native *boiers* resented the intrusion of Greeks who accompanied the Phanariot princes. But in the second half of the eighteenth century the matter had become less acute than earlier because the majority of the Greeks had been assimilated, and thus the *boiers* were for the most part ethnically homogeneous. For example, in Moldavia in 1810, of 465 *boiers*, only seventeen were Greek, and in Wallachia in the 1820s there were but sixty-two Greek *boiers*.

The chief cause of tension within the *boier* class was undoubtedly the view which the great *boiers* had of themselves as an aristocracy, an exclusive group composed of the best elements of society who alone were capable of providing leadership. Such an attitude required a certain style of life. The *boiers* had to live 'nobly'. There were thus certain activities such as commerce in which they could not engage. Ideally, they should live from the land, though not necessarily on it or by managing it themselves. Many *boiers*, in fact, resided in the capital or a provincial town, where they felt obliged to maintain an ostentatious existence befitting their station. Such display was costly, and the debts they incurred and the rewards the prince bestowed upon them bound them more closely than ever to the court.

The last half-century of Phanariot rule witnessed fundamental changes in the lifestyle of the *boiers*. The main cause was contact with the West. Before the adoption of Western European ways *boiers* usually lived easily on the incomes of their estates and comparatively simply. Although the prices of the agricultural products raised on their estates were low, the labour services of peasants and of the *scutelnici* and *posluşnici* and the income from their monopoly on the sale of such items as meat and spirits on their estates provided them with a relatively carefree material existence.

Changes in that way of life became pronounced after the Russo-Turkish War of 1768–74. French influence, which the Phanariot princes had already introduced, became more widespread and intense. It is from this time that the Europeanization of the Romanian upper classes dates, however superficial the process may have been initially. During the war itself the *boiers* came into contact with Russian officers, many of whom were of French, German, or Greek extraction and had a cosmopolitan education. They introduced French dances and European music and card-playing, and they organized evenings of such entertainments. Women regularly attended, and by coming into contact with society outside the family, they began their emancipation. Many *boiers* took to imitating the European nobility not only in lifestyle but also in its symbols, as they eagerly adopted coats-of-arms and drew up genealogies.[8] The upshot of this superficial Westernization was a striving for luxury in all things, from clothing

---

[8] P. Eliade, *De l'influence française sur l'esprit public en Roumanie* (Paris, 1898), 181–90: N. Iorga, *Istoria Românilor prin călători* (Bucharest, 1981), 437–52.

and furniture to amusements. The budgets of many *boier* households were, as a result, severely strained, and bankruptcies became increasingly common.

Such a portrait of the *boiers*, though characteristic, is, nevertheless, incomplete. A number of them were well educated and took an enlightened part in civic and governmental affairs. An outstanding example is the great *boier* Radu Golescu (1746–1818), a large landholder and high official, who possessed a splendid library and provided his sons with as sophisticated an education, including the study of French and Italian, as was possible in the principalities at that time.[9] He and they were imbued with a strong sense of duty to promote the general good. Many other *boiers* led the movements for constitutional reform within the principalities and for independence from Ottoman domination. From their ranks also came the foremost political and economic thinkers of the time.

The old *boier* class, tied to the land and its aristocratic traditions, was gradually being transformed from within. The lower *boier* ranks became more persistent in their demands to share power and privilege with the great *boiers*, and new elements, mainly merchants and bankers, entered the ranks of the *boiers* in increasing numbers, bringing with them social values and aspirations different from those of the settled aristocracy. Many *boiers* from the upper ranks were themselves beginning to engage in commerce and were making investments in industry, and in the process they were adopting the outlook and ethics of their non-noble partners and competitors. Together, they were participating in the formation of the modern Romanian middle class.

In the countryside the peasantry, the overwhelming majority of the population, formed the massive base of the social pyramid. They indeed constituted an estate, but it was of the unprivileged, for the legislation that defined their status put upon them the main burden of supporting the existing social and political order, while depriving them of a voice in managing it, except, perhaps, at the village level. If the peasants were one in sharing taxes, labour obligations, and social disabilities, in other respects they were separated from one another by almost infinite gradations of status, whether they were dependent or free.

In the second half of the eighteenth century the largest stratum of dependent peasants was composed of *clăcași*, that is, those who performed labour services (*clacă*) for a landlord. They were not serfs. In Wallachia in 1746 and in Moldavia in 1749 during the reigns of Constantin Mavrocordat personal servitude had been abolished. The initiative for reform in both principalities had come from the prince and his bureaucracy, who sought to transform the serf (*rumân* in Wallachia: *vecin* in Moldavia) into a regular and reliable taxpayer and a conscientious cultivator of the soil. Otherwise, they reasoned, it would be impossible to meet the growing financial needs of the state, occasioned by an expanding bureaucracy and, especially, by mounting Ottoman fiscal and economic demands. In Wallachia the divan decided on 5 August 1746 that the persons of the *rumâni*

[9] A. Iordache, *Goleștii: Locul și rolul lor în istoria României* (Bucharest, 1979), 13–15.

should be redeemed by a money payment, but that control of the land should remain in the hands of landlords. Thus, the peasant obtained his personal freedom, but had no recognized legal claim to the land. He remained dependent economically upon the landlord, performing labour services for him as rent for the use of land which his family had cultivated for generations. In Moldavia the divan approved a similar settlement on 6 April 1749, but the *boiers* specified that the former *vecini* provide twenty-four days of labour per year. In a sense, then, under the system of *clacă* the economic relations of serfdom continued in fact if not in law in both principalities. Besides labour services, the *clăcaşi* continued to pay various tithes to their landlord and respect his monopolies on the sale of such items as wine and meat and on the milling of grain. They were also mainly responsible for the payment of the *bir* and the numerous other taxes levied by the state.[10]

Many villages still existed where the inhabitants were free of obligations to any landlord and where they themselves controlled the land they worked. These peasants usually had family plots in full proprietorship (*ocina*) and worked the rest of the land in common (*în devălmăşie*) with the other members of the village commune. In law the free peasants were classed with the other 'masters of the land', but, unlike the *boiers*, they were subject to taxation.

The free villages, unlike those which had fallen under the control of landlords, retained ancient rights of self-government. The key institution was the village assembly (*obştia*),[11] where all the adult inhabitants, men and women, took part in the debates and in the making of decisions. Here everyone was equal, but custom often allowed the older male members of the village, 'the good and old men', to take the lead. The village, through the assembly, was the nominal holder of the land that its inhabitants occupied, and the assembly had the responsibility of defending it against encroachments by neighbouring villages and landlords. The village was also a juridical person capable even of selling itself into dependency or engaging itself to perform *clacă*, usually only for a limited period, in return for a loan. At the same time it had collective economic responsibilities towards the state for the payment of taxes and towards its own members for the coordination of their agricultural activities.

As the burden of taxation grew, many free peasants were forced to sell their *ocini* and to accept the status of *clăcaşi*. This practice, which was already evident in the seventeenth century, accelerated in the eighteenth. The *boiers*, who were eager to enlarge their estates, took advantage of the free peasants' need for money by infiltrating the commune and persuading its members to sell their portions to

---

[10] V. Mihordea, *Maîtres du sol et paysans dans les Principautés Roumaines au XVIIIᵉ siècle* (Bucharest, 1971), 79–114; I. Corfus, *L'Agriculture en Valachie durant la première moitié du XIXᵉ siècle* (Bucharest, 1969), 15–37.

[11] On the internal organization of the village commune, see H. H. Stahl, *Contribuţii la studiul satelor devălmaşe romîneşti*, ii (Bucharest, 1959), 25–102.

them, an act of alienation that violated customary law. By the end of the Phanariot period the number of free peasants had been reduced to but a small fraction of the total peasant population.

A discussion of urban society must proceed from the fact that the boundary between the countryside and the cities and towns was far from distinct. Many urban inhabitants retained close ties to the village. As owners of arable and pasture land, they continued to derive a portion of their income from agriculture. The rural areas provided a continuous stream of immigrants to the urban centres. Immigration was, in fact, an essential feature of urban life; it, rather than natural increase, accounted for the growth of population in the cities and towns and imposed upon urban life a more transient, less settled character than the village. Although it is still too early to speak of an urban mentality, the occupations and aspirations of urban dwellers were none the less beginning to create a social consciousness distinct from that of the countryside.

The upper bourgeoisie formed the non-noble élite of the cities. Composed of great merchants who were engaged in long-distance commerce and other large-scale economic activities and of master artisans who produced goods in quantity for an extensive market and employed large numbers of journeymen and apprentices, it dominated the cities in much the same way that the *boiers* dominated the countryside. The one element that characterized all members of this class was wealth. In comparison to the rest of the urban population, no bourgeois was poor; he could afford more than the necessities of life. Another characteristic shared by members of the upper bourgeoisie was a sense of their own rising importance, which gave them social pretensions beyond their origins. Capital, which they accumulated mainly through commerce, but also to some extent from 'manufacturing' (the processing of raw materials in modest establishments or through the putting-out system) and 'banking' (moneylending and money-changing), gave them the wherewithal to rise in the social hierarchy and made them an important component of the machinery of government. The bourgeois already shared a distinctive attitude towards life and work—thrift and industry and a spirit of enterprise in seeking new sources of wealth—which set them apart from the majority of *boiers*. Yet, they had still not developed a consciousness that they belonged to a distinct class with permanent interests of its own. Rather, they were ready to abandon their status and move into the nobility, whose values they accepted as their own. As a result, they invested much of their wealth in land and social climbing.

The great merchants, called *toptangii* in contemporary documents, traded in wholesale quantities of goods, mainly agricultural, which their agents gathered from every corner of the principalities, sometimes at the behest of the princes. Another lucrative enterprise was the leasing of customs duties and salt-mines. The operations of these merchants reached the principal commercial cities of Central Europe, and through a network of correspondents they kept themselves informed of economic trends throughout the continent. Some among them, because of the influence they enjoyed in high places and the large sums they were willing to pay, achieved *boier* rank.

An outstanding figure among the great merchants was Ioan Hagi Moscu.[12] He was the new type of merchant who combined long-distance commerce between Wallachia and the international markets with tax-farming and high administrative positions. Born in 1751 in Salonika into a Greek-speaking Macedo-Romanian merchant family, he expanded its business north of the Danube and through the vast wealth he accumulated he obtained a succession of official positions. Beginning as a supervisor of salt-mines in 1786, within a decade he had risen to *paharnic* (wine-steward to the prince), a *boier* position of the third rank, which he undoubtedly purchased. In 1812 he became Mare Vistier and now exercised extensive powers, notably the collection of the principality's revenues, the disbursement of funds needed to meet its obligations, and the keeping of detailed financial records. At the same time he was busy promoting his own business interests and building his personal fortune by leasing great salt-mines (such as Slănic), various customs duties, and tithes on sheep and pigs. During the Austrian occupation of 1789–91 and the Russian occupation of 1806–12 he made enormous sums by provisioning the two armies.

The liberal professions—lawyers, physicians, teachers—remained small. But the number of clerks, bookkeepers, and others possessing business skills kept increasing as production and trade expanded and the need for complex administrative and legal services grew. After the turn of the century the civil service added significantly to the middle class as government at all levels assumed more varied functions and moved into areas, such as education, which had previously been served by the church.

The poor made up a significant portion of the urban population, but exact figures are lacking. At the top were skilled workers, mainly journeymen and apprentices, but the bulk of the lower classes was formed by domestic servants and casual or day labourers who had drifted in from the countryside. Some were totally dependent upon their employers, the *boier* who lived for much of the year in town or the well-to-do bourgeois permanent resident. Many others retained their contacts with the village and agriculture. All lived a precarious existence and were forced to rely upon family or their own devices in a society which showed little concern for the unprivileged.

The Orthodox clergy did not constitute a homogeneous estate. Significant differences of class, education, and power divided the metropolitans, bishops, and their bureaucracies from a numerous parish clergy. The majority of the higher clergy were recruited from the *boier* class and from among Greek prelates from outside the principalities. They shared with the great *boiers* an outlook on life and certain moral and philosophical assumptions that were characteristic of the Or-

---

[12] D. Limona and E. Moisuc, 'Casa comercială Ioan Hagi Moscu și Stefan I. Moscu din București', *Revista arhivelor*, 37/3 (1975), 256–71.

thodox world of the day. As we have seen, they also sat together on the same government bodies and often pursued the same political and economic goals. In the absence of a regular theological academy, a number of the higher clergy received their training at the princely academies in Bucharest and Iaşi, the most important institutions of learning in the principalities, where admission was usually reserved for the upper classes. Here both secular and religious subjects were taught, and candidates for places in the church rubbed shoulders with fellow *boiers* destined for state service.[13]

The parish clergy was recruited from the humbler strata of society. The peasantry supplied by far the greatest number of priests, and only rarely did a member of the middle class or the lesser *boiers* pursue this vocation. The priesthood, in a sense, formed a closed corporation, since the office was often passed on from father to son, especially in the village. Here the faithful had a decisive voice in the selection of the priest, and cases of church authorities imposing a candidate against the popular will were rare. As general rule, the villagers picked the son of a priest, usually from their village or one near by. In any case, the tradition of election allowed them to choose someone acquainted with local customs and sensibilities. Only if the sons of priests were not available would they request from the bishop the ordination of a local peasant's son and then only if he had served for a time as a church singer (*cîntăreţ*) or sexton (*tîrcovnic*).

Among the peasantry ordination as a priest was eagerly sought. Besides the spiritual calling many undoubtedly felt and the tradition that the 'gift' of the priesthood should not be lost to the family, the material advantages the priesthood offered were a strong attraction. In general, in the eighteenth century priests enjoyed exemption from the *bir*, but the privilege was not absolute and could be modified at will by the prince. The sons of priests, as long as they were preparing for the priesthood and until they reached their majority, were excused from taxes normally owed by peasants. Although priests did not receive a fixed salary, they enjoyed a more or less regular income from fees which their parishioners paid in money or goods for a variety of services performed inside and outside the church, including baptisms, weddings, funerals, and prayers for the dead. The parish priest, especially in the village, usually enjoyed great prestige. He was not only the spiritual guide of his flock, but also often served as their political leader and as the teacher of their children.

The parish clergy was far from homogeneous. A few priests were well off. Those who served the prince's court church or other churches founded by him and those of monasteries, gained significant privileges: they paid no taxes to the state or to their own superiors. Some priests possessed land of their own and employed others to work it. But the majority of priests shared the same hard life as their parishioners. They lived in the same modest dwellings and ate the same

[13] A. Camariano-Cioran, *Academiile domneşti din Bucureşti şi Iaşi* (Bucharest, 1971), 207–15.

monotonous food. They also wore the same clothes, but in the latter part of the eighteenth century, especially in the towns, bishops were making headway in obliging them to wear their priestly vestments, at least in public. Priests who lived in villages where the inhabitants had to perform labour services for the landlord were usually excused from this onerous burden in peacetime, but during war or in other extraordinary circumstances they, too, were called upon to work in the fields.

The majority of priests were subject to an almost endless series of taxes and fees owed to both state and church. As their sporadic obligation to pay the *bir* suggests, they enjoyed tax privileges not because they constituted an estate with a recognized legal status, but because princes occasionally found it advantageous to grant them temporary fiscal relief. Alexandru Ipsilanti's elimination of most state levies on priests is a good example. He was mainly interested in raising the general quality of pastoral care by improving the standard of living and education of priests. But in return he limited the number of priests to 3,500 and stipulated that new priests could be ordained only to replace those who had died. Here he was concerned not so much with spiritual matters as with the maintenance of the taxpaying capacity of the rural population, which an overabundance of priests seriously diminished.[14] During his reign and generally thereafter the main fiscal obligations of priests consisted of regular contributions for the maintenance of schools (payments which lasted until the 1830s) and for poor relief. The payments were made by *lude*, of which there were 3,500 for priests. Thus, officially, each priest formed a taxpaying unit, even though the actual number of priests was much larger. From time to time priests were also subject to special taxes: during the Austrian occupation of Wallachia in 1789–91 they paid for the transport of provisions for the army; in 1794 and 1797 they contributed supplies and money to satisfy extraordinary Ottoman requisitions; and in 1810 each priest was forced to pay into a special fund for the purchase of supplies for the Russian army of occupation. Priests also had to make various payments to their ecclesiastical superiors: a tax when they were ordained and another when a new metropolitan or bishop was installed, an annual 'free-will' offering to their metropolitan and bishop, and a tax to support the district protopope, who did not receive a salary. Occasionally, a priest might avoid a part or all of these obligations by becoming a *poslușnic* of the metropolitanate. In return for fiscal exemptions he performed such services as work in the vineyards or the delivery of correspondence between the metropolitanate and protopopes and parish priests.

Despite all these taxes and fees and the hardships priests often experienced, their number steadily grew because the church offered almost the only opportunity for a peasant to rise above his station. Statistics, however meagre, suggest that for many the long-term advantages of holy orders outweighed the occasional

[14] N. Stoicescu, 'Regimul fiscal al preoților din Țara Românească și Moldova pînă la Regulamentul Organic', *Biserica Ortodoxă Română*, 89/3–4 (1971), 335–54.

inconveniences of taxation and labour services. At the beginning of the nineteenth century an official count showed 3,500 priests in Wallachia and 4,750 in Moldavia, but undoubtedly there were many more. In 1818 the historian Dionisie Fotino put the number of priests in Wallachia at 10,278, a figure that was probably closer to the true state of things than the official census. It was not unusual for a village to support five or six priests when one or two would have served its needs adequately. Discrepancies between the official count and the actual situation were caused by the refusal of superfluous priests to declare themselves. They thus hoped to elude the reforms of princes and metropolitans, who had joined forces to bring order to the parishes. In 1793 Metropolitan Dionisie Filitti of Wallachia, armed with a *hrisov* from Prince Alexandru Moruzi restricting ordinations, required every candidate for the priesthood to furnish a letter from his village justifying its need for a priest. In 1813 Prince Ioan Caragea had to repeat the injunction, because of the drain on the public treasury which unlimited ordinations were causing. He instructed villages to select as priests only men who were not subject to the *bir*, and he withheld permission for the ordination of any candidate until the *ispravnic* had made certain that a new priest was needed. In 1815 Caragea instructed his representative in Craiova, where many unauthorized ordinations were taking place, to subject all priests ordained to the same taxes paid by everyone else. None of these measures proved effective, and by the end of the Phanariot period civil and church officials had made little progress in reducing excessive numbers of priests in rural areas.

A distinct social category in both principalities were the *sudiţi* (Italian, *suddito*), initially foreigners who were engaged mainly in commerce and certain crafts and who enjoyed the protection of their respective consuls in Bucharest and Iaşi.[15] They had come into existence after the Treaty of Kuchuk Kainardji, which, by allowing Russia and later other European countries to establish consulates in Bucharest and Iaşi, had brought the principalities within the system of the so-called capitulations, charters of privileges which Ottoman sultans had granted certain foreign powers. Behind the capitulations was the realization that Muslim law which was essentially religious, could not be applied to Christians. But the extension of the capitulations to the principalities was anomalous, since Muslim law was not in force there. None the less, many foreigners who carried on their business in Bucharest, Iaşi, and other cities enjoyed numerous privileges which set them apart from the rest of the population. The most important economic privilege of these *sudiţi* was the low tariff they paid as merchants on imported and exported goods, a sum not exceeding the 3 per cent *ad valorem* tax specified in the capitulations. They also enjoyed the legal protection of extraterritoriality: disputes between *sudiţi* were judged only by their countries' consuls and in accordance with the laws of their countries of origin; cases involving *sudiţi* and native inhabitants were heard by local authorities, but the consul or his inter-

---

[15] S. Mărieş, *Supuşii străini din Moldova în perioada 1781–1862* (Iaşi, 1985), 40–73.

preter had to be present, and no sentence could be imposed without the assent of the consul. The person and the domicile of the *sudiţi* were inviolable, and they were permitted to own landed property and to engage in retail commerce, rights normally withheld by law from foreigners. The majority of the *sudiţi* enjoyed Austrian protection and thus served to expand Austria's economic and political influence in the principalities. At first, the number of *sudiţi* was small. In Moldavia, for example, there were only 540 heads of household in 1803, but by 1832 they had increased to 4,400, mainly because large numbers of native Moldavians had obtained foreign protection in order to enjoy all the advantages inherent in the status of *sudit*. The number of *sudiţi* peaked at 6,164 in 1859. As the principalities reasserted their autonomy in subsequent decades the protection offered both foreigners and natives was steadily curtailed. Independence in 1877 and the proclamation of the Kingdom of Romania in 1881 brought an effective end to the institution through treaties between Romania and Austria-Hungary, France, and Germany.

The *sudiţi*, along with other foreigners, contributed to the gradual economic emancipation of the principalities. Their own commercial activities helped to undermine the Ottoman trade monopoly and to bring the principalities more fully within the sphere of international trade, and their example encouraged other foreign merchants to establish themselves in the principalities. Yet, the *sudiţi* also symbolized the political and economic dependence of the principalities on the great powers.

Among other foreigners, Jews represented a significant and growing addition to the population, especially in Moldavia. The first Jewish community, formed by immigrants from Turkey, probably settled in Iaşi about the middle of the seventeenth century. From that time until 1834 the Jews of Moldavia enjoyed a separate organization, the *hahambaşie* (*haham*, rabbi) under a chief rabbi. First recognized in 1666 and confirmed on numerous occasions afterwards, it allowed Jews to practise their religion undisturbed and to settle among themselves matters relating to their own community, an organization which resembled the autonomous religious communities of the Ottoman millet system. By the beginning of the eighteenth century Jews, drawn by economic opportunities and relative toleration, had already become sufficiently numerous in certain towns to make possible the formation of their own merchant guilds. By the end of the same century as a result of steady immigration from Austrian Galicia and Bukovina they had also settled in many villages and on the estates of *boiers*, where they engaged in certain occupations—the lending of money at interest and the sale of spirits, particularly *holercă* (brandy) imported from Poland—which Christians had traditionally shunned. The first serious complaints against Jewish immigration now began to be heard.[16] In 1782 a large number of *boiers* urged Prince Alexandru Mavrocordat to drive the Jews from the villages because they were

---

[16] E. Pavlescu, *Economia breslelor în Moldova* (Bucharest, 1939), 320–2.

forcing the peasants into debt by usury and thereby causing serious economic harm to landlords. Although the prince acceded to the *boiers'* request, his successors did not pursue the banishment of Jews from the countryside and the situation thus remained essentially unchanged. Many princes were motivated by self-interest. They found wealthy Jewish merchants and moneylenders useful and depended upon them for loans and other assistance in satisfying Ottoman demands for supplies. As early as 1785 Jewish merchants in Iaşi were lending large sums to the prince's treasury.[17] Many of these merchants, who came from Galicia, became Austrian *sudiţi*, thereby gaining exemption from local laws and putting their indigenous competitors at a disadvantage. They were, for example, able to elude the prohibition against the leasing of land by Jews, which had been enacted on the grounds that it was wrong to allow them to be the 'masters' of Christians. In the early decades of the nineteenth century a number of Jews thus leased the estates of *boiers*, who welcomed the opportunity for profit. These lease-holders were the forerunners of those who founded the great land-leasing trusts at the end of the century.

In the first three decades of the nineteenth century the Jewish population of Moldavia tripled, from 11,732 in 1803 to 36,956 in 1831, 70 per cent of it being urban. The increase in Iaşi in the same period was even more dramatic, from 2,420 to 17,570, or roughly 36 per cent of the total population.

Although Jewish merchants from Turkey settled in Bucharest as early as the latter half of the seventeenth century, Jews in Wallachia remained less numerous than in Moldavia. An official census of 1820 showed only one significant community, that of Bucharest, which was composed of just 127 families. Other documents indicate the presence of a small colony in Craiova and a few individuals in other cities. In 1831 the Jewish population of Wallachia was only 3,316, about 70 per cent of them living in Bucharest. The small number of Jews in Wallachia at this time was undoubtedly owing to the principality's distance from the chief centres of Jewish migration.

Manifestations of anti-Semitism based upon racial hatred were absent during the period. The hostility which Jews encountered was that commonly directed against the foreigner and the economic competitor, although religious antagonism, harking back to an earlier era of religious polemics, was also evident.

At the very bottom of the social scale were gypsies. When the first mention of them appeared in written sources in the fourteenth century, they were already slaves, and they remained so until their emancipation in 1848.[18] They were the property of the prince, monasteries, and *boiers*, and they could be bought and sold and bequeathed like any goods. In the latter half of the eighteenth century princely *hrisoave* eased the rigours of their existence. In 1766 Grigore Ghica of Moldavia forbade sales or bequests of gypsies which broke up families, and in

---

[17] N. Iorga, 'Istoria evreilor în ţările noastre', *Analele Academiei Române*, Memoriile Secţiunii Istorice, 2nd ser. 36 (1913–14), 185.

[18] G. Potra, *Contribuţiuni la istoricul ţiganilor din România* (Bucharest, 1939), 26–65.

1785 Alexandru Mavrocordat removed some of the stigma of being a gypsy when he decreed that a Moldavian who married a gypsy remained free and that the children of such a union were also free. Yet, the economic burdens of the gypsies showed no signs of diminishing. Some gypsies, especially those belonging to monasteries, worked in the fields, while others were employed in *boier* households where they performed a variety of tasks from kitchen work and sewing (for women) to metalwork (for men). Still others exercised a skilled trade and might reside far from their master's residence. Such were the *aurari* (gold-miners), who served the prince, and itinerant artisans who paid their *boier* owners a tax. Foreign in customs, mentality, and appearance from the majority of the population, they lived on the periphery of society. Although they performed valuable services such as metalworking for the population in certain areas, they remained social outcasts.

AGRICULTURE

In the last quarter of the eighteenth century and the early decades of the nineteenth the economy of the principalities rested upon agriculture. In most respects its organization and techniques remained at the level they had known in earlier centuries. The landscape, too, was largely unchanged, for it continued to be dominated by immense expanses of forest, meadow, and pasture. In many parts of Wallachia, for example, great forests extended from the mountains and hilly country of the north over the plains as far as the Danube. Only a small portion of the available agricultural land was under cultivation. In the latter eighteenth century a French observer estimated that only one-fortieth of the arable land was being worked, while the English consul in Bucharest in 1815 put the figure at one-sixth.

Immediately evident about the structure of agriculture and the methods used to work the land is the itinerant nature of production.[19] The very system of cultivation encouraged movement. It was characterized by the continuous opening up of new arable land and the abandonment of old, exhausted fields. This was the practice particularly in areas which were relatively sparsely settled and where the inhabitants had large, almost unlimited amounts of land at their disposal. The peasant ploughed wherever and as much as he wished and simply abandoned the field when it ceased to be productive. Whole villages often moved together, usually over short distances and at relatively brief intervals. But sometimes war or the heavy fiscal demands of the prince or the *boier* landlord caused longer moves. The modest nature of the peasant household made such mobility relatively easy. The peasant could abandon his simple hut with little emotion and easily put

[19] F. Constantiniu, *Relaţiile agrare din Ţara Românească în secolul al XVIII-lea* (Bucharest, 1972), 50.

up a similar habitation elsewhere. Then, too, his main source of wealth—animals—were also mobile.

Peasants treated the land as they had done in previous centuries. The continuous clearing of new land was fundamental to their system of cultivation. Moreover, princes and *boiers* encouraged the practice by guaranteeing those who did so and then worked the new fields full rights of usufruct over the land. But by the end of the eighteenth century the destruction of the forests had become so intense that *boiers* prevailed upon the princes to limit clearing in order to save the forests for other vital purposes. When peasants began to create new arable plots out of pastures and hayfields, princes moved to protect these lands as well.

The right to clear land was essential to the economic health of peasant households, because of their primitive farming methods, which quickly exhausted the soil.[20] They used a wooden plough, or, if they were too poor to own one, a wooden hoe, tools which failed to turn over the soil sufficiently. In the mountains it was customary to plant the same crop, often corn, year after year until the earth could produce no more. Instead of fertilizers, the cultivator used the technique of seed-holes, planting corn seeds mixed with pumpkin and bean seeds in an effort to restore the fertility of the soil. In the plains, where land was more abundant, the usual practice was to plant a field for three years in wheat, for example, and then let it lie fallow for three to six years. Sometimes it was turned into a hayfield, or animals were grazed there for three years and in the fourth year another crop, usually corn, was planted. Such procedures were the only ways of conserving or renewing the productivity of the soil, since regular fertilizing was not practised.

The raising of animals was the most important branch of agriculture. Their sale was the peasant's principal source of income and enabled him to meet his numerous money obligations to the state and the landlord. He also needed work animals to plough his own fields, to perform *clacă*, and to acquit himself of various other obligations such as transport services for his landlord and the Ottomans. Pastures were thus of crucial importance to the peasant, and as they became increasingly scarce in the latter decades of the eighteenth century he and his landlord entered into a fierce competition to control them. Custom obliged the latter to provide the peasant living on his estate with enough pastureland to satisfy his needs, but since neither custom nor written law specified exactly how many animals a peasant needed to maintain himself, the landlord often set his own limit on the number of cattle a peasant might graze on his pastures. Yet, both the peasant and the landlord were eager to expand the production of cattle, sheep, pigs, horses, and goats because animals and animal products were the main items of both domestic and foreign commerce in the later eighteenth and early nineteenth century.

[20] V. Neamţu, *La Technique de la production céréalière en Valachie et en Moldavie jusqu'au XVIIIᵉ siècle* (Bucharest, 1975), 43–208.

The cultivation of vineyards and wine-making were major preoccupations of both *boiers* and peasants. Orchards were also numerous, especially in hilly country, where immense quantities of plums were harvested and used for the making of *ţuică* (brandy). Wines from certain regions, such as Cotnari and Nicoreşti, in Moldavia, were famous for their high quality, but other wines, though good, were in less demand because of uneven methods of processing. From the very beginnings of significant wine production hired labourers, especially *scutelnici* and *posluşnici*, rather than dependent peasants had been employed in the vineyards.[21] Since the Turks did not use alcohol, wine and *ţuică* escaped the Ottoman commercial monopoly and were a key element in the economy of both principalities. The princes took extraordinary measures to protect local producers from foreign competition, since the excise tax on wine contributed significantly to state and princely coffers and the production and sale of alcoholic beverages was a major source of income of *boier* and monastery estates.

Grains dominated crop agriculture.[22] First in importance was corn, the cultivation of which had spread rapidly among the small peasant producers since its introduction into the principalities probably in the latter half of the seventeenth century. In the eighteenth century it became the main source of nourishment of the rural population, replacing millet. Its high yields and multiple uses and the lack of interest in it by the Turks encouraged its cultivation. Wheat also occupied an important place in grain production, because of a steady demand on the international market, especially from Ottoman authorities. There were also large plantings of barley, which ranked just behind wheat as the principal grain of the *zahire* and was used by the peasants to feed their animals. Oats and rye were raised in small quantities. The cultivation of vegetables increased steadily in the eighteenth century, especially near cities and towns. Frequently mentioned in the sources and by travellers were cabbage, beans, onions, cucumbers, melons, tomatoes, and radishes. The potato seems to have made its appearance only after 1800 in Wallachia during the reign of Ioan Caragea (1812–18). So-called industrial crops such as flax and hemp attracted little interest, the peasants preferring to buy goods made of these fibres from Transylvania. Tobacco was grown here and there, but was of poor quality and had to compete with tobacco imported from Turkey and Austria.

In the last half-century of Phanariot rule land continued to be the chief source of wealth and, hence, the basis of political power and social standing. But fundamental changes were taking place in the division of land among the various classes, as the *boiers*, and to a lesser extent the monasteries, expanded their holdings at the expense of the peasantry. Within the peasantry itself processes of social differentiation, accelerated by demographic changes and a slowly developing market economy, altered the distribution of holdings. Both a cause and a result of these changes was a new conception of landholding. The traditional

---

[21] C. C. Giurescu, *Istoricul podgoriei Odobeştilor* (Bucharest, 1969), 121–6.
[22] Columbeanu, *Grandes exploitations*, 20.

belief that all land ultimately belonged to the community as a whole was giving way to the acceptance of land as appropriable by the individual, that is, as private property.

The structure of landholding can be established only in general terms, because of insufficient data. It is impossible, for example, to determine precisely the total amount of land belonging to each of the various categories of landholders, or to know the average size of individual holdings within each category. None the less, an approximate idea of the proportion of land controlled by various social classes may be had from general censuses. In both Moldavia and Wallachia about two-thirds of the land was held by the prince, the *boiers*, and the monasteries, while the rest was in the hands of free peasants (*razeşi*; in Wallachia, *moşneni*), who cultivated their plots within the system of communal property or as proprietors of their own holdings. According to the census made by Russian occupation authorities in Moldavia in 1773–4, there were 1,977 villages (*sate*) and small market-towns (*tîrguri*). Of these, 1,830 were listed as belonging to *boiers* and monasteries (*răzeş* villages, unfortunately, were also included in this category).[23] A register of taxpayers of 1803 was more discriminating. Of 1,711 villages and small market-towns, 23 belonged to the state, 215 to monasteries, 927 to *boiers*, and 526 to *răzeşi* (266 villages in northern Moldavia, or Bukovina, were not included because the territory had been annexed by Austria in 1775). Besides an increase in the number of inhabited places, indicating a growth of population, the figures also suggest an increase in the size of individual *boier* domains; of the 927 *boier* villages, 470 were in the hands of 28 large landholding families.

The prince, as head of state, had ultimate authority over the disposition of land. He exercised the right of eminent domain over all property, regardless of the social condition of the holder. All land not legally possessed by his subjects, all the land around cities, and lands confiscated for acts of high treason or lacking heirs belonged by right to him. But he showed little interest in increasing permanently the amount of state land or in turning it into productive domains. He used it instead to satisfy his family, reward his entourage, and cultivate good relations with the higher clergy and *boiers*. As a result of continuous grants, state land steadily diminished in the eighteenth century. When, towards the end of the century, confiscations, uninhabited places, and other sources no longer provided enough land for his needs, the prince had recourse to other, subtler methods of acquisition. A favourite device was to assert the principle that the right of possession be substantiated by written documents. If these could not be produced, the land was considered to have been acquired illegally and thus subject to recovery by the state. In 1796 Prince Alexandru Callimachi of Moldavia established a commission of *boiers* to seek out such lands. The free peasantry, not the *boiers*, became the primary object of such scrutiny.

[23] Mihordea, *Maîtres du sol*, 46–7.

The prince was also a landlord in his own right. Unlike state lands, his own holdings grew continuously through inheritance, purchases, and dowries. Although he was not one of the largest landholders in the country, he none the less had a sufficiently strong economic base to assure his personal standing with the great *boiers*. As a large landholder he had the same interests as they, and he managed his properties and dealt with their inhabitants in similar fashion. Economic cooperation with the *boiers* suggests that the Phanariot princes did not consider themselves simply Ottoman functionaries, but, rather, identified their interests with those of the country and its leading class.

The church had accumulated vast amounts of land over the centuries mainly through donations from princes, *boiers*, and humbler persons. The two metropolitanates had extensive holdings throughout their respective principalities, and individual monasteries, such as Cotroceni, near Bucharest, possessed numerous properties encompassing arable land, vineyards, and mills. All together, the production from church lands, though less than that of *boier* estates, represented a vital contribution to both domestic and foreign commerce and to the state treasury.

As a class the *boiers* were the largest landholders. By the end of the eighteenth century they controlled somewhat more than half the land in each principality. Some of it had come in the form of grants from the princes. But a more important source were the lands of free peasants, against whom the *boiers* mounted a sustained campaign of appropriation. A highly effective device was the *boiers'* penetration of the communal village. By circumventing the traditional rights to communal property enjoyed by its inhabitants, they became co-proprietors of the village, a status which allowed them to buy up the holdings of everyone else.[24] This method of acquiring peasant holdings seems to have been widespread and the resistance of the villages fierce enough to have led to the promulgation in 1785 of *Sobornicescul hrisov*, which forbade 'gifts' of land by members of the village communes to persons who were unrelated to them. But *boiers* had other means of increasing the size of their holdings. Many used their high administrative offices to good advantage. The most lucrative of these offices was the treasury, which put at the disposal of the incumbent an amount of money far greater than the income from his own estate. It was no coincidence that the largest landholders of the time were usually the high treasurers.

The amount of land held by free peasants steadily diminished during the period. Although statistical evidence of the process is fragmentary, it appears that in Moldavia at the end of the eighteenth century *răzeș* villages represented 32 per cent of the total. A comparable figure probably held true for Wallachia also. The free peasants continued to hold land individually or in common, the size of which rarely surpassed what they and their families could cultivate by themselves. But the latter part of the eighteenth century and the early decades of the

---

[24] Stahl, *Contribuţii*, ii. 232–56.

nineteenth were a period of crisis for the free village commune as traditional forms of landholding broke down.

Under the pressures of an increase of population and an expansion, however modest, of the domestic and foreign markets for agricultural products the old system of absolute joint ownership of land gave way to limited joint ownership and, finally, even to demands among wealthier peasants for the recognition of the rights of private property. Those families who sought change were no longer satisfied to use land simply to assure themselves of the minimum level of subsistence recognized by their community. They now regarded agricultural produce as a commodity, and, as their needs no longer had a theoretical limit, they were eager to take advantage of market conditions to raise their standard of living.[25]

Another use of land which became increasingly common at this time also suggests a weakening of traditional agrarian structures. The leasing of estates by both *boiers* and monasteries had become widespread in the second half of the eighteenth century.[26] Originally a spontaneous act, perhaps based on the practice of farming out state revenues, the leasing of land achieved legal recognition through its incorporation into the *Pravilnicească condică* of 1780. The usual procedure was for the master of the estate to lease his land for a specified period of time in return for a fixed sum. The lessee then had the right to receive all the income and labour services due to the master from the inhabitants. All classes of the population participated in the leasing of land—great and lesser *boiers*, merchants, clergy, and peasants—but the most numerous lessees at this time were *clăcaşi*.

In leasing estates, the *clăcaşi* were exercising their traditional right of preemption, which came into force whenever the lands they worked changed masters, even temporarily.[27] Leasing offered them many advantages. They no longer had to perform obligatory labour services or pay the tithe. Nor could the master of the estate impose new burdens upon them during the term of the lease. The *clăcaşi* also obtained other benefits such as the exclusive right to sell alcoholic drinks on the estate. Leasing was in effect a redemption in money of feudal obligations. Sometimes the whole commune entered into the lease arrangement, but usually a more limited group—the leaders or *fruntaşi*—assumed responsibility and thus took the place of the *boier* or monastery in subsequent dealings with the rest of the village. Such a practice suggests that the process of differentiation among the dependent peasantry was well under way. The leasing of land was popular with peasants also because it enabled them to escape the control of a

[25] On the evolution of the idea of property, see G. D. Iscru, *Introducere în studiul istoriei moderne a României* (Bucharest, 1983), 64–120.

[26] I. Constantinescu, *Arendăşia în agricultura Ţării Româneşti şi a Moldovei pînă la Regulamentul Organic* (Bucharest, 1985), 17–42.

[27] Ead., 'Contribuţii la istoria relaţiilor agrare în perioada destrămarii feudalismului: Arendarea pe baza dreptului de protimisis (preempţiune) în Moldova', *Studii: Revistă de istorie*, 25/2 (1972), 241–56.

third party, who, experience had taught them, would be more exacting than their landlord.

The *boiers* opposed the leasing of estates to *clăcaşi* because they were afraid that eventually they would lose control over both the land and its inhabitants. Their apprehension was justified because the practice tended to make the *clăcaşi* more independent of the *boier*, and when the lease period was over they sometimes refused to resume payment of the tithe or to perform labour services. After 1800, therefore, leasing agreements often stipulated that the *clăcaşi* would again meet all their customary obligations when the lease expired. But the *boiers* saw clearly that leasing was contributing to the emancipation of their peasants. They tried, therefore, first to limit and then to abolish the right of preemption enjoyed by the *clăcaşi* in order to be free to lease their estates to other *boiers* and merchants, who would not threaten their property rights. They finally succeeded in persuading the princes to abolish the right of pre-emption in 1815 in Moldavia and in 1818 in Wallachia, even though the princes had earlier encouraged leasing by peasants as a means both of eliminating a major cause of peasant flight—the abuses of landlords—and of strengthening the economic position of peasants, who would thus be better able to meet their fiscal obligations to the state. The abolition of pre-emption was one of a series of measures being advanced by the *boiers* at this time to free their estates from all the obligations which custom had attached to the land and to transform them into their own private property.

The victory of the *boiers* in the struggle over the leasing of estates to *clăcaşi* was only one aspect of the general decline of the peasants' status. By the latter decades of the eighteenth century dependence upon a landlord, either lay or ecclesiastical, had become a way of life for the majority of peasants. The largest category of dependent peasants was formed by the *clăcaşi*, who, while personally free, were bound economically to their landlords by tithes and labour obligations. But dependency took a variety of forms. For example, two large categories of agricultural workers were the *oaspeţi* (guests), who had been brought in from other countries under conditions specified in a princely *hrisov*, and the *băjenari* (fugitives), who had left one estate for another, usually illegally. Both settled on *boier* or monastery estates in accordance with a contract setting down their fiscal obligations to the state and their dues and services to the landlord, which were generally lighter than those owed by *clăcaşi* and were limited to a specific period of time. Often *clăcaşi* and the newcomers lived side by side, a situation that created widespread dissatisfaction among the former. The example of the *băjenari* encouraged many *clăcaşi* to seek better working conditions elsewhere. Because of the shortage of labour in many places in the latter eighteenth century, they often succeeded in improving their status, despite strict state prohibitions against the employment of fugitive *clăcaşi*. At the same time landlords strove to reduce peasants under contract to the status of *clăcaşi* in order to increase the amount of labour and payments from them.

The evolution of agrarian relations between the 1770s and the 1820s followed similar paths in both Wallachia and Moldavia. Here the discussion is based upon conditions in Wallachia, except where otherwise noted.

The most important single obligation of the *clăcaşi* and other dependent peasants during the period was the tithe.[28] It was also the chief source of revenue from the land. According to ancient custom the landlord was obliged to provide the peasants settled on his estate with enough arable land for their subsistence and enough meadowland to provide hay for their animals, and in return he was to receive a tithe on what these fields produced. The system did not work smoothly, for neither side trusted the other. The peasants never willingly met their obligations to the landlord and never on time, while the latter continually sought ways to increase what was due him and did not hesitate to use the coercive power which the state put at their disposal. The collection of the various tithes was often done in an arbitrary manner, which increased the amount taken from the peasant. For example, landlords insisted upon computing the tithe on corn on the basis of the amount of land sown rather than on the actual quantity harvested. Such a practice often meant disaster for the peasant because he was obliged to hand over a fixed amount of grain, even if the harvest had been lean. Tithes were levied on almost everything which the peasant produced —grain, animals, hay, wine—and on almost everything on the estate which he used—wood from the forests and fish from the ponds. Landlords even took to levying a tax on pastures, which, according to custom, they were required to give the peasants free of charge and in sufficient amount to satisfy their needs. But by 1800, as pastureland diminished, landlords were setting limits to the number of cattle they would allow peasants to graze on the estate's pastures. Their justification was that excess cattle, that is, those which they deemed unnecessary for the maintenance of the peasant household and were thus intended for sale, should not fall under the customary obligation to provide free pastureland. The landlords had their way, since no law stipulated exactly how many head of cattle a peasant household needed.

Compulsory labour was the distinctive feature of dependence, and the amount required by the landlord was the subject of an unending contest between the masters of the land and the *clăcaşi*. In Wallachia between 1780 and 1818 the kinds of labour service and the number of work days were stipulated by the *Pravilnicească condică*. But as with other aspects of landlord–peasant relations, the actual state of things depended less upon the letter of the law than upon the degree to which its provisions could be enforced. There were obscurities in the law itself, but the main cause of non-compliance was the refusal of both landlords and peasants to abide by conditions which they thought inimical to their own interests.

[28] Corfus, *L'Agriculture en Valachie*, 17–24.

The *Pravilnicească condică* stipulated that the *clăcaş* render his landlord twelve days of labour annually, a provision which *boiers* and monasteries insisted be fully enforced. Whenever a dispute between landlords and peasants reached the divan this *boier* committee always sided with fellow landlords. It usually based its decision on an arbitrary interpretation of the law which held as invalid verbal agreements between peasants and landlords calling for less than twelve days of labour. Since almost all the agreements between the two parties were verbal and were based on local custom, which varied from place to place, rather than on written contracts, peasant litigants were at a distinct disadvantage and were invariably forced to perform the number of days set down in the law. *Hrisoave* promulgated by Prince Constantin Ipsilanti on 31 July 1804 and by Ioan Caragea on 12 May 1814 in Wallachia confirmed the numerous court decisions, but allowed the peasant to redeem his labour services, if the landlord was willing, by the payment of a relatively small sum each year.

Another labour obligation of dependent peasants was one day of ploughing per year on the fields reserved by the landlord for his personal use. This practice began in the second half of the eighteenth century, but was not formally enacted into law until the very end of the Phanariot period. Its imposition was simply an abuse of authority, approved by courts dominated by large landholders. The area of land thus to be worked was a *pogon*, or roughly half a hectare. Peasant resistance was fierce and often resulted in the substitution of a money payment, one *leu* at first, but later on whatever sum the landlord could exact, sometimes as much as three *lei*. The Caragea Law Code finally sanctioned these practices in 1818. Another labour obligation of every dependent peasant was the cutting and transport of a cartload of firewood for the landlord at Christmas. This task also had its origins in recent, eighteenth-century practice, but became legally binding through litigation well before its inclusion in the Caragea Law Code.

Beginning in the last quarter of the eighteenth century *boiers* (and to a lesser extent, monasteries) engaged in a relentless campaign to increase compulsory labour services. The course of events was similar in both principalities, but in Moldavia the moral rift between landlord and peasant became sharper and the preponderance of *boier* property over peasant holdings greater than in Wallachia. In Wallachia the twelve days of *clacă* established by Constantin Mavrocordat in 1746 remained the norm, despite constant pressure to increase the amount. Shortly after the end of the Russo-Turkish War in 1774 the *boiers* demanded that Prince Alexandru Ipsilanti grant them twenty-four days of *clacă* per year. He flatly refused, fearing that to do so would cause so much unrest among the peasants that all attempts to restore order and foster prosperity would fail. The agrarian legislation he proceeded to have drawn up in 1775 and 1776, therefore, set the amount of compulsory labour at twelve days, a norm confirmed by the *Pravilnicească condică* in 1780.

Landlords in Moldavia were initially more successful than their counterparts in Wallachia in imposing heavier labour services on the peasants. The act of emancipation of 1749 had stipulated twenty-four days of clacă for the former serfs, but the authors of the reform allowed lăturaşi, peasants who had settled on boier and monastery estates on the basis of a contract, to perform only twelve days. Such a disparity between these two categories of peasants led to widespread unrest and flight among the clăcaşi. In 1766, to restore order, Prince Grigore Ghica set the clacă at twelve days, a decision that apparently signified a peasant victory. But Ghica, to satisfy the boiers, introduced the nart, an amount of labour necessary to count as a full day, which, in fact, took one and a half to two days to perform (in Wallachia the nart represented two days of ploughing, one in the spring and one in the autumn).[29]

The landlords became increasingly aggressive. In 1775 they petitioned the prince to grant them a tithe of the days of labour, or thirty-six days per year. The prince was indeed willing, but he held back, because of the two-year exemption from payment of the tribute stipulated in the Treaty of Kuchuk Kainardji, relief which made it difficult to justify imposing new burdens upon an exhausted peasantry. But in 1777, the immediate economic crisis having passed, he ordered clăcaşi to perform two extra days of labour, which were to be used in building and maintaining fishponds, mills, and various farm buildings. In 1803 the boiers again demanded a tithe of the clacă. As justification they cited recent unfavourable economic conditions and the unrelenting pressure from the princes to satisfy Ottoman economic demands, all of which, they claimed, required the cultivation of new lands and, hence, more labour. They resorted to a novel argument to support their claims by insisting that twelve days of labour was no longer adequate compensation because the number of days had been set at a time when land was abundant and thinly populated and, hence, of little value, and when the cost of living had been low and the expenses of running the estate modest. Now, they pointed out, all that had changed, for land had become a commodity whose value was increasing steadily, because of the rise in agricultural prices. Prince Alexandru Moruzi accepted their argument and issued a comprehensive aşezămînt on agriculture in 1805 which significantly altered the relationship between landlords and peasants. The new obligations which it forced upon the peasantry increased the number of days of clacă to approximately thirty-three, or, in effect, the tithe the boiers had been seeking. The act went even further. It limited the amount of pasture and hayfields which the landlord had been bound by custom to make available to the peasants on his estate and, in so doing, enlarged the reserve, the amount of land directly under the landlord's control.

The boiers in both principalities sought additional days of labour in order to increase their income. Although production and trade statistics are fragmentary, a general pattern of increased activity on the estates at the turn of the century is evident. Besides more clacă, landlords wanted all the days of labour concentrated at times of the most intensive field work, instead of allowing them to be evenly

---

[29] R. Rosetti, Pământul, sătenii şi stăpânii în Moldova (Bucharest, 1907), 326–30, 462–5.

distributed throughout the year, as had been customary, and they sought to replace communal peasant agriculture with methods that would be more responsive to the market. Such *boier* behaviour suggests an expanding local and even international market for agricultural products, especially grain, and a corresponding eagerness to supply it. Undoubtedly, the demands for supplies of foreign armies—Russian, Austrian, and Ottoman—stimulated production, at least in the short run. Western Europe, too, was showing an increased economic interest in the principalities, but direct trade in Romanian agricultural products was modest and cannot at this time account for the actions of the *boiers*. A greater stimulus to production was the rising Ottoman demand for provisions accompanied by greater flexibility in setting prices at the turn of the century. A flourishing contraband trade outside Ottoman commercial restrictions also affected production, but the precise extent of this trade is for obvious reasons unknown.

Fundamental changes in the *boier* way of life at the end of the eighteenth century may also account for their intensified economic activity, but the evidence is contradictory. The growing contact with Europe—the presence of Austrian and Russian officers, the opening of foreign consulates, which served as introductions to Western social life, the influx of aristocratic refugees from Revolutionary France, many of whom became tutors in *boier* households, and the appearance of Western merchants—led to a gradual replacement of old, patriarchal social values by an imitation of Western lifestyles. Adaptation to new ways, however superficial, required large sums of money. Many *boier* families spent their fortunes with little regard for the consequences and sank deeply into debt. Yet, few of them seem to have thought of increasing their incomes by transforming the economic structure of their estates in order to produce more grain and other agricultural crops for the market. They had neither the inclination nor the managerial skills necessary for the task. Consequently, they continued to divide their reserve into smallholdings, which they distributed to peasants in return for the tithe. Nor were they willing to put substantial investments into the land. They chose, instead, a more certain way of obtaining needed funds quickly by leasing their estates, a practice that suggests their lack of interest in directly overseeing agricultural production. Some of the lessees, after 1800 merchants or moneylenders from nearby towns, had the same concern for an immediate return and the same lack of interest in developing an extensive commercial agriculture. If the lessees were *clăcaşi*, they, too, showed little inclination to depart from traditional agricultural methods.

There is a paradox in the *boiers'* quest for more and more labour from their peasants: a large number of days of *clacă* went unused. Instead of the twelve, and sometimes more, days stipulated in the law codes or other princely legislation, the amount of *clacă* actually performed on many estates did not exceed three to nine days per year. Reliable calculations are possible only for church properties, but they show, for example, that on four large estates belonging to the metropolitanate of Ungrovlachia in Ilfov *judeţ*, surrounding Bucharest, between

1782 and 1786, the inhabitants owed a total of 18,562 days of *clacă*, but they actually furnished only 8,030 days.[30] The allocation of this labour also tells us much about the economic character of these estates. Haymaking absorbed the largest amount of labour (3,939 days), while only a relatively few days were devoted to crop agriculture (for example, 96 days for the threshing of grain). An examination of other properties belonging to the metropolitanate between 1780 and 1786 yields similar results—49 per cent of the obligatory days of *clacă* remained unused. The cause does not lie primarily in the resistance of the peasants, but rather in the inability of the estates to absorb all the labour at their disposal. No significant reserve for the raising of grain existed. Instead, the peasants worked at other tasks, the most important of which were wine production and animal husbandry.

Another apparent paradox was the use by both monasteries and *boiers* of hired labour when large amounts of *clacă* went unused. This practice may be explained in part by the need for skilled workers in the two branches of the estate's economy which brought in the largest income—wine-making and the raising of animals. Landlords could not count on an often indifferent or hostile dependent peasantry to perform specific tasks at the appropriate time and found that money wages were a strong incentive to production. The hired workers (*simbriaşi*) were by no means an agricultural proletariat which was forced to sell its labour in order to survive. They were usually peasants who were anxious to earn money with which to meet their fiscal obligations to the state and their landlords. Both the *simbriaşi* and their employers thought of this arrangement as merely a temporary expedient which did not change the fundamental relationship between them.

Besides furnishing *clacă* and paying tithes, peasants residing on *boier* and monastery properties were also obliged to respect their landlords' monopolies. Both lay and ecclesiastical landlords strictly enforced their exclusive right to sell wine, vegetables, and meat on the estate; to build and operate mills and fulling machines; and to regulate fishing. Increasingly, after 1800 landlords also sought to limit the peasants' traditional free use of forests. They still recognized the peasants' right to cut wood in the forest if it was to be used for heating, but they collected a tax or a tithe on wood destined for construction or the making of such items as pails and shingles.

Although the peasants often tried to circumvent the monopolies on wine and food, they seem to have accepted them as matters governed by customary law. But the efforts of the *boiers* to control the forests provoked fierce resistance. The peasants would not renounce the tradition that the forest belonged to everyone and hence to no one. For centuries the inhabitants of an estate had enjoyed the unrestricted right to cut firewood and take lumber for building or even for sale from its forests. The clearing of forests had been the chief means by which the arable land of the estate had been expanded, and, consequently, the landlord had

---

[30] Columbeanu, *Grandes exploitations*, 90–1.

raised no objections to unrestricted cutting. But by the second half of the eighteenth century the forests had begun to shrink dramatically in size and lumber was becoming scarce and, hence, more valuable. The *boiers* wanted to share in the bounty, and the princes were under constant pressure to preserve the great forest which supplied wood for Ottoman naval vessels and for the repair of fortresses along the Danube. Against such powerful adversaries the peasants found themselves engaged in a losing cause.[31]

The *boiers* had begun to reserve certain forests for their own use as early as the fifteenth century, but documentary evidence of the practice becomes abundant only in the eighteenth century. At first, only small forests were at issue, and as late as 1786 the prince of Moldavia ordered landlords not to keep others from using the great forests lying within their estates. But little by little the *boiers* succeeded in imposing a tithe on wood cut from these forests, on the grazing of livestock there, and on hunting and fishing. In Moldavia Prince Alexandru Moruzi sanctioned these taxes in 1792. His decree, which set down in detail the responsibilities of all who used the forests, was the first true forestry code for the principality.[32] But it also interfered with the slash and burn methods of farming used by the peasants. Noting that the forests near the Prut and Siret Rivers had been almost completely destroyed by such practices, Moruzi prohibited peasants from entering the great virgin forests except to clear away fallen trees or get lumber for building houses. But such injunctions had little effect, since the peasants stubbornly refused to relinquish their ancestral rights to the forest. It was a matter of economic necessity. So long as they used traditional agricultural methods, they could not dispense with the forest. Consequently, it was only after major changes in agriculture had taken place in the middle of the nineteenth century, primarily the development of the large-scale production of grain for the market, that the *boiers* finally gained control of the forests.

Landlords also restricted the peasants' access to pastureland. Custom decreed that landlords provide peasants residing on their estates with sufficient pastureland without requiring labour or other payment in return. But in the latter decades of the eighteenth century they began to limit the number of animals which peasants could graze on the common pastures to those they deemed necessary for the maintenance of the peasant household. They imposed a tax on additional animals on the grounds that these animals were intended for sale. The *boiers* had good economic reasons for their actions, for in many areas peasants circumvented the restrictions on pastures by using the lands of their own villages for grazing, while acquiring new cropland on neighbouring estates. In this way they reaped a double benefit: they assured themselves of adequate grazing land and at the same time reduced their obligations to pay the tithe and perform *clacă*, for on the new

[31] Stahl, *Contribuţii*, iii (Bucharest, 1965), 376–86.
[32] D. C. Sturdza-Şcheeanu, *Acte şi legiuiri privitoare la chestia ţărănească*, 1st ser. i (Bucharest, 1907), 41–6.

lands, owing to the shortage of labour, they were usually able to negotiate better terms.

The *boiers* were anxious to limit the long-established right of the peasants to move their animals from one pasture to another over property lines and cultivated fields. But as late as 1804 the princes sided with the peasants, citing the lack of any alternative, since they 'could not go by air' when taking their animals to market.

A landmark in the contest between landlords and peasants over the control of land was the *hrisov* issued by Prince Alexandru Moruzi of Moldavia in 1805 granting the *boiers* the authority to limit peasant pastures to no more than three-quarters of their estates.[33] He also established the size of the hayfield given each inhabitant of the estate at half a *falce* (at the end of the eighteenth century about one and a half hectares in Moldavia and half a hectare in Wallachia) for each head of cattle and limited the number of horned cattle that a *clăcaş* could keep on the estate to from 8 to 16 head, depending upon the region. Moruzi also divided into four parts the hayfields and pastures of narrow, or small, estates which could not provide their peasants with the minimum required by law. One part was henceforth reserved to the landlord, the other three to the peasants. Far more important than the specific provisions of the *hrisov* was the precedent it set of allowing the landlord to assert, in effect, private property rights over a substantial portion of his estate, which had until then been treated as the common inheritance of all its inhabitants.

Newly cleared lands (*curături*) were also in dispute between landlords and peasants. Custom decreed that peasants could clear as much land as they wished as long as they obtained the prior consent of the landlord. Permission, at least before the forests began to be threatened by destruction, was rarely withheld because clearing was the only way of bringing land under cultivation and thereby assuring the landlord of his tithes. Peasants regarded themselves as the absolute proprietors of the land they cleared and, hence, assumed the right to dispose of it as they wished, but landlords objected, and the documents of the time contain frequent references to their seizure of cleared lands. The landlords wanted to collect tithes and other dues by leasing the *curături* to other peasants from their estate or from elsewhere. As in other matters concerning the control of land and the obligations attached to it, the *boiers* eventually prevailed.

The efforts of the *boiers* to restrict the rights of the peasants over the land was part of a broader campaign to free their estates from all obligations towards the inhabitants which custom had imposed and to gain control over production by altering the traditional methods of peasant agriculture. But it is by no means clear that they intended to transform their estates into commercial enterprises based upon a large reserve producing grain and other crops for the market.

---

[33] Rosetti, *Pământul, sătenii şi stăpânii*, 346–57, 488–96.

A reserve of sorts existed on the *boier*'s estate between the fourteenth and the sixteenth centuries in the form of lands separate from peasant holdings. In the seventeenth century such terms as *delniţa boierească* (the *boier* portion) to designate these lands and *lucru boieresc* (work due the *boier*) to describe peasant labour services suggest that the reserve had achieved a permanent place in the rural economy. But the reserve refers not only to land devoted to the cultivation of grain but also to pastures, vineyards, forests, and even mills and distilleries, which were supervised directly by the landlord or his representative and which employed servile labour.

The sources are too fragmentary to permit a detailed description of the reserve in the eighteenth century, of its place within the estate (whether, for example, it was compact or dispersed), and of the number and categories of persons who worked it. Although indirect evidence suggests that the reserve grew in the final decades of the century in response to an increasing demand for grain and other agricultural products, it is impossible to measure by how much production grew because the data, especially about the size of harvests per hectare, are lacking. In any case, the twelve days of labour per year owed by *clăcaşi* were not sufficient to cultivate large amounts of land. Although the day of ploughing in the spring and in the autumn in Wallachia and the introduction of the *nart* in Moldavia, which provided still more labour, may suggest a growth of the reserve, these obligations, like the *clacă* itself, were often redeemed by a money payment. Estimates of the proportion of peasant holdings to the reserve also indicate the modest size of the latter. In a group of estates belonging to the metropolitanate of Ungrovlachia in Ilfov *judeţ*, the very heart of the Wallachian agricultural region, for the period 1772–80 the above proportion varied between 17 to 1 and 27 to 1. A similar situation prevailed in estates of the metropolitanate in other *judeţe*.[34] Other evidence makes clear that the centre of grain production was not the reserve. Rather, the holdings of dependent peasants covered the landlords' needs almost entirely and supplied grain for both the internal and foreign markets, including Constantinople. The status of the reserve does not seem to have changed significantly in either principality between 1815 and 1830. On estates in four different parts of Wallachia the production of wheat on the reserve in relation to that on peasant holdings varied between 1 to 6 and 1 to 25. Moreover, the landlord continued to get the bulk of his grain from the tithe levied on peasant holdings rather than from *clacă* performed on the reserve. Striking evidence of the small importance which landlords accorded the reserve may be found in the registers of income and expenditures of monastery estates. They did not separate the income derived from cultivating the reserve from that obtained from tithes.

Neither the *boiers* nor the monasteries invested significant resources in the raising of grain and other crops, a practice offering further evidence that the

[34] Columbeanu, *Grandes exploitations*, 81–8.

agricultural reserve was small and relatively unimportant. Instead, they invested in those activities which promised the greatest return. Since the bulk of their income came from the sale of wine and spirits and of animals and animal products, they gave particular attention to viticulture, which was practised on almost every estate, whether in the hilly country or in the plains, and to haymaking and the maintenance of pastureland. The cultivation of the vineyards and the gathering and processing of the grapes required skilled labour, and the storage and transport of the wine special facilities and wagons, all of which required sizeable investments. The operation of flour and fulling mills was another major source of revenue for landlords, and their construction and maintenance were, consequently, important items in the budget of the estate. But landlords spent almost nothing on wages and inventory for the raising of grain and other crops. Rather, they depended upon their peasants to supply both and left decisions about planting and cultivation entirely to them, a lack of interest which persisted into the third and fourth decades of the nineteenth century. To derive benefits from their croplands they resorted to methods that required little investment in either salaries or equipment. Leasing, therefore, was especially attractive.

The modest development of the reserve and the continued reliance upon peasant holdings to supply the bulk of agricultural produce suggest that no significant structural changes in agriculture occurred during the period. Other impediments also account for the lack of progress in agriculture. Demographic factors appear to have been decisive. Low population density, caused mainly by a high death rate, resulted in a lack of adequate manpower. Moreover, the number of persons directly engaged in production was in continuous flux, as the rural population showed a remarkable mobility. The frequent wars and military occupations, the unrelenting fiscal demands of the state, and the general deterioration of the legal status of both the free and dependent peasants often caused whole villages to flee to another estate, another district, or sometimes another country. The flight of peasants often brought agricultural production to a standstill because, as we have seen, most of the agricultural inventory was in their hands. When they left the draft animals and tools went with them. The peasants' almost complete monopoly of the instruments of production also meant that innovations in agricultural methods were the responsibility mainly of those who lacked the wherewithal to put them into effect. Agricultural practices—what to plant, how, and when—continued to be determined primarily by the traditions of the communal village, which yielded only grudgingly to change. The peasant usually had little incentive to increase production because endless taxes and requisitions deprived him of a good part of the fruits of his labour. Obligations to the Ottoman suzerain in the form of forced deliveries of foodstuffs for the *zahire*, the taxes to the prince, and the tithe to a lay or ecclesiastical landlord kept the majority of peasants at a subsistence level.

Despite the weight of tradition, agriculture showed signs of change in the latter decades of the eighteenth century. The market for agricultural products was growing, however slowly, and the rural economy generally was expanding beyond the limits of self-consumption. Paradoxically, the very causes of economic hardship stimulated production. The need to supply the Ottomans with larger and larger quantities of foodstuffs and the requirements of Austrian and especially Russian armies accelerated the rhythm of production and increased the exchange of goods and the amount of money in circulation. The gradual weakening of the Ottoman commercial monopoly made Romanian grain and animals more accessible to other countries, but the full effects of the international market would not begin to be felt until after 1830.

The intervention of the princes in economic matters also did much to stimulate agricultural production. The demands for foodstuffs from the Ottomans, Russians, and Austrians had made agriculture a permanent state concern, and princely regulations designed to expand production became a common feature of agricultural activity. Typical were Alexandru Ipsilanti's circulars to his *ispravnici* in 1779 instructing them to make certain that peasants sowed as much grain as possible in the spring and autumn, and not only corn and millet for their own consumption but also wheat and barley for Constantinople. Ipsilanti's *Pravilnicească condică* inaugurated a continuous stream of legislation intended to place agriculture on rational legal and economic foundations.

The repeated intervention of the princes in agrarian relations altered the traditional balance between landlords and peasants. But they did not follow a consistent agricultural policy. Rather, they were motivated primarily by fiscal concerns and had immediate, practical ends in mind. To the extent that a policy did exist, it was one of encouraging the peasants to produce more grain. In such matters the princes addressed themselves directly to the peasants, not to the *boiers*, a practice which indicates once again that the production of grain depended upon the peasant plot, not upon the *boier* reserve.

The immediate goal of princely legislation was to eliminate disputes between landlords and peasants, which often led to the mass flight of peasants and the consequent interruption of the flow of supplies to the Ottomans and of tax collections for the state treasury. The numerous *așezăminte* and law codes promulgated between 1775 and 1818 aimed at reducing friction by clarifying mutual rights and obligations and by making them uniform throughout the country. The princes eliminated some of the abuses to which the peasants had been subjected, but at the same time they gave landlords a legal basis for violating customary law and private agreements with their peasants and even encouraged them to seek state intervention to enforce the new norms.

Princely involvement in agrarian issues in Wallachia, in particular, reveals the slow and uncertain evolution of policy. Alexandru Ipsilanti laid the foundations of a new era in agrarian relations in the first year of his reign (1774) as he struggled with the catastrophic economic and demographic consequences of the just concluded war between Russia and the Ottoman Empire.[35] His main task was to persuade the masses of peasants who had left their villages during the war to return home and to remain there. He realized that he could accomplish neither objective unless the underlying causes of their dissatisfaction—mounting fiscal burdens imposed by the state and tithes and labour services acquired in often arbitrary fashion by landlords—were removed. Consequently, he resisted demands by *boiers* and monasteries to increase peasant obligations, particularly the number of days of *clacă*. He was also anxious to bring uniformity to the welter of arrangements fashioned by landlords and peasants in accordance with local customs and economic circumstances. He had this objective in mind when he promulgated his most important piece of legislation, the *Pravilniceasă condică*. He was only partially successful in imposing uniformity in agrarian relations, for the code itself allowed landlords and peasants to conclude contracts for a varying number of days of *clacă* below the stipulated norm of twelve. Ipsilanti thus seems to have yielded, reluctantly, to both *boiers* and peasants; *boiers* wanted to require fewer days of *clacă* from peasants to attract scarce labour to their estates, and peasants were eager to accept this 'generosity' as a means of lightening their burdens. But such arrangements thwarted the prince's efforts to prevent the movement of peasants from one estate to another.

The code of laws promulgated by Prince Ioan Caragea in 1818 provides a clear measure of the changes in landlord–peasant relations which had occurred over four decades. It marked in particular the victory of the *boiers* in their long struggle to assert their property rights over the estate at the expense of their dependent peasants. Two provisions of the code stand out: the abolition of all contracts calling for less than twelve days of *clacă*, and a sixteenfold increase in the sum a peasant had to pay in order to redeem his labour services—from 30 *parale* per family per year to 480 *parale*. The immediate aim of the first provision was to discourage the movement of peasants from one estate to another in the search for less onerous labour obligations. But the motivation behind the second is less clear. It cannot be explained by a drastic depreciation of the currency. Rather, it may reflect a growing desire on the part of landlords to receive all the stipulated days of *clacă*. If so, it suggests that production was rising, that prices were increasing, and that labour, which remained scarce, had become more valuable than redemption payments in money. Yet, it was not entirely effective because peasants continued to convert their labour obligations into money payments, even though the practice had become more costly.

The *Pravilnicească condică* had reinforced the principle that every person residing on someone else's land and deriving benefit from its use was subject to *clacă*. But

<hr>

[35] Constantiniu, *Relaţiile agrare*, 145–9; V. Georgescu, 'Date noi despre reglementarea relaţiilor agrare în domnia lui Alex. Ipsilanti', *Studii: Revistă de istorie*, 23/3 (1970), 441–68.

in the early decades of the nineteenth century the notion of *clacă* was different from what it had been in the eighteenth century. The view of the *boiers*, who had drawn up the Caragea Law Code, had prevailed. They regarded labour services simply as rent owed by the peasant in return for the privilege of residing on their estates. Consequently, the *boiers* no longer felt an obligation to offer the peasant anything in return for *clacă*—arable land, hayfields and pasture, or wood for construction and heating—as had been customary. The courts, over which *boiers* presided, and the state bureaucracy upheld this interpretation. The Caragea Law Code, therefore, represented a major advance in the *boiers'* efforts to gain full control over their estates and transform them into private property, unencumbered by traditional economic obligations. But the code did not signify a complete victory for the *boiers*. In several important respects it sustained, at least partially, the peasants' claims to some of the land they worked, notably cleared land. They were allowed to dispose of the *curături* freely as before, but the code recognized only their possession of these lands, not their property rights to the soil, which it assigned to the landlords. The only property right allowed the peasants was to the crops they raised on such land, but even this right was contingent upon payment of the tithe.

Princely legislation on landlord–peasant relations, taken as a whole, imposed greater uniformity on the patchwork of relations that had evolved over several centuries. It further undermined the communal village and weakened the traditional rights of the peasant over the plots he worked in favour of the landlords, and thereby furthered the commercialization of agriculture.

Despite changes, the general structure of agriculture in 1829 was not markedly different from what it had been in the 1770s. Overall production had increased, but the rate of growth had been slow. Although this production had become more responsive to market conditions, the trend was discernible only on those estates close to larger cities such as Bucharest, Craiova, and Iaşi. Besides the endemic poverty of the peasantry, the ambivalent attitude of the *boiers* towards agriculture, and the Ottoman commercial monopoly, the absence of dramatic changes in agriculture may also be attributed to more general problems of economic development. Before 1830 neither demographic development nor urbanization had advanced sufficiently to change the organization of agriculture. The population of the principalities in the 1820s was certainly larger than it had been a half-century earlier, but it was still small and unable to provide sufficient labour for agriculture, as is clear from the continuous importation of labour from Transylvania and south of the Danube. Cities were, with a few exceptions, small and did not offer agriculture the stimulus of a large, varied market. The surrounding villages, in turn, were too poor to sustain a vigorous, diversified industry in the cities. Not until the second half of the nineteenth century did population growth and urbanization affect agriculture in significant ways, but by then other forces had already altered the mode of agricultural production.

CITIES AND TOWNS

Urban configurations in the last half-century of Phanariot rule bore the heavy impress of past centuries. None of the processes characteristic of modern urbanization was fully under way, although the population of cities and towns was slowly increasing. Moldavian and Wallachian cities showed little resemblance to their counterparts in Western Europe. Even the two capitals were rural in appearance. They were spread out over a wide area, thus revealing the absence of the discipline imposed elsewhere by old fortifications. The Turks were, in a sense, responsible, for they had forbidden the princes to fortify their cities. But the political autonomy enjoyed by the principalities had spared these cities the Islamization that had overtaken urban centres south of the Danube. Nevertheless, in the later Phanariot period Turkish influence was evident in architecture, clothes, and food.

There were two main types of urban settlements: the old cities (*oraşe*), many of which dated from the fourteenth century, such as Iaşi, Botoşani, and Galaţi in Moldavia and Bucharest and Tîrgovişte in Wallachia, and the market-towns (*tîrguri*), which appeared in the second half of the eighteenth century and the first half of the nineteenth. Official documents of the time did not always distinguish between the two. None the less, cities were generally thought of as having a variety of functions—economic and administrative, cultural and religious; they were usually larger than market-towns, and the structure of their populations was more complex and, to a great extent, engaged in non-agricultural pursuits. The market-towns, on the other hand, were semi-urban; their functions were almost entirely commercial, and the majority of their inhabitants were still linked to agriculture.

The population of both cities and market-towns was small. Estimates by foreign travellers of the size of Bucharest, the largest city in the latter decades of the eighteenth century, varied between 20,000 and 60,000. Other Wallachian cities lagged far behind. In Moldavia, Iaşi was the largest city in 1774 with 9,075 inhabitants, which represented 26 per cent of the total population of Moldavian cities. No other city exceeded 5,000. Botoşani had 2,665 and Roman 1,080. By 1803 only modest increases had occurred. Iaşi still led with 15,995 inhabitants, followed by Botoşani with 4,505 and Roman with 2,235. Significant increases, however, were to take place in the next thirty years. By 1831 the population of Iaşi, for example, had reached 48,000. As for the market-towns, their population cannot be precisely determined mainly because officials tended to count *clăcaşi* who resided there as villagers rather than as *tîrgoveţi* (town dwellers). In any case, in Moldavia before 1832 none had more than 1,000 inhabitants.

The main reasons for the modest level of urban development were economic: the slow pace of industrialization, as evidenced by the perpetuation of guild monopolies over the production and distribution of goods; the lack of investment in new enterprises; and the weak demand for urban goods and services in the surrounding countryside. In Wallachia there was a special problem: the raids carried out by the pasha of Vidin, Pasvanoglu, and other undisciplined Ottoman forces from across the Danube constantly disrupted economic activity, as in 1800, when they destroyed Craiova, the second largest city in the country. There were still other impediments to the growth of cities. In the first place, they were neither healthy nor safe. Because of the lack of urban planning and the failure to provide public health and sanitation services, they were continually ravaged by fires and epidemics.

Although urban growth before the 1820s was limited, certain trends, which were to accelerate the social and economic development of cities later on, were already present. The urban population was increasing, fed by continuous immigration from the countryside. The movement of peasants to the cities and towns seems to have been caused mainly by the deteriorating conditions on the land as a consequence of the *boiers*' successes in extending their control over cropland, pastures, and forests and the steady increases in state taxes.[36] Yet, urban centres offered the skilled and unskilled only modest opportunities for employment. Nor were they safe havens for fugitive *clăcaşi*, who could be returned at any time to their landlord. Neither permanent nor temporary residence within its precincts automatically made one free.

The influx of peasants into the cities was merely part of a much broader and almost continuous movement of rural population from one place to another. In this period the majority of peasants who left their homes did not go to cities and *tîrguri* but to other villages and *boier* estates, a situation that suggests the limited extent of urban development and the general lack of economic opportunity in cities. Those who went to urban centres were often the unskilled who found employment mainly as servants or in other menial occupations, whereas those who had a trade tended to be more selective, usually settling in a market-town where the opportunities to use their skills were greater than in the cities.

Although links between the countryside and urban centres remained strong and were reinforced by the flow of peasants from the villages, the two populations were none the less becoming increasingly distinct. One cause was the greater ethnic diversity to be found in many cities and towns. Those places which took the lead in commercial and artisan activity attracted large numbers of foreigners, especially merchants and skilled workers, who often preserved their ethnic identity through separate guilds. Religion also enhanced ethnic differences. Many of the newcomers—Jews and Germans—were not Orthodox. Although they did not belong to the dominant church, they suffered no significant racial or religious discrimination, which was generally absent from the principalities at this time. The *sudiţi*, as we have seen, played an important role in the life of larger cities where they used their privileged status to acquire wealth and

---

[36] E. Negruţ, 'Despre migraţiile temporare în mediul urban din Moldova în prima jumătate a secolului al XIX-lea', *Anuarul Institutului de Istorie şi Arheologie*, 14 (1977), 301–12.

political influence. Still other foreigners came to Bucharest and Iaşi and other cities as diplomats or travellers. All these groups together imparted a cosmopolitan air to the cities, and in many facets of social and economic life they served as catalysts of change.

The last half-century of Phanariot rule witnessed the beginnings of modern city government. But modern must not be taken as a synonym for self-government. The urban middle class had to wage an uphill struggle against both *boiers* and the state bureaucracy to gain control over their own affairs. The inhabitants of cities were generally subject to the same dues and services required of dependent peasants. Originally, the prince had controlled the cities because they had developed on lands over which he had the power of eminent domain and were, therefore, considered his possessions. In the seventeenth century, for example, the princes had begun to include properties within the boundaries of cities in grants of land to *boiers* and monasteries. At first, such urban grants were small—a house, a pond, a place along a stream for a mill, or a little arable land—but in the eighteenth century they became larger and struck at the vital economic interests of the middle class. Grants of urban property were most numerous between 1750 and 1760, following the decrees abolishing serfdom when landlords were anxious to assure themselves of more land and adequate labour. As commerce and artisan production grew, *boiers* and monasteries also recognized the benefits of controlling the non-agricultural economic activities of cities, and they strove to take over the hitherto free markets of cities.

Sometimes the princely grants encompassed the whole outer territory of the city (*moşie*) as at Bîrlad (1757), Craiova (1765), and Ploieşti (1775), and even the centre (*vatră*) as at Roman (1798). These grants drastically altered the legal status of city-dwellers. From free men whose fiscal obligations were to the prince they had become dependents of the *boier* or monastery whose estates now encompassed the city and its surrounding arable fields. They owed their new landlord tithes and in some instances *clacă* (both were usually transformed into money payments), and they had to respect the traditional landlord monopolies.

The new legal and economic relationships created by princely grants were an added obstacle to the commercial and industrial development of cities. They were also the cause of widespread unrest, as the burghers stubbornly resisted the pretensions of their new masters. They refused to render labour services or pay tithes, and they built workshops and opened taverns without seeking permission of their nominal landlords, for they considered themselves the masters of the land. Some of the disputes lasted for decades and suggest a growing class consciousness among the middle class. Among the more celebrated urban conflicts were those in Bucharest and Ploieşti.[37] The inhabitants of the eastern

---

[37] C. C. Giurescu, *Contribuţii la studiul originilor şi dezvoltării burgheziei române pînă la 1848* (Bucharest, 1972), 69–74; C. Şerban, 'Noi contribuţii la istoria luptei tîrgoveţilor şi oraşenilor moldoveni împotriva asupririi feudale în secolul al XVIII-lea şi începutul secolului al XIX-lea', *Studii şi articole de istorie*, 4 (Bucharest, 1962), 73–91.

periphery (*mahala*) of Bucharest took the monastery of Pantelimon to court in 1785 to defend their property rights, a case which dragged on until 1819, when the prince finally intervened directly in favour of the monastery to quell disorders caused by a frustrated citizenry. In Ploieşti merchants categorically refused to recognize the grant of the *vatră* of their city by Prince Alexandru Ipsilanti to his cousin in 1775. Their resistance, despite repeated decisions of the princely divan against them, was unyielding, until finally in 1809 their leaders were arrested on charges of rebellion. The artisans and merchants of the cities also harboured economic grievances against the prince. They objected especially to the fixing of prices by the central bureaucracy on items of mass consumption. When in 1814 the merchants of Ploieşti closed their shops to protest a reduction of retail prices by the prince to alleviate the hardships caused by war and two years of plague their leaders were arrested and sent to work in the salt-mines. Conflicts of these kinds persisted until the 1830s, by which time the emancipation of cities was well under way.

The leading urban classes were also aggrieved by the loss of self-government to the agents of the prince. The eighteenth century witnessed the steady decline and almost complete disappearance of elective bodies in urban government as a result mainly of the growth of *boier* and monastery property. It has been estimated that by the end of the century 85 per cent of the cities and towns in Moldavia and 60 per cent in Wallachia were totally or partially in a state of dependence upon a lay or ecclesiastical landlord. At the same time the princes used the opportunity to extend their administrative control of the cities by replacing locally elected organs of government by their own appointees. The *ispravnic*, in particular, assumed a paramount role in city government. As the representative of the prince he was involved in all the affairs of the city, administrative, judicial, and fiscal. None the less, in the last quarter of the century modest representative institutions were gradually revived in the form of committees (*epitropii*) charged with overseeing public works, social assistance, and, later on, schools. The initiative for their founding came from the middle class as a means of regaining at least partial control of their own affairs. The princes, whose approval of these bodies was necessary, did not object because the committees performed valuable public services at little or no cost to the state treasury. Yet, the levers of public administration remained in the hands of the state bureaucracy.

The growth of population and the increase of the commercial and industrial activities of cities brought demands for new public services and raised the issue of systematic versus haphazard growth. Before the last quarter of the eighteenth century princes and their officials had paid little attention to cities. They did not figure as distinct entities in the great reforms of the 1740s and in other legal and fiscal legislation. But in the 1770s, as in so many other aspects of public administration, Alexandru Ipsilanti took the lead in formulating an urban policy. His proposals were modest, but they reflected his estimate of the enhanced

economic and civilizing roles cities could play in public life.[38] In 1775 he
instructed Mihail Fotino to insert in the new general code of laws he was drafting
a paragraph urging future princes to concern themselves with the beautification
of cities. He also made valiant attempts to discipline their growth. In 1776 he
appointed a commission of *boiers* to establish clearly the boundaries of Bucharest
in order to prevent 'illegal' settlements by peasants and gypsies, and, concerned
with public health, he forbade the slaughter of animals within the city limits and
ordered the butchers' guild to construct slaughterhouses on the periphery and
bring meat into the city with proper attention to hygiene. The *Pravilnicească
condică* also contained several stipulations that reveal a new sensitivity to urban
problems such as limitations on construction that might affect a neighbour's
property.

All these measures represented the modest beginnings of urban planning.
Generally, however, between the 1770s and 1820s neither the central government nor local authorities gave more than passing attention to the systematic
development of cities. Iaşi is a good example of uncontrolled urban sprawl. As it
expanded by encompassing surrounding villages and receiving a steady influx of
newcomers, city officials made no effort to regulate construction or to systema-
tize streets, even though the periodic destruction caused by foreign armies and
fires offered splendid opportunities to rationalize growth. Instead, individuals,
both rich and poor, were left largely to their own devices.

Officials in Iaşi and elsewhere did concern themselves with such pressing
matters as the water supply, the prevention of fires and epidemics, street-lighting,
and the upkeep of the chief thoroughfares, and they made modest progress in
assuring the populace of these essential public services. In Bucharest the prince
and his bureaucracy took the lead. A *hrisov* of 1782, for example, made the
cleaning of streets a regular obligation of all householders and shopkeepers as a
means of improving sanitation and reducing the incidence of disease. Yet, despite
this and similar measures, health conditions remained unsatisfactory until the
second quarter of the nineteenth century, when streets began to be paved with
stone. Fire protection was provided by a force of 100 men at the turn of the
century, but it was inadequate for a city the size of Bucharest where most of the
buildings were constructed of wood. After the great fire of 1804 workshops
which used fire were moved out of the centre of the city, and construction with
stone and plaster was encouraged. Systematic street-lighting began in 1814 in
response to a princely instruction to place a street-lamp every seven houses along
the principal thoroughfare. In Iaşi similar projects were under way. The upkeep
of streets, which were paved with wooden planks, was supervised by an *epitropie*
created specifically for the purpose, and the city administration financed their
maintenance by farming out the various taxes levied for the purpose to great

[38] V. A. Georgescu and E. Popescu, *Legislaţia urbană a Ţării Româneşti 1765–1782* (Bucharest,
1975), 71–2.

boiers. A special concern of yet another *epitropie* was the improvement of the city's water supply to satisfy the needs of its growing population. Funds to dig new wells and build new conduits were taken from the tax on sheep and the tax used to maintain the postal system.[39] Little, however, was done to improve health services, which remained inadequate to meet the needs of the general public. Only one hospital, that of the monastery of St Spiridon, was in operation at the turn of the century, and the only doctors were foreigners who served the prince's court. As a result, terrible epidemics like those of the latter 1790s and in 1819–20 swept unchecked through the city.

Despite some progress in urbanization and a certain *esprit de corps* among the middle class in its struggles with princes and *boiers*, it is difficult to discern the existence of a distinct urban mentality before the end of the Phanariot regime. Merchants and artisans were indeed anxious to gain control of their own economic and political affairs, but they did not yet express a way of looking at the world that was peculiar to the bourgeoisie. Urban culture continued to be dominated by the *boiers* and the church and thus, despite a certain degree of Europeanization, it tended to reflect traditional, one might almost say rural, values.

INDUSTRY AND COMMERCE

Agriculture, as we have seen, dominated the economy of the principalities. But by the turn of the century industry and commerce were expanding. New methods of processing agricultural products and other raw materials made their appearance in the form of manufactories, and the international market for Romanian goods grew. Increased production and the growing complexities of the market, in turn, required more systematic and rational ways of doing business, and the period thus witnessed an expansion of credit, the beginnings of a more modern banking system, and efforts to create a stable currency. Although these changes came slowly, they reveal the path which the principalities were to follow towards more modern forms of industry, commerce, and finance in the nineteenth century.

Between the 1770s and the 1820s the production of goods was in the hands mainly of individual artisans working alone. Some had a helper. Still others owned a shop and employed a number of journeymen and apprentices, but they were the exception. Whatever the size of their business, the majority were engaged in the making of common household items such as pots, candles, and soap for the general market, but others—millers, smiths, painters, and tailors—worked primarily to fill specific orders. Many artisans had permanent workplaces,

---

[39] D. Berindei, *Oraşul Bucureşti: Reşedinţă şi capitală a Ţării Romîneşti, 1459–1862* (Bucharest, 1963), 151–4; C. Cihodaru and G. Platon (eds.), *Istoria oraşului Iaşi*, i (Iaşi, 1980), 429–41.

but large numbers still travelled far from home, setting up shop wherever they could find work. Artisans in the villages generally satisfied local, peasant needs, but some of what they produced—coarse cloth and wool, tanned hides, and pots and pans made of wood and clay—were sold at fairs and even exported, especially south of the Danube. Much of this work was done in the home and was intended to satisfy immediate household needs and supplement the main family income, which came from agriculture. This tradition helps to explain the lack of specialization of many craftsmen.

Village crafts were already in decline by the turn of the century. The causes are complex, but have to do mainly with the inability of artisans to satisfy the requirements of their clientele. They found it difficult to reserve raw materials for themselves, because of requisitions for the *zahire* and the increase in the tithes; they lacked the time away from agriculture to produce goods in sufficient quantities; and their rudimentary tools and methods restricted their productive capacity. As a result, peasant households turned increasingly to the specialized craftsmen who brought their wares to local and regional fairs.

The persistence of a natural economy and the relative abundance of raw materials and cheap labour favoured the maintenance of crafts on *boier* and monastery estates.[40] Here artisans were expected to provide almost everything needed by the master and his household, and clothing, household goods, wagons, and tools were regularly produced. The estate also usually had a complement of skilled artisans to run its mills and distilleries. Landlords were generally eager to acquire and retain a large force of artisans as a means of reducing the expenses of running their estates, and competition among them for skilled workers was as fierce as for *clăcaşi*, a situation that again suggests a small population and a shortage of labour. The majority of artisans on many estates came from the ranks of gypsy slaves, and to increase their number landlords saw to it that gypsy boys were taught trades. Other important sources of skilled labour were the *scutelnici* and *posluşnici*, who would often be hired to make items for the *boier* household in return for exemption from state taxes. Occasionally, landlords also engaged foreign artisans, especially to construct the mills that provided a substantial share of the estate's revenues. Yet, as in the village, crafts on the estates also suffered a decline. The immediate causes were the often poor quality of the articles produced on the estate and the easy access to goods of better quality and at lower prices from artisans in nearby cities and towns or from itinerants.

In contrast to the countryside, crafts in the cities and towns were prospering. New branches were being established, older ones were becoming more specialized, and new products and larger quantities were being made in response to a growing demand in both the cities and, to some extent, in the surrounding countryside. The crafts in the cities and towns were superior in tools and techniques to those in the countryside and had the urban markets almost com-

[40] Ş. Olteanu and C. Şerban, *Meşteşugurile din Ţara Românească şi Moldova în evul mediu* (Bucharest, 1969), 339–48.

pletely to themselves, because of the general absence of manufactories and mechanization and the still limited circulation of foreign goods. The majority of urban crafts were engaged in processing foodstuffs, making clothes, shoes, and household goods, and producing various construction materials. Although a modest foreign market existed for their products, mainly south of the Danube, urban artisans sold most of their goods locally.

The production of goods in the cities was dominated by the guilds.[41] Called *bresle* or *isnafuri*, they were associations of master artisans formed to promote their own economic interests by regulating production and limiting competition. From the beginning of the eighteenth century until the 1820s the number of guilds increased steadily. Fear of foreign imports and encouragement from the princes, who saw in the guilds a source of social and fiscal stability, persuaded large numbers of artisans to organize.

Authorization to establish guilds had to come from the prince, but since they were both economic associations and brotherhoods (*frăţii*) with religious or social responsibilities, the church exercised extensive rights of patronage. In order to heighten the members' sense of responsibility and cohesion it was customary at this time, when faith was strong and the prestige of the church high, for them to submit their charter for approval to the metropolitan or bishop in whose eparchy they lived. If the clergyman found its moral and spiritual content satisfactory, he would then give it his blessing. The prince's sanction came in the form of a *hrisov*, which contained comprehensive dispositions concerning the organization of production in the artisan workshop, the selling of goods on the market, the conditions of membership, and the duties of guild leaders and members. The prince himself retained the right to intervene in the affairs of the guild at any time and even to dissolve it.

Membership in a guild was, in principle, open to anyone who met the requirements set down in its charter, although there were closed associations which strictly limited the number of members. In general, guilds were formed by men, but a number of them also admitted women, usually those engaged in the making of clothing. Widows were sometimes granted the rights of membership held by their husbands. Neither the laws of the land nor the guild charters prohibited the admittance of women, but the acceptance or rejection of any candidate was up to the general assembly of the guild members. Not even personal liberty was a criterion for membership, since gypsy slaves were received into the guilds of fiddlers (*lăutari*) either together with free men or in separate associations of their own. Gypsies who were organized in guilds usually had considerable freedom. They lived off the earnings of their craft in their own houses and paid their masters an annual fee for the privilege.

Master artisans were the true members of the guild. Only they could administer its affairs, and only their names appeared in the guild register, which

---

[41] Pavlescu, *Economia breslelor în Moldova*, 179–255.

authorized them to practise their trades. Those who operated larger shops employed journeymen for a wage specified in a contract. Those journeymen who possessed the means could open their own shops, but only after they had spent a number of years under the supervision of a master and had passed a professional examination. Masters also hired apprentices, boys of from 6 to 12 years old, who performed menial tasks for varying lengths of time, depending on the craft, before they had their own professional examination. If they passed it, they were hired to work alongside the journeymen for a specified period, usually a year, after which they could be promoted into the ranks of the journeymen. Neither journeymen nor apprentices enjoyed much independence while they were in the employ of a master.

The spirit of the guild system was hierarchical, since guilds were, strictly speaking, composed only of masters, who were usually persons of solid financial standing. The wealthier masters had pretensions beyond their profession. They usually acquired property in the countryside in the hope of gaining some of the exemptions accorded the lower *boier* ranks. Yet, a certain degree of democracy permeated the guild, for the general assembly of its members chose its head (*staroste*) and had a voice in all matters of common concern. The *staroste* was elected annually by a majority vote of the members and was confirmed by the prince or his representative. Originally, in the seventeenth century, the *staroste* had exercised considerable power, which had made him the equal of the *boiers*, but by the second half of the eighteenth century he had lost much of his authority and prestige as a result of the general decline of representative institutions and the corresponding increase in the prince's power and the rise of a centralized bureaucracy. The *staroste* still had authority to enforce established rules of production and employment in all workshops and to collect the tax owed by the guild to the state treasury. He was assisted in these tasks by a number of councillors (*epitropi*) who were also elected by the general assembly.

The guilds carried on a variety of activities. They were, first of all, economic associations whose purpose was to assure members a monopoly of the production and, often, the sale of goods on the local market by forbidding non-members to practise their trade in the guild's city. But the guilds also regulated the economic activities of their members in order to maintain a rough equality among the master artisans. They sought to assure all their members an adequate supply of raw materials by enforcing the right of pre-emption, which, for example, allowed the soap and candle-makers to be the first to buy animal fat. The guilds maintained a division of labour between potentially competing associations such as bootmakers and shoemakers by stipulating what they could and could not do. The guilds also performed a number of social and religious functions.[42] They provided death benefits for families and even organized the poor through beggars guilds. Religion was often intimately connected with the guild. Each usually had

[42] Ibid. 397–418.

a patron saint and regularly celebrated his feast day and even built or maintained a church dedicated to him, activities which were intended to strengthen the feelings of solidarity among its members. There were also guilds based upon nationality, especially those of the Armenians and Jews, who found in these associations a means of furthering their economic interests and at the same time of protecting their ethnic identity.

In the last half-century of Phanariot rule the regulation of guild activities by the state became increasingly strict. Princes Alexandru Ipsilanti in Wallachia and Mihai Suţu in Moldavia initiated a policy of close supervision by granting the guilds new, uniform charters, which governed every aspect of their economic activity, including the size and quality of their products, the status of journeymen and apprentices, and the promotion of new masters. At the same time princes assumed a key role in the marketing of goods through their power to set prices and determine weights and measures. They took all these measures because they recognized the vital importance to both the state treasury and the public welfare of a social class which was chiefly responsible for the production and distribution of essential consumer goods.

The guild system has often been cited as a hindrance to the development of the principalities' productive capacity. The guild charters indeed limited the number of journeymen and apprentices a master could employ and tended to discourage competition from outsiders by enforcing a monopoly on production and by asserting the guilds' privileged access to raw materials. State regulation tended to reinforce all these restrictions. Yet, these obstacles to development were never so stringent in practice as they seemed on paper. A master could usually engage as many journeymen as his economic position would allow so long as he did not upset the general equilibrium within the guild. Nor could his production be strictly controlled because the hours which he and his helpers could work were unregulated. A master worked in accordance with the orders he received from customers. The viability of the guild system and the strength of its 'monopoly' began to be tested after the turn of the century by competition from foreign imports and by new forms of production—the manufactories. The fundamental causes of the slow increase of productive capacity must be sought first of all in the general economic condition of the principalities—the lack of capital, the weakness of the domestic market, and economic and fiscal subordination to foreign powers—rather than in the workings of the guild system.

The guilds were, none the less, an important force in economic and social life, as their increasing numbers suggest. They supplied the general public with the bulk of processed goods for everyday use, and their well-being was crucial to the development of cities, since they created economic opportunities, which drew newcomers to the growing urban centres. The guilds sat astride two worlds. They were the repositories of tradition, and, yet, at the same time their members displayed a mentality which combined in a curious way the immobility of the past with a spirit of enterprise that pointed to the future.

Another form of production which arose in the last quarter of the eighteenth century was the manufactory. It differed from the more traditional artisan shops in the larger number of workers employed and the greater division of labour. But it was not yet a true factory, even though contemporary sources occasionally referred to it as a *fabrică* (factory), because it depended upon manual labour and a workforce that still spent much of its time in agriculture. There were two kinds of manufactories—dispersed and centralized. A classic example of the former was the cloth manufactory of Pociovalişte, near Bucharest.[43] At first, its owners, *boiers*, operated a putting-out system, employing in the 1770s about forty spinners on different estates. Later on, the work was concentrated in one place and by 1794, the last year of operation, 243 workers were employed. The typical manufactory brought all its workers together under one roof on a *boier* or monastery estate, where it could obtain abundant raw materials and cheap, servile labour, or it might be located in a larger city or town, especially Bucharest, Iaşi, Galaţi, Botoşani, and Tîrgovişte, where it could benefit from closeness to important markets and a skilled workforce.

The majority of manufactories were founded by *boiers* and merchants, the classes which possessed the necessary capital. Occasionally, the prince might invest some of his own funds, but the initiative came from private individuals rather than the state. Although some of these undertakings were little more than experiments, and many more were short-lived, they none the less suggest a burgeoning spirit of enterprise, as capital, derived mainly from commerce, was placed at no little risk in a novel undertaking for that time and place. The investors could count upon the patronage of the prince, who always welcomed an opportunity to increase his tax revenues. The list of concessions they might receive was impressive: the exclusive right to produce the item in question for a given period of time; exemptions from taxes on raw materials and imported tools; authorization to bring in skilled workers from abroad; and even the power to administer justice to the workers in the manufactory. But the prince lacked the resources to make direct subsidies to encourage new industries. Nor could he decree an end to the Ottoman commercial monopoly and the *zahire*, both of which impeded the development of local industry. Ottoman tariff policies made it impossible for the prince to protect enterprises from foreign competition, for the sultan had granted extensive trading privileges to foreign merchants through-out the empire, including the Romanian principalities, and unrelenting Ottoman demands for foodstuffs, timber, and other items reduced the quantities of raw materials available for processing by local industry. The development of manufactories and more advanced forms of industry was also hindered by the low level of technology and the persistent shortage of skilled workers. As a result,

---

[43] C. Şerban, 'Intreprinderea manufacturieră de postav de la Pociovaliştea şi Bucureşti', *Studii: Revistă de istorie*, 5/3 (1952), 86–105. See also Serap Yilmaz, 'La Manufacture de draps de Chipereşti (Moldavie) (1766)', *Südost-Forschungen*, 48 (1989), 107–39.

local manufactories found it difficult to compete with foreign imports and, at the beginning, even with the traditional craft industries.

The majority of the workers in the manufactories were recruited from among the peasantry. In the countryside they were usually *clăcaşi* or contract agricultural labourers who fulfilled at least a part of their obligations towards their landlords by working in his 'factory'. Free peasants, eager to supplement their incomes, also sought employment there. But whatever their social condition, the peasants remained attached to agriculture. Their work contracts show that they retained plots of land, which constituted their primary source of income, and that they usually received two out of every three weeks for agriculture, except during the winter months when agricultural activity practically ceased. Women, children between the ages of 12 and 16, and convicts were also employed in the manufactories, doing the same kind of work as others, but being paid less. In the cities the majority of the workers were free men, who received their wages partly in money and partly in goods. Many were artisans, some of whom maintained contact with the village and continued to engage in agricultural pursuits.

Most of the manufactories were engaged in making textiles or processing food, mainly for the local market. The modest amount of available capital flowed easily into these industries because they promised quick returns on relatively small investments. Another industry which attracted intense interest was distilling. In the eighteenth century the importation of *holercă* (brandy) from Austria and Poland had provided the prince with important revenues from customs duties and the *boiers* with a steady income from its sale to peasants on their estates. After the turn of the century a number of *boiers* sought a larger share of this lucrative trade by establishing their own distilleries. To meet the objections of the prince, who feared the loss of customs duties, they offered to pay a tax on each *vadră* (pail; about 13 litres in Wallachia, 15 in Moldavia) of *holercă* they produced. He agreed, and the industry developed rapidly after the war of 1806—12, when grain, which had been in short supply, again became available for the making of alcohol.

The most important centre of the manufacturing industry was Bucharest, where paper and cloth factories, founded by *boier* officials, were functioning as early as the 1760s.[44] The number of these enterprises, especially food-processing plants, grew steadily after the turn of the century. A few, like a suburban cloth factory in 1803, employed as many as 150 workers. These were the modest beginnings of what was to become the country's major industrial centre.

Mining, with the exception of salt, contributed only slightly to the economies of the two principalities. Iron- and copper-mining had been abandoned in the first half of the eighteenth century because these metals, which were used primarily by artisans, could be imported in ample quantities and at advantageous prices from Transylvania. To import was cheaper than to explore for new deposits at home. Only in the 1830s and 1840s, as a result of systematic

[44] C. Şerban, 'Breslele bucureştene în secolul XVIII', *Studii: Revistă de istorie*, 12/6 (1959), 55—89.

prospecting by Romanian and foreign mining engineers, were new reserves of ore discovered and their exploitation begun. There was some mining of coal in Wallachia at the end of the eighteenth century, and small quantities of sulphur, amber, and mercury were noted by foreign travellers, but none of these minerals added significantly to the commerce of the two countries. Of the precious metals, only gold had some importance. It was taken, as it had been for centuries, from the rivers of both Moldavia (the Bistriţa and the Moldova) and Wallachia (the Argeş and the Olt). The work was done primarily by gypsies, who, using traditional methods and tools, were obliged to produce a minimum amount each year, in return for which they were excused from the *bir* and all other labour services.

Salt was the main product of the mining industry.[45] The most important mines, such as Slănic and Ocnele Mari (Wallachia) and Tîrgu Ocna (Moldavia), were located on *boier* and monastery as well as princely estates, but their income, which was invariably leased and was substantial, belonged to the prince's treasury. In the second half of the eighteenth century the mines at Slănic produced about 8,000 tons each year, most of which was transported by ship to Constantinople and the Black Sea ports of Asia Minor. Tîrgu Ocna produced annually about double the output of Slănic, which was exported mainly to Poland and the Ottoman Empire. The methods of extraction were those of past centuries, and labour was provided by free men, *clăcaşi*, gypsies, and convicts.

The exchange of goods intensified as a result of the general increase in population, the growth of cities and towns as artisan and administrative centres, and new contacts with foreign countries. The spread of fairs and the increase in the number of merchants were clear signs of an expanding domestic commerce. Peasants, who supplied much of the stuff of commerce, also had compelling reasons for entering the market. They had, in fact, never been absent from it, for they had always had to sell some of their produce in order to pay the *bir*, which was a tax in money, and to redeem labour services owed landlords. Although payment of the tithe in kind and obligatory sales to Ottoman merchants curtailed the amount of produce peasants could bring to market, these very obligations (and the possibility of selling what was left over) seem to have spurred productivity. The princes constantly admonished them to raise more grain, as Alexandru Ipsilanti did in 1779 when he reminded local officials that peasants were free to sell as much of their produce as they wished as soon as Ottoman merchants had taken their quota. Peasants in the vicinity of cities and towns were drawn into the market more readily than others by the demand for food from the growing urban population. They raised not only the traditional corn and wheat but also a variety of vegetables intended for sale to city-dwellers.

The steady increase in the number of fairs suggests a burgeoning commerce. Some fairs appeared spontaneously, while others carried on a tradition which

---

[45] D. Vitcu, *Istoria salinelor Moldovei în epoca modernă* (Iaşi, 1987), 34–47; Hurmuzaki, *Documente*, xix/1. 64–9, 553–9.

extended back for centuries. Anyone—*boier*, monastery, town-dweller, free peasant, even a *clăcaș*—could hold a fair. But a fair of any consequence had to have
the authorization of the prince.[46] In any case, it was advantageous for the fair's
sponsor to have official sanction, since it guaranteed him the maximum return on
his investment. Although the prince saw the fair as a source of income and
therefore rarely withheld his approval, he was often obliged to limit the sponsor's
freedom of action in order to prevent economic harm to others: the
fair could not be held in a place close to another, older fair or on the same
date as other fairs in the district, and the fair had to be necessary and 'desired by
the inhabitants' of the locality. The prince also tried to prohibit the holding of fairs close to the Danube frontier in order to discourage Turkish
merchants from crossing over in great numbers and monopolizing the buying and
selling.

*Boier*s were the chief beneficiaries of fairs. There was hardly a *boier* estate that
did not play host to some kind of fair during the year. Monasteries and bishoprics
also benefited from the prince's favour. There were regular fairs in the larger
cities, and even *clăcași* occasionally obtained permission to hold small village fairs.
The eagerness of *boier*s and churchmen to organize fairs suggests that they were
good business. As sponsors, they were entitled to collect a fee from each
participant and were granted the exclusive right to sell wine and brandy (*rachiu*)
and sometimes even bread and meat at the fair. The sales tax (*vamă*) belonged to
the prince, but often he transferred it to the *boier* or churchman to gain his
goodwill. Sometimes he also granted the *boier* or the *egumen* of a monastery a
diploma of immunity, which forbade state officials to interfere in the operation
of the fair.

There were two types of fairs. The *tîrg* was usually local and attracted peasants
and artisans from the surrounding area who exchanged modest quantities of
goods. Most of the fairs held on *boier* and monastery estates fell into this category,
even though they might be known by other names. Their main function was to
assure landlords a convenient place to sell the products of their estates under
conditions approaching a monopoly. At the *bîlciu* (in Moldavia: *iarmaroc*), on the
other hand, in addition to peasants and artisans, there were foreign and native
merchants, sometimes coming from great distances to engage in wholesale buying
and selling. At the larger fairs—Ploieşti, Buzău, Botoşani, Iaşi—which might last
several weeks, large quantities of goods from Leipzig, Transylvania, and the
Ottoman Empire changed hands. Merchants used the occasion to amass large
stocks of goods, which they sold later in the Ottoman Empire when market
conditions were favourable. The fairs sponsored by monasteries were often held
in conjunction with the patron saint's day when larger crowds than usual could
be expected to attend. The main items of commerce at both Moldavian and
Wallachian fairs were animals. They were the most valuable possessions the

---

[46] G. Penelea, *Les Foires de la Valachie pendant la période 1774–1848* (Bucharest, 1973), 28–40.

peasant could bring to market, and it was their sale that enabled him to pay his taxes and, no less important for the local economy, to become a customer of others at the fairs. The buying and selling of animals was big business. Even the governments of Prussia and Saxony regularly sent merchants to the great fairs of Iași to replenish stocks of horses for their light cavalry.

The outskirts of cities provided a favourite setting for the ordinary fairs; these were the so-called outer markets (*tîrguri de afară*), as opposed to the inner markets (*tîrguri din lăuntru*), the permanent shops within the city limits. The suburban fairs operated under much the same conditions as those sponsored by *boiers* and monasteries, but they were mainly places for exchanges between town-dwellers and the surrounding peasants. The former provisioned themselves with food-stuffs, while peasants and even *boiers* used the opportunity to acquire various consumer goods at advantageous prices. The poorer inhabitants of the cities and the suburbs also frequented these fairs to buy artisan goods produced in the villages, which, though of poorer quality, were usually cheaper than those made in the urban shops.

Fairs were thus indispensable for the exchange of goods. At a time when there were few large centres of population, when transport and communications were rudimentary, and when a strong monetary system, modern credit facilities, and a central exchange to regulate prices were lacking, they provided a regular and convenient setting where buyers and sellers could conduct their business.

Much of the activity at fairs and in the permanent shops in towns and cities was in the hands of professional merchants. Their share of this trade was gradually increasing, even though artisans and *boiers*, and especially peasants, continued to sell their own goods. In the absence of adequate statistics, it is impossible to say precisely how numerous professional merchants were and how much of the domestic commerce was theirs.

Divisions within the merchant profession are strikingly evident. The most important distinction was between natives and foreigners. It was not merely ethnic; it also reflected the dimensions of their respective operations and the kinds of goods and services they provided. Native merchants, with few exceptions, limited their activities to the retail trade. Their business was small-scale and local and rarely extended beyond the boundaries of the district. Large-scale commerce was carried on almost exclusively by foreign merchants. They enjoyed numerous advantages over their local competitors, because of the capitulations which the Ottoman Empire had granted the major European powers, not the least of which was the regular intervention on their behalf by the foreign consuls in Bucharest and Iași. As *sudiți*, as we have seen, they were exempted from many of the onerous taxes and regulations imposed upon Moldavian and Wallachian merchants. They also simply ignored the laws of the land. Although forbidden to sell goods in their own shops and to buy land, many became leading retailers, especially in the larger urban centres, and amassed extensive properties in the countryside.

Foreign merchants were not new to the principalities, but in the latter decades of the eighteenth century the size and variety of their operations changed significantly. Typical of earlier times were the merchants of Braşov, in Transylvania, who kept their businesses and families in their home city and maintained retail stores in Bucharest and smaller towns in Wallachia. The volume of their trade was relatively modest. They imported the bulk of their goods from Braşov and only rarely from the larger cities of Central Europe. But by the end of the eighteenth century these merchants had been superseded by large merchant companies whose founders had come from south of the Danube (Macedo-Romanians, Greeks, and Bulgarians) and had built up thriving businesses throughout the Habsburg monarchy. In the principalities they operated as Austrian *sudiţi*, importing goods in large quantities from Vienna, Breslau, Leipzig, and other major European cities. They inundated the mass market with low-priced manufactures, and at the same time they satisfied the growing demand of the *boier*s for luxuries. They also exported grain and animals from the principalities to Central Europe, in spite of Ottoman restrictions, and more than any other group they were responsible for bringing the economies of Moldavia and Wallachia into contact with the international market. Typical of these entrepreneurs were the 'Greek' companies of merchants in Sibiu and Braşov, just across the border from Wallachia in Transylvania. 'Greek' was a synonym for Orthodox rather than an ethnic term, since these companies included Romanians, Macedo-Romanians, and Bulgarians as well as Greeks.[47]

A leading representative of the great merchants was Hagi Constantin Pop. For three-quarters of a century (1768–1836) his company, with its headquarters in Sibiu, dominated Wallachian commerce in all its varied aspects—imports, exports, transit, and credit. Pop and his son Zenobie, who assumed direction of the firm upon his father's death in 1808, represented the new class of businessmen in the principalities who had passed from local commerce to large-scale international trade and financial operations and who had agents in all the important centres of Central and South-eastern Europe.[48] The core of Pop's business was the export of raw materials, especially wool, hides, dyes, and wax, from Wallachia to Pest and Vienna, but the monetary chaos in the principality, caused by the circulation of the most diverse currencies and the absence of a modern banking system, gave him the opportunity to provide such services as money changing and transfers and credit. The execution of commissions such as subscribing to Western journals and procuring scarce food items and other luxuries for *boier*s was an important part of his business and assured him of goodwill in high places. The variety and extent of the operations in which Constantin and Zenobie Pop engaged exceeded anything Moldavian and Wallachian merchants

---

[47] O. Cicanci, *Companiile greceşti din Transilvania şi comerţul european în anii 1636–1746* (Bucharest, 1981), 96–118; E. and D. Limona, 'Negustori bucureşteni la sfîrşitul veacului al xviii-lea: Relaţiile lor cu Braşovul şi Sibiul', *Studii: Revistă de istorie*, 13/4 (1960), 107–40.

[48] A. Oţetea, *Pătrunderea comerţului românesc în circuitul internaţional* (Bucharest, 1977), 119–32.

knew. They lacked the capital and the experience to challenge the Pops' control of the principal markets on both sides of the frontier and could not overcome the privileges the Pops enjoyed as foreign subjects. Such disadvantages help to explain why the native merchant class remained relatively small well into the nineteenth century and why, more generally, a Romanian middle class was slow to form.

Native merchants also faced formidable competition from the *boiers*. *Boiers* of a certain rank (and monasteries) did not have to pay the tax (*vamă*) on the sale of animals, foodstuffs, and alcoholic beverages from their estates, and the great *boiers*, the metropolitanate, and the great monasteries could maintain retail shops in Bucharest without payment of the usual tax (*fumărit*) to which merchants generally were subject. The *boiers* could also ignore the long-standing rule at fairs and other markets that the purchaser paid the sales tax. The catalogues of excise duties for 1792 and 1803 show that when a *boier* (or a monastery) bought wheat, horses, or cattle for the needs of his own estate it was the seller who paid. Many *boiers*, especially those who held high office and, hence, could draw on a ready supply of capital from the public till, often extended their commercial activities beyond the sale of goods produced on their estates. Some were true entrepreneurs, gathering and marketing animals and certain foodstuffs from an entire district. Still other *boiers* entered into partnerships with established merchants.

The very privileges enjoyed by the *boiers*, which enhanced their opportunities for economic gain, thus drew them into middle-class occupations. As a result, a blurring of social distinctions and a gradual merging of the *boiers*' predominantly agrarian interests with the new business ethos occurred, a process which contributed significantly to the emergence of the modern Romanian middle class.

Both native and foreign merchants were organized into companies or guilds, whose number grew steadily in the eighteenth century. Besides speciality, guild membership was often based upon nationality or the region where its members were most active. Foreign merchants—Greeks, Armenians, and Jews—tended to have their own companies in each city where they did business. The merchant guilds were similar in organization and functions to those of the artisans. But merchants, as a rule, were wealthier than the master artisans, and they were chiefly responsible for accumulating investment capital. They also had higher social aspirations and were closer to the princely throne, circumstances which were evident in their purchase of estates and titles of nobility, rare occurrences among the master artisans.

The accelerated exchange of goods put an extraordinary strain upon an already inadequate transportation network. Roads were in a deplorable state and became impassable at certain times of the year. Bridges, too, were often poorly maintained or did not exist at all over many streams. As a result, goods moved slowly and uncertainly, and passengers often had to make part of their journey on foot. The only regular overland transportation system was the postal service (*menziluri*), which was operated by the state to carry officials, *boiers*, and foreign travellers.

Merchants had to rely upon their own devices to transport their goods, usually in heavy wagons drawn by oxen or in lighter carts pulled by horses, sometimes in caravans of a hundred wagons or more. Princes in both Moldavia and Wallachia, vigorously supported by the Austrian consuls, tried to repair old roads and build new ones in order to stimulate the economy, but they could not overcome the resistance of Ottoman authorities, who regarded bad roads as a natural barrier to invasion from both Austria and Russia.

The Danube served as the major artery of commerce for the principalities. The Ottomans depended upon it to move large quantities of supplies to the Black Sea and Constantinople, and Austria, as we have seen, was eager to make the river and its tributaries her economic gateway to the East. After the turn of the century other powers, notably France and Britain, began to seek regular entry into the Danube and took a serious interest in regulating navigation on it. Romanians, too, saw advantages in expanded use of the river. In 1793 Prince Alexandru Moruzi of Wallachia, citing the inability to move bulky agricultural produce and artisan goods overland as a major impediment to the economic development of the country, obtained permission from the sultan to construct merchant vessels for service on the river. But the new Wallachian commercial fleet had only a short existence. The predatory bands of Pasvanoglu, the rebellious Turkish pasha of Vidin, destroyed many of the small vessels, and the rest disappeared during the Russo-Turkish War of 1806-12. Subsequent attempts by Moldavians and Wallachians to reconstitute a merchant fleet were unsuccessful until after the Treaty of Adrianople of 1829.

The foreign trade of the principalities during the period experienced no dramatic changes in either volume or direction. None the less, commercial activity benefited from European economic interest in the principalities, as is evident in the increasing numbers of foreign merchants in Bucharest and Iaşi and at the major fairs.

Interest in trade between Europe and the principalities was by no means one-sided. Wallachian and Moldavian princes constantly encouraged native and foreign merchants to expand exchanges as a means of increasing their revenue. Many *boiers* eagerly cooperated. Already engaged in selling the products of their estates, they became good customers of merchants who could supply them with new products from Western Europe to enhance their style of life.

Despite the wishes of princes and *boiers*, the direction and amount of foreign trade were determined mainly by the economic and political requirements of the Ottoman state as manifested in the capitulations and supplementary treaties between the sultan and the major European powers. The first such commercial agreement had been concluded with France in 1535, which guaranteed French subjects freedom of commerce, extraterritoriality, and consular protection throughout the Ottoman Empire. Renewed on five separate occasions, the privileges they granted remained in force until 1923. Similar treaties were made with Britain (1580), Holland (1612), Austria (1615), Prussia (1761), and Russia

(1774), all of which granted freedom to trade and to export all articles not expressly prohibited in return for payment of a 3 per cent *ad valorem* tax paid once either upon the entry or the exit of the goods or at the place where they were sold. This rate could not be increased by either Ottoman authorities or local customs officials. Since all the capitulations included a provision for most favoured nation status, a concession to one country could automatically be applied to all the others. Consequently, the tariffs assessed on foreign merchants doing business in the principalities, including the *sudiţi*, were often reduced to practically nothing. Native merchants, however, rarely enjoyed such benefits, unless they became *sudiţi*.

The princes of Moldavia and Wallachia had little direct control over foreign commerce. The provisions of the capitulations were automatically applied to their countries, even though they and the *boiers* had had no part in drafting them. The sultan simply communicated their provisions to the princes with instructions to carry out his wishes. Ottoman restrictions on commerce in sheep, grain, honey, saltpetre, wax, and lumber, which favoured official Ottoman merchants, remained in force and were the main limitations on trade between Europe and the principalities. Although the Treaty of Kuchuk Kainardji and the *hatti-sherif* of 1802 softened Ottoman constraints on the commerce of the principalities, they had little practical effect. To ensure an uninterrupted flow of supplies, the sultan continued to require every new prince before his installation to guarantee their delivery at favourable prices.

The Ottoman commercial monopoly was never as comprehensive as it seemed on paper. The ingenuity of merchants, the greed of princes and their subordinates, the persistence of foreign consuls, and the complicity of Ottoman officials allowed a thriving commerce to operate outside the bounds of its regulations and prohibitions. Moreover, the princes exercised considerable discretion in carrying out instructions from Constantinople concerning the *zahire* and tariffs. Sometimes they ignored them completely, and sometimes they charged higher tariffs than those specified and pocketed the difference. Princes also regularly allowed the export of prohibited items by secretly giving licences to merchants willing to pay for the privilege, and they often halted the export of non-prohibited goods, such as wool and pigs, on the grounds that they were needed for internal consumption, and then relented when merchants paid a special tax. The denunciations of such practices by foreign consuls, who demanded the abolition of all taxes above the 3 per cent *ad valorem* duty, rarely brought relief to the aggrieved parties.

Of all the foreign states which had sought to extend their commerce into the Black Sea and the lower Danube, Russia was the first to gain formal Ottoman economic concessions. As we have seen, the Treaty of Kuchuk Kainardji allowed Russian trading vessels to sail unhindered in the Black Sea and gave Russian merchants freedom of movement on the lower Danube and in the principalities. Subsequent treaties with the Ottomans brought Russia still further advantages. The Treaty of Bucharest of 1812, in particular, enhanced Russia's commercial opportunities in the principalities, because for the first time it extended her political boundaries to the Danube. She acquired the Chilia, or northern, channel of the Danube delta, established a vice-consulate at the port of Chilia, and obtained the right of free navigation on the Danube for her merchant vessels and warships as far as the mouth of the Prut.

In spite of these substantial advantages, Russia's trade with the principalities was modest.[49] The main reason was the similarity of their economies, which were essentially agricultural and, hence, competitive rather than complementary. Russia's principal export to the principalities was furs, but after 1800 even this trade declined, because of the changes in taste among the *boiers*. The Russo-Turkish War of 1806–12 dramatically affected fashions in the principalities. Russian officers and their families introduced Western styles, which, according to numerous foreign observers, took Bucharest and Iaşi high society by storm. Of other Russian exports, cloth (from Moscow), iron and other metal products (from Tula), and hides were the most important. Russia's chief imports from the principalities (Moldavia was the more active trading partner) were salt, which was sent to the Ukraine, and wine. But after the annexation of Bessarabia in 1812, the importation of Moldavian wine was greatly curtailed, since Russian authorities wished to develop the wine industry between the Prut and Dniester and imposed high tariffs on foreign imports to discourage competition.

Russia's trade with the principalities was by no means negligible. At the turn of the century she ranked third behind the Ottoman Empire and Austria in total volume, a position she maintained until the Treaty of Adrianople in 1829. Yet, it was already evident in the 1820s that Romanian commerce owed its dynamism to expanding contacts with Central and Western Europe. Trade with Russia continued to be modest throughout the nineteenth century and failed to provide a basis for close political relations.

The trade of the principalities with Austria was more extensive than that with Russia, thanks in large measure to the activities of the *sudiţi*. In the 1790s the prospects of expansion seemed favourable as officials in Vienna, the governor of Transylvania, and the Austrian consuls in Bucharest and Iaşi promoted closer commercial relations with both Moldavia and Wallachia.[50] But well into the 1820s, perhaps because of war and the economic dislocations it brought, trade languished. It was also largely one-sided. Austria imported cattle and horses, wine, brandy, hides, wool, and cheese, but found only a small market for such Austrian manufactures and 'luxuries' as dishes, eyeglasses, mirrors, fine textiles, sugar, and coffee. Competition from other European exporters, the modest size of the Moldavian and Wallachian markets, and the lack of attention to them on

---

[49] C. C. Giurescu, *Relaţiile economice dintre Români şi Ruşi până la Regulamentul Organic* (Bucharest, 1947), 35–40.

[50] H. Heppner, *Österreich und die Donaufürstentümer, 1774–1812* (Graz, 1984), 61–8, 94–102; S. Marieş, 'Activitatea lui Ignaţiu Ştefan Raicevich, primul consul al Austriei în Ţările Române (1782–1786)', *Cercetări istorice*, 6 (1975), 123–39.

the part of Austrian businessmen and merchants impeded the development of trade. None the less, Austria was second only to the Ottoman Empire as a trading partner of the principalities.

In comparison with the Ottoman Empire, Austria, and Russia, trade between Western Europe and the principalities was in its infancy. Commercial relations with Britain were negligible and with France sporadic and one-sided. From the latter the principalities imported manufactured goods and luxuries. Among the most sought-after items was cloth from Lyons, which was stocked by shops in Bucharest and was very expensive. None the less, French products could not compete with those of Austria because they did not benefit from the low tariffs and other advantages enjoyed by the Austrian *sudiţi* and because they did not come directly from France, but were transhipped from some intermediate point such as Constantinople or the Leipzig fair, a procedure which added substantially to their cost. The principalities sent nothing in return to France. Despite the interest of the French government and individual French entrepreneurs in trade with the principalities, exchanges of goods did not rise above modest levels until after the Treaty of Adrianople, when a direct sea route between Marseilles and Brăila and Galaţi was finally opened.[51]

Trade between Moldavia and Wallachia themselves does not appear to have been extensive, mainly because of the similarity of their economies. They produced essentially the same things—agricultural products, craft goods, and salt—and thus had to rely upon foreign countries to satisfy additional needs.

The principalities lacked a modern banking system. Moneylenders and money-changers operated in its stead, and under prevailing fiscal conditions theirs was a thriving business.[52] An astonishing variety of social groups participated: foreign merchants, the more affluent *boiers*, and the clergy, to mention only the most important. All classes of the population were borrowers, from the prince and the great *boiers* to the peasant. The usual rate of interest was 20 per cent, but it fluctuated widely in response to changing economic and political circumstances.

The princes were in constant need of money, first, to gain their thrones and then to retain them. Once in office they were often obliged to contract huge loans to cover the immediate needs of the country. Since the usual ways of raising money, such as a new tax, were too cumbersome and uncertain, they turned to moneylenders, who could supply the necessary funds promptly. Until the beginning of the nineteenth century, when princes began to seek loans in Vienna, their chief foreign creditors were the moneylenders of Constantinople. They negotiated loans in the Ottoman capital through their official representatives, or they obtained money directly from Ottoman merchants during their purchasing expeditions in the principalities and from Greek and other merchants

[51] G. Lebel, *La France et les Principautés Danubiennes* (Paris, 1955), 309–43.
[52] I. Caproşu, 'Camăta şi cămătari în Moldova în epoca fanariotă', *Anuarul Institutului de Istorie şi Arheologie*, 8 (1971), 27–59; Lia Lehr, 'Camăta în Ţara Românească pînă în secolul al xviii-lea', *Studii: Revistă de istorie*, 23/4 (1970), 706–14.

who did business there. As a return on their loans merchants expected not only interest but favours from princes and *boiers*. Some wanted exemptions from taxes or dispensations on the export of certain goods. The more pretentious among them strove to enter the ranks of the *boiers*, sometimes as a reward for services rendered, but more often through the purchase of high offices.

The princes also turned to the great *boiers* for funds. Although few *boiers* possessed the amount of ready capital available to Ottoman and other foreign merchants, they none the less made loans to all segments of the population. A few even became regular moneylenders and developed a predilection for speculative activities quite unlike the *boier* stereotype. The princes also obtained loans from the church. According to a custom that had achieved almost the force of law in the eighteenth century, high churchmen and monasteries were compelled to grant the ruler loans, even if they themselves had to borrow the necessary sums. The prince was expected to pay interest on his loans, but sometimes, as in the case of a sudden departure from the throne, he defaulted altogether.

The peasantry offered moneylenders extraordinary opportunities for profit. Ottoman merchants, in particular, took advantage of the poverty of the small agricultural producer to obtain grain and animals often for a pittance. They readily loaned money to all comers on condition that it be repaid in produce at harvest time. This practice was often disastrous for the peasant, who had had no experience with this method of financing his production.

In the first three or four decades of the nineteenth century Jews, particularly in Moldavia, less so in Wallachia, acquired an important share of the moneylending (and money-changing) business. They owed their position in part to the limitations placed on their other economic activities and in part to their international connections. But their very success in these occupations did much to create a general resentment against them at all levels of society. It is by no means coincidental that modern anti-Semitism gathered momentum in Moldavia as Jews gained prominence in the financial affairs of the principality.

The Jews acquired their predominance in commerce and moneylending in a relatively short time. But Jewish immigrants from Galicia and Bukovina did not arrive in Moldavia with fortunes. The majority were poor. Yet, they brought with them an outlook and practices which gave them a distinct advantage over their competitors.[53] The typical Moldavian merchant of the day waited for the customer to come to him, and he always had time for amusements and social life. The Jewish merchant disregarded such traditions; experience had taught him how to compete for business, and he actively sought customers on the premiss that every passer-by was a potential purchaser of his wares. Of particular importance for the development of commerce was the Jewish merchant's willingness to sell goods on credit. That practice had already been in use, but mainly among the larger merchants and only for important sales. The Jewish merchant introduced

[53] G. Zane, *Economia de schimb în Principatele Române* (Bucharest, 1930), 329—44.

credit between the small retailer and the everyday customer, a practice which soon became widespread and allowed the Jewish merchant and moneylender to extend his business into the village. This type of credit proved extremely popular among the peasantry.

Moneylenders were at the same time money-changers. The latter occupation was indispensable for commerce in the principalities, because of the almost infinite variety of monies in circulation. Gold coins mingled with silver, strong currencies with weak, and Ottoman with Austrian and Russian.

Neither Moldavia nor Wallachia had a monetary system of its own, since the Ottoman government had consistently denied them this attribute of sovereignty. As a result, they had become dependent upon Ottoman monetary policy and the fluctuations of the Ottoman currency, a situation which led to continuous economic insecurity, speculation, and fraud.[54] Perhaps in no other area of economic life was Ottoman domination more destructive. Particularly harmful were attempts by Ottoman authorities to set artificially high exchange rates for their currency as a device to stem the relentless depreciation of the piastre between 1783 and 1820. The main effect in the principalities of such measures was to discourage foreigners from investing large sums out of fear that the rate would continue to fall and the value of their assets would decline accordingly.

The development of industry and commerce in the principalities thus had to overcome major obstacles: an insufficient supply of capital, a reluctance to invest, except in land, and the lack of public confidence in credit institutions. The great *boiers* were in the best position to accumulate investment capital, but the majority lacked the entrepreneurial spirit. They consumed both their incomes and their capital (their estates) in the pursuit of luxury and the maintenance of a lifestyle they thought befitting their station. Many other persons of wealth, *boiers* and merchants, preferred to keep their money in cash or other easily accessible forms rather than invest it in long-term undertakings. Habit and the uncertainty of the times, caused by the vagaries of Ottoman suzerainty and foreign invasion, were responsible for this attitude. For centuries Romanian society had regarded metallic money as the only certain kind of wealth and had displayed a persistent reserve towards paper. These sentiments had been reinforced in the eighteenth century by the chronic instability of government, resulting from frequent and arbitrary changes of princes and the ineffectiveness of law. In the final analysis confidence in credit and in credit institutions and the social stability upon which they rested were the prerequisites for fundamental change in the way business was conducted.

---

[54] M. N. Popa, 'La Circulation monétaire et l'évolution des prix en Valachie, 1774–1831', in *Bulletin de l'Association Internationale d'Études du Sud-est Européenne*, 13–14 (1975–6), 157–67, 172–98.

3

The Spirit of the Times, 1774–1829

THE second half of the eighteenth century and the early decades of the nineteenth witnessed unusual intellectual and spiritual ferment in the principalities of Moldavia and Wallachia. As the Phanariot regime, the form Ottoman domination had taken in the eighteenth century, was gradually undermined, and as contacts with Europe grew the intellectual horizons of educated Romanians expanded. The mental climate they created was extraordinarily diverse, as the adherents of both tradition and innovation tested their theories against changing social and economic circumstances. Yet, even in such diversity two ideas gave their thought direction and cohesiveness—nation and Europe.

TRADITION AND INNOVATION

Intellectual and cultural life in the principalities remained within long established bounds for most of the eighteenth century. The leading social classes—the *boiers* and the higher clergy—were faithful to the religious and didactic tradition of written literature, while the majority of the population—the peasantry—were beholden to an ancestral, mainly oral literature. The Romanians thus maintained largely intact their adherence to the Byzantine-Orthodox cultural world, and their intellectual and spiritual aspirations were turned towards the south-east rather than to the west. The idea of nation was still amorphous, and educated Romanians considered themselves first of all members of the international Orthodox community.

Ottoman suzerainty reinforced these venerable foundations of Romanian thought and expression. Inside the principalities it helped to maintain an economic and political system that impeded institutional change and retarded the emergence of new classes. Outside, it discouraged contacts between Romanians and Western Europeans, thereby delaying those intellectual and social connections that were to have such a leavening effect on Romanian culture after 1830.

Literature, in particular, accurately reflected the persistence of tradition in intellectual and cultural life until the final decades of the eighteenth century. The structure of literature remained what it had been in past centuries, except for the works of Dimitrie Cantemir at the beginning of the century. It lacked original works of fiction and poetry in the modern sense, while narrative prose was limited to history, religious works, and the political pamphlet. Prose had a utilitarian purpose. If religious, it was either apologetic or exegetic, and if it dealt with lay subjects, it was didactic or moralizing. History, too, respected traditional formulas. Ion Neculce (1672–1745), whose *Letopisețul Țării Moldovei* (Chronicle of Moldavia) represents the high point of old Romanian literature, thought that the purpose of history was to register events for contemporaries and future generations and to teach men how to behave in both their public and private lives. He also conceived of history as a product of the divine will, and he invoked God at every step in order to explain great and small events. *Belles-lettres*, except for those few persons who could read the ancient classics or Western literature in the original, meant the 'popular books' (*cărți populare*). Typical of this genre were the adventure 'novels' about Alexander the Great (*Alexandria*) and the Trojan War (*Istoria Troadei*) and the oriental romances *Sindipa* and *A Thousand and One Nights* (*Halima*). They had large audiences among all strata of the population and circulated widely in Romanian translation, mainly in manuscript.

Yet, traditional institutions and mentalities had already been breached. New currents of ideas, already manifest in the middle of the eighteenth century, had begun to affect the way Romanians viewed themselves and meditated on the organization and ends of human society. The higher clergy of the Orthodox Church served as an effective instrument of innovation, a vocation that at first glance appears paradoxical. None the less, while retaining their role as preservers of the Christian tradition, they displayed a keen receptivity to ideas and institutions that were essentially secular. A similar ferment also stirred Romanian lay intellectuals, who contributed substantially to the rising tension between the old order and the emerging notion of progress.

The Orthodox clergy in the eighteenth century remained the keepers of tradition in the sense that they strove to maintain Christian ethical values and defended the religious interpretation of man's history. This attachment to tradition was particularly strong among the rural parish clergy, whose modest training and isolation from broad cultural currents left their intellectual world largely untouched. The higher secular clergy, on the other hand, were peculiarly open to innovation. While by no means renouncing their religious calling, they could not but be influenced by European learning. From the same class as the *boiers*, they enjoyed the same opportunities for education and shared similar aspirations to enlightened reform, but within a Christian context. The monastic clergy was also touched by the general spirit of renewal within the church. But its sources were the mystical traditions of the Eastern Church; it looked inward rather than towards Europe.

The main centre of innovative intellectual activity within the church in Wallachia was at Rîmnic, a small town on the Olt River. Gathered at the diocesan see was an unusual group of clerics who, without breaking with ecclesiastical tradition, took a fresh look at man's relationship with God and his purposes on earth. They cherished learning and within the limits imposed by their faith and religious training they displayed a remarkable openness to new ideas and, in a modest way, merit the title of *Aufklärer*.[1]

The principal animator of the group and its leading figure was Chesarie, bishop of Rîmnic from 1773 to 1780.[2] The date of his birth is unknown, and the details of his early life are sketchy. He received his education at the princely academy in Bucharest, where theology and classical antiquity dominated the curriculum and where he acquired a knowledge of Greek, Latin, Slavonic, and French. He became a monk in 1761 and thereafter held various administrative posts at the metropolitanate in Bucharest. While there he served as a member of the delegation which travelled to St Petersburg in 1770 to bring the grievances of the Wallachian nation against Ottoman rule to the attention of Catherine II.

As bishop, Chesarie was esteemed in his own time, and is remembered today, as a translator and publisher of church books and as a writer of pithy introductions. He completely renovated the old printing house at Rîmnic, which dated from 1705, with equipment obtained in Sibiu through his friend, the merchant Hagi Constantin Pop. He published new editions of indispensable liturgical works—an *Octoih* (a book of hymns, which were sung each week in one of the prescribed eight keys) in 1776, a *Triod* (a book of songs for the great fast from the tenth Sunday before Easter until Easter), and a *Ceaslov* (book of hours) and a *Psaltire* (book of psalms) in 1779—but his major accomplishment was the publication of the translations of six *Mineie* (a *minei* is a church book indicating the daily services for the respective month) for October to March. The publication in Romanian of the remaining six (April to September) by his successor, Filaret, meant that the entire church service could now take place in the native language. In a sense, they brought to a conclusion the process of translating the service books and of extending the use of Romanian in the liturgy, which had begun in the fifteenth century.

The prefaces which Chesarie wrote for his *Mineie* mark him as a man imbued with the spirit of his own time. They reveal a breadth of vision and a commitment to the new learning that was shared by growing numbers of Romanian intellectuals. Chesarie read French journals—*Journal encyclopédique de libre propagande philosophique* and *Mercure historique, littéraire et politique*—and acquired a set of the great *Encyclopédie*, all through Sibiu and his friend Pop. But he remained a man of the church. He never doubted God's influence over the lives of men and never ceased to impress upon his fellow Christians the efficacy of prayer. For him, traditional teachings about the reciprocal relationship between God and man retained their validity in an age of growing scepticism. Although he thus believed time to be subordinate to the will of providence, he was no less

---

[1] On the circle at Rîmnic, A. Duţu, *Coordonate ale culturii româneşti în secolul XVIII* (Bucharest, 1968), 119–70, is indispensable.

[2] M. Manolache, 'Viaţa şi activitatea episcopului Chesarie al Rîmnicului (1773–1780)', *Biserica Ortodoxă Română*, 84/1–2 (1966), 129–51.

certain that men could control their own destinies on earth. His view of history was thus far removed from the passive and the contemplative. Rather, he considered transformation, or change, to be not only inherent in nature but also a law that dominated human affairs. In his view, life on earth was connected to the overall divine plan for men, but it was not, as his medieval predecessors had taught, simply a preparation for eternal life. Historical time, he argued, should be used to improve men's lot on earth and to promote the general welfare.[3] His idea of time thus differed from that found in such popular traditional works as *Pildele filosofeşti*, a book of maxims translated from Greek into Romanian in 1713, where time is likened to a wheel, which, once set in motion, brings man ever closer to death. Time, for Chesarie, was an opportunity to promote the public good. But it is unclear whether he believed in progress, for he conceived of change in human affairs as an unending cycle of rise and fall.

Chesarie also shared the growing interest of his fellow intellectuals, lay and ecclesiastical, in the nation or, as he called it, the *patrie* (fatherland). Although he was by no means abandoning the international Orthodox community and still thought of mankind's development in broad Christian terms, the frequency with which the term *patrie* recurred in his writings none the less suggests a subtle shift from an Orthodox to a national consciousness. For example, he referred to the metropolitan of Ungrovlachia as the spiritual mentor and the son of the fatherland, and seemed to suggest that the role of the higher clergy could be defined in national terms.[4] When he meditated on the obligation of men to use time to promote the common good the *patrie* was his usual frame of reference. His disparate thoughts on the matter could hardly be described as nationalism, but they none the less contained certain elements, such as the descent of the Romanians from the ancient Dacians and the Romans, which eventually were to form the core of the ideology of modern Romanian nationalism. In the *Minei* for November he noted the Romanians' illustrious ancestry, and in the *Minei* for December he compared certain customs of the Romans to those practised by the Romanians of his own day.[5]

Grigore Rîmniceanu (*c.*1763–*c.*1828) was one of Chesarie's disciples and shared his intellectual preoccupations.[6] He, too, used the prefaces to new editions of the church service books as a vehicle for his own ideas, and his preface to the *Triod* of 1798 is a characteristic expression of the new world-view. Like his mentor, he tried to reconcile traditional religious teachings with the new currents of thought. He praised the human mind as an instrument that had allowed man

[3] Preface, *Mineiul pe Ianuarie* (Rîmnic, 1779), in BRV ii. 234–6.

[4] Preface, *Mineiul pe Noemvrie* (Rîmnic, 1778), in BRV ii. 228. On the idea of *patrie* held by Chesarie and his contemporaries, see Ş. Lemny, *Originea şi cristalizarea ideii de patrie în cultura română* (Bucharest, 1986), 61–92.

[5] Preface, *Mineiul pe Noemvrie*, 227–8; M. Basarab, 'Prefeţele mineielor de la Rîmnic, 1776–1780: Problema originei latine a poporului şi a limbii române', *Mitropolia Olteniei*, 19/9–10 (1967), 763–8.

[6] Duţu, *Coordonate*, 155–63.

to penetrate the deepest secrets of heaven (he had astronomy in mind) and earth. But he was quick to add that the mind and the intelligence it exhibited were gifts to man from God, and he cited the Bible as his authority. Like his fellow clerics at Rîmnic, he was also concerned with history and *patrie*. His thought took a decidedly modern turn in his meditations on the place of the Romanians in Europe. Specifically, he wondered why the Romanians had not accomplished the same marvellous 'feats of the mind' as their neighbours to the west, who had made Europe the 'jewel' of the world. He found the answer in the Romanians' concentration on the 'inner life': they indeed had had learned men, 'some of whom had studied in distant lands', but they had devoted themselves to carrying out the word of God rather than to pursuing 'exterior things' (presumably, science and business).[7] The Romanians, he concluded, were essentially a religious people, a quality, he thought, that had been mainly responsible for their survival: their country had often been a battleground and had been afflicted by other calamities, but, in the end, they had always found peace because they had been faithful to God and, hence, He had watched over them. But, Grigore insisted, the Romanians, despite the special path they had taken, were no less Europeans.

In Moldavia, groups of clerics, centred mainly in Iaşi, were preoccupied with intellectual and cultural concerns similar to those of the circle at Rîmnic. But the Moldavians produced fewer original works and seemed less inclined to tackle the complex problems of history that had attracted Chesarie and Grigore. None the less, their interests were broad, and the stimulus of European currents of thought no less strong.

Here, too, a high churchman presided as the mentor of a younger generation of activist clerics. Leon Gheuca (*c.*1735–88), bishop of Roman in 1769 and then metropolitan from 1786 until his death, was a characteristic figure of Moldavian intellectual life.[8] He was committed to the idea of reform and the dissemination of new cultural values. Because of his ecclesiastical office, he could not express his ideas directly, but tried to influence others by patronizing translations and composing small anthologies of the writings of authors congenial to him. Many of these books purveyed the enlightened ideas of the time. He himself may have translated *Despre ştiinţa stihiilor* (1780; On the Nature of Things), an anthology juxtaposing, among other works, the *Pensées sur differents sujets* of Jean Baptiste Massillon (1663–1742), the noted French preacher; fragments from Fénelon's *Traité de l'existence et des attributs de Dieu*; citations from Cicero; and a speech by Seneca before Nero. The encyclopedic character of the anthology corresponded to the taste and spirit of the time. It dealt with universal questions—the limits of despotism, the accountability of the great before history, the essence of nature, and the well-being of man on earth.

---

[7] Preface, *Troid* (Bucharest, 1798), in BRV ii. 406–8.
[8] A. Ciurea, *Figuri de ierarhii moldoveni: Leon Gheuca* (Chişinău, 1942); *Istoria filozofiei româneşti*, i (2nd rev. edn., Bucharest, 1985), 289–90.

Gheuca's cultural initiatives were not intended simply for the delectation of intellectuals. They expressed his own dissatisfaction with the prevailing order of society and his certainty that the spread of knowledge and the cultivation of reason were the keys to beneficial change. His activities were of a piece with the general ferment within *boier* society.

Among the next generation of enlightened clergymen in Moldavia none represented the national side of the new current of ideas more consistently than Veniamin Costache (1768–1846).[9] A member of a distinguished *boier* family, he chose the monastic habit, despite strong objections from his parents. Bishop of Huşi in 1792 and of Roman in 1796, he was chosen metropolitan of Moldavia in 1803. Like Leon Gheuca, he was a firm believer in knowledge as the key to man's earthly progress. But whereas Gheuca and his generation had thought of education in universal terms without regard to nationality, Costache argued that to be beneficial it must take place in a Romanian context.

Costache's most important early accomplishment in education was the founding of the seminary of Socola, near Iaşi, in 1803. His primary objective was to improve the training of the clergy to enable them to perform their spiritual and didactic responsibilities more effectively, but he was also eager to establish higher education on a national basis and, by introducing Romanian as the language of instruction, he sought to diminish the influence of Greek and the Greek professors at the princely academy in Iaşi. For him, the seminary was only one aspect of a master plan to modernize Moldavian education that would eventually touch all elementary and secondary schools.[10] Recognizing the need for teachers trained in up-to-date pedagogical methods and thoroughly grounded in their respective disciplines, he began to send talented students abroad at his own expense. He also used the printing press to good advantage. In 1804 he reorganized the metropolitan press in Iaşi and in 1807 established a new one at the monastery of Neamţ where he planned to publish works in Romanian which would 'illumine the mind and awaken the spirit of the reader for good things'. They were to be mainly religious in content.

Although Costache was an innovator and an individualist throughout his long career, he remained within the limits of traditional Christian teachings. Unlike some of his colleagues, he was not an admirer of such figures of the Western European Enlightenment as Voltaire. Rather, he adhered to the admonitions of the patriarchate of Constantinople that revolutionary ideas were foreign to the Christian Church. Yet, he was a warm admirer of the ideas of Eugenios Vulgaris, of the Athenian Academy, and Nikiforos Teotokis, of the princely academy in Iaşi, both well known for their enlightened views, and he never wavered in his faith in knowledge as the key to human progress.

[9] M. Păcurariu, *Istoria Bisericii Ortodoxe Române*, iii (Bucharest, 1981), 7–25.
[10] C. Erbiceanu, *Istoria Mitropoliei Moldaviei şi Sucevei şi a catedralei mitropolitane din Iaşi* (Bucharest, 1888), pp. lxiv–lxvi; N. C. Enescu, 'Veniamin Costachi ctitor şi indrumător al şcolilor naţionale din Moldova', *Mitropolia Moldovei şi Sucevei*, 43/1–2 (1967), 32–48.

Parallel with the spread of the new currents of thought about education, language, and fatherland patronized by the higher secular clergy, an equally pervasive spiritual revival gathered momentum among the monastic clergy. If the ideas and programmes espoused by the metropolitans and bishops may be characterized as openings to the West and essentially social in their aims, then the movement for monastic renewal may be thought of as the continuation of older traditions and as other-worldly in its ultimate purposes. The one was turned towards Europe; the other conceived of the Romanians as part of the Orthodox world.

The reinvigoration of monastic life in the principalities in the eighteenth and early nineteenth century was strongly influenced by the asceticism practised in a number of Russian monasteries in accordance with the rules laid down by St Dimitry, the metropolitan of Rostov (1651–1709). One of his disciples was the Moldavian Pahomie, the bishop of Roman (1707–13), who withdrew from his see and lived for a time in the skete he himself had founded near the monastery of Neamţ. Another great ascetic was Vasile, the *stareţ* (abbot) of the monastery of Poiana Mărului (d. 1767), near Rîmnicu-Sărat, in Wallachia, where he and a few followers pursued a life of prayer, study, and manual labour.[11] Pahomie and Vasile were isolated figures, whose influence was limited to their immediate circles. The inspiration for a general monastic revival came from a more charismatic figure, Paisie Velicicovschi (Velichkovskii).

The career of Paisie Velicicovschi reveals the supranational character of Orthodoxy on the eve of modern national movements in South-eastern Europe.[12] He was born in Poltava in the Ukraine in 1722, the son of a priest, and from an early age he was attracted to asceticism and meditation. He took holy orders in 1741 and began his quest for a true life of the spirit, which took him first to the Romanian principalities, where he spent four years in small monastic communities, notably at Poiana Mărului where he met the *stareţ* Vasile, then to Mt. Athos (1746–63), and finally back to Moldavia, where his communities became major centres of a reinvigorated monasticism and of intense intellectual labours. In 1763 Metropolitan Gavriil Callimachi of Moldavia offered Paisie's community the monastery of Dragomirna, in northern Moldavia, and the income of its numerous estates. Here, attracting large numbers of novices and others who felt a higher spiritual calling, Paisie introduced the monastic rule he himself had elaborated at Mt. Athos. It was severe, requiring all members of the community to pursue a life of poverty, obedience, humility, and work. When Austria annexed northern Moldavia (Bukovina) in 1775, Paisie and a majority of his followers moved south to the monastery of Secu and then, in 1779, to Neamţ, the most brilliant centre of monasticism in Moldavia. It was from here that Paisie exerted his greatest

[11] Păcurariu, *Istoria*, ii (Bucharest, 1981), 579–80.

[12] On Paisie Velicicovschi's life and career, see S. Chetverikov, *Starets Paisii Velichkovskii*, trans. V. Lickwar and A. J. Lisenko from the 1933 Russian edn. (Belmont, Mass., 1980), and A. N. Tachiaos, *O Paisios Velitskofski (1722–1794) kai ē askēlikofilologikē scholē tou* (Thessalonike, 1964).

influence over the monastic life of both principalities,[13] and it was here that he died in 1794.

Under Paisie Neamţ became renowned for its translations from Greek into Slavonic and Romanian of the works of the great ascetics of the Eastern Church and of other fundamental theological works.[14] These translations were of immense importance for the Romanian church, for they made available in Romanian the works of the Church Fathers and other theologians who had not previously been translated. The combination of deep spirituality and sustained intellectual labour drew to Neamţ monks and novices from monasteries all over Moldavia and Wallachia and made the members of its community welcome wherever monks were engaged in their own work of spiritual renewal. Among the great churchmen who passed through Paisie's school was Veniamin Costache, and among the great monasteries which developed under the tutelage of Paisie's disciples were Căldăruşani and Cernica in Wallachia. Yet, Paisie served the church, not a nationality. He attracted Russians, Ukrainians, and Byelorussians as well as Romanians, and he gave equal place to Slavonic, Greek, and Romanian.

The enlightened intellectual concerns of the higher clergy and the revival of asceticism among the monastic clergy stimulated general efforts at reform within the church. A notable example were the measures taken by Metropolitan Dositei Filitti of Wallachia (1793–1810) to improve the training and standard of living of parish priests. Yet, it appears that the religious life of the great peasant majority went on much as it had for centuries, initially only slightly affected here and there by the currents of change among the clergy.

THE GREEK CONNECTION

Greek learning fulfilled a dual role in intellectual life similar to that of the Orthodox higher clergy. The widespread influence of Greek culture and use of the Greek language in the eighteenth and early decades of the nineteenth century strengthened the traditional bonds between the principalities and the Byzantine-Orthodox world. But at the same time they offered Romanian intellectuals a vital opening to Western European literature and thought.[15] Modern Greek was one of the languages of higher culture in the principalities. It was the principal language of instruction and, together with classical Greek, a major component of the curriculum in the princely academies of Bucharest and Iaşi, the highest

---

[13] A. Eftimie, 'Influenţa paisiană în mănăstirile româneşti', *Mitropolia Ardealului*, 11/4–6 (1966), 331–48.

[14] Chetverikov, *Starets Paisii*, 227–38; Tachiaos, *O Paisios Velitskofski*, 72–108.

[15] A valuable guide to the problem under discussion is C. Papacostea-Danielopolu, *Literatura în limba greacă din Principatele Române (1774–1830)* (Bucharest, 1982). See also ead., 'Formaţia intelectualilor greci din Ţările Române (1750–1830)', in A. Duţu (ed.), *Intelectuali din Balcani în România, Sec. XVII–XIX* (Bucharest, 1984), 68–113.

institutions of learning in the principalities.[16] The intense cultivation of antiquity in the academies greatly enhanced the prestige of modern Greek literature, which many intellectuals in the principalities regarded as the lineal descendant of classical Greek literature. Among the upper classes Greek enjoyed the same degree of prestige as French in the West at the same period. Many *boiers* spoke and wrote Greek as their sons and grandsons would do French in the 1830s and 1840s. A knowledge of Greek was also a practical necessity. It was the second official language after Romanian, being used in the prince's chancellery and in the judicial system, and it served as a lingua franca in international commerce.

The acceptance of Greek by the Romanian upper classes had been voluntary. No stigma was attached to the use of a foreign language, since the culture for which Greek served as the main vehicle was treated as the common property of all the Orthodox peoples of South-eastern Europe. As in the time of a common Slavonic culture up to the sixteenth century, intellectual and literary activity was not yet judged to be a singular expression of a national soul. The Phanariot princes did not deliberately try to Hellenize the Romanians or stifle manifestations of Romanian culture. Rather, many of them and of the Greek prelates who occupied episcopal and metropolitan sees actively promoted Romanian culture by establishing printing houses and publishing books in Romanian and by insisting that the parish clergy learn to read Romanian, the language of their faithful.

None the less, dissatisfaction among the native clergy with the predominance of Greek ecclesiastics led to tension within the church. The accession of the Phanariots to the thrones of the two principalities had reinforced the links between the Romanian churches and the Greek patriarchate in Constantinople and had resulted in a certain degree of Hellenization, particularly in the Wallachian church. Between 1716 and 1821 of twelve metropolitans, six were of Greek origin, and of the eleven bishops of Buzău, five were Greek.[17] Many Greek churchmen who came to the principalities held honorary titles of metropolitans and bishops of sees in areas which were under Ottoman control and no longer existed. They were maintained at the metropolitanate of Bucharest or became egumens of numerous monasteries. These clerics were conscious of the superiority of Greek culture and sought to preserve the unity of the Greek cultural world and to use the wealth of the Wallachian church to aid the Eastern patriarchates.

The Romanian clergy reacted to Greek predominance in various ways, especially by contesting the election of Greeks to vacant sees. The dispute over the

---

[16] A. Camariano-Cioran, *Academiile domneşti din Bucureşti şi Iaşi* (Bucharest, 1971), 114–88; G. Cronţ, 'L'Académie de Saint-Sava de Bucarest au XVIIIᵉ siècle: Le Contenu de l'enseignement', *Revue des études sud-est européennes*, 4/3–4 (1966), 459–68.

[17] On the opposition of the Romanian clergy to Greek predominance in the church, see A. Elian, 'Legăturile Mitropoliei Ungrovlahiei cu Patriarhia de Constantinopol şi cu celelalte Biserici Ortodoxe', *Biserica Ortodoxă Română*, 77/7–10 (1959), 931–2; Păcurariu, *Istoria*, ii. 325–7.

choice of a new bishop of Buzău in 1793 was typical. Romanian *boiers* and clergy demanded that he be a Romanian, but Metropolitan Dositei Filitti wanted a Greek. To win over his opponents he persuaded the prince to create a new bishopric at Arges, which would be headed by a Romanian, a strategem that worked.[18] Yet, tension between the two clergies continued to mount in the following decades. Not surprisingly, Romanian laymen and clergy hailed the election of a fellow Romanian, Dionisie Lupu, as metropolitan in 1819 as a victory for their movement to autochthonize the church. As later events would show, the accession of a Romanian as head of the church after three successive Greek metropolitans inaugurated a new, national orientation in the conduct of church affairs.

Greek influence in the Moldavian church never achieved the same level it had in the Wallachian. A tradition of independence going back to the fifteenth century and based upon the conception of its autocephalous character was reinforced in the eighteenth century by strong native metropolitans. The Moldavian clergy closed ranks behind them to oppose foreign penetration of their church. As a result, only two Greeks gained high ecclesiastical positions and then only because of heavy political pressure exerted by the princes.

The significance of Greek culture and the Greek language for the 'progress', or Europeanization, of Romanian society has been a matter of controversy since the eighteenth century. Many historians in the nineteenth century particularly, in a reaction to Phanariot rule, held that the language and culture of the Greeks, by preserving the bonds between the principalities and the Orthodox world south of the Danube and in Constantinople, had reinforced tradition and had thus delayed the entrance of the Romanians into the more 'advanced' intellectual and cultural life of Western Europe. The weight of the evidence, however, suggests a more positive role for Greek culture and language. They served, first of all, as intermediaries between Romanian intellectuals and the West, especially through the princely academies and numerous translations of major works of literature and political commentary.

The main body of ideas thus disseminated were those of the Enlightenment. Although a few Romanian *boiers* and clergy became acquainted with the works of the Enlightenment in the original languages, such direct contact with the sources often occurred only after the same books had already circulated in Greek translations.[19] Romanians who knew Greek were more numerous than those who could read Western languages, and although a few had Western books in their libraries, these works probably had less influence than translations into Greek, which circulated far more widely and in greater numbers of copies. This was true, for example, of the works of Christian Wolff, the *Logic* of Heineccius, and the *Logic* of Condillac. In literature Fénelon's *Télémaque* was translated into

---

[18] Păcurariu, *Istoria*, ii. 447–8.

[19] D. Popovici, *La Littérature roumaine à l'époque des lumières* (Sibiu, 1945), 59–74; Papacostea-Danielopolu, *Literatura şi limba greacă*, 45–65.

Romanian in 1772, but Romanian intellectuals had had access to it well before that time in a Greek translation, which had been published in 1742 and had been disseminated in hundreds of copies. Moreover, the Romanian translator used the Greek intermediary rather than the French original for his version. Some of the classics of eighteenth-century thought became known to Romanian intellectuals first in Greek translation, notably John Locke's *An Essay concerning the Human Understanding* and *Some Thoughts concerning Education*; Fontenelle's *Entretiens sur la pluralité des mondes*, which popularized the theories of Copernicus and Descartes about the universe; and Montesquieu's *Considérations sur les causes de la grandeur des Romains et de leur décadence*. The translation of such works into Greek continued well into the 1820s. A striking example is the activity of Iordache Golescu, a great *boier* and the son of Radu Golescu and one of the chief promoters of education in Wallachia.[20] He justified his own translations into Greek on the grounds that they were for the 'general good', a phrase which suggests that such works were widely read.

Exactly how widely works in Greek penetrated Romanian society cannot be known with certainty. But since the principalities had preserved at least a semblance of political autonomy, books and manuscripts of the most diverse kinds could be imported and read without hindrance by Ottoman authorities and the conservative elements at the Greek Patriarchate in Constantinople. This was especially true in the latter part of the eighteenth century and the beginning of the nineteenth when Greek works were suspect, because of the leading role Greek intellectuals were playing in the social and political ferment in South-eastern Europe. Greek books printed in Venice and Vienna often circulated more freely in Moldavia and Wallachia than in Greece proper or Constantinople. The great *boiers*, small groups of intellectuals, and the upper middle class were the buyers and readers of these works. But Greek books were not restricted to Bucharest and Iaşi. Private libraries in smaller towns such as Huşi, in Moldavia, and Ploieşti, in Wallachia, possessed respectable collections.[21]

The growing receptivity of educated Romanians to European thought in Greek translation and, to a lesser extent, in the original French and German suggests a general shift in the mental climate in the principalities. Even more striking evidence of this is to be found in the literary taste of the second half of the eighteenth century.

LITERATURE

Changes in the content and forms of literary expression were signs that literature had ceased to be primarily a means of instruction. Authors now sought to

[20] N. Camariano, 'Primele traduceri din B. de Saint-Pierre în literatura neogreacă', *Revista Fundaţiilor Regale*, 9/6 (1942), 644–6; Perpessicius, 'Iordache Golescu, lexicolog, folclorist, scriitor', in Perpessicius, *Menţiuni de istoriografie literară şi folclor, 1948–1956* (Bucharest, 1957), 257.

[21] See e.g. M. Carataşu, 'Catalogul bibliotecii unui mare negustor din veacul al XVIII-lea: Grigorie Anton Avramie', *Studii şi cercetări de bibliologie*, 12 (1972), 189–206.

entertain. New genres, which satisfied the tastes of rising social classes, appeared. The very status of literature was different. It had acquired a certain autonomy and was becoming a mirror of national life, and writers were beginning to find in it a permanent vocation.

Up to the middle of the eighteenth century Romanian literature had had a mainly utilitarian purpose: chronicles were written to teach later generations the ways of politics or to instil loyalty to the prince or to the *boiers*; church books were intended to provide moral and religious training (the Lives of Saints indeed resembled imaginative literature, but they were not supposed to be read for amusement); medieval romances, like the legend of Alexander the Great, continued to be accepted as history by many readers; and other 'popular books' were used to explicate obscure passages in the Bible and were received as religious works (*Varlaam and Joasaph* was, after all, a saint's life and not a piece of fiction). All these works had been written or translated in order to accomplish some common social purpose, not to give pleasure to the individual reader. Prose, moreover, except for history, did not reflect immediate reality, and cultivated poetry, as opposed to folk poetry, shied away from purely secular themes.

Sometime between 1750 and 1780 the taste of the reading public showed signs of change, first among the town inhabitants (*tîrgoveți*) and the lesser *boiers*, rather than among the aristocracy and the peasantry. Literature produced by and for the aristocracy remained conventional in themes, images, and composition. The same may be said about the village, where folklore flourished, drawing inspiration from customs and myths handed down from generation to generation. Between these two levels lay the petty functionaries, teachers, and small merchants of the towns, who displayed their literary vitality by cultivating two genres—the *cîntec de lume* (love-song) and the rhymed chronicle.

The *cîntece de lume* were modest creations, poems that in style lay between folklore and the cultivated poetry of intellectuals.[22] Their themes were the joys and sorrows of love and the consolation of wine, and their tone ran the gamut of elation, sentimentality, and melancholy. They circulated orally (the more popular ones were written down) and, often accompanied by music, had as their most popular interpreters the *lăutari* (fiddlers). The composers of the *cîntece de lume* made use of folklore, especially of its trochaic rhythms, but they adhered more closely to the disciplined structures of cultivated verse than did the folk poets. This type of poetry suggests a distinct change of feeling in the towns. In contrast to the solemn accents of the Enlightenment in vogue among the intellectuals and the myth and fantasy of folk creations, the *cîntece de lume* expressed a sense of release from traditional social forms and moral pressures, which the middle class, in particular, was experiencing. Its members displayed a new joy of living, the desire to taste the good things of life.

---

[22] O. Papadima, *Ipostaze ale iluminismului românesc* (Bucharest, 1975), 114–20.

The rhymed chronicles appealed to the same audience as the *cîntece de lume*, that is, to those who could read, but had no formal literary education. These chronicles told of recent historical events such as the assassination of Prince Grigore Ghica of Moldavia in 1777, or the wars between the Russians and the Turks in the 1770s.[23] Their anonymous authors seem to have taken their models from Greek literature of the period, but, apparently unacquainted with cultivated literature or the rules of versification, they adopted the forms of contemporary folklore, favouring the same characteristic assonances and the same strained rhythms. The rhymed chronicle also shared with folklore the exaggerated, often satirical, portrait of the hero. These short pieces exude the same joy of living as the *cîntece de lume*. Both are remarkable revelations of a change of mental climate seemingly unaffected by the general invigoration of intellectual life taking place under foreign influences.

The first attempts at authentic poetic creation were made by a handful of writers in the final years of the eighteenth century, but a new conception of what literature should be about came more slowly. Until around 1820 traditional moral and didactic values continued to inform both poetry and prose. None the less, expanding international economic and political relations, a gradual integration into European cultural life, and the emergence of an ethical system no longer inspired solely by religion already promised to free literature from its heavy baggage of the past.

The characteristic style of cultivated literature at this time can best be described as classicism. The verses of such poets as Gheorghe Asachi (1788–1869) and, to some extent, Alecu Văcărescu (1769–99) and Costache Conachi (1778–1849) showed greater respect for craftmanship and established models than for the lyric impulse and favoured reason over sentiment. But they were not conscious of themselves as classicists because a true literary life, that is, one which generated an exchange of aesthetic ideas and created distinct groups of writers, did not exist. As a consequence, Romanian classicism lacked a programme. To be sure, Văcărescu and Conachi recognized the need for rules and models, but they stopped short of formulating a theory. None the less, they made important contributions to the development of a modern literature through the conscientious practice of their craft. For the first time in a systematic way they attempted to transform the language of everyday speech into literature, and they brought a certain discipline to the massive infusion of folklore found in existing genres.

An obvious connection existed between classicism and the Enlightenment, a compelling influence among intellectuals of the period. Reason, order, and utility were hallmarks of both. The fable, which enjoyed great popularity in the principalities between 1790 and 1820, illustrates perfectly the correlation

---

[23] M. Anghelescu, *Preromantismul românesc* (Bucharest, 1971), 61–4; D. Simonescu (ed.), *Cronici și povestiri românești versificate, Sec. XVII–XVIII* (Bucharest, 1967), 5–32.

of subject matter, form, and purpose.[24] The collections of Aesop's and La Fontaine's fables were much in vogue because they offered a means of expressing political and philosophical ideas which could not be stated directly, and because they satisfied the prevailing taste of the educated for literature that was moral and instructive. The treatment which writers accorded folklore also fitted in with classical, enlightened ideals. Văcărescu and Conachi ignored the inherent qualities of folklore, disdaining its substance as the work of crude, superstitious men and thus as raw material to be reworked.

Within the dominant current of classicism the leading poets expressed sentiments that were often romantic. They showed a persistent concern for the individual in the contemporary world. In examining his inner life and sensibility, they were often overcome by intuitions of deeper truths, the melancholy drift towards death, and the feeling of loneliness in a hostile world.

The mingling of classicism and the new romantic impulses is evident in the poetry of Alecu Văcărescu and Ioan Cantacuzino (1757–1828). Both poets were indebted to foreign models and both had a greater knowledge of European poetry than any previous generation of intellectuals. European influence as yet meant little to them in matters of form, mainly because of the absence of a standard literary language, but in theme and atmosphere Romanian poetry now achieved at least a degree of independence from didactic, religious, and historical functions. Văcărescu's poetry displays an intimate tone, which suggests the emancipation of the individual artist. He experimented with the emotions with an intensity and ambiguity unthinkable for a classicist, and he expressed poignantly his feelings of isolation as a poet in an uncomprehending world. Cantacuzino probed individual spirituality and simple human virtues as he sought to discover the nature of man freed from all external rules. In 'Veacul de aur sau cel scump' (c.1796; The Golden or Precious Age) he presents the existence of primitive man in an idyllic, Rousseauistic vision critical of modern society. Both he and Văcărescu insisted on the personal character of their work and on their own pleasure as their chief creative motivation. They thus no longer represented the ideas and aspirations of the collectivity as the old chroniclers, for example, had. Yet, the transition to the new sensibility was by no means sudden or complete. Classical attitudes and rhetorical devices, the grandiloquent tone, and the solemn invocations are still prevalent, but the straightforwardness and passion of the two poets clearly belong to a different vision of man and his emotions.[25]

Costache Conachi is also a transitional figure. Brought up on the prose of the Enlightenment and neo-classical poetry, he remained a man of the eighteenth

---

[24] G. Loghin, 'La Fable en prose, oeuvre-témoin dans le processus de l'évolution de la mentalité et de la formation du goût littéraire à la fin du XVIIIᵉ et au début de XIXᵉ siècle', *Revue des études sud-est européennes*, 17/3 (1979), 623–6.

[25] Anghelescu, *Preromantismul românesc*, 69–88.

century.[26] Yet, he expressed a restlessness clearly out of step with classical restraint as he continually sought his own poetic voice. His inspiration was primarily erotic, and his most popular works were adaptations of the *cîntece de lume*. In his love poems he evokes a wild and grandiose nature, which for the first time in Romanian poetry becomes native, as he describes what he sees, not what literary tradition recommended be seen.

A younger poet, Iancu Văcărescu (1792–1863), the son of Alecu, brought a fresh sensibility to bear on the great questions about nature and man's fate.[27] His was a poetry of observation, which described what was, not what ought to be, and thus he contributed to the undermining of classical models. No longer satisfied to have his art serve frivolous amusements, he focused his attention on contemporary moral attitudes. His verse was still stiff as he twisted language to fit preconceived patterns, but he brought new, universal themes to Romanian poetry, linking the tragedy of human destiny not to the inevitability of death but to the fact of existence itself.

In the absence of an abundant original literature translations played a decisive role in moulding taste and preparing the reading public for original works in Romanian.[28] Translations responded to the need for a broader culture and a more diversified fare and reflected more or less accurately the tastes of the period. Those who favoured the Romanesque were treated to new versions of the popular books. Others who sought moral and socially constructive reading were drawn to Fénelon's *Télémaque* and Marmontel's *Bélisaire*. There was also a growing audience after 1800 for works in a sentimental or preromantic vein such as Bernardin de St Pierre's *La Chaumière indienne*, and the Abbé Prévosts's *Manon Lescaut*, but, surprisingly at first glance, Rousseau, Edward Young, Goethe, and other pre-Romantics of the first rank were absent. Perhaps the Romanian audience was unprepared aesthetically for their subtleties and sophistication, but it seems more likely that the translators had simply decided to promote civic virtue and moral uplift, which they thought the public wanted, through modest and straightforward works.

THE ROMANIAN ENLIGHTENMENT

Striking evidence that the principalities were drawing closer to Western Europe was the pervasive influence of the European Enlightenment among intellectuals.[29] It helped to modify political doctrines and traditional thinking about nature and

---

[26] P. Cornea, *Originile romantismului românesc* (Bucharest, 1972), 304–20.

[27] Ibid. 343–64.

[28] Ibid. 95–114; Anghelescu, *Preromantismul românesc*, 91–118.

[29] Valuable overviews are Popovici, *La Littérature roumaine*, and P. Teodor (ed.), *Enlightenment and Romanian Society* (Cluj-Napoca, 1980). See also A. Duțu, 'Mişcarea iluministă moldoveană de la sfîrşitul secolului al XVIII-lea', *Studii: Revistă de istorie*, 19/5 (1966), 911–28, and N. Isar, 'Aspecte ale mişcării luministe din Moldova la începutul secolului al XIX-lea (pînă la 1821)', *Studii: Revistă de istorie*, 22/6 (1969), 1127–44.

the relationship between God and man; it provided incentives for educational reform; and it reinforced the tendencies towards classicism inherent in
Romanian literature. But the Enlightenment should not be seen solely
in terms of Westernization or an awakening. Such a view assumes that before the
second half of the eighteenth century intellectual and cultural life in the principalities languished in a kind of oriental torpor, to be stirred only by
light from the West. Such an approach ignores the fact that Romanian cultural
and intellectual life had a dynamic of its own, which, moreover, helps to
explain the particular course taken by the European Enlightenment in the
principalities.

The changes in literary taste and creative sensibility and the growing receptivity to European thought and culture, as we have seen, were aspects of a general
movement of ideas in Moldavia and Wallachia which can best be described as the
Romanian Enlightenment. It resembled the European movement in its critical
attitude towards established institutions and in its reliance upon reason and
education. Intellectuals in both principalities subjected the existing economic and
political order and the ideological assumptions underlying it to relentless scrutiny.
Their critical spirit had its primary source in the realization that alternative ways
of life existed outside the principalities. Acquaintance with Western Europe
offered dramatic contrasts to their own 'backward' existence. So did classical
Greece and Rome. The cultural values and civic virtues of antiquity, taught in
the princely academies of Bucharest and Iași and a part of every educated man's
intellectual baggage, were a potent source of social relativism. The progress of the
printed word and the increase in the size of the reading public steadily expanded
the range and influence of the critics.

Characteristic of the Enlightenment in the principalities was a preoccupation
with the specific problems of Romanian society. For the *boiers* and the higher
clergy ideas were first of all a means to practical ends. The cultivation of ideas for
their own sake and abstract theories of political and social reform had less
attraction for Romanian intellectuals than for their counterparts in the West
because the Romanians faced the constant threat of foreign political and cultural
domination. To remove it absorbed the energies of all who had committed
themselves to the general welfare of the *patrie*. While the European philosophers
tended to ignore national boundaries and ethnic differences, Romanian intellectuals focused attention on reform at home and gave relatively little thought to
other nations.

The Romanian Enlightenment, unlike the European, was generally free of
anticlericalism. Although lay intellectuals harshly criticized individual church
leaders from time to time, the motivation was political—the clergy's support of
the great *boiers*, for example—rather than religious. Largely absent was the idea
that the chuch had to be combated as a force for obscurantism and an impediment to progress. Laymen readily acknowledged that many ecclesiastics were as
receptive to innovation and as vigorous in promoting educational reform and the

general welfare as they were. Equally important in blunting criticism of the clergy was the pre-eminent role of the church in public life. The church provided indispensable social services and was the guardian of public morality at a time when an ethical system separate from traditional religious teachings had only begun to form among intellectuals, but left the great mass of the population untouched.

One of the salient characteristics of Romanian thought and higher culture of the period was its gradual secularization, at a time, paradoxically, when the spiritual renewal inspired by Paisie Velicicovschi was reaching its culmination. Theological questions and even God receded into the background as the majority of lay intellectuals strove to understand the mechanisms that moved human society and adapt and reform institutions in accordance with these new 'laws'.

The clergy remained steadfast in their faith, and the revival of monasticism under Paisie Velicicovschi and the increased publication of church service books suggest no slackening of militancy on their part. But there was no fresh theological debate. Doctrine remained what it had been and went unchallenged from within the clergy. Such fundamental questions as the relationship between God and man or the role of the church in continuously changing social conditions elicited only the repetition of familiar formulas. Through its inability to keep pace with the curiosity and imagination of the growing stratum of lay intellectuals, the higher clergy, and with it the church as an institution, gradually relinquished the intellectual leadership which it had exercised during much of the eighteenth century.

Religion was by no means absent from the writings of lay intellectuals. They often invoked the deity as an explanation for the course of human events, but their appeals sound formal, almost routine. Few would have accepted the bald proposition of Naum Rîmniceanu, a noted cleric of the period, that God was 'the cause of all things',[30] that truth was attainable only through faith, and that science could shed only a partial light on the problem of existence. Lay intellectuals were attracted, instead, to rationalist explanations of phenomena in both nature and human society. The majority could best be classified as deists. They conceived of God as a first cause who had set the world in motion and then let it run in accordance with the immutable laws he had legislated. They were not given to speculating about the nature of God or about the extent to which he could be known, but they had no doubt that men could discover his laws and bring their institutions into harmony with them. That certainty lay at the heart of the optimism that pervaded their writings. They had abiding faith in the powers of reason to guide the course of human affairs. It was a faculty they defined as unique to man, which endowed him with the capacity to develop as an autonomous being and to order the world in ways that were congenial to

---

[30] N. Rîmniceanu, *Despre originea Românilor*, in C. Erbiceanu, *Cronicari greceşti carii au scris despre Români în epoca fanariotă* (Bucharest, 1888), 235.

him. Such unabashed anthropocentrism suggests strong affinities with the European Enlightenment.

AN AGE OF CRITICISM

The changes in the way Romanian intellectuals viewed themselves and the world are strikingly evident in their critical attitude. They sought new solutions to fundamental problems of social and political organization by drawing upon their own countries' historical experience and their growing acquaintance with Europe. They indulged, as none of their predecessors had, in self-examination, which in turn brought a heightened ethnic awareness and a compelling need to define their place in Europe.

A small number of Romanian writers and public figures, *boiers*, and a few bourgeois and clergy turned a critical eye on the state of society and its institutions and found them wanting. Despite harsh judgements, their approach was essentially constructive, for they shared the faith of the times in the ability of reasonable men to provide for the general good. They also drew strength from a growing ethnic awareness and the conviction that they were about to join an enlightened and progressive Europe.

In no previous period had the whole system of values upon which society and politics in the principalities were based been subjected to such a sustained questioning as in the latter years of the eighteenth century and the early decades of the nineteenth.[31] The very pillars of society were attacked. The *boiers* as a class, especially the great *boiers*, were blamed for their lack of initiative in economic matters and their general failure to lead, and, most reprehensible of all, their unwillingness to share power. *Boiers* of the second and third ranks distinguished themselves in this kind of criticism, but even a representative of the great *boiers*, Mihai Sturdza, a future prince of Moldavia, qualified his own class as parasitical.[32] Nor was the higher clergy immune from scrutiny. Anonymous pamphlets rebuked the metropolitans and bishops for their cooperation with the Phanariots and their constant fiscal demands upon the poor. Yet, none of these critics went so far as to demand the abolition of the *boier* ranks or the replacement of the traditional church by some sort of rational religion. Instead, they urged a reform of existing institutions.

These critics were unrelenting in their attacks on Ottoman suzerainty and Phanariot administration, for they saw in this dual subservience the main cause of the decline of the principalities. The majority blamed 'the Turks and the Greeks' for the pervasive insecurity of individual lives and property

---

[31] Indispensable for the political thought of the period is V. Georgescu, *Ideile politice și iluminismul în Principate Române, 1750–1831* (Bucharest, 1972).

[32] Hurmuzaki, *Documente*, suppl. 1, pt. 5 (Bucharest, 1894), 30: a memorial by Sturdza on the condition of the peasantry, written perhaps in 1829.

and the disarray in public affairs.[33] In their view, foreigners had not only corrupted political institutions and retarded economic development, but they had also severely warped the psyche of the great mass of the population. Not surprisingly, the reforms the critics advocated gave priority to stability and order.

They drew their ideas from a variety of sources. The core came from the writings of their predecessors of the seventeenth century and the first half of the eighteenth. The great chroniclers—Grigore Ureche (1590–1647) and Miron Costin (1633–91) of Moldavia and Constantin Cantacuzino (1640–1716) of Wallachia—bequeathed to them fundamental political ideas and a historical framework for their thought. Ureche's chronicle was used by Ion Tăutu (1795–1830), the most original political theorist of the 1820s, and Costin's by the monk Naum Rîmniceanu (1764–1838), one of the most progressive thinkers of the time, to establish the ethnic identity of the Romanians and reinforce claims to independence from Ottoman domination. Dimitrie Cantemir (1673–1723), an advocate of enlightened, absolute monarchy of the sort that Peter the Great had introduced in Russia, was most influential. Although he was prince of Moldavia only briefly (1710–11), having lost his throne as a result of Peter's disastrous Prut campaign, and spent his remaining years in exile in Russia, his ideas were well known to Romanian political thinkers in the later eighteenth and early nineteenth century. The demands of the *boiers* to limit Ottoman suzerainty, the theory of the capitulations, and various arguments in support of the historical rights of the principalities owed much to Cantemir.

While native sources provided continuity, Western thought offered Romanian intellectuals new ways of organizing historical experiences. Besides the Enlightenment, the French Revolution and the events of the Napoleonic period also expanded the Romanians' view of themselves and of Europe.[34] In the great-power struggles of the period they saw themselves as mere objects of barter, but they also sought to take advantage of international rivalries to gain independence from Ottoman rule and even to bring about internal political reorganization. Revolution itself had few supporters among Romanian intellectuals, but they adapted to their own purposes various ideas contained in the revolutionary literature that found its way into the principalities. Among the first such works to reach Bucharest and Iaşi were *De la souveraineté du peuple* (Paris, 1790) and *Le Manuel du citoyen* (Paris, 1791). These and other pamphlets were brought to the principalities by French republican agents and, after 1796, by French consuls, who enjoyed easy access to the highest levels of Moldavian and Wallachian society through the salons of *boiers* and metropolitans. A number of Greeks, who used the principalities as a base for their own anti-Ottoman activities, and Polish *émigrés* also disseminated revolutionary ideas among the *boiers*, while booksellers

---

[33] Georgescu, *Ideile*, 31–2, 147–9.
[34] A. Camariano, *Spiritul revoluţionar francez şi Voltaire în limba greacă şi română* (Bucharest, 1946), 59–63; A. Zub (ed.), *La Révolution Française et les Roumains* (Iaşi, 1989), 17–52, 95–117, 147–62.

who catered to the tastes of *boiers* found it profitable to stock books on the recent events in France.[35]

With the exception of a few Romanians, mainly in Bucharest and Iaşi, who were caught up in the enthusiasm of the moment, revolutionary ideas and conspiracies found no fertile ground in the principalities. Rather, the great *boiers* and the higher clergy took their ideas about government and social organization primarily from their own country's historical experience. Of foreign influences, the most congenial were those of the conservative Enlightenment with its emphasis upon reason, knowledge, and, especially, order. To be sure, the principle of national sovereignty proclaimed by the French revolutionaries found immediate favour with the *boiers*, but the social and political programmes of French republicans filled them with apprehension. Those persons in Moldavia and Wallachia who might have welcomed the extension of political equality and economic justice were few in number and had no following. The Romanian bourgeoisie lacked both the numbers and the cohesion necessary to formulate and carry out public policy. The same may be said of the intellectual élite. It existed as a sum of individuals rather than as an organized group pursuing common goals.

Liberal thought, too, had its admirers in the principalities, though its overall influence was less than that of other currents. Its main source was England, but few Romanian intellectuals had direct knowledge of English political thought and institutions.[36] The first to visit England was the great *boier* Nicolae Rosetti-Rosnovanu in 1818. During this visit he may have become acquainted with the works of Adam Smith and David Ricardo, which seem to have had a lasting influence on his own economic thought. But the majority of Romanian intellectuals made contact with English liberalism through France, particularly Montesqieu, whose *De l'Esprit des lois* was known to almost all the reforming *boiers*.

Romanian *boiers* were eager to establish their new political institutions on a firm theoretical foundation and thus gave much attention to the beginnings and subsequent evolution of civil society. Their thought displayed little originality, as they were satisfied to draw upon ideas current in Europe at the time. The majority accepted the contract theory of the origin of political society, but their formulations were so general that it is impossible to say from whom they borrowed. In any case, the idea of a social contract had become a commonplace by the beginning of the nineteenth century and can be found in princely *hrisoave* and in the political programmes of 1821. Romanian writers agreed that the contract had been entered into because men by nature were social beings and because they understood that this bond afforded them the most favourable

---

[35] Hurmuzaki, *Documente*, xix, pt. 1 (Bucharest, 1922), 814–16.

[36] E. Vîrtosu, 'Les Idées politiques de I. Tăutul, candidat au trône de Moldavie en 1829', *Revue roumaine d'histoire*, 4/2 (1965), 279; id., *Napoleon Bonaparte şi proiectul unei 'Republici aristo-democraticeşti' în Moldova, la 1802* (2nd edn., Bucharest, 1947), 34.

conditions for their development. They accepted the general idea of evolution.[37] Neither social and political institutions nor nature itself, in their view, had assumed a single form for all time, but they showed little inclination to speculate about the causes of change.

In applying the idea of evolution to their own history, Romanian *boiers* discerned three distinct periods, which they designated gold, silver, and bronze, in that order. They obviously regarded this succession as one of decline and were certain that the contemporary world was neither better nor happier than the ages that had preceded it. Their sombre view of things had its origin in the recent history of the principalities. They showed no hesitation in classifying the Phanariot regime as a bronze age of decadence, which they contrasted with the golden age of the second half of the seventeenth century, a period of relative political stability and cultural bloom. This notion of decline appeared often in projects of reform and other political writings between the 1770s and 1830s. Yet, despite this pessimistic assessment of their own recent history, *boiers* and intellectuals by no means looked to the future with resignation. On the contrary, they were doers and reformers. They had before them the example of Western Europe, whose high level of civilization and strong political institutions greatly impressed them, and they were persuaded that, once free of foreign domination, they themselves would be equal to the task of building a modern society.

Although the majority of Romanian political thinkers recognized the social contract as the origin of civil society, they by no means accepted the notion that all its members should be equal. Theirs was a hierarchical view of society. Basing their ideas upon existing structures at home, they divided society into two strata—privileged and commoners. They usually referred to the latter as 'the people' (*popor* or *norod*), which encompassed everyone except *boiers* and clergy. To refer to the *boiers* they sometimes used the term *stare* in the sense of 'estate' or 'order', as in the phrases 'the estates of Wallachia' and 'all the orders of the nation', but it is not always clear whether 'estate' referred to a narrow, privileged stratum like the *boiers* or was merely a broader, general term for social category. All the political thinkers of the period treated the *boiers* as an estate, but none accorded the same distinction to the clergy, preferring instead to include them among the *boiers*, a practice which suggests a lack of understanding of social class.[38] By lumping the entire clergy together with the *boiers*, they ignored the sharp economic and social differences between the higher clergy and the parish priests. Moreover, their failure to recognize the clergy as a separate estate originated in the historical evolution of the Orthodox Church itself, whose leaders, as we have seen, identified themselves with the *boiers* in public affairs. For these reasons the *boiers* and intellectuals of our period

---

[37] Id., *1821: Date şi fapte noi* (Bucharest, 1932), 183–6: a memorandum of 1822.
[38] Hurmuzaki, *Documente*, ns i (Bucharest, 1962), 99–100: Moldavian *boiers* to Prince Repnin, 27 July 1775; ibid. 110–11: metropolitan of Wallachia to Repnin, Aug. 1775.

accorded the clergy a purely spiritual role in society, denying it political importance.

The majority of the *boiers* were convinced that their class was by right the leading political force in the country, and they tended to identify their interests with those of the country as a whole. But they were divided on the question of who precisely was entitled to *boier* status. *Boiers* who considered themselves natives (not Greek Phanariots) insisted that only those whose lineages went back to the period when the principalities themselves were formed and who had been rewarded for services rendered at that time could be called *boiers*. But those *boiers* who were of Greek origin and who owed their status to the Phanariot princes argued that nobility had its origins in high political functions performed. None the less, both parties readily agreed on the distinctiveness of noble rank.[39] It was a sentiment that grew stronger during the first decades of the nineteenth century, undoubtedly as a result of increasing contacts between the *boiers* and the West European nobility. The use of coats of arms, for example, was adapted from Western practice and represented an attempt by the old, established *boier* families to differentiate themselves from the new *boiers*. Yet, the great *boiers*, native and Greek, closed ranks against the lesser and middle *boiers* and persons without noble lineage who sought to enter the élite. Iordache Rosetti-Rosnovanu and Mihai Sturdza urged the maintenance of an aristocracy as necessary for social stability and continuity. But *boiers* of lesser rank argued that there was only a single *boier* class and complained that its division into separate categories on the basis of state service was artificial and unfair. Occasionally, the great *boiers* could be critical of themselves, precisely because they were conscious of the responsibilities they had assumed as an élite. Iordache Rosetti-Rosnovanu warned the privileged not to let themselves become a burden to society by living off the country and giving nothing in return. In particular, he found irrational a fiscal system which exempted the wealthy from taxes and urged the enactment of a single tax payable by all regardless of social status.[40]

The majority of the *boier* social thinkers were by no means unaware of other classes. They showed genuine sympathy for the peasantry and approved of the abolition of serfdom in 1746 and 1749. Several even suggested that more should be done because, as the suppliers of food, the peasants were the most valuable segment of the population. All the *boiers* tended to blame the persistence of poverty in the countryside on excessive fiscal burdens and a corrupt administration, but they did not yet conceive of a peasant problem and had no plan to deal with underlying economic and social ills. They had little to say about the bourgeoisie as a class because it did not yet represent a significant social force. But they showed some concern about cities and their inhabitants because of their role in stimulating economic activity.

[39] Rîmniceanu, *Despre originea Românilor*, 242–5; D. Fotino, *Istoria generală a Daciei*, iii (Bucharest, 1859), 139.

[40] D. Greceanu, 'O închipuire a lui I. Rosetti-Rosnovanu', *Arhiva*, 1–2 (1898), 603–5.

The true vocation of the *boier* writers was political thought. They elaborated projects of constitutional and administrative reform of much originality, but they made no attempt to conceal their class bias and reserved to themselves the exercise of power. They were persuaded that the most suitable form of government for the principalities was monarchy, which they accepted as a natural product of European constitutional development from the Middle Ages to the beginning of the eighteenth century. But they could not agree on precisely what kind of monarchy would bring the greatest benefits in the new age.

The majority favoured enlightened absolutism, a choice that accorded with their obvious admiration for Catherine II. But the Phanariot regime was odious to them. They saw little hope of introducing enlightened government as long as the principalities were administered by foreigners, even though they recognized that several princes, such as Alexandru Ipsilanti, were by intention and deed enlightened monarchs.

Many *boiers* also favoured constitutional monarchy, by which they simply meant a *boier* state. The great *boiers*, in particular, favoured this form because they were certain that it would enable them to extend their own power and limit that of the prince. Characteristic was a programme of action drawn up in Iaşi in 1782 entitled 'The Union of Native *Boiers*' (*Unirea boierilor pămînteni*), in which the authors, who prudently chose anonymity, declared their intention to resist all efforts from inside or outside the country to diminish the 'honour' of the *boier* class and the 'welfare' of the *patrie*. Significant here is the identification of their own privileges with the prosperity and good order of the country at large, a formula that was repeated in numerous *boier* writings in the early decades of the nineteenth century.

The idea of a republic also had its advocates, but almost all of them were great *boiers* who conceived of it, as they had constitutional monarchy, as a means of limiting the powers of the prince and of ensuring the predominance of their own class. They really had in mind an aristocratic oligarchy, an idea which they set forth for the first time in the Moldavian memorials to Catherine II in 1770. They proposed that the government of the principality be entrusted to twelve great *boiers*, half with legislative powers and half with judicial functions. Their immediate aim was clearly to prevent the return of the Phanariot princes after the conclusion of hostilities between Russia and Turkey. Broader in its representative character was the 'Plan of an Aristo-democratic Republican Government', probably drawn up by Chancellor (*logofăt*) Dimitrie I. Sturdza in 1802, which represented the thinking of the more liberal *boiers*. They had no intention of diminishing their role in public affairs, but they made provision for representation in government of elements from the country at large in a lower council (*divan de jos*), which would share certain executive and legislative functions with the great *boiers* sitting in the grand council (*divanul mare*). The liberal *boiers* also expressed concern for the education and health of the general populace and urged equal treatment for both great and small in the courts and the elimination of abuses in tax assessment and collection.

Sturdza's ideas represented the extreme limit of republicanism during the period; all the authors cited adamantly opposed government by the common people. Ion Tăutu spoke of the 'anarchy of the mob' and was highly critical of the events of 1789 in France and the republic that had followed; Mihai Sturdza expressed certainty that 'rule by the many' would in time lead to social upheaval; and Naum Rîmniceanu was alarmed by the extent of popular unrest in Wallachia in 1821, which he classified as anarchy.

Although the great *boiers* and others might differ on forms of government, they were of one mind on the need to improve its machinery. Their reforms were aimed primarily at a corrupt and inefficient administration and inequalities of taxation. They were unanimous in urging that public functionaries be appointed for fixed terms and be removed only for sufficient cause. The main reason for corruption was clear to them: the irregular manner in which officials were paid. They were therefore eager to abolish the *havaieturi* and introduce fixed salaries for all ranks in the bureaucracy. These innovations would, they thought, also lead to fundamental changes in the role of officials; henceforth, they would cease to be servants of the prince, treating their posts simply as sources of income, and would become employees of the state with responsibilities towards the public and accountable to it for their actions. It followed from this line of reasoning that merit and education, rather than wealth and birth, would be the criteria for appointment to public office. They saw no contradiction between these sentiments and the principle of *boier* rule because they themselves monopolized higher education and experience in government and had no doubts about their own merits. Opinions on taxation were more diverse. Some *boiers* held that taxes should, in keeping with tradition, be levied on the person, but a growing number thought a single tax on property and income, without exemptions based upon class or rank, would be fairer and would produce a greater amount of revenue. All advocates of fiscal reform argued that the main purpose of taxation should be to provide the state with the means necessary to carry out its functions.

A number of *boiers* looked beyond political and fiscal reform as the means of assuring good order and prosperity. The great *boier* Dinicu Golescu was typical of this group. Critical of the backwardness into which the principalities had sunk, he drew upon what he had seen during his travels in Central and Western Europe between 1824 and 1826 for remedies.[41] He noted particularly the advance of technology and the wide diffusion of education as the foundation of European civilization and had no doubt that they could serve also as the sources of a renaissance in the principalities. His observations confirmed his belief that human progress ultimately depended upon reason and a vigorous moral and

---

[41] On Golescu, see the introd. by Mircea Anghelescu in Dinicu Golescu, *Scrieri* (Bucharest, 1990), pp. v–lxi.

spiritual life, and thus he carried the traditions of the Romanian Enlightenment into the third decade of the new century.

A significant sign of change in mental attitudes was a growing concern for individual rights. Such a point of view ran counter to the almost exclusive preoccupation in Romanian law with collective rights, a position especially evident in attitudes towards property. An early indication of change was the definition of law itself contained in *Sobornicescul Hrisov* (Council's Code) of 1785 as an instrument for guaranteeing private property.[42] The comprehensive *Cod Calimach* (Code of Callimachi) of 1817 made the point more forcefully, declaring the ownership of property to be an absolute right.[43] Romanian intellectuals after 1800 generally subscribed to this view. For example, in 1822 Ion Tăutu called the individual ownership of property an imprescriptible right and opposed confiscation of it without due process of law, and Nicolae Rosetti-Rosnovanu spoke repeatedly about the 'sacred rights of individual property'. Such ideas also reflected the militant position on property taken by *boier* landlords, who were engaged in transforming their traditional limited control over their estates into full private ownership. The same idea of property was enthusiastically embraced by the emerging middle class.

A changing conception of law also lay behind the defence of personal liberties. For most of the eighteenth century Romanian princes and jurists had treated law as a tool of government instituted by God, but after 1800 the idea that law was a natural phenomenon, that is, an institution created by man out of his social experience, gained increasing currency. Social theorists demanded guarantees of personal security and respect for basic freedoms, and in numerous projects for constitutions and other reforms drawn up between 1800 and 1830 they included provisions ensuring equality before the law, freedom of speech and of the press, and the right to travel abroad freely.[44]

The advocates of individual rights imposed no religious qualifications for their enjoyment, except for Islam, which they associated with Ottoman rule, because they considered religious liberty as natural an attribute of man as freedom of speech. The neglect of religious observances and the growth of secularism among the educated in the eighteenth century furthered this spirit of toleration. The opposition of Romanian intellectuals to Islam (unanimous) and to Catholicism (widespread) had little to do with religious beliefs. Rather, they opposed these religions mainly on the grounds that an increase in their influence

---

[42] *Sobornicescul Hrisov* (crit. edn., Bucharest, 1958), 20.

[43] *Codul Calimach* (crit. edn., Bucharest, 1958), 223, 225 (paras. 461–5).

[44] I. Rosetti-Rosnovanu, 'În scurt luare aminte pentru oareşcari îndreptări . . . în administraţie de acum a Moldovei' (1818), in *Documente privind istoria României: Răscoala din 1821*, i (Bucharest, 1959), 121–4; D. Sturdza, 'Plan sau o formă de oblăduire republicească aristo-democraticească' (1802), in Vîrtosu, *Napoleon Bonaparte*, 35–6; D. V. Barnoschi, *Originile democraţiei române, Cărvunarii: Constituţia Moldovei dela 1822* (Iaşi, 1922), 155–8, 223–5, 232–9; A. D. Xenopol, 'Primul proiect de constituţiune a Moldovei', *Analele Academiei Române*, Memoriile Secţiunii Istorice, 2nd ser., 20 (1897–8), 136–60.

would lead to the extension of Ottoman and Austrian political and economic power. The 'Jewish question', which became acute in the second half of the nineteenth century, was still of little concern, because of the relatively small number of Jews in either principality. Except for Islam, all other religions enjoyed a broad measure of toleration—the right to construct houses of worship, the enjoyment of certain fiscal exemptions, and admittance to public schools. The *Cod Calimach* put the matter succinctly: 'Religious differences do not affect individual rights.'[45]

A constant preoccupation of Romanian writers was the search for an ideology that would link their past with the present and reconcile individual rights with collective responsibilities. Increasingly, they were drawn to the idea of nation. Although their writings on the subject did not constitute a coherent doctrine of nationhood, let alone a national ideology, their ethnic consciousness, which was the foundation of both, was already sharply defined. It had two main sources: Byzantine-Orthodox and, gradually overshadowing it, the theory of the Roman origins of the Romanians and the Latinity of their language. The authors of memorials to Russian officials during the war with the Ottoman Empire in 1768–74 referred to themselves as Roman colonists, doubtless a suggestion that such an ancestry entitled them to be heard at the future peace negotiations. The anonymous author of a memorial of 1807 to Napoleon urging support for an independent Moldavia described the wars between the Dacians and the Romans, the Romanization of Dacia, and the continuity of Roman settlement there after the withdrawal of the Roman legions by the Emperor Aurelian in the latter half of the third century.[46] Still other writers—Chesarie of Rîmnic, Naum Rîmniceanu, and the *boier* Dinicu Golescu—cited Roman origins as a compelling reason for the re-Europeanization of the Romanians and contrasted the glories of Roman times with the decadence ushered in by Ottoman suzerainty and Phanariot administration. The idea of Roman origins was, of course, not an invention of the eighteenth century. Moldavian and Wallachian chroniclers of the seventeenth century had accepted their ancient heritage as self-evident. The novelty of our period was their use to sustain political demands and to stimulate a national renaissance.

Another novelty was the attention that a few Romanian intellectuals paid to the Dacians.[47] The Romans, they recognized, had bestowed nobility upon the Romanians but the Dacians, as the original inhabitants of the land, had given them priority over all the other peoples who had settled on the territory of ancient Dacia. By claiming the Dacians as ancestors alongside the Romans,

[45] *Codul Calimach*, 81 (paras. 45, 47).

[46] V. Georgescu, *Mémoires et projets de réforme dans les Principautés Roumaines, 1769–1830* (Bucharest, 1970), p. xix; E. Vîrtosu, 'Napoleon Bonaparte şi dorinţele Moldovenilor la 1807', *Studii: Revistă de istorie*, 18/2 (1965), 411–12.

[47] Rîmniceanu, *Despre originea Românilor*, 245–7; I. Văcărescu, pref. *Observaţii sau băgări dă seamă asupra regulelor şi orînduelelor grammaticii rumîneşti* (Rîmnic, 1787), in BRV ii. 319; T. Codrescu, *Uricariul*, ii (Iaşi, 1852), 198–9: *Anaforaua pentru pronumiile Moldovei* (1827).

Romanian writers could point to an uninterrupted presence on both sides of the Carpathians of over 2,000 years. This Dacian sentiment was a product of the eighteenth century; the chroniclers of the seventeenth century had dismissed out of hand the notion that sophisticated Romans and barbarian Dacians could have intermingled.[48]

Growing ethnic awareness was accompanied by a heightened sense of patriotism. For most of our writers, the term meant love of country. But for some, a patriot was also someone who worked actively to promote the public good and the general happiness. This obligation sometimes took on romantic overtones, as in Naum Rîmniceanu's *Despre originea Românilor* (*c*.1801–2; On the Origins of the Romanians): 'Fatherland, sweet name, like an old family memory, an inheritance from our beginnings, which our heart embraces, you surpass every desire and are forever in my memory.'[49]

At the heart of the burgeoning ethnic consciousness of Romanian intellectuals and their optimistic vision of the future lay a certainty that the principalities were a part of Europe. They cherished the old idea that the principalities had served for centuries as the defenders of Europe against the Ottoman tide, and they viewed Phanariot rule, which had intensified their subjection to the Ottomans, as a grievous break in their natural connection with Europe. Now, in the latter part of the eighteenth century they sought to re-establish their old links with Europe, as Ottoman suzerainty waned and the principalities slowly resumed commercial and cultural relations with the West. An image of enlightened Europe was formed, a world in which science and learning had opened the way to unparalleled material well-being and advances of the human mind. The first to write in praise of Europe as the 'source of culture and light' had been Metropolitan Gavriil Callimachi of Moldavia in 1733, but after 1800 such thoughts became commonplace.

A number of writers went further. They conceived of Europe and the East as two supremely different worlds culturally and politically: the former was dynamic and stood for innovation and progress, while the latter was synonymous with routine and stagnation. They placed the principalities squarely on the side of Europe. If, they argued, Moldavia and Wallachia appeared so different from France and Austria, the cause lay in their long isolation from the rest of the continent and in institutions and customs ill-suited to their nature which had been forced upon them. They used such reasoning to justify demands for an end to Ottoman domination, pointing out that the structures of an oriental civilization could not possibly guarantee the progress of a European people.

[48] O. Babu-Buznea, *Dacii în conştiinţa romanticilor noştri* (Bucharest, 1979), 5–29.
[49] Rîmniceanu, *Despre originea Românilor*, 247–8.

4

The Beginnings of a Modern State

BETWEEN the outbreak of the Greek War for Independence in 1821 and the revolutions of 1848 the contours of modern Romania became perceptible. Moldavia and Wallachia moved closer to union and independence through the efforts of a new élite of *boiers* and bourgeoisie and through the intervention of the great powers. Institutional changes brought order to government administration, led to experiments with representative assemblies, and stimulated the formation of political groupings separated as much by ideology as by social status. Society itself became more cosmopolitan and complex as cities grew in number and size and ethnic diversity and as social differentiation and mobility accelerated under the impress of changing economic and cultural patterns. In the economy production increased in both industry and agriculture, but structures continued to resist innovation. Underlying economic and social change lay burgeoning contacts with the West. No significant aspect of the public and private life of the élite and of those who aspired to join it was left untouched by Europe.

THE UPRISING OF 1821

In the spring of 1821 Wallachia was the scene of a complex social and national movement. A large-scale, mainly peasant, uprising, originating in Oltenia, encompassed most of the principality. Its causes lay partly in the unbearable conditions on the land and partly in the fiscal and administrative abuses of local officials. At another level a number of *boiers* sought to bring an end to Ottoman suzerainty, while others concentrated on driving out the Phanariots. Their actions were the overt responses to the strong sense of patriotism and a national consciousness which had already found theoretical expression in the projects of the reforming *boiers*. The economic and social demands of the peasants and the political aspirations of the *boiers* intersected in the movement led by Tudor Vladimirescu, one of the most influential figures of early modern Romanian history.

Vladimirescu, the *boiers*, and the peasants were stirred to action by the general rising against Ottoman rule in South-eastern Europe initiated by Greeks united in a secret organization, the Philike Hetairia (Friendly Society). Founded in Odessa in 1814, the society increased its membership steadily and by the spring of 1821 it had formed branches in almost every major commercial centre in the eastern Mediterranean and South-eastern Europe. At first, it was exclusively Greek, but soon its leaders recognized the need for wider support to achieve their aims. They therefore called for a union of all the Christians of European

Turkey to ensure the victory of the Cross over the Crescent. To win over the leaders of the Romanians, Serbs, and Bulgarians they let it be known that their project had the full support of Russia, whose prestige among them was enormous, because of her traditional defence of Orthodoxy and her military victories over the Turks. The leaders of the society went so far as to portray Tsar Alexander as the founder of their organization. The first branches of the Hetairia in the principalities were established in Galaţi, Bucharest, and Iaşi, but their membership was mainly Greek. Significantly, only a few Romanian *boiers* joined.[1]

The Philike Hetairia took the initiative in organizing an uprising in the principalities in 1821, but, at first, it relegated action there to a secondary role, that of a holding operation, while the decisive encounter took place between Greeks and Turks in the Peloponnesus. Nevertheless, throughout 1820 the society made preparations for possible military action in both Moldavia and Wallachia, and by autumn military leaders who were committed to the cause of the Hetairia—Iordache Olimpiotul, the commander of the prince of Wallachia's guard, and his associates, Ioan Farmache and Sava Fochianos (Bimbasha Sava)— were ready to move at the appropriate signal. The leaders of the Hetairia, who met in Ismail, on the lower Danube, in October to plan for a general rising of the Balkan peoples to assist the Greek cause, decided that Hetairists and their sympathizers in the principalities should enter the conflict only if Ottoman forces crossed the Danube. At the time such action seemed unlikely, for it would have violated existing treaties with Russia and would thus have offered a pretext for Russian intervention. But Hetairist leaders thought it wise to continue the mobilization of sympathizers and the gathering of supplies in Iaşi, Bucharest, and other strategic points. They were also at pains to win over at least one of the princes in order to guarantee the uninterrupted flow of supplies from Russia to themselves and other insurgents south of the Danube.

The most important decision taken at Ismail was to send Alexander Ipsilanti to Greece to initiate the long-awaited uprising. He was the son of Constantin Ipsilanti, prince of Wallachia (1802–6, 1806–7), and a major-general in the Russian army and an adjutant to the tsar. He was well connected with the families of the Phanar and the great *boiers* in the principalities and was thus a vital link between the Hetairia and its supporters in South-eastern Europe and, so it seemed to many, a guarantor of Russian aid. Ipsilanti was the 'guardian' of the society. He had not assumed the title of 'leader', for the Hetairists thought it essential for the success of their recruiting activities among the other Orthodox peoples that the tsar be seen as the head of the society. Moreover, Ipsilanti considered himself to be the agent of the tsar.

In the weeks following the meeting at Ismail Ipsilanti drastically altered the

---

[1] N. Camariano, 'Planurile revoluţionare ale eteriştilor din Bucureşti şi colaborarea lor cu Tudor Vladimirescu', *Studii: Revistă de istorie*, 20/6 (1967), 1165.

original plan of operations. He decided to begin the Greek war for independence in the principalities, for reports from Greece had made it clear that preparations for the uprising there were far from complete and that Greek forces would have little chance of success against the better organized and equipped Turkish army. Moreover, the use of Moldavia and Wallachia as a springboard for military operations had much to recommend it. Ipsilanti was convinced that the Greek cause would be supported enthusiastically in both principalities. He and others thought of the great *boiers* by education and by long association with Phanariot families as belonging to the Greek world, and they were certain that the *boiers* would use their political power and economic resources to further the cause of Hellenism. They were thus confident that the entire administrative apparatus of the two principalities would quickly fall into their hands. They were no less sanguine about the military contributions they could expect. Besides the *boiers* and Iordache Olimpiotul and his allies, they also relied increasingly upon an emerging leader from Oltenia, Tudor Vladimirescu, who had acquired a devoted following among the humbler ranks of society. The proximity of Russia to the principalities also boded well for the undertaking, for the Hetairists had linked their success to the immediate and unstinting support of the tsar. To coordinate their own activities with Russian aims in the region they had initiated the Russian consuls in Iași and Bucharest, Andrei Pisani and Alexander Pini respectively, into the secret plans of the Hetairia. Both consuls had already used their considerable influence with the Moldavian and Wallachian princes to secure the appointment of Hetairist sympathizers to key positions in the central administration and the *judeţe*.[2] Thus, *boiers* who had accommodated themselves to Ottoman rule were replaced by younger, more liberal *boiers* such as Nicolae Rosetti-Rosnovanu, who became treasurer at the age of 24. Perhaps the most important recruit of all to the Greek cause was Prince Mihai Suţu of Moldavia, who placed his personal fortune and the resources of his country at the disposal of the Hetairia. In return, he hoped to be made prince of both Moldavia and Wallachia as soon as Russian troops entered Moldavia.

Ipsilanti and his colleagues made final preparations for the uprising in November 1820. They planned to assemble a small force in Bessarabia and to initiate armed action by crossing the Prut River and rallying large numbers of *boiers* and others to their cause. They regarded these operations as a means of diverting Ottoman forces away from Greece, which was still to be the centre of the insurrection. After entering Moldavia, Ipsilanti then intended to march as quickly as possible through the principalities, gathering men and supplies as he went, cross the Danube, and lead a general rising of Christians against Turkish rule.

Ipsilanti and his followers had good reason to believe that Moldavian and Wallachian *boiers* would support them, since many were eager to bring an end to Ottoman political and economic domination. The *boiers* themselves were

---

[2] M. T. Radu, *1821: Tudor Vladimirescu și revoluția din Țara Românească* (Craiova, 1978), 242–61.

especially impressed by the apparently close relations between the Greeks and Russian officials in the principalities and the imminence of Russian military intervention, for they continued to base their hopes for liberation from the Turks on Russian armies. The Hetairists were well aware of these expectations on the part of the Romanians (and the other Balkan peoples) and continually exaggerated the degree of Russian support for their cause.

As events were to show, the Hetairia had seriously overestimated the sympathy for their cause among the Romanian upper classes. Although a number of prominent *boiers*—among them Grigore Ghica, the future prince of Wallachia, and members of the Filipescu, Văcărescu, and Sturdza families—and church leaders in both principalities welcomed the insurrection as a means of ending Ottoman rule once and for all, they also intended to abolish the Phanariot regime and eliminate Greek competition for political office and economic advantages. Still other *boiers* thought such action a necessary prelude to long overdue political and social reform. Practically all the *boiers*, conservatives and liberals alike, were deeply influenced by the new patriotism, which had made foreign predominance especially intolerable. As a consequence, few Romanian *boiers* (and few Romanians generally) came to the support of the Hetairia.

The initiative for an armed uprising on the Romanian side did not come from the cautious *boiers* in Bucharest and Iaşi but from a provincial leader of humbler origins, Tudor Vladimirescu. Born about 1780 into a family of free peasants in Oltenia, as a boy he entered the service of a *boier* from Craiova, where he learned to read his own language and acquired a working knowledge of Greek. At the age of 18, following local custom, he joined the *panduri*. Later, he became the administrator of two of his patron's estates and, as such, had the responsibility of taking animals to market in Transylvania. He gradually accumulated enough money to go into this business for himself. At the same time he entered state service as a *vătaf de plai* in Gorj *judeţ*, a post which he purchased. He was now relieved of all *podvezi* (transport services) and *angarale* (labour services), which officials might require of free peasants, and was himself entitled to an annual day of labour (*clacă*) from all heads of households in his *plai*. As *vătaf* he gained valuable military experience at the head of a corps of volunteers in service with the Russian army during the war of 1806–12. After the war he purchased another *vătaf* office and gradually accumulated a considerable wealth from commerce, mainly the export of animals and grain to Transylvania and Hungary, and from the leasing of *boier* estates. He also began to buy land for himself and thus entered the ranks of the lesser *boiers*. He was strong-willed and ambitious and in his dealings with others reserved.

Vladimirescu was drawn into the planning of the Greek uprising in the principalities by Iordache Olimpiotul, with whom he had been in close contact since the war of 1806–12, and by Constantin Samurcaş, a great *boier* and the prince's high commissioner, or *caimacam*, in Oltenia. They and others who were determined to overthrow Ottoman rule considered Vladimirescu the most capable Wallachian military commander and the one best able to mobilize a sizeable army.

Vladmirescu carried on extended negotiations with both the Hetairists and the *boiers* in Bucharest between November 1820 and the end of January 1821. He was initiated into the Hetairia's plan of operations in the principalities and was introduced to the Russian consul, Pini, who had placed the contacts and prestige of his office at the disposal of the Hetairia. Despite Vladimirescu's close co-operation with the Hetairists, he did not become a member of the society.[3] Nor did he intend to subordinate his own aims to theirs. He viewed the uprising as an opportunity, first of all, to end Ottoman rule and reassert the independence of Wallachia. But he also sought to bring about economic and political change, in particular to further the political interests of the lesser *boiers* against the great *boiers* and to ease the economic burdens of the peasantry. His pursuit of these national and social goals brought him into bitter and ultimately tragic conflict with the Greeks and great *boiers*.

Vladimirescu's negotiations with the *boiers* in Bucharest were complicated. He recognized that his own success would depend upon the support of others, especially those *boiers* who had committed themselves to freeing the country from Phanariot rule and Ottoman suzerainty and who stood for reform. For their part, the *boiers* welcomed the mass support Vladimirescu could deliver to further their political objectives, but they opposed any attempt to change the political and economic structure of the country from below. The two sides finally reached an understanding on 27 January 1821. The three great *boiers*—Grigore Brâncoveanu, Grigore Ghica, and Barbu Văcărescu—designated Vladimirescu as the head of the *panduri* and the leader of an 'armed rising of the people', which was to coincide with the advance of Ipsilanti through the principalities to Bucharest. The support of these *boiers* was crucial, for they held key positions in the Comitet de Oblăduire (governing committee), which had taken over the temporary admin-istration of Wallachia on 27 January from Prince Alexandru Suţu, who was gravely ill and died three days later. The committee remained in office until 7 March, during which time preparations for the insurrection were completed.

Vladimirescu left for his native Oltenia on 30 January to organize an army and gather supplies. From Tismana on 4 February he issued a general procla-mation to the inhabitants of Wallachia, promising all who joined his army membership in his Adunarea norodului (Assembly of the People), a representa-tive body empowered to take action for the common good. He denounced all oppressors, but stopped short of attacking the *boiers* as a class. He drew a sharp distinction between 'tyrannical' *boiers*, whose 'ill-gotten gains' he made fair game for his followers, and members of the Hetairia and all other

[3] D. Berindei, *L'Année révolutionnaire 1821 dans les pays roumains* (Bucharest, 1973), 106–10; A. Oţetea, 'Legămîntul lui Tudor Vladimirescu faţă de Eterie', *Studii: Revistă de istorie*, 9/2–3 (1956), 125–33.

*boier*s who joined his movement and whose persons and property, he urged, should thus be spared. He blamed the rampant hardship and oppression in the countryside on unscrupulous individuals who had taken control of government for their own private ends, but, significantly, he absolved the sultan of such responsibility. He was conciliatory. He sent an *arz* (report) to the sultan denouncing the misrule of the Phanariots and requesting the dispatch of an imperial representative (but not a Greek) to investigate the sad state of affairs.[4]

Neither the proclamation nor the *arz* reflected Vladimirescu's true intentions. The former was an attempt to cover over fundamental differences between himself, the *boier*s, and the Hetairists, and had, in fact, been drawn up before he left Bucharest. The message to the sultan, which had been drawn up at the same time, was intended to lull the Turks into thinking that his uprising was directed against the Greeks and *boier*s and thus did not threaten Ottoman suzerainty. But Vladimirescu's subsequent actions showed that he was fully committed to freeing Wallachia from both Phanariot and Ottoman rule and was willing to cooperate with Alexander Ipsilanti and the Hetairia as long as was necessary to bring about the expulsion of the Turks. It was also evident that he had no intention of prolonging Greek administration, for he insisted that Ipsilanti and his forces leave the principality as quickly as possible. The extent of the social and economic reforms he was prepared to carry out is less clear. Conscious of the need for *boier* support, he said nothing in his proclamation about the abolition of *clacă* or the recognition of the peasants' property rights to the land they worked. Instead, he promised general relief—an end to the 'abuses' of officials and the 'tyranny' of *boier*s and their exemption from taxes.

Despite the vagueness of Vladimirescu's social programme, even the promise of reform was enough to bring peasants from all over Oltenia to his side. Many even thought that he had proclaimed the end of the old agrarian order and proceeded to take matters into their own hands. They swarmed over the estates of *boier*s and monasteries, destroying vineyards, emptying wine-cellars, and cutting down trees, direct action intended to abolish landlord monopolies and reassert their old rights to the forests. From Oltenia the violence spread first to the Danubian plain, where large numbers of peasants, most of whom were *clăcaşi*, stopped paying the tithe, and then it engulfed Buzău *judeţ* in eastern Wallachia, where the peasants, mainly from free villages, refused to perform any sort of labour service.

In Bucharest the Comitet de Oblăduire took no action to suppress the spreading violence and withheld information about the state of affairs from Ottoman authorities. In full sympathy with the expressed aims of the Hetairia, it bided its time until the uprising in Oltenia had reached the point of no return and Ipsilanti and the Russians had arrived. Only on 14 February, when the

----

[4] *Documente privind istoria Romîniei: Răscoala din 1821*, i (Bucharest, 1959), 207–10.

committee learned that the Pasha of Vidin was aware of the true state of things in Oltenia, did it send a report to Constantinople, but, to delay Ottoman military intervention, it passed the violence off as simple brigandage.

Other *boiers*, particularly those on the divan, which was not controlled by Hetairist sympathizers, took a different view of events. Fearing social upheaval, they decided to request the sending of Ottoman troops to protect property and restore order, and on 16 February they informed the Russian consul of their intention. Pini had authorization from the Russian ambassador in Constantinople to approve their request, but he placed full responsibility on the *boiers* for what might happen if Turkish troops entered the country. Thus sobered, the divan decided to postpone action and, instead, sent an emissary to Vladimirescu to persuade him to disband his army. Vladimirescu rejected their summons out of hand and continued to increase his force, which now numbered 8,000, including 2,000 *arnăuţi* (mercenaries).

Moldavia was now the scene of decisive events. On 6 March Ipsilanti, at the head of a small group of supporters, crossed the Prut River and entered Iaşi. He immediately took charge of the administration and police, and on the following day he issued a proclamation to all the inhabitants of the principality, announcing the beginning of the war for the liberation of all the Christian peoples of South-eastern Europe from Turkish rule and guaranteeing the Moldavians their peace and security. He reassured them that there would be no Turkish invasion because 'a mighty power' (which everyone understood to mean Russia) would punish any violation of the principality's territory. On the 8th he and Prince Mihai Suţu sent a joint letter to Tsar Alexander, who was in Laibach attending a congress of the great powers, reminding him of Russia's traditional support of the Orthodox and the Greeks and appealing for the immediate dispatch of Russian troops to protect the inhabitants of Moldavia from Turkish vengeance.[5]

Ipsilanti's crossing of the Prut and the initial welcome he received from the prince and various *boiers* were based upon the expectation of swift Russian military intervention. The aim of the Hetairia and its Romanian supporters all along had been to create a situation in the principalities that would have justified Russian intervention on the pretext of restoring order and maintaining the general peace of Europe. Such action, they calculated, would have been fully in accord with the tsar's international obligations toward his partners in the Holy and Quintuple alliances. The existence of such a plan is suggested in a letter of 29 July 1821 from John Capodistrias, one of the tsar's principal advisers on foreign policy, to the former Metropolitan of Ungrovlachia, Ignatie, in which he noted that Russia could intervene on behalf of the Greeks only in the case of 'imperious necessity', a situation he defined as one which the Turks could not

---

[5] Ibid. 304–5; V. Georgescu, *Mémoires et projets de réforme dans les principautés roumaines, 1769–1830* (Bucharest, 1970), 101–2.

control and which, therefore, threatened European peace.[6] But Ipsilanti assumed that such a situation existed in March and that, consequently, Russian troops would soon follow him across the Prut. But he committed a grave error in announcing publicly that he expected Russian aid. By so doing, according to Stroganov, who warmly advocated intervention, Ipsilanti had undone 'all the calculations of Russia', and, hence, she was forced to remain inactive.

In the mean time, in Iaşi Ipsilanti was feverishly gathering supplies and enrolling recruits in preparation for the march south. The *boiers* and the higher clergy lent their support so long as they believed that Russian intervention was at hand. Iordache Rosetti-Rosnovanu, the wealthiest landholder in the country, contributed 10,000 Holland ducats and 300 horses, and other *boiers* contributed horses, weapons, and the enormous sum of 3,000,000 *lei*. Thus fortified, Ipsilanti set out on 13 March at the head of an army of about 2,000 for Bucharest where he planned to link up with Vladimirescu.

On the day of his departure from Iaşi support for the Hetairia in Moldavia had already begun to crumble. The prince learned that some 4,000 Turkish troops had arrived in Brăila and that another 6,000 were on the way. Then, he and the *boiers* discovered that the tsar had condemned Ipsilanti's actions and would apparently not oppose Turkish intervention. The behaviour of Russian diplomats caused a state of near panic. Stroganov admonished the consul, Pisani, for his failure to protest against Ipsilanti's crossing of the Prut and instructed him to close the consulate and leave Iaşi. Pisani immediately broke off relations with Suţu, and from the safety of Bessarabia on 28 March he invited all Moldavians in the name of the tsar to submit to the 'legitimate authority of the suzerain power'. On the following day Suţu abdicated and left the country, followed by those *boiers* and Metropolitan Veniamin Costache, who had signed the original appeal to the tsar to send troops. The divan, anxious to save the country from a Turkish invasion, hastily drew up an address to the sultan placing the entire blame for what had happened on Suţu. Desperate attempts by the Hetairists to take over the administration of the country failed, and in the resulting anarchy the principality could offer no effective resistance to the Turkish army of occupation.

In Oltenia, meanwhile, upon receiving news of Ipsilanti's arrival in Iaşi, Tudor Vladimirescu moved his army eastward to Slatina on the Olt River, which he reached on 18 March. In a public statement he now openly declared his objective to be the independence of Wallachia. Clearly, like the Moldavian *boiers*, he regarded Russian support as crucial to the success of his movement. He even went so far as to announce that he had undertaken his mission on instructions from the tsar, a statement which probably had its source in Ipsilanti's assurances that the tsar knew about the plans of the Hetairia and approved them. Vladimirescu went on to say that the arrival in Bucharest of Ipsilanti's 'large

---

[6] A. Oţetea, *Tudor Vladimirescu şi revoluţia din 1821* (Bucharest, 1971), 290. On Russian involvement in the actions of the Hetairists, see Radu, *1821*, 168–76.

army' would be followed shortly by Russian troops and that the Russians and Wallachians together would assist Ipsilanti in crossing the Danube and would take back the *raya*s of Turnu, Giurgiu, and Brăila from the Turks. He promised that the Russians would then withdraw back across the Prut, leaving the Wallachians free 'to govern themselves in accordance with their own laws'.[7]

Vladimirescu set out for Bucharest on 22 March, determined to assert his authority over the political and military situation in the principality. He covered the distance in a week, his army of 8,000 making 25 km. a day, the average progress for an organized force in that region of poor roads. There was no effective opposition to his advance. Two provisional commissioners, Constantin Negri and Stefan Vogoridi, representing the newly appointed prince, Scarlat Callimachi, had superseded the Comitet de Oblăduire, but they took no action against Vladimirescu because they sympathized with the aims of the Hetairia and knew about his role. When Vladimirescu reached the outskirts of Bucharest on 28 March, they left the city for Giurgiu. Many followed their example. As Vladimirescu's and Ipsilanti's armies converged on the city the Russian consul and numerous *boiers* who felt that they had compromised themselves with either the Turks or the Russians fled to Braşov and Sibiu in Transylvania. Only a few *boiers* remained behind because either they were firmly committed to Ipsilanti or they did not wish to arouse the suspicions of the Turks by fleeing. These were the *boiers* with whom Vladimirescu had to deal.

The two parties, acknowledging the perilous circumstances in which they found themselves, concluded their negotiations quickly. Hopes for Russian intervention had vanished. Vladimirescu's appeal to the tsar in Laibach had been summarily rejected, and his own agents had verified the absence of any Russian troops or other aid for Ipsilanti. The *boiers* and Vladimirescu also had other compelling reasons to cooperate. For his part, Vladimirescu wished to become prince, a goal he was certain he could not attain unless he demonstrated his ability to preserve order and respected the traditional forms of the office. With these thoughts in mind he agreed to moderate the social and economic demands of his followers, specifically, to stop their attacks against *boier* property and to ensure the peasants' fulfilment of labour and other obligations to landlords. He thus renounced, at least temporarily, the promises contained in the proclamation of Tismana, which had aroused such widespread enthusiasm. In return, the *boiers* accorded his movement legal recognition, and, in so doing, held out the hope of modest social reform later. Both sides readily agreed on the abolition of Phanariot rule and the restoration of native princes, but Vladimirescu was determined to keep the administration of the country in his own hands for an indefinite period, using the *boiers* as technicians, while he himself oversaw the carrying-out of political and economic reforms.[8]

---

[7] Radu, *1821*, 285–94; D. Berindei, *Revoluţia română din 1821* (Bucharest, 1991), 124–5.
[8] On Vladimirescu's relations with the *boiers*, see the ample discussion in Radu, *1821*, 303–36.

Vladimirescu now turned his attention to Ipsilanti, who had reached Bucharest on 6 April. Their relationship had changed dramatically in the preceding month from one of tacit cooperation to open rivalry for control of the principality. The immediate cause was Russia's failure to aid the Hetairia. Ipsilanti was now no longer certain that he could carry out his planned march south of the Danube, for his army, even though it had grown to some 5,000 men, would be no match for superior Ottoman forces, and he himself was bitterly disappointed by the failure of Moldavians and Wallachians to rally to his cause. Vladimirescu had also been counting on Russian troops, and when Ipsilanti could not guarantee their appearance, he refused to commit his own forces to an unequal contest with the Turkish army. He also demanded that Ipsilanti and his men leave the principality as soon as possible in order to avoid provoking an Ottoman invasion. But for the time being, until Ipsilanti could arrange his withdrawal, they decided to separate their forces, the hilly districts falling to Ipsilanti, those in the plains and along the Danube to Vladimirescu. Accordingly, Ipsilanti moved northward to Tîrgovişte, while Vladimirescu remained in Bucharest in effective control of the government.

Vladimirescu, as suggested earlier, aspired to become prince, but he intended to ascend the throne in the traditional manner, elected by the *boiers* and blessed by the metropolitan, not as a revolutionary. Once that had happened he was certain that he would be able to carry out the promises of economic justice he had repeatedly made to his followers.

He was prevented from undertaking any significant social reform, because of the unsettled internal situation and the constant threat of foreign invasion, but some idea of what he hoped to accomplish may be gleaned from *Cererile norodului român* (The Demands of the Romanian People), a combination of political programme and constitution which he drew up and made public in the middle of April.[9] It contained an unsystematic and sometimes vague series of reforms, which, none the less, expressed the same dissatisfaction with the old regime as that contained in the more sophisticated writings of the reforming *boiers*. Vladimirescu did not, however, contemplate the immediate removal of the Phanariots, for he allowed the new prince to receive his appointment as usual from the sultan and to bring four Greek councillors with him from Constantinople. But before the prince could cross the Danube Vladimirescu insisted that he swear to respect a diploma of rights, which would include a reduction in the number and amounts of taxes, an end to the purchase of public offices, the abolition of *havaieturi* and the introduction of regular salaries for all officials, the removal of Greeks from all ecclesiastical offices, the ordination of only those priests who possessed the necessary training, the abolition of privileges enjoyed by foreigners, an end to excise taxes on goods entering cities and on exports from Wallachia to the Ottoman Empire, and the establishment of a permanent army of

---

[9] Oţetea, *Tudor Vladimirescu*, 387–91; Berindei, *Revoluţia română*, 221–8.

4,000 *panduri* to guard the country's frontiers. Perhaps the most important provision of all defined the role which Vladimirescu reserved for himself. He would assume the position of 'supreme chief and governor' of 'all the Romanians' with responsibility for both internal and foreign policy. But he left unresolved his relationship to the prince and how he and the Phanariot would work together to promote the common good.

The most immediate problem Vladimirescu faced as *de facto* head of government was the threat of a Turkish invasion.[10] To save himself and his movement he strove to convince the sultan that he had had nothing to do with the Hetairia and that he had in fact led his uprising against the Phanariot regime, which, he pointed out, had brought only hardship and oppression to his people. At this stage he still did not regard his situation as desperate and thought that if Russia and the Ottoman Empire remained at peace, the sultan would respect the territorial integrity of Wallachia and would be satisfied with sending an emissary to investigate the abuses committed by the Phanariot princes and the Hetairists. Vladimirescu thus perceived a common interest between himself and the Turks in suppressing the Hetairist movement, an endeavour that would, he was certain, enhance his standing with both the *boiers* and his peasant followers. But if the Turks did invade Wallachia, then, he reasoned, such a blatant violation of their treaties with Russia would force the tsar to intervene, and he himself would once again lead a general uprising of his people.

In the end, Vladimirescu achieved none of his objectives. Negotiations with the Turks failed because the sultan was determined to reclaim his full rights of suzerainty over the principalities. From the first, the Ottomans had regarded the Hetairist invasion of Moldavia and Vladimirescu's movement as two distinct undertakings pursuing different aims. But they had never had any doubts about the involvement of Russia in both and summarily rejected all of Stroganov's protestations about his government's good intentions. They also rejected overtures from Vladimirescu and petitions from the *boiers* as mere stratagems, 'in accordance with Russian practice', to undercut attempts to reassert Ottoman suzerainty.[11] But the Turks refrained from sending their troops across the Danube immediately because they feared war with Russia. By May, however, they had received the tsar's authorization to restore order in the principalities. Alexander was anxious to avoid complications with the Ottoman Empire, which might lead to the collapse of the European order he had been so assiduous in creating and, in any case, he had no intention of aiding 'rebels', but he insisted that the Ottoman government guarantee the lives and property of its Christian subjects.

Ottoman armies marched into Wallachia and Moldavia on 25 May. Even at this late hour Vladimirescu tried to parley, but he refused the invitation of the

---

[10] On Vladimirescu's relations with the Ottoman government, see A. Stan, 'Revoluţia de la 1821 şi statutul internaţional al Principatelor Române', *Revista de istorie*, 33/5 (1980), 850–7.

[11] V. Veliman, 'Noi documente turceşti privind evenimentele din 1821–1822', *Revista arhivelor*, 43/1 (1981), 67–9.

sultan's representatives to join in the campaign against the Greeks. He preferred to remain neutral, keeping his army intact for use later as a bargaining chip. On the 27th he left Bucharest, heading for his native Oltenia, where he hoped to use the monasteries and the rugged terrain to hold off the Turkish advance. On the following day Turkish troops occupied the city.

The Turkish invasion exacerbated relations between Wallachians and Greeks. Vladimirescu's refusal to aid the Hetairists and Ipsilanti's suspicions that his erstwhile ally was about to join the Turks in attacking his retreating forces led him to order Vladimirescu's arrest. At a sham trial Vladimirescu was condemned to death and executed on 8 June. Almost at once his army began to disintegrate. Although most of its roughly 4,000 men reached Oltenia and held their own against superior Ottoman forces until running out of ammunition, the disappearance of their leader and the lack of clear goals brought about their final dissolution as a fighting force. They had no intention of sacrificing their lives for the Hetairist cause, which was completely foreign to them.

The end of Ipsilanti's movement was also near at hand. He left Tîrgovişte on 9 June to avoid capture by the Turks and headed toward Oltenia. On 19 June his small force was defeated by the Turks at Drăgăşani, on the Olt River, and a few days later he crossed the border into Transylvania, where he was interned. What was left of his army melted away. In Moldavia isolated groups of Hetairists held out until October, when their last stronghold, the monastery of Secu, fell to Turkish occupation forces.

Although Vladimirescu's movement had been short-lived, the goals he sought to achieve were firmly rooted in the Romanians' recent historical experience. His proclamation of the right of self-determination embodied the general will to be free of Turkish and Phanariot domination; his promises to relieve the peasant of unbearable burdens to landlord and tax-collector and the enthusiastic response he provoked revealed the depths of the agrarian problem; and his proposals to ease restrictions on commerce and abolish the privileges of foreign merchants spoke to the aspirations of the rising middle class. His defeat by no means discouraged the movement for independence or stifled the currents of political and economic reform.

OTTOMAN SUZERAINTY AND RUSSIAN PROTECTION

The Ottoman army had entered the principalities in May 1821 ostensibly to drive out the remnants of the Hetairists and restore order, but after these tasks had been accomplished, instead of leaving, its commanders set up a military administration, whose manifest purpose was to reinforce Ottoman suzerainty. This regime, which lasted until the autumn of 1822, was a heavy economic burden for the population to bear, since it had to pay the full occupation costs of the 11,000 Turkish troops in Moldavia and the 9,000 in Wallachia. Although violent acts against the local population were rare, as Turkish commanders strove to enforce discipline among their troops, the military government was, none the less, all-encompassing and arbitrary.[12] There was no significant public activity in which it was not involved. The old administrative institutions such as the divan continued to function, but no important decisions could be taken without the approval of the military governor. He was also responsible for the appointment of the *ispravnici* and other officials of the *judeţ*. Venality was rife, as public offices went to the highest bidders. It was a lucrative business. An *ispravnic*, for example, who ordinarily had an income of 5,000 piastres a year, could take in as much as 80,000 piastres from the sale of offices to subordinates and from various types of extortion practised on the local population. As insurance he shared his bounty with Ottoman officials, who in return allowed him a free hand with the local population.

Other elements of society also benefited from the occupation, notably those *boiers* who had remained in the country or had returned quickly from self-imposed exile. They cooperated with the military government because, as the only stable political authority in the country, they relied upon it to maintain order and prevent new peasant violence. They themselves manned a civil administration set up to perform normal tasks such as taxation. The Turks were also interested in an accommodation with the *boiers*. They wanted a base of support in the country in order to solidify their political control and assure an uninterrupted flow of supplies to Constantinople. The military government, therefore, took all necessary measures to protect *boier* property and privileges and to force the peasants to fulfil their obligations of labour and tithes. The *boiers* reciprocated by refraining from openly opposing the military administration.

A significant number of *boiers*, however, took a different view of the situation. Their pursuit of political independence had lost none of its ardour after the defeat in 1821. From places of refuge in Austria and Russia they minced no words in denouncing the military occupation and Ottoman suzerainty in general. From Chişinău, in Bessarabia, Nicolae Rosetti-Rosnovanu summed up their feelings in a memorandum to the Russian ambassador in Constantinople in July 1821 in which he vigorously defended the principle of Moldavian autonomy and once again condemned the Phanariot princes for their complicity in destroying it. He was at pains to point out that Moldavia had freely entered into a vassal relationship with the Ottoman Empire (he dated the event in 1512) in order to gain the protection of a great power and to maintain the country's territorial integrity. For these services Moldavia had agreed to an annual money payment, but, he argued, that act did not give the sultan the right to interfere in her internal affairs.[13] Other *boiers* raised the same historical and legal points and demanded a complete restoration of Moldavian and Wallachian autonomy under native, not Phanariot, princes. The reforming *boiers* also had as their goal economic self-determination:

---

[12] Oţetea, *Tudor Vladimirescu*, 450–67.   [13] Georgescu, *Mémoires et projets*, 103–6.

a reduction of the tribute to the amount stipulated in the original treaties between the principalities and the sultan; unhindered commercial relations with other countries and a separate tariff policy that would protect native industry and agriculture; and control over the revenues of such public institutions as the dedicated monasteries.

The *boiers* did not propose to rely solely upon historical right and reasoned argument to achieve their ends. Nor did they intend to entrust their fate to the goodwill of a single great power (Russia). The unhappy experiences of half a century, during which the two principalities had been the object of war and haggling between Russia and the Ottoman Empire, had taught them the folly of such a policy, for the result had not been greater autonomy, but only increased Russian domination. Thus, their primary aim was to internationalize the status of the principalities. To accomplish their ends they intended to undermine Ottoman suzerainty still further and to limit the Russian protectorate by persuading the great powers collectively to be the guarantors of Moldavian and Wallachian autonomy.

The *boiers* linked the restoration of autonomy to the replacement of the Phanariots by native princes. This objective they achieved quickly, in part because of Ottoman rage at the 'perfidy' of the Greeks, but also because the fate of the principalities had, in fact, become an international question. The uprising of Tudor Vladimirescu alongside the Greeks had obliged Austria, France, and Britain, in addition to Russia and the Ottoman Empire, to take a more active role in settling the political affairs of Moldavia and Wallachia, which, the powers now saw, could not be ignored as they sought solutions to the Eastern Question.

The Turkish occupation of the principalities had precipitated a new crisis in Ottoman–Russian relations. The tsar considered the future of the principalities a strictly Russian affair and in June 1821 demanded that the sultan respect existing treaties and withdraw his troops. When a satisfactory response was not forthcoming, he broke off relations in July and made their re-establishment conditional upon the evacuation of the principalities. The outcome of subsequent negotiations hinged mainly upon a settlement of military questions and the appointment of native princes.

The Turks were determined to obtain an agreement that would strengthen their own position in the principalities and reduce Russia's capacity to intervene. Showing little inclination to compromise, they rejected an attempt at mediation by Metternich. Anxious to prevent Russia from using the continuing unrest in the Ottoman Empire as a pretext to occupy the principalities or take other action that would cause complications with the European powers, the Austrian chancellor proposed in January 1822 an immediate evacuation of the principalities and a conference of Turkish and Russian commissioners to discuss their future form of government. The sultan refused, for military successes in Greece proper, where the struggle of the Hetairists for independence continued, and the rivalries of the powers persuaded him that concessions were unnecessary. He also thought that the powers, to protect their own vital interests in the region, would prevent Russia from launching an attack.

The fulfilment of two conditions was uppermost in the minds of Ottoman officials: first, Greeks would not again be allowed to occupy the thrones of Moldavia and Wallachia because Muslim hatred had been so inflamed by the Greek uprising that the appointment of Phanariots would almost certainly lead to new turbulence in Constantinople; and second, Russia must at all cost be prevented from occupying the principalities again. As a solution to both problems the sultan and his advisers preferred an indefinite extension of the military government, but they finally concluded that worsening relations with Russia, the growing impatience of Britain and Austria, and persistent unrest in the principalities made such an outcome unlikely.

At this point the aims of the Ottoman government and Romanian *boiers* converged. A memorandum by Nicolae Golescu, the *Vornic* (minister of the interior) of Wallachia, to the grand vizier concerning the banishment of the Greeks and the appointment of native princes in their place was favourably received and led to invitations to the civil administrations of both principalities to send delegations of *boiers* to Constantinople in April 1822. Out of these negotiations a kind of Turco-Romanian condominium emerged which excluded Russia, an aspect of the settlement that was congenial to both parties.[14] The Turks were satisfied with the arrangement because it would allow them to maintain their political influence in the principalities by strengthening the role of Ottoman officials, especially of the divan-effendi. For their part, the *boiers* could take comfort from the fact that from this time on princes would be appointed from among their own ranks, even though Ottoman negotiators withheld formal recognition of the *boiers*' pre-eminence in political life.

The political restoration began in 1822. The new princes—Grigore Ghica in Wallachia (1822–8) and Ioan Sandu Sturdza in Moldavia (1822–8)—were appointed on 1 July, and the Ottoman occupation forces left the two countries later that year. The old political structures were revived, but neither the princes nor the *boiers* were satisfied. The most burning domestic issue quickly became constitutional reform. *Boiers* of all ranks intensified their demands for the enactment of fundamental laws that would limit the powers of the prince and guarantee their own predominance in political life. The princes themselves were by no means averse to reform, but their main concern was to preserve and, if possible, extend their prerogatives. Their resulting contest with the *boiers* dominated domestic politics for the rest of the decade.

Prince Grigore Ghica of Wallachia belonged to one of the most distinguished families of the principality. During the uprising of 1821 he had been a member of the Comitet de Oblăduire and had cooperated with Tudor Vladimirescu in

[14] M. A. Mehmet, 'Acţiuni diplomatice la Poartă în legătură cu mişcarea revoluţionară din 1821', *Studii: Revistă de istorie*, 24/1 (1971), 63–76.

order to drive out the Phanariots. But the social goals of Vladimirescu's followers coupled with the tsar's denunciation of his movement had caused Ghica to flee to Transylvania in March 1821. He returned in November and was welcomed by the Turks, who were eager to use this great *boier* to consolidate their position.

Ghica tried to rule as an eighteenth-century enlightened despot. He was receptive to innovation, especially in economic and cultural matters, and he established a committee in 1827 to undertake administrative reform. But at the same time he ruled in absolutist fashion and would not hear of any limitation of his powers. The result was a growing estrangement from the *boiers* and a political stalemate.[15]

The political ferment was even more pronounced in Moldavia than in Wallachia. Prince Ioan Sandu Sturdza, from an illustrious *boier* family, faced internal political problems similar to those of Grigore Ghica, but in Moldavia the *boiers* were deeply divided among themselves. The result was a continuous struggle between the great *boiers*, who dominated political life, and those of the second and third rank, who demanded a place for themselves in governing the country and, hence, a share in the material benefits that accompanied the exercise of political power. Sturdza made the mistake of choosing sides. He supported the lesser *boiers* as a means of keeping in check the great *boiers*, whom he regarded as the chief threat to his own position.[16]

The great *boiers* simply arrogated to themselves the decisive role in managing the affairs of the principality. The memorials which they drew up in 1821 and 1822 on political and economic reorganization left no doubt about their intentions. Mihai Sturdza (no relation to the reigning prince) was their most eloquent spokesman. He called for the establishment of a monarchical form of government, but with limitations on the powers of the prince and recognition of the great *boiers* as the leading force in the country. He objected vehemently to the appointment of men from the 'lower strata' to positions of influence and demanded constitutional guarantees of the historical political and economic privileges of the *boiers*.[17]

The lesser *boiers* had pretensions of their own, which in 1822 they set down in one of the most radical political documents of the period—the Constitution of the Carbonari, a name bestowed upon its authors by the great *boiers*, who compared them disdainfully to the revolutionary 'charcoal burners' of Italy. In it they urged the enactment into law of fundamental rights of citizenship such as freedom of the press, speech, and assembly and equality before the law. They also recommended strict limitations on the powers of the prince and sought to

---

[15] A. Iordache, *Principii Ghica: O familie domnitoare din istoria României* (Bucharest, 1991), 111–36.

[16] I. C. Filitti, *Frământările politice şi sociale în Principatele Române de la 1821 la 1828* (Bucharest, 1932), 150–70.

[17] M. Sturdza, 'Considérations sur la Moldavie et la Valachie au commencement de 1825', in Hurmuzaki, *Documente*, suppl. 1, pt. 4 (Bucharest, 1891), 65–9.

transfer final authority to a representative *sfat obştesc* (general council). But they had no more intention than the great *boiers* of sharing power with other classes and restricted rights and privileges to their own class. They differed from the great *boiers* mainly in their emphasis upon collegiality. They wanted decisions to be made at all levels of government by a majority vote of all *boiers*, without regard to rank, a procedure that they were certain would ensure their own predominance.[18]

The debate between the great and lesser *boiers* paled by comparison with the irreconcilable rift between the prince and the great *boiers*. The latter adamantly opposed Sturdza's growing fiscal demands and were alarmed by the large number of new *boiers* he was creating from among the merchant class. In their frustration they repeatedly went over his head to the sultan, an act of disloyalty which Sturdza repaid with arrests, fines, and banishment from the capital.

In foreign policy the princes gave the sultan no overt cause to question their loyalty, but they continued to seek ways of reducing their dependence on Constantinople by courting Austria and Russia. Both princes had to be circumspect in their relations with foreign countries, for they were under the constant surveillance of the divan-effendi and the Turkish commander of the prince's personal guard. Yet, it is a measure of the decline of Ottoman authority that they were able to maintain extensive relations with a host of countries, Ghica even going so far as to appoint his own secretary for foreign relations in 1823. The three conservative powers—Russia, Austria, and Prussia—exerted the greatest political influence, while relations with France and Britain were of little importance.

Both princes pursued essentially the same foreign policy, but Ghica was the more active. At first, he looked to Austria for support of his efforts to loosen the ties to Constantinople. He followed the advice of Metternich, which was regularly conveyed to him by Friedrich von Gentz, Metternich's trusted secretary, with whom he maintained a correspondence until he left the throne in 1828.[19] Metternich and other Austrian officials were primarily interested in the broader issues of the Eastern Question. Aware that one of the duties of the prince was to collect information from the capitals of Europe and relay it to Constantinople, they used the link between Gentz and Ghica to influence Ottoman policy. For his part, Ghica often consulted the Austrian consul in Bucharest on matters of foreign policy and was represented in Vienna by his own agent. But despite these close personal relations, Austria enjoyed little popularity among the *boiers*, who criticized her policies as self-serving.

The leading *boiers* continued to look to Russia to support their strivings for autonomy, mainly because every significant limitation of Ottoman suzerainty

---

[18] V. Şotropa, *Proiectele de constituţie, programele de reforme şi petiţiile de drepturi din ţările române* (Bucharest, 1976), 65–79.

[19] V. Georgescu (ed.), *Din corespondenţa diplomatică a Ţării Romîneşti (1823–1828)* (Bucharest, 1962).

over the principalities since 1774 had come as a result of Russian intervention. Intensely anti-Ottoman, they hoped for an outbreak of war that would bring Russian troops once again across the Prut. That event was closer at hand than they realized.

Neither the terms nor the manner of the settlement after the events of 1821 in the principalities had met with Russian approval, for there were no guarantees that Russian interests would be protected, while Ottoman suzerainty, at least on paper, had been fully restored. Particularly objectionable were the direct negotiations between the *boiers* and Ottoman officials over autonomy without Russian participation. Other issues also exacerbated relations between Russia and the Turks—territorial disputes in the Caucasus, the prolonged fighting in Greece, and alleged violations by the Turks of old treaty commitments. But war did not break out, mainly because of the continued restraint exercised by Tsar Alexander, who tried to fit Russia's immediate ambitions in the Near East into a broader framework of international cooperation. But his brother Nicholas, who succeeded him in 1825, was of another mind. Determined to pursue Russia's interests in the area vigorously with or without the cooperation of the Western powers, he did not long delay a confrontation with the Turks. On 17 March 1826 the Russian government sent an ultimatum to Constantinople demanding that the provisions of the Treaty of Bucharest of 1812 be fully carried out and that the Ottoman government send plenipotentiaries at once to a place on the Russian border to negotiate a permanent settlement of outstanding differences. Failure to accede to these demands within six weeks, the note warned, would lead to hostilities. Sultan Mahmud II (1808–39) yielded and in May dispatched a delegation to the small port of Akkerman on the estuary of the Dniester River.

The result of these negotiations was the Convention of Akkerman (7 October 1826), which reaffirmed Russia's prerogatives as the 'protecting power' in Moldavia and Wallachia. It prescribed the method of electing the prince by the *boiers* and stipulated a seven-year term of office; it reiterated the fiscal obligations of both principalities towards the suzerain power in accordance with the terms of the *hatti-sherif* of 1802; and it declared the commerce of the principalities to be free, except for those limitations necessary to assure the provisioning of Constantinople. In all matters relating to the privileges of the principalities it required the prince, the *boiers*, and the Ottoman government to take into account the observations of the Russian ambassador in Constantinople and the Russian consuls in the principalities, a mechanism that had ensured respect for Russian interests in the past and, as events were to show, would be equally effective up to 1848.

The Russian government evidently regarded the convention as simply one step in a process that would eventually remove the principalities completely from Ottoman suzerainty, for it called upon the princes and the divans to begin work at once on a general statute with the object of reorganizing internal political and economic life. In order to make certain that this work went according to plan the Russian foreign ministry reopened its consulate in Bucharest. The new consul-general, Matei Minchakii, enjoyed enormous influence, as the *boiers* returned to a pro-Russian stance, but his initial popularity was soon dissipated by frequent and forceful meddling in Wallachian affairs as he sought to further Russia's interests.

Russo-Turkish relations steadily deteriorated after the conclusion of the Convention of Akkerman. Mahmud II carried out its provisions only half-heartedly and rejected offers by Russia and other powers to settle the Greek War for Independence by negotiation. The disastrous defeat of the Turkish-Egyptian fleet at Navarino on 20 October 1827 stiffened his resistance to great-power mediation. On 30 November he repudiated the Convention of Akkerman, and shortly afterwards the tsar and his army chiefs decided on war. They considered fulfilment of the terms of the convention more important at the moment than the international settlement of the Greek question.

Russia declared war on Turkey on 26 April 1828. Her armies crossed the Prut on 7 May and moved swiftly southward, meeting no significant resistance until they reached the Danube. They occupied Bucharest on 12 May and laid siege to Brăila on the 15th. The fall of Brăila on 6 June opened the way south to what appeared to be a quick victory, but Turkish defences held, and military operations came to a halt until the following spring.

While fighting was going on south of the Danube the principalities were placed under a provisional civil administration headed by Count Feodor Pahlen, privy councillor to the tsar. Since the two princes had shown little zeal in carrying out Russia's wishes, Russian authorities had removed them in May and Pahlen assumed almost dictatorial powers. Both countries were soon filled with Russian officials of every kind. The immediate tasks of this large and unwieldy bureaucracy was to provide the army with foodstuffs and maintain supply lines. The tsar had instructed Pahlen and the army commanders to be guided by no other thought than success on the battlefield. Thus, supplies were requisitioned, prices were fixed, exports were curtailed, and even the treasuries of the two principalities were put at the disposal of the Russian army. Neither the *boiers* nor anyone else had a say in these matters. The winter of 1828–9, when large numbers of Russian troops were quartered in Wallachia during the lull in operations south of the Danube, was especially hard on the local population, and discontent with the Russian occupation among all classes mounted. The *boiers* had particular reasons to be dissatisfied. Pahlen had begun to reorganize the administration of the country on his own. He introduced principles and regulations which conflicted with the easygoing manner of governing practised by the majority of *boiers* and gave little thought to their political sensibilities and economic well-being.[20]

---

[20] I. C. Filitti, *Principatele Române de la 1828 la 1834* (Bucharest, 1934), 25–6.

Despite his ceaseless activity, Pahlen was viewed in St Petersburg as lacking firmness, perhaps because of continued problems of supply and bitter opposition among the *boiers* to the provisional government. He resigned on 25 January 1829 and was replaced by General Peter Zheltukhin, the former military governor of Kiev. Zheltukhin was a vigorous administrator who carried out faithfully his instructions to press ahead with the drafting of new administrative regulations for the principalities, but he lacked the diplomatic talents of his predecessor, and in no time his brusqueness had thoroughly alienated the great *boiers* and the higher clergy. His inability to cooperate with the leading elements of Romanian society, upon whom the achievement of Russian aims in the principalities depended, led to his resignation on 14 September.

Russian armies resumed their advance in June 1829. By July they had broken through Ottoman defences in the Balkan mountains and had reached the plains of eastern Thrace. Adrianople fell on 20 August, and Constantinople was but a further two or three days' march away. The Turks sued for peace and, forgoing their usual delaying tactics, quickly signed the final peace treaty on 14 September.

The Treaty of Adrianople, which regulated numerous matters long in dispute between Russia and the Ottoman Empire, proved to be a milestone in the political and economic development of the principalities.[21] The sultan agreed, once again, to abide by the provisions of earlier treaties with Russia concerning the principalities, notably the Treaty of Bucharest and the Convention of Akkerman. He recognized the administrative autonomy of Moldavia and Wallachia, accepted life appointments for the princes, and undertook to return to Wallachia the Turkish fortresses on the left bank of the Danube (the old *raya*s of Turnu, Giurgiu, and Brăila) and the islands attached to them. The economic provisions of the treaty in time brought about dramatic changes in agricultural production and foreign commerce, for the Turks renounced all claims to the provisioning of Constantinople by the principalities and recognized the right of their inhabitants to trade freely in all their agricultural and industrial goods. They also agreed to confirm new administrative statutes for the principalities, which were to be drawn up under Russian supervision. As a condition for the withdrawal of their troops from the principalities the Russians obliged Turkey to pay a large indemnity. They apparently contemplated a long stay because they demanded such an enormous sum that the Turks could not possibly have paid it at once. Thus, in diverse ways the treaty solidified the Russian hold on the principalities, but at the same time it went far toward satisfying the aspirations of the reforming *boiers* to be rid of Ottoman domination. The only vestiges of Ottoman suzerainty that remained were the annual tribute and the sultan's right to confirm the election of the princes.

---

[21] On the final negotiations of the treaty, see V. I. Sheremet, *Turtsiia i Adrianopol'skii mir 1829g.* (Moscow, 1975), 129–56.

RATIONAL GOVERNMENT

The Russian occupation brought major changes to public life in the principalities. Of crucial importance was the introduction of a new fundamental law for
each, the Organic Statutes, which offered a framework for orderly and efficient
government. But the motives of Russian officials were hardly altruistic. They
promoted order and efficiency, to be maintained by the possessing classes, as the
most effective way of achieving their long-term goals in the principalities.

Tsar Nicholas entrusted Count Pavel Kiselev, an energetic officer and enlightened administrator who had distinguished himself in the Napoleonic Wars
and in the recently concluded conflict, as his representative in the principalities
with responsibility for carrying out the terms of the Treaty of Adrianople. Kiselev
wasted no time in getting to work. On the day he arrived in Bucharest, 24
November 1829, he met with the divan. Admitting to the assembled *boiers* that
many of their complaints against the previous military administration were
justified, he assured them that he would act differently from his predecessors.
That statement was reassuring to the *boiers*. Although Kiselev's official title was
plenipotentiary president of the divan, he was in all but name the prince of each
country.

During his tenure, which lasted until April 1834, Kiselev used his almost
unlimited power to reorganize political and economic life in accordance with the
accepted principles of the day. Although many of his acts seemed revolutionary
at the time, he had no intention of overturning the established social order.[22] He
sought, in fact, to perpetuate it by defining precisely the rights and obligations of
all classes and by providing the administrative and legal machinery to enforce
them. Unlike his predecessor, he was anxious to understand the countries whose
institutions he had been called upon to overhaul. He thus assembled a vast
collection of documents dating back to the sixteenth century and solicited the
active participation of leading, younger *boiers* in his work. He chose well. Mihai
Sturdza, Barbu Ştirbei, Gheorghe Bibescu, all future princes, and Ion
Cîmpineanu, a leading reformer, were among his closest advisers.

Kiselev could not afford the luxury of waiting for new laws and institutions to
take effect. He found the principalities in an almost hopeless condition as a result
of the military occupation: disease raged unchecked; famine was widespread; the
administrative apparatus and the finances were in complete disarray; and stocks of
farm animals, upon which the peasants depended for ploughing and transportation, had been dangerously depleted. He therefore took immediate steps to
control the plague which had broken out in 1828 by appointing sanitary commissions in Bucharest and Iaşi to coordinate the effort in each principality, by
setting up hospitals and dispatching doctors to the most affected areas, and by

---

[22] V. I. Grosul, *Reformy v dunaiskikh kniazhestvakh i Rossiia (20–30 gody XIX veka)* (Moscow, 1966),
200–37.

establishing a strict quarantine along the Danube.[23] These measures brought results, and by the spring of 1830 no new cases were being reported. To overcome the critical shortages of food Kiselev had grain brought from Odessa, and, as a long-term measure, beginning in 1830, he had part of each harvest set aside in storehouses as a reserve. He initiated fiscal reform by abolishing the *scutelnici* and *poslușnici*, a measure which added about 40,000 families to the tax rolls. As a preliminary to a comprehensive reorganization of the finances and of the administrative and judicial systems he carried out a general census of the population in 1831. But agriculture proved intractable, and he confessed that he could do little with its complexities until comprehensive agrarian legislation had been enacted.

Kiselev's most important accomplishment was the elaboration of a fundamental law, in effect, a constitution, for each principality. These Organic Statutes (Regulamente Organice) were the product of close cooperation between Russian authorities and Romanian *boiers*.

In the winter of 1828–9, while the war was still in progress, guidelines for the drawing up of the statutes had been discussed at length in St Petersburg. Among the Romanians who participated was Mihai Sturdza, who represented the great *boiers*. The tsar approved the guidelines in May 1829, and in July a commission, composed of four *boiers* from Wallachia and four from Moldavia, half chosen by the divans and half by their plenipotentiary presidents (Kiselev), began the task of drawing up the statutes. They had two main tasks: to reform institutions without overturning fundamental structures and to eliminate in so far as possible institutional differences between the principalities. Drafts were ready by March 1830 and were sent to St Petersburg, where another commission, composed of three Russians and two Romanians (Mihai Sturdza for Moldavia and Alexandru Vilara, a great *boier*, representing Wallachia), examined them and made minor changes. They were then submitted for discussion to Extraordinary Assemblies in Bucharest and Iași, the majority of whose members were great *boiers*. The assembly of Wallachia approved the text of its statutes in May 1831, and they entered into force on 1 July of that year, while the assembly of Moldavia acted in October, its statutes becoming law on 1 January 1832. Kiselev, who was well acquainted with the dilatory tactics of the Ottomans, did not bother to wait for the sultan's approval of the statutes, as required by the Treaty of Adrianople, but proceeded to apply them immediately.

The statutes (they were so named at least in part to avoid using the term 'constitution', which had revolutionary connotations in St Petersburg) had as their overall objective the strengthening of the existing social order and the maintenance of the *boiers*' privileges.[24] They assured the continued dominance of

[23] D. Panzac, *La Peste dans L'Empire Ottoman, 1700–1850* (Louvain, 1985), 459–60.

[24] For a detailed analysis of the Organic Statutes, see Filitti, *Principatele Române de la 1828 la 1834*, 101–222. A critical edn. of the statutes was prepared by P. Negulescu and G. Alexianu, *Regulamentele organice ale Valahiei și Moldovei* (Bucharest, 1944).

the *boiers* in political life by recognizing their exclusive right to be represented in the new legislature, by according them the leading positions in the central administration, by exempting them from taxes, and by confirming their property rights over their estates. But the authors of the statutes also felt constrained to accept at least a limited participation of the middle class in the conduct of the country's affairs and saw the wisdom in creating a more favourable climate for the development of its economic activities. Such indulgence did not, however, extend to the peasantry, whose social and economic status remained as precarious as before. The statutes also introduced drastic changes in every branch of government in the principalities. Old practices and institutions were modified or abolished, as the political, judicial, and fiscal functions of government became more orderly and systematic. In this way the long-held aspirations of the reforming *boiers* were at least partially fulfilled, and the transition from essentially medieval to modern forms thus became a striking feature of public life in the 1830s and 1840s.

The statutes introduced crucial innovations in public administration. One guiding principle was the separation of powers. Legislative authority was vested in the Ordinary General Assembly (Obişnuita Obştească Adunare), whose approval was required before a bill could become law. Even though the assembly lacked the power to initiate legislation, it could make representations to the prince and, as a last resort, bring the grievances of the country to the attention of the suzerain and protecting powers (the Ottoman Empire and Russia respectively). It was by no means a representative body, but was, rather, the instrument of a narrow élite intent upon maintaining its privileges. Elected for a period of five years, it was composed in Wallachia of the metropolitan of the Orthodox Church, who served as president; the bishops of Rîmnic, Buzău, and Argeş; 20 *boiers* of the first rank; and 18 *boiers* chosen from among those of the *judeţe*, a total of 42 deputies. Voting rights were extremely limited: 70 great *boiers* elected 20 deputies, and 3,000 *boiers* of the second and third ranks, 18 deputies. The four ecclesiastics served by right. The general assembly of Moldavia was organized in similar fashion. The composition and functions of the two assemblies were thus more precisely defined than those of their eighteenth-century predecessors, and in a sense they represented a transition between the princely council of the old regime and the parliament of the latter nineteenth century.

The statutes maintained the tradition of a strong executive. The prince thus retained considerable powers, despite the inroads of the legislature, and remained the key figure in the political system. As the head of the executive branch of government he appointed and dismissed ministers and other public officials, who were thus responsible to him rather than to the assembly. Although he was obliged to share legislative power with the assembly, he alone possessed the right to introduce bills, and his sanction was necessary before a bill passed by the legislature could become law. He continued to be the representative of the upper classes, for he was elected for life from among the great *boiers* by the Extraordi-

nary General Assembly (Adunarea Obştească Extraordinară), which was composed largely of *boiers*. The middle class, represented by delegates of the artisan
and merchant guilds, participated, but exerted little influence.

The judicial system underwent a thorough reorganization from the
village board to the prince's council (*divan domnesc*). Although it was separated
from the executive, on the grounds that justice for the individual could thus
be better served, judges were still responsible to the prince, for it was he
who appointed them for renewable three-year terms and he who could remove
them as it suited his purposes. Yet, the statutes declared the irremovability
of judges to be highly desirable and provided that the principle be introduced
within ten years. At the local level village courts of conciliation (*judecătorii
de împăciuire*) were created, composed of a priest and three jurymen selected by
the villagers, to settle minor disagreements. Provincial tribunals, one for each
judeţ, became courts of first instance. In Wallachia appeals could be made
to the judicial council (*divan judecătoresc*) in Bucharest or, in Moldavia, to the
council of appeal (*divan de apelaţie*) in Iaşi. The final court of appeal was the
prince's council, whose decision was now declared to be final. This stipulation
put an end to the sometimes interminable litigation which custom had allowed
whereby a plaintiff who had lost his case under one prince could reopen it under
another. The new procedure was also a boon to economic activity because it
stabilized property relations and ensured the validity of commercial and financial
contracts.

Government administration was expanded and became more precisely struc-
tured. Its most striking feature was the tendency towards centralization, which
was everywhere apparent. To aid the prince the Extraordinary Administrative
Council (Sfat Administrativ Extraordinar), in effect, a council of ministers,
composed of six executive officers (interior, finance, foreign relations, justice,
cults, and the army), was created. Their competence extended over the whole
country, and, thus, those great administrative officers of the past like the Ban of
Craiova in Wallachia or the Mare Vornic of Ţara de Sus and of Ţara de Jos in
Moldavia, who had been appointed in the sixteenth century and had exercised
authority (mainly judicial) only over certain portions of the principality, had
ceased to exist. At the local level the *judeţe* and the *plăşi* (*ocoale* in Moldavia)
remained largely intact and were administered by *ocîrmuitori* (administrators) and
subocîrmuitori respectively, in Wallachia (*ispravnici* and *privighetori* in Moldavia), all
of whom were chosen from among *boiers*. These officials were no longer replaced
every year, and they no longer exercised judicial powers, as they had in the
eighteenth and early nineteenth century. But they served at the pleasure of the
prince, who appointed them for terms of three years and could remove them at
any time.

Central authorities also supervised village affairs through monitors, called
pîrcălab de sat in Wallachia and *vornicel* in Moldavia. Although their responsibilities

were primarily fiscal—to ensure that the various local taxes were collected on time and properly disbursed—as representatives of the prince their influence was wide-ranging. In the villages themselves councils of elders, which were chosen by the heads of families, as in the past, attended to minor, everyday matters. But these activities did not constitute self-government, for the rural commune as a juridical person had not yet come into existence. Village government remained under the tutelage of *județ* administrators and local landlords, since they had the power to confirm the election of elders.

In the cities full self-government continued to elude the middle class, as the central government maintained close supervision over urban administration: the general assembly of the principality selected the president of the city council, and the prince appointed a commissioner 'to protect the interests of the state'. Yet, the leading merchants and artisans were gaining ground. Through their guild corporations, which chose the five members of the *sfat orășenesc* (city council), they assumed the responsibility for managing the day-to-day affairs of their city.

The statutes brought new efficiency to the fiscal system and enabled each principality to formulate, if not carry out fully, its own fiscal policy.[25] The tax structure was simplified through the replacement of the numerous indirect taxes (the *rusumaturi* and *huzmeturi*) and the fees levied by functionaries (*havaieturi*) by a single capitation tax on each head of family. Gone were the *ludă* and collective responsibility for the paying of taxes, as individuals shouldered the burden. Yet, certain categories of the population, notably *boiers* and the clergy, were exempted from ordinary taxation. Besides the capitation tax, the state treasury continued to derive revenue from mining, tariffs on foreign trade, a part of the income of monasteries, and a tax (*patentă*) on merchants and artisans. Through the abolition of the prince's personal treasury, whose funds had often been intermingled with those of the state, and the introduction of up-to-date bookkeeping methods the new treasury department undertook to provide each principality with the systematic management of its finances. (As compensation for his loss of revenue the assembly granted the prince a civil list.) Perhaps the most important fiscal innovation of all was the adoption of modern budget-making procedures. An annual budget was introduced based upon projected revenues and expenditures and drawn up by the executive and approved by the assembly. The statutes also initiated modest attempts to use fiscal policy to stimulate the economy, as numerous internal tariffs were abolished and provision made for the establishment of a national bank. But little progress was made in stabilizing the currency, because of continued Ottoman opposition to the establishment of a national monetary system.

The statutes accelerated the subjection of the Orthodox Church to the state.

---

[25] Filitti, *Principatele Române de la 1828 la 1834*, 139–57.

Although they enhanced the order and efficiency with which church affairs were conducted, at the same time they offered the prince and his bureaucracy greater opportunities to interfere in ecclesiastical matters by expanding and formalizing their supervisory powers. The statutes regulated the election of metropolitans and bishops (the higher clergy and all *boiers* of the first rank took part, and the prince confirmed their choice) and prescribed the norms for the selection of priests and egumens (the prince had the final word). The separation of church and state (or, rather, of the religious and the secular) deepened. Although the metropolitans and the bishops in their dioceses remained masters in spiritual matters, their participation in civil affairs was now drastically reduced. With the abolition of the old *divan domnesc* they lost their judicial and administrative powers, retaining only their membership in the general assembly. Gone also was their power to dispose of the property and income of their dioceses as they wished. Under the old regime the prince had intervened in these matters only when he sought an extraordinary contribution, but now, under the statutes, church lands could be leased only by auction in the legislative assembly, and a committee of clergy and laymen were given the power to decide how much the dioceses should contribute to charitable foundations. The immediate responsibility for overseeing all these matters and coordinating state policy towards the church rested with the new secretary for religious affairs (*logofăt al credinţei*), who was the prince's man. He had to make certain that the clergy conformed to the new legislation and refrained from interfering in public administration, activity which the statutes specifically forbade. The financial dependence of the clergy on the state grew. Priests received a kind of salary from the state in the form of 2 *parale* for every *leu* in taxes paid by their parishioners (100 *parale* = 1 *leu*), but they continued to receive the bulk of their income from landlords, who were obliged to provide them with land, and from villagers, who supplied labour and paid fees in return for the performance of necessary religious ceremonies.

All in all, the Organic Statutes opened the way to profound change in the principalities. They enhanced the predictability of government, especially in fiscal matters, and thus offered more reliable guarantees than before for investments and contracts, essential conditions for economic progress. They also brought the union of Moldavia and Wallachia closer by endowing them with almost identical political institutions and according their inhabitants joint citizenship. Yet, despite these innovations, the statutes did not constitute a sudden break with the past. Rather, in many areas of public life they expanded upon ideas and projects, such as rational management of the finances, put forward by the reforming *boiers* during the preceding decades. The concentration of power in the hands of the prince and the expansion of the central bureaucracy at the expense of regional and local administration also fitted in with trends already well under way.

The Russians continued to occupy the principalities after the adoption of the Organic Statutes, ostensibly because the Ottoman government had failed to pay the indemnity specified in the Treaty of Adrianople. But in fact the tsar and his advisers were anxious to keep Kiselev and his staff in place to supervise the implementation of the statutes. They had sponsored these constitutions in the first place in order to gain the sympathy of the *boiers* and thereby consolidate Russia's predominance in the principalities. Their treatment of Moldavia and Wallachia thus fitted in with a new policy towards the Ottoman Empire, which emphasized peaceful ascendancy rather than conflict as the most effective way of maintaining stability in the region and avoiding international complications. The tsar thus rejected proposals to annex the principalities. He preferred to maintain a protectorate over them, using the princes to keep order and the consuls to ensure that Russia's interests would be well served.

A mere protectorate, however, ran counter to Kiselev's own objectives. He tried to convince the ministry of foreign affairs in St Petersburg and his friend Alexei Orlov, who was appointed ambassador to Constantinople in 1833, that Russia's best interests required the incorporation of the principalities and the extension of her frontiers to the Danube.[26] Only in this way, he argued, could Russia be certain of retaining her influence over the Christians of the East, who had traditionally looked to her for protection against the Turks. He was certain that if Russia could prolong her occupation of the principalities for at least ten years, the powers would become accustomed to the situation and annexation would, consequently, be a mere formality. But his urgings received scant attention in St Petersburg, as the Russian court stuck to its plan for a protectorate and cultivated friendly relations with Austria, Russia's chief rival in the principalities.

The occupation of the principalities came to an end as a result of improved relations between Russia and the Ottoman Empire. The tsar's policy of conciliation coupled with the military threat to the sultan from the powerful ruler of Egypt, Mohammed Ali, led to a new relationship, which was formalized in the Treaty of Unkiar-Skelessi (8 July 1833). By establishing what was in effect a Russian protectorate over the Ottoman Empire, it offered satisfactory safeguards of Russian interests in the principalities which made their annexation unnecessary. The treaty was followed by the Convention of St Petersburg (29 January 1834), by which the sultan sanctioned the Organic Statutes and the tsar promised to evacuate the principalities within two months after the publication of a *hatti-sherif* implementing the terms of the convention. Kiselev returned to Russia in April, and under his successor, General Feodor Mirkovich, the Russian administration came to an end and the governments of the principalities were handed over to the new princes—Alexandru Ghica in Wallachia and Mihai Sturdza in Moldavia. At the beginning of September 1834 Mirkovich and the remaining Russian troops, except for a small garrison at Silistria, on the Danube, left the country.

---

[26] A. P. Zablotskii-Desiatovskii, *Graf P. D. Kiselev i ego vremia* (St Petersburg, 1882), i. 415, and iv. 90–8.

POLITICAL PRACTICE

Between the end of the Russian occupation and the outbreak of revolution in 1848 Romanian society was in a state of flux. It was a period of curious juxtapositions. Remnants of Ottoman suzerainty survived alongside the surge towards independence; representative government won new ground even as Russian interference intensified; and Eastern tradition continued to clash with Western innovation. Striking contrasts were everywhere manifest—in dress, language, and customs.

The political life of the period bore witness to pervasive restlessness and expectation. In Wallachia Prince Alexandru Ghica (1834–42) found himself continuously at odds with Russian diplomats, on one side, and the *boiers* in the assembly, on the other. His position was made all the more delicate by the fact that he owed his position to appointment, as demanded by Russia, rather than to election, as specified in the Organic Statutes. Yet, he came to the throne at the age of 38 with impressive credentials. During the reign of his brother Grigore, he had acquired valuable administrative experience in a number of high positions and later had been a close associate of Kiselev. Yet, as prince he was frustrated by his inability to rule as he thought tradition required. Proud of his family, which had produced no fewer than seven princes, he also chafed under Russia's tutelage, for he could take no serious action on his own without the approval of the resident consul. He was anxious to be a national monarch standing above parties, but his idea of a strong ruler made cooperation with the liberal and patriotic *boiers* in the assembly impossible.

Ghica's troubles with the *boiers* came from both the left and the right and originated, in part, in the suspicion of the great *boiers* that the prince was more interested in increasing his own powers than in defending the privileges of his class, a charge not without substance. But their disputes also arose out of the very nature of the statutes, which had placed two proud rivals face to face—a sovereign prince and a sovereign assembly—without adequately defining their respective powers.

Characteristic of the relationship between Ghica and the *boiers* was the dispute over the so-called 'additional article' of the statutes.[27] During negotiations in 1833 with the Ottomans over confirmation of the statutes Russian representatives had attached a clause, which, in effect, prevented the prince and the assembly from modifying the statutes without the express approval of the Russian and Ottoman governments. Thus, the freedom of the assembly and the prince to legislate was gravely undermined, and the power of Russia to intervene in all areas of public life dramatically enhanced. When the additional article was laid before the assembly for ratification, the majority of *boiers* rejected it after stormy

---

[27] I. C. Filitti, *Domniile române sub Regulamentul Organic, 1834–1848* (Bucharest, 1915), 38–58.

debate in June and July 1837. Only extreme pressure from Russia and Turkey in the form of a *firman*, issued by the sultan but drawn up in St Petersburg, ordering the assembly to approve the legislation at once, ended the *boiers*' opposition. On 21 May 1838 the assembly grudgingly complied. Russia had triumphed, but at the cost of alienating the liberal *boiers*, who were to form the core of the anti-Russian generation of 1848.

The opposition in the assembly took a radical turn in the late 1830s. Led by Ion Cîmpineanu (1798–1863), an enthusiastic champion of independence from both Russia and the Ottoman Empire, liberal *boiers*, who had formed a National party in the assembly, drew up a declaration stating bluntly their determination to defend Romanian sovereignty against foreign encroachments and to restore Wallachia as a free and independent country.[28] They denied the legitimacy of a prince (Ghica) who had been 'imposed' on the country by an Ottoman *firman* and they rejected the validity of a fundamental law (the Organic Statutes) which had been drawn up during a foreign occupation and ratified by a national assembly chosen in an arbitrary manner. They also denounced continued vassalage to the Ottoman Empire and demanded the free election of a hereditary prince, whose first act would be to secure the country's independence and the recognition of its sovereignty by the great powers. Cîmpineanu, who was their choice for prince, and Felix Colson, a former attaché of the French consulate in Bucharest, proceeded to draw up a liberal constitution for the new, independent state which mandated universal suffrage and the personal emancipation of the *clăcaşi*. Cîmpineanu, aware that little could be accomplished without international support, travelled to Constantinople, Paris, and London in 1839 to plead the case of the liberal *boiers* for a change in the status of the principalities.[29] It was all to no purpose. He simply compromised himself in the eyes of Russia and Turkey, and upon his return home he was exiled to a monastery until 1841.

Even more radical solutions to the political and social problems of the principality came from a small, secret group headed by Dimitrie Filipescu (1808–43), a great *boier* with a law degree from Paris.[30] Their stand on independence resembled that of the National party, but in social and political reform they went much further: emancipation of the *clăcaşi* with land and only a symbolic indemnity for the landlords; the abolition of all ranks and privileges and the equality of all citizens before the law; and the replacement of the existing *boier* state by a democratic republic. Filipescu, like Cîmpineanu, recognized the impossibility of accomplishing any of his goals as long as the Ottoman Empire and Russia held sway. Pinning his hopes on the outbreak of a new international crisis in the Near East to shake the status quo, he welcomed the Turco-Egyptian War

---

[28] C. Bodea, *Lupta Românilor pentru unitatea naţională, 1834–1849* (Bucharest, 1967), 17–18, 216–24.

[29] C. Vlăduţ, *Ion Câmpineanu* (Bucharest, 1973), 163–75.

[30] G. Zane, *Le Mouvement révolutionnaire de 1840* (Bucharest, 1964), 55–94.

in 1840 as providential. It seemed to open the way to active British and French involvement in Ottoman affairs and perhaps even a territorial division of the empire, which, he was certain, would bring freedom at last to its subject peoples. But all his activities were abruptly halted by his arrest and imprisonment in 1840.

The discovery of such conspiracies and the increasing acrimony between Ghica and the *boiers* in the assembly, which led to repeated denunciations of him in St Petersburg and Constantinople finally persuaded the Russian and Ottoman governments that the prince was incapable of maintaining order and furthering their interests. They thus removed him from the throne in October 1842.

Gheorghe Bibescu, Ghica's successor, was one of the wealthiest *boiers* in the country and had been elected by the Extraordinary General Assembly, as stipulated in the Organic Statutes. But his relations with the *boier*-dominated legislature were no more congenial than his predecessor's had been, and for essentially the same reasons. As the strife showed no signs of abating many *boiers*, conservatives and liberals alike, began to doubt whether the political system inaugurated by the Organic Statutes was suited to Wallachian society. To counter the opposition Bibescu turned increasingly to Russia. With the approval of St Petersburg and armed with a *firman* from the sultan sanctioning drastic action, Bibescu prorogued the assembly *sine die* and ruled by decree from March 1844 to December 1846. He assured himself of Russian backing by working closely with the consul in Bucharest.

The years of Bibescu's personal rule were productive and suggestive of how he intended to bring his country closer to European standards of civilization. Accepting the notion that the prosperity of a nation depended upon trade, he took vigorous measures to improve roads, which were in a lamentable state, and strove to eliminate the remaining tariffs between Wallachia and Moldavia, action which would, in effect, bring a customs union into being and inevitably draw the two countries together politically.[31] He tried to protect the economic interests of the country, including the artisan crafts and the fledgeling manufactories, by prevailing upon the Ottoman government to allow a rise in duties fron 3 to 5 per cent on imported processed goods. Although he was much concerned with education, his solution to cultural backwardness, as he called it, differed substantially from the plans of the younger generation of liberal *boiers*. Rather than enhance the role of Romanian, which he disdained as unsuitable for a modern culture, he proposed to introduce French as the language of secondary and higher education and to transform the Academy of St Sava in Bucharest into a French college.

Despite all Bibescu's good intentions, opposition to him would not abate, but now its most liberal elements were concentrated outside the country, mainly in

---

[31] A. Macovei, *Moldova și Țara Românească de la unificarea economică la unirea politică din 1859* (Iași, 1989), 46–55.

Paris, among the growing numbers of *boiers'* sons who had come to study law and history. When elections for a new assembly were held in November 1846 Bibescu left no device unused to crush the opposition and thus secured a compliant body composed almost solely of his supporters. It dutifully followed his lead and would undoubtedly have completed its normal five-year term in 1851, if revolution had not broken out in the spring of 1848.

In Moldavia Prince Mihai Sturdza faced opposition similar to that of his colleagues in Wallachia, but he was more successful in overcoming it. Born in 1795 into one of the most illustrious families of Moldavia and a large landowner, he easily persuaded the great *boiers* that he was a defender of class privilege.

Despite Sturdza's feelings of solidarity with the great *boiers*, he had no intention of allowing himself to become dependent upon their goodwill. He had a sharply different vision of a ruling prince, which harked back to the enlightened absolutism of the eighteenth century. His classical education and aristocratic inclinations, which were reflected in the numerous memoranda he had drawn up in the 1820s on government and society, had turned him away from representative institutions, even limited ones like the Moldavian general assembly, because he thought they were incompatible with efficient and beneficial government. Yet, his ideal prince was never a despot, for he felt a strong obligation to govern in accordance with the laws of the land. Nor was he opposed to constitutions—he was, after all, one of the authors of the Organic Statutes and favoured such a fundamental law as providing a stable framework within which public officials could work for the general progress of the country—but he insisted that constitutions not infringe upon the absolute power of the prince to carry out his responsibilities.[32]

Sturdza steadfastly pursued two objectives during his long reign (1834–49): the extension of his own powers and the maintenance of good relations with Russia. Both inevitably brought him into conflict with the *boiers*. Condemning the political pretensions of the *boier* aristocracy as intolerable, he sought the authority to appoint and remove all officials and to dissolve the assembly whenever it displayed 'seditious tendencies'. He also advocated the complete separation of the legislative and executive branches of government. But he had no intention of sharing power. He sought, rather, to prevent the assembly from interfering with princely prerogatives. Yet, the assembly never mounted serious opposition to him, and, hence, he never had to resort to the extraordinary measures used by Bibescu in Wallachia. He could usually count upon Russian officials in St Petersburg and the consuls in Iaşi to join him in opposing any manifestation of liberalism, for they shared the notion that the prince had a duty to discourage all activities which might undermine the existing political and social order. Nevertheless, Russian support of Sturdza was not unconditional. The consuls intervened in political matters whenever they thought it necessary, but not always on

---

[32] For an overview of Sturdza's reign, see D. Ciurea, *Moldova sub domnia lui M. Sturdza* (Iaşi, 1947), 52–99.

the side of the prince.[33] They were adept at playing the *boier* opposition off against the prince in order to enhance Russian influence, but in the end this practice proved counter-productive because it alienated both the prince and the *boier*s.

As a latter-day enlightened despot Sturdza was anxious to overcome irrational and outmoded practices and customs and to bring a measure of Western order to his country's traditional chaotic society. Such concerns lay behind his emancipation in 1844 of the gypsy slaves belonging to the state and monasteries, his further subordination of the church to state supervision, his constant preoc-cupation with health and sanitation, and his efforts to expand educational oppor-tunities, at least for the well-to-do, which were marked by the founding of a college, Academia Mihăileană, in Iaşi in 1835. Thus, during Sturdza's reign the general public in Moldavia for the first time felt the good side of government administration and no longer had to bear just the burdens it regularly imposed.

Despite his own good intentions and considerable powers, which included the manipulation of elections and a strict censorship, Sturdza could not stem the growing restlessness among the élite. Once a reformer himself, he had failed to keep pace with fundamental changes taking place in Moldavian society. As a result, the incomprehension between him and the young, mainly Western-educated sons of *boier*s grew into open conflict. The latter saw in Sturdza only the defender of the old order, of the flawed political system of the Organic Statutes, and of the humiliating deference paid to a foreign power.

SOCIETY AND THE ECONOMY

Between Tudor Vladimirescu's movement and the restoration of the native princes in 1821 and 1822 and the revolution of 1848 Moldavian and Wallachian society moved further away from eighteenth-century social and economic norms towards those that were to characterize the united national state of the latter nineteenth century. Change was gradual and uneven, but it was marked by two events which were to have profound consequences for the development of modern Romania: the accelerated growth of population and the expansion of economic ties with Western Europe. Yet, despite resulting pressures on the productive capacity of the land, the structure of agriculture, which determined the economic health of the principalities, remained essentially unchanged. The dire consequences of immobility in this vital area were to be borne by all segments of society.

Perhaps the most striking social development of the period was the increase of population. This European-wide phenomenon thus began in the principalities

---

[33] Filitti, *Domniile române*, 462–6, 501–5.

later than in the West. It was characterized by a more than twofold increase in the urban population during the first half of the nineteenth century. The movement of people from the countryside to the cities and towns and the expanded immigration from foreign countries, which also continued to be directed primarily towards urban centres, was unrelenting.

These demographic changes undermined the social equilibrium which had prevailed in the eighteenth century. They also opened the way to a restructuring of the economy by stimulating the development of the country's material resources and productive capacity. The pressure of population was felt most keenly in agriculture. At the beginning of the century the land available for agriculture had been adequate to feed the existing population even with traditional methods of cultivation, since, as we have seen, the amount of arable land seemed inexhaustible. But by the middle of the century, as forests and other reserves dwindled, it had become apparent that without fundamental changes in its organization and methods agriculture could no longer satisfy the needs of an expanding population or supply the increasing demands of the international market, upon which the economies of both principalities had increasingly come to depend.

Demographic change was everywhere evident.[34] The population of Moldavia rose from 1,115,325 in 1826 to 1,463,927 in 1859, and that of Wallachia from 1,920,590 in 1831 to 2,400,000 in 1860. Population density grew significantly: in Moldavia in 1803 there were only 11.8 persons per km^2, but in 1859 the figure was 36.1. The number of inhabited places, particularly villages, also increased: in Oltenia in 1831 there were 1,189 villages, and in 1848, 1,350. The trend in Moldavia was similar, as the number of villages rose from 1,647 in 1826 to 2,135 in 1859, and the number of cities from 35 to 81.

The exact causes of these striking changes remain obscure, once again because of insufficient data. Undoubtedly, the main cause of population growth was the decline of the death rate, which, none the less, remained high in comparison with other European countries. The end of foreign wars on Romanian soil and of burdensome military occupations after 1812 (the Russian occupation of 1828–34 must be considered beneficial) removed a major cause of death in earlier periods. Disease, which periodically swept South-eastern Europe, still claimed many lives in the principalities, especially in the cities, but health and sanitary measures taken after 1821, notably the creation of the strict quarantine along the Danube, began to have some effect. The plague was eradicated, and cholera epidemics (in 1831 and 1848) were no longer so virulent as in the past. Vaccination also made headway; in Moldavia between 1834 and 1844, for example, 197,000 children were immunized against smallpox.

Accelerated economic activity and greater fiscal stability also undoubtedly

---

[34] On demographic change in the countryside between 1821 and 1848, see E. Negruți, *Satul moldovenesc în prima jumătate a secolului al xix-lea; contribuții demografice* (Iaşi, 1984).

affected population growth. The abolition of Ottoman commercial restrictions and the growing economic interest of Austria, Britain, and France in the principalities after 1829 contributed to a new dynamism in agriculture. Although the resulting prosperity affected only part of the population directly, it may, none the less, have offered many others new hope for the future and thus may have encouraged larger families. Restraints on heavy and haphazard state fiscal exactions, especially after the accession of the native princes in 1822 and the introduction of the Organic Statutes a decade later, reduced the emigration of peasants to Transylvania and south of the Danube. A more orderly administration enhanced social stability and even helped to attract foreign immigrants. Especially important were the settlement of Slavs from south of the Danube in Wallachia and of Jews from Galicia in Moldavia. The flow of population into the principalities from abroad was substantial, and by the middle of the nineteenth century in Moldavia, for example, foreigners constituted roughly 19 per cent of the population.

Significant changes occurred in the number and character of urban centres. In Wallachia new cities developed along the Danube or near it—Alexandria in 1834 and Turnu Severin and Turnu Măgurele in 1836—mainly because the abolition of the Turkish *raya*s and the improved security stimulated economic activity in this naturally rich area. Older cities on the river underwent a renaissance. The best example is Brăila, which was rebuilt on the site of the demolished Turkish fortress in accordance with new ideas about urban planning. In Moldavia numerous semi-urban centres, *tîrguri* or *tîrgușoare* (market-towns), appeared where there had previously been only temporary fairs.[35] They owed their existence to the agricultural character of the Moldavian economy and to changes in the domestic market, which had reduced the need for periodic large fairs. Neither occasional fairs nor existing larger urban centres, which were located far from most villages, could satisfy the consumer needs of a growing population. The market-town, on the other hand, concentrated the exchange of goods from a given rural area in one place and offered artisans a stable and convenient centre from which to serve their clientele. In the first half of the nineteenth century some sixty market-towns were established, the most dynamic period of growth being from 1831 to 1838. Market-towns did not develop on the same scale in Wallachia. Here the domestic market maintained its traditional character longer than in Moldavia because the non-agricultural population was growing more slowly than in the neighbouring principality, owing to less intense immigration from abroad, and because access to existing urban centres from the countryside was generally easier than in Moldavia, where hilly country predominated.

Population figures testify eloquently to the growth of urban centres. In Wallachia between 1835 and 1853 the population of Bucharest rose from 50,370

---

[35] V. Tufescu, 'Tîrgușoarele din Moldova și importanța lor economică', *Buletinul Societății Regale Române de Geografie*, 60 (1942), 92–131.

to 64,860, Buzău from 2,860 to 6,805, and Giurgiu from 2,105 to 7,140. The same trends are evident in Moldavia: between 1832 and 1859 the total population of cities and market-towns increased 122 per cent from 129,413 to 288,161, up from about 50,000 at the beginning of the century, and between 1832 and 1845 the population of Iaşi rose from 48,314 to 68,655, Botoşani from 13,796 to 28,290, and Galaţi from 8,606 to 22,635. Of the total population of Moldavia 8.8 per cent resided in cities and market-towns in 1803, 10.2 per cent in 1832, and 23 per cent in 1859.

The causes of this unprecedented urban growth were diverse. Natural increase, however, was not among them, for in a number of cities, notably Iaşi and Galaţi, mortality exceeded the birth rate. Urban population expanded primarily because of the constant flow of people from the countryside. As in the period 1774–1821, villages formed the great reservoir of population for the cities. The patterns of migration between the 1820s and the 1850s had already been set in the latter decades of the eighteenth century, and the causes remained essentially the same: shrinking amounts of cropland and pasture available to peasants in many regions and growing labour and fiscal obligations caused by the slow but relentless commercialization of agriculture. Foreign immigration also remained a regular source of urban inhabitants.

As the urban population grew, its social composition was substantially altered.[36] At the beginning of the century merchants and artisans were in the minority, and persons engaged in agricultural or mixed agricultural and commercial or artisan occupations formed the clear majority. Even as late as 1831 agriculturists made up approximately 48 per cent of the population of cities and *tîrguri* in Moldavia and Wallachia (merchants and artisans accounted for 24 per cent, servants (*slugi*) 15.1 per cent, gypsy slaves 6.4 per cent, *boiers* 3.6 per cent, and clergy 2.3 per cent). But by 1845 in the five leading cities of Moldavia merchant and artisan families constituted 64 per cent of all families.

By the 1840s the middle class had become the most dynamic force behind the development of cities and market-towns. The liberal professions contributed significantly to its growth. The number of teachers steadily increased as a result of the impetus given education by the Organic Statutes; engineers, especially surveyors, found themselves in great demand by landlords, who were eager to delimit their holdings in order to take advantage of the rise in land prices since the latter decades of the eighteenth century; and doctors, pharmacists, and lawyers became indispensable components of urban society. There were also moneylenders, money-changers, and a few modern bankers. But artisans and merchants were the dominant element of this nascent bourgeoisie.

The numerical relationship of merchants and artisans and their ethnic compo-

---

[36] E. Negruţi-Munteanu, 'Date noi privind structura demografică a tîrgurilor şi oraşelor moldoveneşti în 1832', in *Populaţie şi societate*, i (Cluj, 1972), 239–57; E. Negruţi, 'Factorul demografic urban şi dezvoltarea social-economică a Moldovei în prima jumătate a secolului al XIX-lea', *Revista de istorie*, 28/8 (1975), 1183–96.

sition provide useful criteria for judging the general course of urban development. In Moldavia in 1832 their numbers were almost equal—5,602 merchants and 5,080 artisans—but by 1845 artisans outnumbered merchants 8,139 to 5,952, and in 1859 16,445 to 4,015. These numbers suggest that the processing rather than the exchange of goods had come to dominate the economies of cities and tîrguri. Figures for Iaşi lend support to this generalization. In 1831 there were 2,313 merchants and 2,164 artisans, but by 1845 artisans outnumbered merchants 3,381 to 2,765. As for ethnic relations, foreigners, particularly Jews, formed a majority of the merchants in Moldavia. In 1845 3,901 native merchants were engaged in 24 branches of commerce, but there were 6,049 Jews in 41 branches and 1,066 foreign subjects, mostly sudiţi, in 40 branches. The situation among artisans was approximately the same: 4,620 natives, most of them belonging to the third rank (as determined by the amount of the patentă, or business tax, they paid and engaged in 61 different trades, 5,153 Jews were active in 85 trades, and 1,091 foreign subjects in 101 trades.

Merchants and artisans, both natives and foreigners, did not yet constitute a bourgeoisie in the classical sense.[37] The majority belonged to the third rank. They carried on a modest business and, with a few exceptions, had no direct connection with industry and possessed little capital. The large and middle-size bourgeoisie (first and second ranks) were smaller and less cohesive. In Moldavia, particularly, they lacked homogeneity. They were divided by ethnic and religious allegiances and by economic and social rivalries between merchants and artisans, who found it impossible to act together on important social and political issues. In Wallachia, on the other hand, ethnic and confessional divisions were less pronounced, and the bourgeoisie was thus able to exert greater influence over public affairs, as it was to demonstrate in the spring of 1848. Yet, in both principalities boier status continued to be the ideal to which merchants and others of the middle class aspired. Many continued to purchase boier ranks and land as a means of achieving higher social status (land was also a profitable investment because the growing demand for grain had increased its value significantly). The consolidation of a true bourgeoisie, marked by a heightened sense of class consciousness, was to come about only in the second half of the century.

Other changes also occurred in the composition of the urban population. Servants and, especially, clerks, who had been almost completely absent before 1800, became more numerous as other classes depended upon them to perform myriad new tasks. Merchants and artisans, for example, needed persons to tend their shops as business expanded, and boiers who had begun to live much of the year in town required household servants of all kinds. None had any trouble hiring all whom they needed because more labour was generally available than

[37] C. C. Giurescu, Contribuţiuni la studiul originilor şi dezvoltării burgheziei române pînă la 1848 (Bucharest, 1972), 156–202. On the genesis of the middle class, see also Ş. Zeletin, Burghezia română; originea şi rolul ei istoric (Bucharest, 1925), 33–81.

the cities could absorb. Serving, moreover, was usually the first occupation for persons newly arrived from the countryside without a skill. In 1832 servants, together with gypsy slaves, constituted perhaps 20 per cent of the stable urban population of the two principalities.

Another result of the rapid and undisciplined growth of cities was the appearance of a large floating population without permanent occupations or domiciles. In Iaşi in 1845, for example, there were at least 1,000 such persons. Population had grown so quickly that old urban structures could not accommodate all who arrived. The unfortunate consequences were begging, prostitution, and abandoned children on a scale not seen before in Moldavian and Wallachian cities.

The village was also undergoing important changes in social structure. Dependent peasants, particularly the clăcaşi, represented the great majority of the population in both principalities—75 per cent in Wallachia and 70 per cent in Moldavia—and the size of the free peasantry continued to shrink, as the boiers consolidated their control over the land. Within each of these broad categories of peasants differentiation, caused by economic change and official acts, had become more pronounced. The distance between a narrow stratum of wealthy peasants and the rest of the village became greater as its poorest members sank to the level of a rural proletariat. On the other hand, a small rural middle class was on the rise.[38] In addition to the clergy, it included schoolteachers, who gained prominence in village affairs as public education expanded, and the neamuri and mazili. Although this class was composed of heterogeneous elements, all its members had in common education and property and, particularly, aspirations to improve their social status and play a role in political life.

Significant changes in the social composition of the boier class were also taking place.[39] To be sure, the Organic Statutes had consolidated the political power of the great boiers, but social and economic forces, which the statutes could not control, were undermining their predominance. In the first place, the boier class as a whole was losing its exclusive character as the number of boiers increased steadily (in Moldavia, for example, from 902 in 1828 to 3,325 in 1853), mainly through the purchase of offices. The majority of the new boiers came from social classes on the rise such as merchants or the sons of merchants, government functionaries, and individuals who had become wealthy managing the estates of boiers. Differences of outlook between the new and the old boiers were often striking. The former were turned towards the future and maintained at best a tenuous link to the values of the old regime, whereas the majority of the great boiers continued to extol the virtues of the aristocratic style. Within the limited circle of the great boiers itself an unbridgeable generation gap had appeared. Many of the sons of boiers who had returned home after study and travel in Western

---

[38] Giurescu, Contribuţiuni, 217–28.

[39] G. Platon, 'Consideraţii privind situaţia numerică şi structura boierimii din Moldova în preajma revoluţiei de la 1848', Populaţie şi societate, ii (Cluj-Napoca, 1977), 351–442; P. Barbu, 'Oltenia în perioada premergătoare revoluţiei de la 1848', Revista de istorie, 32/1 (1979), 144–6.

Europe could no longer accept the leisurely style, without reflection, of their fathers' way of life.

The process of embourgeoisement, already evident before 1821, accelerated in the 1830s and 1840s. The *boiers* of the lower ranks who managed their own properties were eager to develop commerce and improve agriculture. Many invested in small individual enterprises. Nor were such interests foreign to the great *boiers*. But it was the lesser *boiers* who stood closest to middle-class values and aspirations and who contributed to the foundation of that liberal bourgeoisie which successfully challenged the ascendancy of the great *boiers* in the second half of the century.

The steady influx of foreigners led princes and *boiers* to devise legislation to deal with the complex economic and social problems immigration caused. In a period of burgeoning national feeling demands came from many social groups for action to regulate the activities and limit the rights of the newcomers. Legislation was passed in Wallachia in 1847 which established the procedures to be followed by those who sought naturalization. The so-called 'lesser naturalization' (*mica împămîntenire*), which had been included in the Organic Statutes and granted foreign merchants and artisans the ordinary rights of native citizens, was left in place. But to obtain the 'greater naturalization' (*marea împămîntenire*), which had also been provided for in the statutes and accorded the successful applicant all the political rights of citizenship, the foreigner had to follow a long and complicated procedure which ultimately required the assent of the prince and a vote by the legislature on each individual case.[40]

Authorities in Moldavia found the problems raised by Jewish immigration especially acute. Prince Alexandru Ghica took the first serious measures to discourage Jewish immigration in 1834 when he ordered local officials to keep a record of all Jews in the country, to expel those who could not prove they had the means to support themselves, and in the future to allow only those who had passports to enter the country and then only for a month. In response to the growing complaints of native merchants about 'unfair' Jewish competition and the 'moral concerns' of others a series of laws were proposed in 1844 curtailing the economic activities of Jews. Only one measure, forbidding Jews to lease taverns in the villages and to sell alcoholic beverages there on credit, was passed, but it does not seem to have been enforced. The assembly rejected another law which would have prevented Jews from operating taverns at fairs mainly because it would have diminished the sponsors' profits.[41]

In the 1830s and 1840s modest economic changes were taking place in both principalities. The volume of agricultural production increased steadily, and industry struggled to meet the demands of a growing consumer population. But the structure of both agriculture and industry remained essentially the same. Agriculture still depended upon the peasant for labour, animals, and tools, and

[40] Filitti, *Domniile Române*, 356–8.   [41] Ibid. 495–7, 533–5.

the spirit of enterprise had yet to affect the behaviour of the majority of landlords and lessees. In the cities capital accumulation remained slight, and investments, except in land, were few, and the production of goods was still largely in the hands of artisans.

The Organic Statutes affected agriculture in several decisive ways. Its authors had attempted to place the relations between landlords and peasants on a rational basis of reciprocal rights and obligations. But they had had no intention of striking a balance between the two parties. On every important issue they took the side of the landlords against the peasants, who, naturally, had not been consulted during the drafting of the statutes.

The statutes, expanding upon the provisions of Prince Alexandru Moruzi's *hrisov* of 1805, recognized the full, absolute property rights of the landlord over one-third of his estate. Thus, they legally sanctioned the transformation of a significant portion of the feudal domain, over which the peasant inhabitants had for centuries exercised customary rights of usufruct, into private property, a goal, which, as we have seen, the *boiers* had been pursuing since the second half of the eighteenth century. The statutes no longer spoke of *stăpîni de moşie* (master of the estate) but of *proprietar* (property-owner). These changes had dire consequences for the *clăcaşi*. Their traditional, hereditary right of possession over the land they worked (now reduced to that two-thirds of the estate not recognized as the landlord's private property) was replaced by the obligations of a renter. Nor did the amount of land they were now allotted depend upon their needs, as earlier, but upon the number of animals the family possessed, or, in other terms, the amount of labour and other benefits the landlord could expect to receive from them. Accordingly, the *clăcaşi* were divided into three categories: *fruntaşi* (leaders), who had four draught animals and a cow; *mijlocaşi* (middle-sized), who had two draught animals and a cow; and *codaşi* (tail-enders), who had no work animals and could thus offer only themselves. Each category received an amount of arable land, hayfield, and pasture in keeping with its capacity to provide labour: *fruntaşi* approximately four and a half hectares, *mijlocaşi* somewhat less, and *codaşi* neither hayfield nor pasture. Overall, the *clăcaşi* had one-third to one-half the amount of land they had worked before the introduction of the statutes. Not only had the statutes thus brought about an extensive expropriation of the peasantry, they also allowed the landlord to decide by himself which land was to be given to the peasants, a right which would enable him not only to reserve the best land for his own use, but even to offer the peasants less than the statutes required.[42]

All these provisions increased the dependence of the peasants on the landlords. Those who had more animals than the number stipulated or who had too little land were permitted to obtain additional land (*prisoase*) through contracts (*învoieli*)

---

[42] Mitiţă Constantinescu, *L'Évolution de la propriété rurale et la réforme agraire en Roumanie* (Bucharest, 1925), 83–91.

with landlords. The latter were free to impose any conditions they wished, the only serious limitation being their need to retain an adequate labour supply. Yet, the authors of the statutes provided landlords with insurance against peasant flight by severely limiting movement from one estate to another. They realized that peasants had strong incentives to move, since their labour obligations under the statutes were more onerous than those specified in the Caragea Law Code of 1818. Although the number of days was still set at twelve, they were now measured in accordance with norms which effectively doubled or tripled the days of *clacă*.

Agricultural production expanded largely in response to the growing commercial relations between the principalities and Western Europe after the Treaty of Adrianople. Landlords, lessees, and peasants were encouraged to plant more of those crops that were in demand on the international market. Grain, particularly wheat, offered the highest return, and merchants and the state continuously exhorted *boiers* and monasteries to bring more and more land under cultivation. Peasants, too, increased the amount of land sown in grain which they worked for themselves in the hope of sharing in the prosperity.

Wheat was the main cereal crop and was raised primarily for export, as it had been before 1821.[43] But instead of being used to satisfy Ottoman demands for provisions, it found its way into the free, international market and thus became subject to all manner of economic fluctuations. In Wallachia in 1829, seven times more land was sown with corn than wheat, but by 1840 the amount of land devoted to wheat equalled that of corn and continued to increase over the next decade. In Moldavia, on the other hand, corn held its own. Although the planting of wheat almost tripled between 1832 and 1848, that of corn doubled.

Despite the pressure of the market, no significant change occurred in the organization or methods of agriculture. The bulk of the grain continued to be produced by the small peasant, who was responsible for decisions about planting and harvesting, as in the past. He increased his wheat lands not at the expense of fields planted in corn, but by clearing new lands or, more commonly now, by renting additional land (*prisoase*) from landlords. The latter, and those who leased their estates, were also satisfied in the main to entrust production to the peasant, who possessed almost all the draught animals and tools. At the same time landlords stepped up efforts to extend their property rights over the two-thirds of their estate which the Organic Statutes had set aside for the peasants. They were eager to take advantage of the rise in land values by leasing their estates to the highest bidder unencumbered by traditional social and economic obligations towards the peasantry. A few were also motivated by a desire to improve the production of their estates, but to do so they had to wrest control of the land from the peasants. Evidence of their enterprise may be found here and there in

[43] I. Corfus, *L'Agriculture en Valachie durant la première moitié du XIXe siècle* (Bucharest, 1969), 61–2, 172–4.

the expansion of the reserve and a modest increase in wheat production on it in the 1840s.

A few landlords and businessmen recognized the long-term benefits to be gained from a reform of agricultural practices. As early as 1830 an entrepreneur named Krateros had requested financial support from the Wallachian government to import new agricultural implements into the country and to demonstrate their usefulness in improving production. The government, in turn, instructed the *ispravnici* to persuade landlords to contribute to the project, but the latter showed no interest and the matter was dropped. In 1834 an agricultural society was formed in Wallachia for the purpose of introducing the latest techniques from Western Europe. It was responsible for bringing the first agricultural machines to the country in 1835, but their use was sporadic until after 1850. Occasional attempts were made in the 1840s to increase the yield of wheat and corn by introducing new varieties of seed and to improve the quality of cattle and sheep by importing breeding stock, but the initial results were disappointing.

The reserve, that part of the estate which the landlord retained for his own use, developed only slowly as a commercial farming enterprise. In the 1830s the provisions of the Organic Statutes concerning the separation of peasant holdings from the landlord's one-third of the estate appear to have been applied only in a few places. Landlords and lessees favoured allowing the peasants to cultivate as much land as they could and wherever they wished, and they still preferred to collect the tithe and receive money payments in place of *clacă*. They were influenced in part by the wishes of the peasants themselves, who insisted upon converting their obligations into money payments, because of widespread irregularities in computing labour services, and who vehemently opposed limitations on their use of the land. Many landlords were afraid to act otherwise because strict adherence to the statutes on their own estates would probably have caused a massive flight of peasants in search of better conditions. But the majority of landlords were also willing simply to let tradition govern agrarian relationships because they (and their leaseholders) were not interested in making the substantial investments necessary to commercialize the reserve. They thought it wiser to obtain a regular and guaranteed income in the form of tithes and money payments in place of labour, and they were justifiably reluctant to risk investing in the reserve, an enterprise prejudiced from the start by primitive tools and techniques and the constant hostility of the peasants.

Only in the 1840s was a noticeable effort made to extend the production of grain on the reserve, a move apparently related to three consecutive drought years—1839, 1840, and 1841—which caused a shortage of grain for the market and a steep rise in prices. Indications of a changed attitude on the part of a few landlords are to be found in the leasing contracts of the non-dedicated monasteries of Wallachia in 1841, which specified that peasants were to perform at least one-half the days of *clacă* which they owed and would not be allowed to substitute money payments. Such limitations on the conversion of *clacă* into money coincided with increased demands for Romanian grain in Western Europe, but they did not significantly change the character of the reserve.

Under conditions of intensified agricultural production and of a general overhaul of economic and political institutions the peasants were on the defensive not only in matters relating to the possession of land and labour services but in almost every aspect of traditional village life. Especially striking were changes in the configuration of the village introduced by the Organic Statutes. Before this time the simplicity of households and the relative ease with which their owners moved were characteristic of peasant life, particularly in the plains. In both the plains and the hills and among free and dependent peasants individual habitations tended to be scattered and isolated from one another and far from whatever village centre there may have been. The statutes, however, mandated the organization of villages along modern lines. They required landlords to group all the holdings they distributed to their peasants in one part of the estate, and the government itself undertook to promote a rational arrangement of the village under the direction of the new department of the interior. The aim of this legislation was to enable landlords to keep track of their dependent peasants more easily and thus discourage attempts to escape tithes and labour services. It would also allow a more systematic allocation of holdings and, no less important, would facilitate the collection of state taxes. The peasants, however, saw no advantage to themselves in such a drastic reordering of their way of life and strenuously opposed being moved by either landlord or government agent, neither of whom they had any reason to trust. Short of the use of force, which was forbidden by law, the programme of village systematization could not be carried out in accordance with the original grand design. Rather, it emerged only here and there as local conditions permitted and without coordination by the government.[44]

Industry retained its modest dimensions in the 1830s and 1840s. Although the volume of production grew and technological improvements were introduced, the organization of production remained largely what it had been in previous decades. Capital accumulation was small and was used mainly to finance commerce and provide individuals with loans for personal needs and, especially, the purchase of land. To invest in 'factories' was still considered risky business. Such caution was in fact justified because the persistence of the 'capitulatory regime', the system of Ottoman commercial treaties with European countries, prevented the governments of the principalities from offering new enterprises protection from foreign competition, while the low level of purchasing power of the mass of the population continued to deprive native industry of a strong domestic market for its products.

[44] Ibid. 180–9.

The preservation of the guild system discouraged innovation. Although the Organic Statutes had proclaimed the principle of economic liberty, the guild system with its myriad regulations became more powerful than before.[45] The statutes, in fact, encouraged monopoly in almost every branch of production by stipulating that all master artisans had to belong to a craft guild (*breaslă*). Otherwise, they were forbidden to practise a trade or to buy raw materials and sell the finished product. Such drastic limitations on economic enterprise were justified on the grounds that it was wrong for someone to enjoy the benefits of a guild without sharing in its responsibilities. Although these provisions were intended to protect and invigorate the guilds, they in fact opened the way to their destruction in the latter decades of the century because they encouraged their members to resist change and thereby weakened their ability to compete with other forms of domestic industry and foreign imports.

Manufactories increased in number, and several achieved a high level of technical efficiency—ceramics in Tîrgu-Jiu, textiles in Ploieşti, tobacco in Craiova, and the shipyards at Galaţi and Giurgiu.[46] Food-processing enterprises remained the most numerous, for they could draw on abundant and cheap agricultural raw materials, had a ready market for the staples they produced—pasta, oil, sugar, and meat—and could, therefore, offer investors a quick and certain return. Merchants and lessees of estates owned most of the manufactories, a situation which suggests where the bulk of investment capital was being generated. The workers in these enterprises still came mainly from the countryside, but they were now free, salaried labour, no longer dependent peasants. Many workers continued to engage in agriculture, since a number of manufactories, especially those which processed food, operated for only part of the year. Few manufactories, despite favourable conditions, survived for long, owing, it seems, partly to a lack of capital and credit for expansion and technological improvements, and partly to growing foreign competition.

Factories using machines instead of manual labour began to be established in the 1840s. Their founders had been impressed by the success of certain manufactories and tended, therefore, to limit their enterprises to the processing of easily available raw materials and to the satisfying of the immediate bulk needs of consumers. Noteworthy were the paper factory founded by Gheorghe Asachi at Petrodava, in Moldavia, in 1841, which received support from the government in the form of a monopoly on paper production for twelve years; the factory established in 1841 in Iaşi to manufacture agricultural machines; the slaughterhouse at Tighina, near Galaţi (1844), which used steam-powered machinery from Britain and exported canned meat to Britain and later to France and Austria; and

---

[45] V. Diculescu, *Bresle, negustori şi meseriaşi în Ţara Românească, 1830–1848* (Bucharest, 1973), 65–70.

[46] S. Vianu, 'Cu privire la problema descompunerii feudalismului în Ţările Române', in *Studii şi referate privind istoria Romîniei*, i (Bucharest, 1954), 829–33; L. Boicu, 'Despre stadiul manufacturier al industriei în Moldova', *Studii şi cercetări ştiinţifice* (Iaşi), historical ser. 11/1 (1960), 127–37.

the flour mill established at Păcurari, near Iaşi, in 1846 with equipment brought from Paris, an enterprise which initiated the regular investment of French capital in Moldavia.[47]

The number of manufactories and 'factories' increased steadily between 1830 and 1850, during which time 4,025 were established. Mills (2,443) and distilleries (458) were the most numerous. But industrialization, in the true meaning of the word, was still in its infancy, for almost all these enterprises were small, often one- or two-man operations, and many did not survive. All together in 1850 they employed only 8,432 workers, or, if clerks and other salaried personnel are included, about 11,000. There were notable exceptions—the slaughterhouse at Tighina, for example, employed 150 workers—but the modern factory system as the basis of industrial production was still decades away.

The general growth of the economy stimulated the mining industry. The processing and export of food products required increased amounts of salt; the need for oil in industry and transportation led to the exploration for new sources and to increased production; and the construction of roads and bridges and a new concern for city planning expanded the quarrying industry. Salt-mining was the most important of these enterprises. In Moldavia, for example, the number of workers doubled from 511 in 1810 to 1,006 in 1852, and production rose from approximately 18 million *ocale* (1 *ocă* = *c.*1.3 kg.) in 1810 to 20 million at mid-century, two-thirds of which was exported. The state treasury drew substantial revenues from salt-mining and maintained exclusive control over all deposits in the country. Crude oil was second in importance, but exploration was limited to deposits near the surface, as in the region around Buzău, in Wallachia, because of inadequate technology. None the less, production grew from 2,841 hectolitres in 1832 to 14,762 in 1848. Unlike salt, oil was not a state monopoly, and landowners, consequently, were free to work their deposits as they chose.[48]

The exchange of goods intensified, but few modifications in the organization of commerce occurred. Fairs retained their importance on both the local and international level, and in the cities and larger towns merchants carried on largely as before. But a significant professionalization of the merchant class was well under way as the state's regulation of their activities became more systematic. The Organic Statutes provided for a more uniform organization of merchants, grouping them into corporations and requiring them to pay a tax (*patentă*) based on their volume of business. The great majority of merchants paid the *patentă* of the third class; they were almost all natives and engaged in small, retail trade. The large-scale commerce in grains and animals continued to be in the hands primarily of foreign merchants, who benefited enormously from their connections with the great international merchant houses. But many of the old impediments

[47] G. Platon, *Geneza revoluţiei române de la 1848* (Iaşi, 1980), 222–4; A. Macovei, 'Prima intreprindere din Moldova pentru fabricarea uneltelor şi maşinilor agricole, Iaşi, 1841', *Cercetări istorice*, 4 (1973), 207–22.

[48] C. M. Boncu, *Contribuţii la istoria petrolului românesc* (Bucharest, 1971), 70–5, 311–56.

to internal commerce had still not been overcome. The weak purchasing power of the mass of the population, inadequate communications and transport, and elementary banking and credit facilities hindered the growth of the domestic market.

Commercial relations between Moldavia and Wallachia expanded, stimulating their economies and bringing them closer to political unification. The economic agreement of 8 July 1835 protected the major products of one from competition from the other, especially grains and cattle. Even more important was the convention of 1846, which made Moldavia and Wallachia essentially one market, protected by a single tariff barrier. It abolished customs duties between them and, modifying the 1835 agreement, it allowed all products, except salt, to be transported freely across their frontiers and stipulated that foreign goods would pay a duty only once, at the frontier of the country they entered.[49]

The most dramatic economic development in the principalities at this time was undoubtedly the expansion of foreign trade. Britain and France now joined in the competition for Romanian raw materials and markets alongside the Ottoman Empire and Austria, which until then had dominated the commerce of the principalities.[50] Romanian exports to the West were, of course, agricultural, primarily grain and animals. Imports consisted mainly of consumer goods destined for the wealthy such as textiles, glassware, and furs, but few items contributed to the development of industry or strengthened the economic base of the principalities. The value of foreign trade mounted steadily—in Wallachia from 21,514,000 *lei* in 1835 to 64,448,000 in 1847, and in Moldavia from 26,000,000 *lei* in 1843 to 52,000,000 in 1847. Volume also increased, as is indicated by the number of foreign ships docking at Brăila: 480 in 1832, 685 in 1839, and 1,002 in 1846. Galaţi experienced a similar increase: 1,383 ships arrived in 1847, 418 of them British. Ottoman control over this trade was gradually being loosened. Although the treaties of commerce between the Ottoman Empire and foreign countries still governed the commercial relations of the principalities, after 1843 import and export duties were collected by Romanian rather than Ottoman customs officials.

FROM ENLIGHTENMENT TO ROMANTICISM

Two generations of intellectuals—those who adhered to the traditions of the Enlightenment and the classicism of the previous century and the Romantics and

---

[49] A. Macovei, 'Unificarea vamală între Moldova şi Ţara Românească (I)', *Anuarul Institutului de Istorie şi Arheologie,* 7 (1971), 201–44.

[50] P. Cernovodeanu, *Relaţiile comerciale româno-engleze în contextul politicii orientale a Marii Britanii (1803–1878)* (Cluj-Napoca, 1986), 51–132; T. Ionescu, 'L'Échange maritime de marchandises entre les Principautés Danubiennes et la France durant la période 1829–1848', *Revue roumaine d'histoire,* 13/2 (1974), 269–84.

revolutionaries, who were turned towards the future—placed their stamp on cultural life and political thought between the Treaty of Adrianople of 1829 and the outbreak of revolution in 1848. The boundaries between them were blurred. Both were energetic and prepared to confront any challenge, however daunting. Their often naïve enthusiasm and strong sense of patriotism, their grandiose projects and encyclopedic ambitions were beholden to the spirit of the age, which is best referred to simply as 'forty-eightism' (*paşoptism*). They were inspired by a single, all-encompassing goal—to raise the Romanian nation out of its 'backwardness' and to bring it into communion with Western Europe.

The differences between the two generations were manifest in the means by which they sought to attain their common goal. The older generation had reached maturity in the final years of the Phanariot regime. Convinced of its decadence, they set out to eliminate all its remaining traces as the prerequisite for social and cultural progress. But at the same time they strove to preserve traditional values, for their own ideal society was not unlike the patriarchal rural community presided over by a benevolent and patriotic *boier* class. Their ambition was to turn the ideas of the Enlightenment into institutions, and thus their methods were classical and their thought aristocratic. They were wedded to the idea that reasoned reform and education, which would transform the individual, were the keys to social progress. Not surprisingly, Tudor Vladimirescu's uprising left them cold—they would have no truck with revolution. The hard lot of the peasantry aroused their humanitarian feelings, but they could not bring themselves to put the abolition of *clacă* and crushing tithes on their agenda. Nor did they judge the privileges of patriotic *boiers* excessive.

Their younger contemporaries by no means renounced the cultural goals of the Enlightenment, but their methods were, by comparison, revolutionary, their attitude democratic, and their taste romantic. This generation had come to maturity in a period of social and economic change following the events of the 1820s. In their youth the ideas of nationality, personal liberty, and social justice had been widespread, thanks in large measure to the older generation of reforming *boiers*. For them, Tudor Vladimirescu towered above all his contemporaries as the champion of the common people and a defender of the national dignity. Their education, first with tutors and then in new national schools, such as the Academy of St Sava in Bucharest and the Mihăileană Academy in Iaşi, reinforced their sense of civic responsibility and patriotic militancy. But new elements proved decisive in their intellectual formation. They were the first generation to study abroad and thus to confront exciting, and unsettling, social theories and models of development. In politics they were strongly attracted to liberalism, and they gave Romanticism their aesthetic and sentimental allegiance. In their ways of thinking they were remarkably integrated into Europe, and they spoke and wrote French with ease. They showed neither the cautious reserve of the old, Orthodox *boier* class nor the naïve, uncritical admiration of the West of such enlightened *boiers* as Dinicu Golescu. In short, they no longer thought of themselves as being outside Europe. They encountered Western civilization with understanding and a critical spirit.

Literature faithfully reflected the differences and the evolution of individual mood and of collective social and political aspirations of the two generations. The most representative writers of both came from the upper classes, but not from among the Phanariots or Hellenized natives, as in the eighteenth century. Rather, middle, and even lesser *boiers*, who had risen in the social scale in the first decades of the new century through state service or commerce, took the lead. They had been educated in the West or at least in the spirit of the West, its books and ideas forming a common intellectual bond among them. In their reading of current Western, mainly French, literature they showed a distinct preference for the products of Romanticism. Although many still conformed to the tenets of classicism in their own writing and had yet to experience the inner world of the Romantics, it was, none the less, through Romanticism that a synchronization occurred for the first time between Romanian culture and Europe.

The external response of Romanian intellectuals to Romanticism was conditioned largely by their ideas about the role they themselves should have in society. They obviously sensed that they were pioneers and that they would have to rebuild institutions from their foundations. Conscious of the desperate need for reform and nearly overwhelmed by the responsibility for the common good which they had assumed, they devoted little time to introspection. Their literary works, therefore, were usually of a practical nature which left their own inner selves unexplored. They were political leaders and men of action, and they were concerned about the present and its needs, even though they did homage to the past and hoped for a better future.

The poetry and prose of the 1830s and particularly of the 1840s was a literature with a message. Creativity, on the whole, was subordinated to the ideals of national unity and independence, to sympathy for the lower classes, especially the peasantry, and to efforts to nativize inspiration by directing it towards history, folklore, and the local landscape. Much of the writing of this period was also inspired by a belief inherited from the Enlightenment that literature had an inherently didactic value, and thus authors emphasized the useful over the aesthetic and thought first of the general good rather than of personal satisfaction. All these tenets were essential ingredients of *pașoptism*.

Such concerns determined the choice of authors from French and other European literatures, which were to influence *pașoptist* literary doctrine so decisively. Romanian intellectuals were attracted especially to those authors who could help them understand their own age and show them the proper direction to take in bringing the principalities into Europe. They sought a clear message applicable to their own condition, not metaphysics. Hence, conservative Catholicism, utopian socialism, or the delirious Romanticism of a Nerval had little appeal. They preferred Lamartine, Hugo, Michelet, and Lamennais, writers who spoke to the submerged peoples of Europe in humanitarian and sentimental tones and who valued ethnic distinctiveness.

The most important literary influence on Romanian writers was Romanticism,[51] but it was typical of intellectual life in general that no single current predominated, even in the work of an individual author. Literary ideas were in a state of flux, mainly because of the absence of well-defined schools, which could have assured a certain uniformity of thought and have aroused creative reactions to rival tendencies. Neither classicism nor Romanticism in the principalities was governed by rigid doctrines, for their adherents were individuals rather than groups. Individual writers, thus left to themselves, selected what was pleasing or useful at a given moment and showed little inclination to respect abstract principles divorced from prevailing social and political conditions. As a result, they were receptive to everything, and the most diverse currents—classicism, pre-Romanticism, and Romanticism—existed side by side or were mingled together in sometimes bizarre combinations.[52]

Despite such practical concerns on the part of authors, literature was undergoing fundamental change. It had ceased to be merely an emotional appendage to the Enlightenment. Now, authors whose main intent may still have been didactic also produced works that explored the personal and hidden sides of spiritual life or were simply meant to entertain. Although literature had not yet achieved an autonomous status, writers were careful to observe the distinctions between *belles-lettres* and other prose. The professional or semi-professional writer, who made his appearance about 1830, played an important role in the process.[53] Few could yet live off writing alone, but those who practised it as a craft had to concern themselves with what was specific to literature and thus had to differentiate it from other writing.

A new element intruded upon the literary scene after 1830: the reading public. It was still small, but it became increasingly democratic in its composition. The percentage of great and middle *boier*s declined, while the number of merchants, artisans, state functionaries, and village intellectuals (priests, schoolteachers, notaries) grew rapidly. The readers of newspapers, for example, came mainly from the middle class. In 1834 there were 200 subscribers to *Curierul Românesc* (Romanian Courier), which had been founded in Bucharest in 1829 by Ion Heliade Rădulescu (1802–72), the leading literary figure of the period. Although their number was modest by later standards, they were a presence to be reckoned with. Even men like Heliade Rădulescu, whose motivation was not primarily commercial, had, none the less, to take into account their readers' tastes, which were often unsophisticated, in order to preserve their newspapers and printing houses for their real work of education and enlightenment. The distance between

---

[51] On European Romantic influences among the Romanians, see E. Tacciu, *Romantismul românesc; un studiu al arhetipurilor*, i (Bucharest, 1982), 217–512.

[52] P. Cornea, *Originile romantismului românesc* (Bucharest, 1972), 512–74.

[53] L. Volovici, *Apariția scriitorului în cultura românească* (Iași, 1976), 11–18, 87–122.

what the entrepreneurs or 'directors' of culture, like Heliade, envisaged as desirable for society and what the reading public wanted was often vast. Heliade, for example, nurtured an ambitious plan to translate the important works of world literature into Romanian because he thought them indispensable for raising the intellectual and spiritual level of his countrymen. But the broad reading public had simpler tastes. It sought a literature of escape and compensation: the sentimental story with a happy ending, and sensation. Readers were more interested in what was said than in how. Such tastes were the primary reason why Heliade's grandiose 'Universal Library' failed.

The emergence of modern Romanian literature coincided with the flourishing of Romanticism in both principalities. Although the example of French Romanticism was compelling, Romanian writers did not experience directly its inner ambivalence.[54] For them, Romanticism was primarily an external influence. They did not pass through a demoniac or egoistical crisis like the followers of Byron and Chateaubriand in other countries. Yet, in Wallachia, for example, the poets of the 1830s and 1840s gradually introduced a striking novelty into their work— the discovery of the inner self. Henceforth, they made the self the determining factor in their creativity. By giving primacy to the subject instead of the object, which was fundamental to the aesthetics of classicism, they brought a new perspective to Romanian poetry. Increasingly, they sought truth in the inner life of consciousness and emotion rather than in external events. Yet, they could never free themselves from their sense of responsibility for the general good. On the one hand, they indulged in the melancholy of solitude, but, on the other, they embraced the cause of national independence; they might rail against the absurdity of life one instant, and then, the next, compose patriotic verse, which implied that life had a purpose after all. Historical context thus gave Romanticism in Wallachia (and Moldavia) its peculiar turn.

Four poets in particular embodied its essential character. Foremost among them was Ion Heliade Rădulescu. As a publisher, journalist, and patron of new talent he, more than any of his contemporaries, gave direction to literature. As a literary entrepreneur his chief aim was to bring Romanian literature and culture into the modern world as quickly as possible. He was himself bursting with projects, and he enthusiastically called others to action on all fronts.[55] Europe was always his model; it was his stimulant and his measure of accomplishment. Guided in all his undertakings by the didacticism and optimism of the Enlightenment—that man was perfectable, that progress was one of the laws of history, and that literature and the theatre could contribute to both—he was at the same time a man of his own time, for in him a powerful national sentiment took the place of the cosmopolitan humanitarianism of the eighteenth century. As a poet he showed talent and versatility. His masterpiece is 'Sburătorul' (1844; The

[54] N. I. Apostolescu, *L'Influence des romantiques français sur la poésie roumaine* (Paris, 1909), 14–130.
[55] M. Anghelescu, *Ion Heliade Rădulescu* (Bucharest, 1986), 38–71.

Winged Spirit), a typically Romantic ballad of tragic love. The sonnets in *Visul* (1836; The Dream), which is autobiographical, are remarkable for the time, because of their analysis of the subconscious. Heliade was a Romantic by temperament. A visionary, he yearned to be both a bard and a prophet, like Hugo and Lamartine, and to undertake the sacred mission of preaching the twin gospels of patriotism and philanthropy.

Vasile Cârlova (1809–31), the first poet to enjoy Heliade's patronage, displayed a remarkable ability, given the state of the Romanian poetic language, to communicate his feelings in clear, flowing verse.[56] His poems were no longer simulations or moral lectures, like those of the classicists of the eighteenth century, or declamations, in the manner of many Romantics, but monologues as natural in their appeal to God as in their expression of the heavy burdens of the individual soul. 'Înserare' (1830; Twilight) shows Cârlova as a true Romantic poet. It is eloquent testimony to the dominance of Lamartine and the assimilation of the Romantic elegy, which undermined the popularity of the *cîntece de lume* of Conachi and the Văcărescus. 'Ruinurile Tîrgoviştii' (1828; The Ruins of Tîrgovişte) is his best-known poem. But the contemplation of ruins did not become a source of melancholy and of pessimistic philosophical meditations, as it did for the French Romantics. Rather, past glories reawakened feelings of patriotism and evoked criticism of the public inertia of the day.

Grigore Alexandrescu (1810–85) and Cezar Bolliac (1813–81) represent other sides of Wallachian Romanticism.[57] Burdened with the idea that God was absent and man was alone, Alexandrescu was obsessed with the imperfections of human existence. His vacillation between scepticism and resignation gives an impression of modernity. Whereas he sought some point of equilibrium in the world and seems to have found it in his lucid and realist analysis of human nature in his justly famous *Fabule* (1832 and 1838; Fables), his contemporary, Bolliac, exhibited a kind of Byronian satanism. He expressed his defiance of the Christian solution to the human dilemma and derided the consolations offered by reason, by no means solitary acts, in his *Meditaţii* (1835; Meditations).

Moldavian writers pursued objectives similar to those of their colleagues in Wallachia, but their embrace of Western literature was more restrained and their Romantic *élan* more subdued. This reticence reflected the nature of Moldavian society, which, less advanced economically than Wallachian, was more conservative in taste and mores. Moreover, there was no one of Heliade's forceful character to promote new ideas. The leading literary figure, Gheorghe Asachi, who occupied a place similar to Heliade's, was a classicist and conservative and incapable of exciting young talent. The leading Romantic author was Costache Negruzzi (1808–68). His poetic skills and sensibility were modest, but his 'Aprodul Purice' (1837; The Prince's Page Little Flea) introduced a new genre—

---

[56] V. Muşat, *Vasile Cârlova* (Bucharest, 1981), 35–95.

[57] E. Lovinescu, *Grigore Alexandrescu: Viaţa şi opera lui* (Bucharest, 1928), 91–151; O. Papadima, *Cezar Boliac* (Bucharest, 1966), 95–147.

the historical poem—which raised its heroes to legendary proportions and transformed battles into epic encounters, all against a vivid local background. Yet, it
is as a short-story writer that Negruzzi secured his place in Romanian literature.[58]
His masterpiece, *Alexandru Lăpuşneanu* (1840), the dramatic and impassioned tale
of a sixteenth-century Moldavian prince, was Romantic, but he displayed stylistic
and emotional restraint in keeping with his own lightly sceptical and epicurean
philosophy.

The salient characteristic of Romanticism in both Moldavia and Wallachia,
and of cultural and intellectual life in general, was an overriding concern for
nation. The idea of nation itself was undergoing a significant transformation from
what it had been in the eighteenth century. An earlier generation of scholars had
spoken with pride about the Roman, and sometimes even the Dacian, origins of
the Romanians and had used such an association as a measure of their own
character and nobility. But in the works of writers after 1800 the idea of nation
began to assume modern contours. For Naum Rîmniceanu, membership in the
Romanian nation was determined by consanguinity and religion (Orthodoxy),
and, hence, it transcended political boundaries, which he dismissed as temporary,
to include Romanians everywhere.[59] In the memorials which the lesser *boiers*
drew up after 1821 to persuade the great *boiers* to share political power with them
they pointed out that they all belonged to the same nation. Their claim, put
simply, was that equal political rights followed naturally from the sharing of a
common history and membership in the same ethnic community. By the 1840s
such thoughts had lost their novelty. The old juridical conception of nation,
based on privileges which set one social class above all the others and thus assured
the political and social ascendancy of the *boiers*, had given way to an ethnic
conception which embraced all social classes, even *clăcaşi*. The young generation
of intellectuals, in particular, no longer used rank or wealth as criteria for
membership in the nation. For them, ethnic communities had become the
primary cells of humanity.

Indicative of the heightened concern for the ethnic nation was a change in the
attitude of the intellectuals towards folklore.[60] In the principalities the discovery
of folklore occurred relatively late—about 1840—in comparison with Western
Europe. The main reason for the delay seems to have been the intellectuals'
unwillingness to treat the products of humbler imaginations as anything more
than ignorance and superstition. They were conscious of their duty to disseminate useful information and promote good habits among the mass of the people,
and they thought of folklore and village traditions as simply perpetuating backwardness. They were certain that only the élite—they themselves—could im-

---

[58] L. Leonte, *Constantin Negruzzi* (Bucharest, 1980), 119–53.
[59] On Naum Rîmniceanu's idea of nation, see Ş. Bezdechi, 'Protosinghelul Naum Rîmniceanu
despre originea neamului şi limbii noastre', *Transilvania*, 74/3–4 (1943), 231–7.
[60] On the concern for folklore of Ion Heliade Rădulescu and Mihail Kogălniceanu, see A.
Bistriţianu, *Teorie şi inspiraţie folclorică la predecesorii lui V. Alecsandri* (Bucharest, 1977), 154–243.

prove society and that, consequently, they had nothing to learn from the common people. Gradually, under the influence of Romanticism and the modern idea of nation, a new appreciation of folk creativity emerged. An atmosphere of sympathy and understanding for the way of life of the village and for its cultural products replaced the earlier disdain. Folklore ceased to be judged according to the criteria of the Enlightenment—truth and reason—and was eventually accepted as another, valid conception of the world and a manifestation of a distinctive, not necessarily inferior, way of life.

The writing of history in the 1830s and 1840s was also influenced by Romanticism and the new idea of nation. Historians continued to study national origins in order to add to the evidence of Roman descent, although the theory was by now universally accepted among the educated. But an equally compelling attraction of history was the mystery of beginnings and the thrill of deciphering the past through ruins and inscriptions that had survived almost as a miracle. Historians were also drawn to ages of glory. The focusing of attention on Prince Michael the Brave, who had briefly united Moldavia, Wallachia, and Transylvania under his rule in 1600, was by no means accidental, but mirrored perfectly the heightened preoccupation with national unity and independence. In the hands of its best practitioners history became the story not simply of rulers and heroes but of the entire people. The outstanding example of the new history was *Histoire de la Valachie, de la Moldavie et des Valaques Transdanubiens* (Berlin, 1837) by Mihail Kogălniceanu (1817–91), a young Moldavian who had studied history at the University of Berlin and who was to occupy a central place in Romanian public life for the next four decades. The idea of nation had made a striking impression upon him. He conceived of history as the creation of an entire people, not just of their leaders, and, hence, he argued, it was essential to undertake a many-sided investigation of the past in order to reveal fully the activities of peoples and, especially, their spirit. For him, society was not a simple juxtaposition of individuals or classes but an organic, interdependent whole which in myriad ways forged the unity of the ethnic community.[61]

History, then, for the intellectuals of the period could not be a detached, scholarly exercise. On the contrary, it was a weapon which they used to strengthen national consciousness and to mobilize support for the achievement of national unity and independence. History served such purposes well not only through works of erudition but also by imbuing literature with new, patriotic ideals. Through poems, short stories, and plays a national historical consciousness became second nature to the growing literate public.

Romanian intellectuals also viewed language from their new perspective of nationhood. The collapse of the Phanariot regime and the decline of Greek as an administrative and cultural language and the rapid growth in the importance of Romanian stimulated theoretical interest in the native language. In the 1820s

---

[61] A. Zub, *Mihail Kogălniceanu istoric* (Iaşi, 1974), 393–439.

intellectuals (and princes and aristocrats) had expressed sharply divergent views on whether Romanian could serve as the vehicle for a sophisticated culture, but after 1830 the vigour of national feeling had silenced the doubters. The old reticence rapidly gave way to pride in what were perceived to be the superior qualities of the language. The main preoccupation of such cultural figures as Ion Heliade Rădulescu and Costache Negruzzi was not to investigate origins—the Latinity of Romanian was not in dispute—but rather to discover the genius of the language. Writers and scholars sought its specific character and inherent peculiarities in order to know how best to modernize its syntax and expand its vocabulary.[62] But what lay behind all these efforts, even if not yet explicitly stated, was the idea that language was not simply a convention, but rather expressed the essential traits of the national spirit.

The task of fashioning the disparate strands of thought on history, language, and literature into a coherent cultural doctrine, what might be called literary *paşoptism*, was taken up by the writers gathered around *Dacia literară* (Literary Dacia), a review founded by Mihail Kogălniceanu in Iaşi in 1840. Its title was symbolic of his and his colleagues' aims: to promote a sense of unity and purpose among all Romanians living within the historical boundaries of ancient Dacia by cultivating a genuinely national literature. To be national, Kogălniceanu insisted, literature had to reflect the distinctive traits of the Romanian people, as revealed in history and folklore, and had to have as its principal sources of inspiration the historical experiences and the contemporary aspirations of their own people.

These concerns brought the editors of *Dacia literară* face to face with two widely perceived dangers to a robust national literature. One was external: '*franţuzomania*' (Gallomania), which threatened 'to swamp the Romanian spirit' in a tide of translations and imitations. Kogălniceanu denied any intention of banning foreign works or of promoting xenophobia. He reiterated his conviction that regular contact with other cultures was beneficial for the development of a healthy national literature. But he insisted that the main criterion for the selection of French and other foreign works as models be their compatibility with the native spirit and the general cultural level of the country. The other danger he saw was internal: the subordination of artistic creativity to immediate social or political goals. He rejected the notion that a work was good simply because of its national content or message, and, urging greater aesthetic discernment, he declared an end to the era of 'write, write, good or bad', which had lasted for thirty years. None the less, he (and his colleagues) remained committed to a literature that was socially aware and the ideal creator he himself tried to embody was the citizen-author.[63]

Dacia literară was closed down after only three issues on orders of Prince Mihai

---

[62] I. Gheţie and M. Seche, 'Discuţii despre limba română literară între anii 1830–1860', in *Studii de istoria limbii române literare: Secolul XIX*, i (Bucharest, 1969), 261–90; I. Heliade Rădulescu, *Opere*, ed. D. Popovici, ii (Bucharest, 1943), 185–403.

[63] M. Platon, *Dacia literară* (Iaşi, 1974), 36–55.

Sturdza. The pretext seems to have been an article by Kogălniceanu criticizing the upper classes for their disdain of literary works in Romanian and their servile attitude towards foreign cultures. Sturdza, who was promoting education in French at the time, took the criticism personally.

Kogălniceau was undeterred. With redoubled energy he continued the programme of *Dacia literară* in other publications and from his chair at Academia Mihăileană. History remained for him the prime stimulus of national consciousness. Between 1840 and 1845 he edited *Arhiva românească* (Romanian Archive), the first Romanian journal to publish historical studies and original sources. In the introduction to the first volume he put the case for history succinctly: if anyone wanted to know who the Romanians were, where they had come from and where they were going, he need only look at their history, which was 'our whole being'. In 1844 he founded *Propăşirea* (Progress), which, however, had to appear as *Foaie ştiinţifică şi literară* (Scientific and Literary Journal), because the censor rejected the original title as subversive.[64] Kogălniceanu's stated purpose was to arouse within his readers a sense of patriotism, and he himself published a number of articles dealing with major events in Romanian history. He also opened its pages to leading poets and prose writers in order to encourage the development of an original national literature. But his preoccupation with contemporary political and social issues led the authorities to close down this journal, too, in 1844.

The programme of *Dacia literară* had numerous adherents in Wallachia. One of the most enthusiastic was Nicolae Bălcescu (1819–52), who had been implicated in the Filipescu conspiracy in 1840 and had been a contributor to *Propăşirea*. Like Kogălniceanu, he was an ardent student of history who had unlimited faith in its capacity to educate the nation and mobilize its resources to achieve political and social goals. Combining the best qualities of the scholar and the political activist, he was eager to raise Romanian historical research to a level equal to that of the advanced nations of the West.[65] The subjects that attracted his attention especially were military history and contemporary social issues, notably the agrarian problem. Together with a colleague from Transylvania, August T. Laurian, he founded *Magazin istoric pentru Dacia* (1845–8; Historical Journal for Dacia), through which he intended to carry on the programme of *Dacia literară*. It took the form of a scholarly review because the censor would not allow publication of a political journal. But the title suggested what the political objectives of its founders were, and in such pioneering works of social history as 'Despre starea socială a muncitorilor plugari în Principatele Române în deosebite timpuri' (1846: On the Social Condition of the Peasants in the Romanian Principalities in Different Periods) Bălcescu did not hesitate to attack the prevailing order of things which enabled a few individuals to enslave a whole nation.

[64] On the censorship of periodicals during Sturdza's reign, see R. Rosetti, 'Despre censura în Moldova', *Analele Academiei Române*, Memoriile Secţiunii Istorice, 2nd ser. 29 (1906–7), 351–61.

[65] G. Zane, *N. Bălcescu: Opera, omul, epoca* (Bucharest, 1975), 23–62.

The institutionalization of culture was also characteristic of the time. Societies and associations of all kinds sprang up, bringing like-minded individuals together to promote a wide variety of causes. During the 1830s and 1840s the theatre became a regular part of social and literary life; the foundations of a modern educational system from the village primary school to the university were laid; and the newspaper began its mission as a moulder of public opinion.

The theatre as an institution owed its origins in the 1830s to the spirit of the Enlightenment. Its chief promoters, Gheorghe Asachi in Moldavia and Ion Heliade Rădulescu in Wallachia, prized it as a civilizing agent, a powerful means of moral and aesthetic education especially suited to a nation just entering the world of modern culture. Heliade also thought that the new theatre could serve even broader social goals by becoming a forum where the most diverse groups in urban society could come together to consider the burning issues of the day. Despite the efforts of ardent supporters, the theatre in Bucharest and Iaşi did not prosper during its first decade.[66] It had to compete with both foreign travelling companies, which enjoyed more prestige than local aggregations, and itinerant native troupes, which catered to the simple taste of the mass audience. The financial position of the theatre never ceased to be precarious, as audiences were small and the government provided no support. In Moldavia an added problem was the vigilance of the censorship. Asachi's Conservatorul Filodramatic (Philodramatic Conservatory), founded in Iaşi in 1836, experienced all these difficulties, and despite mounting such ambitious productions as Bellini's *Norma*, had to close after a short time. The success of the Romanian theatre would ultimately depend upon the creation of a national repertoire inspired by the indigenous experience and by recognizable characters. This was to come in the 1840s with the plays of the first great modern Romanian poet, Vasile Alecsandri.

Typical of the organizations created by intellectuals and liberal *boiers* during the period was the Societate Filarmonică (Philharmonic Society) of Bucharest. Founded in 1833 by Ion Cîmpineanu and Heliade Rădulescu, it declared its purpose to be the promotion of the Romanian language, literature, and music. In particular, the society sought to give the theatre an institutional base by establishing a school of 'music, declamation, and literature' in 1834. The following year Heliade began to teach courses in dramatic literature and the art of acting, and students were soon performing such plays as Voltaire's *Mahomet sau fanatismul* (Mohammed or Fanaticism) and Alfieri's *Saul*. But other members of the society also had a political agenda which included such radical notions as the union of the principalities, equality before the law, and an equitable sharing of the tax burden. The society ceased its activities in 1838 probably because of divergences over cultural policy among its diverse membership of great *boiers*, liberal intellectuals, and the middle class.

Among numerous other associations were those devoted to economic

---

[66] I. Massoff, *Teatrul românesc: Privire istorică*, i (Bucharest, 1961), 145–234.

improvement and public health. Cîmpineanu and Petrache Poenaru (1799–1875), the director of national schools of Wallachia, founded the Societate de Agricultură (Society for Agriculture) in Bucharest in 1835 and a school of agronomy in nearby Pantelimon. In Moldavia, which under Prince Mihai Sturdza was inhospitable to societies because they were suspected of being liberal and, hence, potentially subversive, Gheorghe Asachi and a few friends established the Societate de Medicină şi Istorie Naturală (Society of Medicine and Natural History) in Iaşi in 1833. All these organizations and the general tendency towards association represented a burgeoning spirit of private initiative aimed at reforming society and raising the nation out of its acknowledged backwardness. After 1840 the character of many of these organizations changed. They became avowedly political as young radicals took the places of older moderates. Their goals were national and democratic, as Romanticism absorbed the Enlightenment.

Education after 1830 became a regular concern of the state, which provided the administrative framework and modest funding. But the success of the early initiatives depended mainly upon the work of dedicated individuals, notably Asachi in Moldavia and Poenaru in Wallachia, the heads of their countries' respective school committees. Receptive to innovation at every level, they planned to create in the chief cities of every judeţ a network of Lancasterian schools, which, by training older students to help younger ones, would make the best use of the small number of teachers available, and they founded normal schools in Bucharest (1831) and Iaşi (1832) for the professional training of teachers.[67] A general effort was also undertaken to improve higher education. In Iaşi the old princely academy was reorganized in 1835 as Academia Mihăileană with sections for philosophy, theology, and law. Later, courses in agronomy and Romanian history were added. In Bucharest the curriculum of the Academy (now, College) of St Sava was expanded in 1840 to include six classes in the humanities instead of four. The advocates of reform sought to create a system of higher education that would serve the needs of a people intent upon achieving national independence and creating a national culture. But their progress was impeded by influential boiers, who rejected the notion of equal opportunity and sought to impose French as the language of instruction. The boiers prevailed and in 1847 the assemblies in both principalities voted to turn the higher schools of Bucharest and Iaşi into French colleges, but their plans were undone by the outbreak of revolution in 1848.

The newspaper made its appearance in modern form in 1829 in Wallachia with Heliade Rădulescu's Curierul Românesc and Asachi's Albina Românească (1829–49; The Romanian Bee). The Russian occupation authorities allowed both to be published as a means of cultivating support for their regime among the

---

[67] N. C. Enescu, Gheorghe Asachi, organizatorul şcolilor naţionale din Moldova (Bucharest, 1962), 47–174; G. Potra, Petrache Poenaru, ctitor al învăţămîntului în ţara noastră (Bucharest, 1963), 77–163.

educated public, but they admonished both editors to respect the state, venerate religion, and uphold 'morals and decency'. Within the limits of censorship, rigorously applied in Moldavia, but only mildly so in Wallachia, the editors brought the important public issues of the day before their readers, kept them informed of the general course of European events and the latest scientific discoveries, and offered them new works by Romanian authors. Asachi was a convinced social conservative who favoured stability and reform exercised from above. His principles remained those of the Enlightenment—reason and the dissemination of knowledge. Heliade was more closely attuned to the ideals of the young generation and opened the columns of his paper to all who stood for beneficial change and were willing 'to debate [diverse] opinions and find truth'. These two papers enabled public opinion to form and express itself and prepared the way for the vigorous and diversified newspaper press of subsequent decades.

Paşoptism represented above all a new, comprehensive vision of nation. Its theoreticians not only brought together the disparate strands of thought about autonomy and political reform that had been circulating since the final decades of the eighteenth century, but they also gave full attention to the social and cultural dimensions of nation-building. Through institutions of all sorts, not the least of which were literary associations, schools, and newspapers, they strove to bring their idea of nation to an audience beyond their own narrow circles. In so doing, they moved closer to 'the people' than any previous generation and thus endowed the vision of nation itself with a distinctly modern content. The first great test of their new vision came during the springtime of peoples in 1848.

5

The Romanians of the Habsburg Monarchy

MANY Romanians lived outside the principalities of Moldavia and Wallachia, in Transylvania and Bukovina, both possessions of the House of Habsburg. Since these Romanians were overwhelmingly peasant, they played no significant role in the aristocratic political structures of the day, even though they formed a majority of the population in both territories. Among the Romanians of Transylvania a small intellectual élite assumed direction of cultural and political life and displayed concerns similar to those of the reforming *boiers* and the *paşoptist* generation in Moldavia and Wallachia. Their energies, too, were absorbed by the idea of nation, and under conditions of foreign rule they struggled to achieve political and cultural autonomy. Like their counterparts in the principalities, they were drawn into the major European currents of ideas of the time—the Enlightenment, Romanticism, and liberalism—and strove to adapt them to their particular circumstances. Their preoccupation with nation and their use of language and history to awaken national consciousness among a wider public were perfectly attuned to the spirit of the times. The situation of the Romanians of Bukovina, the northern *judeţe* of Moldavia annexed by Austria in 1775, was different. They had been abruptly cut off from the sources of their political and cultural traditions, and their history during the period is thus one of integration into the structures of the multinational Habsburg monarchy. Seen in broad perspective, the advent of the Habsburgs in both Transylvania and Bukovina represented an intrusion by the West into the world of the patriarchal Romanian village. In Transylvania it provided a stimulus to national consciousness, but in Bukovina it undermined the compact ethnic community.

RELIGION AND NATION

The position which the Romanians occupied in the political and social life of Transylvania between the final decades of the eighteenth century and the 1840s was determined in great measure by the structure of Romanian society itself.[1] Various statistics show them composing over 50 per cent of the population during this period, and in 1850–1, according to one calculation, out of a total population of 2,062,000, there were 1,227,000 Romanians (59 per cent).[2] Over

---

[1] See the exhaustive analysis in L. Gyémánt, *Mişcarea naţională a Românilor din Transilvania între anii 1790 şi 1848* (Bucharest, 1986), 336–431.

[2] E. A. Bielz, *Handbuch der Landeskunde Siebenbürgens* (Hermannstadt, 1857), 159–61. See also

90 per cent were peasants, and, of these, three-quarters were dependent upon a landlord or were day-labourers, and the rest were free. Few could read or write. Their way of life, still dominated by a curious mixture of folk and religious traditions and still largely impervious to outside cultural and intellectual influences, had changed but little since the beginning of the eighteenth century. A Romanian commercial and industrial middle class hardly existed. Of all the cities of Transylvania, only in Braşov did the Romanians have even a relative majority of the population. Elsewhere, Romanian merchants and artisans were few in number and weak economically and, hence, could play only a modest role in local affairs. A Romanian landowning nobility, the class which provided leadership in an agrarian, hierarchical society like that of Transylvania, had for all intents and purposes disappeared, having been assimilated by the Magyar nobility before the fifteenth century. The remnants of a Romanian noble class were still to be found in certain areas, mainly in southern Transylvania, among the gentry (who were known as *boiers*), but they had little power except in village affairs and, in general, pursued a way of life that differed only slightly from that of the free peasantry.

In the eighteenth and early nineteenth century the higher clergy of the Romanian Orthodox and Uniate (or Greek Catholic) Churches played a more crucial role in the political life of the Romanians of Transylvania than did the Orthodox clergy in Moldavia and Wallachia. They assumed leadership almost by default, since no other group or class possessed comparable prestige and cohesion, and the two churches themselves, in the absence of Romanian political institutions, provided the Romanians with their sole framework for community life. The higher clergy, especially of the Uniate Church, were the initial bearers of national consciousness and the formulators of a new idea of nation based upon ethnicity rather than legal charter or social caste.

During the reigns of Maria Theresa (1740–80) and Joseph II (1780–90; co-ruler with his mother, 1765–80) the Romanians were excluded from the political life of Transylvania, a condition that had prevailed at least since the fifteenth century. In 1437 the leaders of the so-called three nations—the nobles (essentially Magyar), the Szeklers, a people akin to the Magyars who spoke Magyar and had settled in eastern Transylvania; and the Saxons, the name by which German settlers who had first arrived in Transylvania in the twelfth century were commonly known—formed a union to protect their rights against a massive uprising of peasants. Subsequent legislation in the sixteenth and seventeenth centuries reinforced their predominance. At this time membership in a nation was not determined by ethnicity. The idea of nation (*natio*) implied quality rather than quantity; it did not encompass everyone of the same ethnic origin, but only those persons who possessed special rights and immunities. Hence, Magyar, Szekler, and Saxon peasants did not belong to their respective nations. A Romanian *natio*

Erdély története, iii (Budapest, 1986), 1195–7, and I. I. Adam and I. Puşcaş (eds.), *Izvoare de demografie istorică*, ii (Bucharest, 1987), 53–7, 77–8, 106–16.

did not exist at all because the Romanians were mainly peasants and, thus, being of low social status and unprivileged, they had not been passed over in silence in the legislation establishing the system of nations.[3]

The Romanians had been excluded from political life also because of their religion. The Protestant Reformation, which had won many converts to the Lutheran, Calvinist, and Unitarian Churches—the Saxons to the first, the Magyars and Szeklers to the latter two—made a redefinition of religious privilege necessary. In the second half of the sixteenth century the Transylvanian diet recognized the full equality of the Protestant Churches with the Roman Catholic Church: the members of each were guaranteed freedom of worship; each church was granted equal representation (at least in theory) in all the branches of the central government and allowed to administer its own affairs with a minimum of interference from the state; and the clergies of all four 'received', or constitutional, churches enjoyed the same rights and privileges as nobles. No mention was made of the Romanians. The Orthodox Church, to which they belonged, and its clergy shared none of these benefits.

The incorporation of Transylvania, an autonomous principality under loose Ottoman suzerainty since the sixteenth century, into the Habsburg monarchy at the end of the seventeenth century brought significant changes in the intellectual and cultural life of the Romanians. The court of Vienna considered the acquisition of Transylvania an inheritance of the Hungarian Crown, but it was at pains, none the less, to legitimize its rule by negotiating a sort of contract with the three nations. The so-called *Diploma Leopoldinum* of 1691, which was to serve as the basis of public law in Transylvania until the Revolution of 1848, recognized the political autonomy of the principality and confirmed the rights and privileges of the three nations and their churches. Yet, despite these solemn assurances, Habsburg officials set about at once to integrate their new acquisition fully into the imperial political and economic system. Planning and decision-making were gradually shifted from the provincial administration and legislature to the central governing bodies in Vienna, such as the new Transylvanian chancellery. In its work of centralization the court of Vienna relied upon the expanding bureaucracy, the army, and the Roman Catholic Church as its chief instruments.[4]

The Romanians assumed a new importance with the coming of the Habsburgs. The court regarded the Romanian Orthodox as a potential counterweight to the Magyar Calvinist nobility, who formed the backbone of the opposition to centralization. The pursuit of political objectives coincided with the eagerness of the Roman Catholic hierarchy of Hungary to press forward with the Counter-Reformation in the eastern territories of the monarchy.

---

[3] D. Prodan, *Supplex Libellus Valachorum: Din istoria formării naţiunii române* (rev. edn., Bucharest, 1984), 94–101.

[4] Z. Trócsányi, *Habsburg-politika és Habsburg-kormányzat Erdélyben, 1690–1740* (Budapest, 1988), 218–71, 315–56, 398–413.

Negotiations between the Romanian Orthodox Bishop Atanasie, on the one hand, and the Jesuits, who served as the intermediaries of the court, and Leopold Cardinal Kollonich, the primate of Hungary, on the other, led in 1700 to the acceptance by Bishop Atanasie and a portion of his clergy of a union with the Church of Rome. In return for their recognizing the pope of Rome as the visible head of the Christian Church and their acceding to several unobtrusive changes in doctrine, Emperor Leopold I (1657–1705) issued two diplomas, in 1699 and 1701, granting all Orthodox priests who accepted the union the same rights and privileges enjoyed by the Roman Catholic clergy, including exemptions from labour services and tithes to landlords.[5] The new Uniate Church came into being when Bishop Atanasie formally severed his ties with the metropolitanate of Ungrovlachia in Bucharest and on 25 March 1701 was consecrated bishop of the new church. The court of Vienna and Cardinal Kollonich assumed that the Orthodox Church in Transylvania had thus ceased to exist. But, in fact, it carried on its activities at the village level throughout Transylvania for nearly sixty years until the appointment of a new bishop in 1759.

The church union brought few substantive changes to Romanian religious life. In matters of doctrine and practice the two Romanian churches remained Eastern. But the union had a profound effect on the political development of the Romanians. The imperial diplomas of 1699 and 1701 provided the Romanian clergy with the legal basis for challenging the monopoly of power exercised by the three nations. The union also gave a new direction to Romanian intellectual life. By opening Roman Catholic educational institutions in Transylvania and elsewhere in the monarchy to Romanian students, the union contributed directly to the creation of an intellectual élite, which in the 1730s assumed a dominant role in both the church and the social and cultural life of the Romanians. In the final analysis, the union represented the thrust of the West into traditional Romanian society, and, as a consequence, the Uniate clergy became the mediator between two distinct cultural worlds.

Bishop Ion Inochentie Klein[6] (1700–68; bishop, 1729–51) was the first Uniate leader to undertake a systematic campaign to obtain the rights that had been promised the Uniate clergy in the two imperial diplomas. At first, he emphasized clerical rights because they had been clearly set forth in the diplomas and thus offered him a solid constitutional foundation from which to pursue his case. But he did not think of the clergy as separate from the people at large. His distinction was simply a legal one made for tactical reasons in response to the prevailing aristocratic climate of opinion.

---

[5] N. Nilles, *Symbolae ad illustrandam historiam Ecclesiae Orientalis in Terris Coronae S. Stephani*, i (Innsbruck, 1885), 224–7, 292–301. For an analysis of the 2nd diploma, see Z. I. Tóth, *Az erdélyi román nacionalizmus első százada, 1697–1792* (Budapest, 1946), 34–44.

[6] When he received a title of nobility from the emperor in 1729 he followed the practice of the day of Germanizing his family name Micu (small).

Klein's conception of the union seems, at first glance, paradoxical. On the one hand, in a continuous stream of petitions to the court he professed complete devotion to the union and contributed no little to its administrative consolidation. But on the other hand, he made no effort to proselytize among the rural population, leaving village religious life undisturbed, and he resisted all attempts to draw the Uniate Church into a closer communion with Rome. The explanation lies in his idea of nation. It had been moulded by a deep sense of community based upon the beliefs and customs of Orthodoxy that formed the bedrock of social life in the village. Thus, for him, the union was always subordinate to community.

Klein got nowhere with his petitions to the Transylvanian gubernium (the executive council of the principality headed by the governor) and diet, which were dominated by the three nations. He therefore concentrated his efforts on the court of Vienna, where, he hoped, broad imperial interests would carry the day against the provincialism of the Transylvanian estates. Although at first the court sympathized with his campaign because it regarded him as a loyal promoter of the union, in the end it rejected all his entreaties to raise the Romanians to the rank of a fourth nation because it had no intention of undermining the social structure of the principality and of risking an open rebellion of the estates, Protestant and Catholic alike. By 1744 the court had come to regard Klein as an enemy of the union and forced him into exile in Rome.[7]

The court's suspicions of Klein were only partially justified. His conception of nation was unquestionably ethnic rather than religious.[8] His petitions on behalf of Romanian rights amply demonstrate that he regarded all the Romanians of Transylvania as a distinct national entity, regardless of their church affiliation. His identification of the Romanians with the union was thus primarily a device to achieve political and social goals rather than a confession of faith. As he pursued these goals his commitment to the union wavered, and he drew closer to Orthodoxy, but it was to an Orthodoxy that represented the spirit of community rather than a set of religious principles. None the less, he never lost sight of the realities of his situation: Orthodoxy could not serve the cause of Romanian political rights because it lacked legal status and had no place within the estates system. He was convinced that only through the alliance with Catholicism could he hope to achieve his objectives.

In the year that Klein began his exile a massive uprising of the Orthodox rural population led by the monk Visarion Sarai, shook the union to its very foundations and inaugurated a period of fifteen years of almost continuous unrest in the countryside. The ferment culminated in an even more massive uprising, headed by another monk, Sofronie of Cioara, which lasted from the autumn of 1759

---

[7] F. Pall, *Ein Siebenbürgischer Bischof im Römischen Exil: Inochentie Micu-Klein, 1745–1768* (Cologne, 1991), 21–42.

[8] Tóth, *Az erdélyi román nacionalizmus*, 121–2; Hurmuzaki, *Documente*, vi (Bucharest, 1878), 575–6.

until the spring of 1761. The objectives of Visarion and Sofronie and their followers were religious—freedom of worship and the right to choose their own priests and to have a bishop of their own.[9] They displayed uncompromising hostility towards the union with Rome and felt a closer kinship with Orthodox Serbs than with Uniate Romanians. Their movement ended relatively peacefully, although in the aftermath the Austrian military commander systematically destroyed the small monasteries in southern Transylvania that had served as centres of the uprising. The Orthodox achieved a notable victory: recognition by the court of Vienna of the legal existence of their church and the appointment of a bishop in the person of Dionisie Novacovici (Novaković), the Serbian bishop of Buda.

The movements roused by Visarion and Sofronie offer valuable insights into popular notions of community. The climate of opinion prevailing in the village, as revealed by the Orthodox resistance to the union, strikes one as ahistorical, non-national, and to some extent millenarian. Those who followed Visarion and Sofronie had little sense of history. To be sure, they knew that they were Romanian and from tradition may even have heard that they were descended from the Romans, but they did not place themselves in a historical context. They still saw their own lives in terms of the biblical drama of man's fall and redemption. The Christian past was thus their present, continually made real by religious ceremonies. In a sense, they lived in a continuous present, in which ancient beliefs and practices were the models for everyday life. Religion determined their earthly frame of reference, for whenever they thought about membership in a larger community beyond the family or the village they considered themselves to be part of the Orthodox world. An ethnic consciousness clearly existed—they were instinctively aware of the differences between themselves and the Serbs, for example, and they clung to their 'Wallachian religion'—but the idea of nation as the natural context within which they should live was foreign to them. The form their resistance to the union took also suggests certain affinities to millenarianism. Their numerous petitions to the court of Vienna and appeals to Transylvanian authorities constituted a protest against an evil world and a cry for salvation. Yet, like millenarians elsewhere, they had no precise idea of what the future would be like and no effective strategy to achieve their goals. Rather, they hoped for sudden, miraculous change as found in the lives of saints or in the exploits of folk heroes, and they looked to some holy man, a Visarion or a Sofronie, to show them the way.

This was not the path of development the Romanian nation was to take. While Uniate intellectuals shared many of the religious convictions of the rural population, men like Bishop Klein possessed a keen sense of history and of their own place in the evolution of human society. They recognized the capacity and

[9] I. Lupaş, *Două anchete oficiale în satele din scaunul Sibiului, 1744 şi 1745* (Sibiu, 1938), 15–19; S. Dragomir, *Istoria desrobirei religioase a Românilor din Ardeal în secolul XVIII*, i (Sibiu, 1920), annex, 222–4.

the responsibility of men to exercise some control over their destiny rather than remain the plaything of unseen forces. Uniate intellectuals thought increasingly in terms of 'nation', that is, of an institution which gave meaning and scope to man's earthly existence. In the middle decades of the eighteenth century they thus offered the Romanians of Transylvania a new path of development.

The union with Rome survived the massive shocks delivered to it by Visarion and Sofronie, in part, because the court of Vienna refused to abandon its half-century of labour on behalf of Roman Catholicism. But more important in the long run was the perseverance of a dedicated clergy who had come to view the connection with Rome from a perspective that transcended religion to embrace a new idea of nation.

The church union provided a theoretical justification of their faith in progress and gave substance to the idea of a Romanian nation. It explained the history of the Romanians since the Roman conquest of Dacia—their rise and fall—and presaged a new age of glory. The weaving of these ideas into a coherent doctrine signified nothing less than a reconciliation between East and West, which, moreover, provides the key to an understanding of all modern theories of Romanian nationalism. In trying to harmonize the patriarchal Orthodox tradition of an essentially rural world with the dynamic spirit of urban Europe, Uniate intellectuals made an indispensable contribution to the creation of a new, distinctive entity: Romanian.

Their ideas were given clear form for the first time in *Despre schismaticia grecilor* (On the Schism of the Greeks), written in 1746 by Gerontie Cotorea, later vicar-general of the Uniate Church.[10] Cotorea asserted the direct descent of the Romanians from the Roman conquerors of Dacia. This idea was common among Romanian intellectuals of the period. The novelty of Cotorea's argument lay in his identification of the ancient Romans with the Church of Rome and his linking of the decline of the Romanian nation in the Middle Ages to their abandonment of the Western Church in favour of Eastern Orthodoxy. He discerned a striking analogy between the 'decadence' of the Romanians during the Middle Ages and the widely accepted explanation of the fall of Constantinople to the Ottoman Turks. The cause of both tragedies, he argued, had been the separation of the Romanians and the Greeks from Rome. It was too late for a revival of Byzantium. But Cotorea was certain that the Romanians stood on the threshold of a renaissance, if only they would return to the Mother Church. He thus saw the union as a reaffirmation of the inherent Latinity of the Romanians. But he had no intention of abandoning the spiritual culture of Eastern Orthodoxy, for he (and his colleagues) recognized it as a determinant of national character at least equal to Romanness. The task Cotorea had set for himself, then, was to connect the Rome of Trajan with the Rome of Peter and Paul and to reawaken in his fellow Romanians a consciousness of their Western

---

[10] Z. I. Tóth, 'Cotorea Gerontius és az erdélyi román nemzeti öntudat ébredése', *Hitel*, 9/2 (1944), 89–91.

origins without at the same time requiring them to sacrifice their Eastern heritage.

Cotorea and his colleagues thus conceived of their church as an entity quite different from Bishop Klein's. Whereas he had treated it as something imposed from the outside and as a device to achieve social and political goals, they revered it as a peculiarly Romanian institution. Such an interpretation is suggested by their use of 'Romano-Valachus' beginning in the 1740s to describe Romanians who had united. They clearly accepted an identification with Eastern Orthodoxy, which is inherent in the word 'Valachus', for it differentiated Romanians from the other inhabitants of Transylvania—the Lutheran Saxons and the Calvinist and Roman Catholic Magyars. But, in their minds, the link to Rome ('Romano'), established by the union, further differentiated the Romanians from the surrounding Slav Orthodox—the Serbs, in particular. Thus, by removing the Romanians of Transylvania from the international Orthodox community, Cotorea and company placed ethnic interests, represented by the Uniate Church, ahead of religion.

Such a stand is also evident in their opposition to any attempt to Latinize their church. On the one hand, they took immense pride in the union as a return to their Roman heritage, but, on the other, they refused to make their church more Roman. Their reasoning suggests an ethnic and cultural conception of nation fully in accord with the modern spirit.

ENLIGHTENMENT AND NATION

The reign of Joseph II exercised a striking influence on Romanian intellectuals and decisively affected the fortunes of their nation. In the course of reorganizing and centralizing the administration of his vast realm, he shook the old order in Transylvania to its foundations. His cavalier treatment of the three nations convinced Romanian intellectuals that there was room for them and their people in a system that had stubbornly resisted change. His reforms touched every significant aspect of Romanian social and economic life—agriculture, education, civil rights, and religion—and admiration for his enlightened absolutism among Romanian intellectuals endured long after his death.

Joseph initiated a major reform of agrarian relations in Transylvania, which had remained largely unchanged since the beginning of Habsburg rule, during a tour of the principality in 1783.[11] On 16 August he issued a preliminary decree of emancipation of the serfs, which modified the harsh regime which the mass of Romanian (and other) peasants had had to endure. It forbade landlords to take from their peasants the plots of land they worked or to transfer peasants from one village to another, except after due process. It also gave peasants a measure of

[11] On Joseph II's agrarian reforms in Transylvania, see D. Prodan, *Problema iobăgiei în Transilvania, 1790–1848* (Bucharest, 1989), 147–99.

personal freedom by allowing them to marry and to practise any trade of their choice without the consent of their landlords. However beneficial these measures may have been, they did not deal with the fundamental causes of poverty and discontent among the peasantry: inadequate allotments of land, diminished by a growing rural population and encroachments on common lands and individual holdings by landlords, and crushing economic obligations to landlords and the state in the form of tithes, labour services, and taxes.

The peasants expressed their frustration in a massive uprising in the autumn of 1784 led by Horea, a peasant himself who had represented their cause in Vienna on several occasions. The violence was directed primarily at noble landlords, and the objectives of the peasants were mainly economic, although the pitting of Romanian peasants against Magyar landlords suggests national overtones.[12] By January 1785 the uprising had been suppressed, and in February Horea and one of his lieutenants were executed in the presence of 2,500 peasants who had been assembled from over 400 villages to witness the consequences of disobedience.

Joseph was not satisfied merely to suppress the uprising. He sought to discover its causes and to take measures to prevent new violence in the future. A commission of inquiry in 1785 attributed the uprising to the harshness and injustice with which landlords had treated their peasants, the failure of provincial and local authorities to enforce existing regulations governing peasant–landlord relations, and the almost total absence of 'moral and religious training' among the Romanians. It recommended the immediate introduction of a comprehensive set of rules (*urbarium*) regulating conditions on the land with provisions for strict enforcement, the establishment of a system of state-supported schools for Romanians, and the construction of a seminary to improve the training of Orthodox priests.

Joseph acted at once to implement these recommendations. On 22 August 1785 he issued a second and final decree of emancipation of the serfs. It granted the peasant his personal freedom, allowing him to move from one village to another, if he had fulfilled all his obligations to his landlord. He could now acquire landed and personal property and could dispose of it as he wished. Yet, despite these measures, his emancipation remained incomplete, for Joseph had failed to provide him with land. Consequently, he was still obliged to perform labour services for his landlord as rent for the land he worked, a system that would serve the landowning class well as a means of coercion.

The recommendations of the commission for an overhaul of Romanian education coincided with a programme of school construction and textbook publication already under way. The *Ratio Educationis*, a plan to expand elementary education among the non-German peoples of the monarchy, including Hungary, but not Transylvania, had been promulgated in 1777. It provided for centralized direction and a uniform curriculum, but allowed the respective native

---

[12] D. Prodan, *Răscoala lui Horea*, ii (2nd rev. edn., Bucharest, 1984), 709–21.

languages to be used in instruction. None the less, German was to be a special object of study, because of its pre-eminence in cultural life and its use as the official state language, and for this purpose bilingual textbooks were to be introduced into the schools as quickly as possible. Joseph extended the provisions of the *Ratio Educationis* to Transylvania in 1781. He took steps to organize an elementary school system for Romanian Uniates, and within a decade the number of schools had reached several hundred. Joseph also approved plans in 1786 for a network of Orthodox schools, but here progress was slower, owing to the lack of financial resources available to the Orthodox Church and the absence of adequate facilities for the training of teachers. Before Joseph's reign neither the court nor the Transylvanian gubernium had shown any interest in the education of 'schismatics', and, consequently, they had rejected all Orthodox requests for aid in building schools and paying the salaries of teachers.

If the education of Romanians presented a long-term, and uncertain, challenge to the dominance of the three nations, Joseph's open disregard of political tradition in Transylvania struck at the very foundations of the old order. The Saxons were the first to suffer a curtailment of their privileges. According to Joseph's decree of *Concivilität* of 4 July 1781, all the inhabitants of the Fundus regius (the area in southern Transylvania between Sibiu and Braşov where the Saxons enjoyed self-government and almost exclusive rights of citizenship) were henceforth to enjoy equal civil rights. It thus opened the way for Romanians to participate fully in political life, since they were now to be permitted to acquire landed property and enter the guilds in Saxon towns and cities. Joseph delivered an even more stunning blow to the governmental structure of the principality on 3 July 1784, when he decreed the abolition of the old county and district system of local administration, in which the local aristocracy had held sway, and put in their place eleven new counties, in which the word of an *Obergespann*, or prefect, appointed by and responsible to the central government, would be law. The boundaries of the new counties took little account of ethnic divisions and historical traditions. Henceforth, all nationalities were to receive equal treatment before the law, and the main criterion for holding public office was to be merit, not social position or family connections. In the interests of efficiency German was to be introduced as the language of administration as rapidly as possible. The immediate effects of these sweeping changes on the Romanians proved to be slight, since the privileged orders fiercely resisted their implementation.

Joseph further challenged the power of the three nations by proclaiming the principle of religious toleration. The Edict of Toleration, issued on 13 October 1781, granted non-Catholics freedom of worship in their own homes and the right to build churches and to open schools in those places where they numbered at least 100 families. As for the Orthodox, it stipulated that their faith would no longer exclude them from public office or from equal treatment under the law. Yet, the Edict of Toleration did not usher in an era of complete religious freedom, for it produced results which Joseph had not anticipated. In certain areas large numbers of Uniates began to return to the Orthodox Church. Although he was hardly a loyal son of the Roman Catholic Church, Joseph, none the less, had no wish to jeopardize the unity it represented. On 20 August 1782 he issued a decree threatening severe punishment for all who tried to persuade others to leave the Roman Catholic or Uniate Churches for Orthodoxy and making a six weeks' course of instruction in Catholicism mandatory before any Roman Catholic or Uniate could be received into the Orthodox Church.[13]

Although Joseph thus continued his mother's policy of hindering the growth of the Orthodox Church, he also sought to introduce order and stability into its affairs. He proposed to do this by investing it with a full-time bishop to replace the temporary bishop-administrators appointed by Maria Theresa beginning in 1759. His purpose was not to allow the church greater autonomy, but to use its network of parishes to influence public opinion and to keep the peasant masses under control. In 1783 he appointed Ghedeon Nichitici (Nikitić), a Serbian monk, as bishop, and by decrees of 30 September and 9 October of that year he made the bishop of Transylvania dependent upon the Serbian metropolitan of Karlowitz in questions of dogma and ritual. He made no secret of the fact, however, that the church remained subordinate to the state in all other matters, and he pointedly excluded the Romanians from the political privileges granted the Serbs by Leopold I at the end of the seventeenth century.

In every part of his empire Joseph's disdain for local tradition had aroused opposition to his reforms from the privileged. In Transylvania by 1790 Magyar nobles and Saxon burghers had begun to hold public meetings of protest and were withholding supplies from the army until their grievances had been satisfied. A financial crisis brought on by an extended war against the Ottoman Empire together with uncertainties in international relations caused by the French Revolution forced Joseph to undertake a reconciliation with the privileged orders. As a consequence, shortly before his death he reluctantly signed a decree revoking all his reforms except those concerning serfdom and religious toleration.

In Transylvania this act signified the restoration of the system of the three nations. Yet, the effects of Joseph's reforms persisted in every area of public and private life. For the Romanians, the most tangible immediate benefits of his reign were the impetus he had given to education and the formal recognition he had granted the Orthodox Church, which could now represent the Romanian community more effectively. But perhaps the greatest benefits were intangible. By shaking the political and social structure of the principality, he encouraged (unintentionally) Romanian intellectuals to redouble their efforts to gain constitutional status for their nation. He had thus made a return to an earlier era unthinkable.

---

[13] T. V. Păcăţian, 'Contribuţiuni la istoria Românilor ardeleni în sec. xviii', *Anuarul Institutului de Istorie Naţională*, 3 (1924–5), 174–8.

Joseph had won the allegiance of a new generation of Romanian intellectuals. Often referred to as the 'Transylvanian School', because of the similarity of their ideas on social progress and nation, the majority were the products of Uniate secondary schools, which flourished at Blaj, the diocesan see, in the second half of the eighteenth century, and of Roman Catholic institutions of higher learning in Vienna and Rome. They were receptive to the ideas of the Enlightenment, especially in its Austrian incarnation. Placing great store by education and reason to solve human problems, they were uncommonly optimistic about the future. Conscious of their own leading role in society, they were certain that beneficial change must come from above, from the 'enlightened', by which they meant themselves. Characteristic also of this generation was their practicality. Its members were little given to abstract speculation, as their attention was absorbed by the immediate problems of Romanian society—political emancipation and education. Their enormous production of works of all kinds—histories, grammars, theological treatises, sermons, and schoolbooks—were intended to further the general welfare. Such preoccupations suggest another significant trend in Romanian society—the secularization of the intellectual class, a process that was well under way, despite the fact that the majority of its members were priests. In the end, a single element gave their diverse activities and encyclopedic interests cohesion and direction—the idea of nation, which they themselves endowed with a modern historical and linguistic foundation. Ethnic rather than religious, their new conception of nation found its purest expression in the theory of Daco-Roman continuity.

Samuil Micu (1745–1806), historian, linguist, and Uniate priest, was the first to expand upon the theory in a series of historical works culminating in his monumental four-volume *Istoria și lucrurile și întîmplările Românilor* (The History of the Affairs and Events of the Romanians), which he finished in the later years of his life. He sought to prove that the Romanians of the eighteenth century were the direct descendants of the Romans who had settled Dacia in the second century, and he equated the beginnings of Romanian history with the founding of Rome by Romulus and Remus. He also insisted that the Romanians were the pure descendants of the Romans, since their war against the Dacians, in his view, had been one of extermination. He showed how Christianity had also come from Rome as Roman colonists filled up a Dacia devoid of other inhabitants. When the Emperor Aurelian withdrew the Roman administration and army from Dacia in 271, Micu insisted that the bulk of the population remained in place. In the following centuries, so his argument ran, when Dacia was overrun by one barbarian invader after another, its Roman inhabitants survived by taking refuge in the mountains; it was their descendants whom the Magyars found when they entered Transylvania in the tenth century. These Romanians, as Micu now called them, who were organized into a duchy under Duke Gelu, made an alliance with the Magyars and chose the latter's chieftain, Tuhutum, as their prince. Micu pointed out that this treaty did not subordinate the Romanians to the Magyars, but rather established a condominium of equals. Yet, he sadly admitted, referring to the union of the three nations in the fifteenth century, the legal and social status of the Romanians inexorably declined. He detected a reversal of their fortunes only at the end of the seventeenth century with the arrival of the House of Habsburg, and he had only praise for Leopold I and his successors.[14]

In composing his account of the glorious beginnings and subsequent fall of the Romanians, Micu drew upon a wide variety of manuscript and published sources, both foreign, especially Hungarian, and Romanian, notably the great Moldavian and Wallachian chroniclers of the seventeenth century. His works display many of the qualities of modern historiography, but the critical attitude he tried to maintain towards his sources faltered whenever the nobility of the Romanians' lineage and their historical rights came into question. His insistence upon the purity of Romanian descent from the Romans is a case in point. He allowed the other peoples the Romans conquered, such as the Gauls, to survive, but he categorically denied the same boon to the Dacians. He also insisted that all the colonists who repopulated Dacia came only from Rome or the Italian peninsula. Modern scholarship has shown just the opposite—that large numbers of Dacians continued to inhabit the province of Dacia and its periphery after its conquest by Trajan and that the Roman military and civil population of the province was drawn from every part of the empire. Micu's contention that a Romanized population remained in Dacia after Aurelian's evacuation has been a subject of dispute down to the present, but the growing accumulation of evidence, especially archaeological, supports Micu's thesis.

Deficiencies in Micu's work may be attributed in part to the prevailing state of historical scholarship, but his general attitude towards his craft was greatly influenced by the prevailing political and social circumstances. As in the time of Bishop Klein, nobility, or quality, rather than numbers, was the main criterion for the enjoyment of political rights. Consequently, Micu strove to prove Romanness in order to place Romanian claims to status as a fourth nation on a solid foundation.

The ideas which Micu espoused were shared by his contemporaries. Gheorghe Şincai (1754–1816), Uniate school director during the reign of Joseph II, priest, historian, and linguist, marshalled an impressive array of first-hand sources in his three-volume *Cronica Românilor* (Chronicle of the Romanians), which he wrote between 1805 and 1812 to prove the validity of the theory of Daco-Roman continuity.[15] By far the most influential Romanian historical work of the period was *Istoria pentru începutul Românilor în Dachia* (The History of the Origins of the Romanians in Dacia), published in 1812 by Petru Maior (1756–1821), Uniate protopope, historian, and linguist. His work differed substantially from those of

---

[14] S. Micu, *Istoria şi lucrurile şi întîmplările Românilor*, i. 49, 64–5, and iv. 18–19, Biblioteca Academiei Române, Cluj, MS rom. 436–9; id. *Scurtă cunoştinţă a istorii Românilor* (Bucharest, 1963), 9–10, 18–23, 36.

[15] G. Şincai, *Hronica Românilor*, i (Bucharest, 1967), 13, 48–50, 65–7, 136–7, 263–6, 337–8.

Micu and Şincai. It was a synthesis in one volume from which all matter not relevant to the main theme had been excised. It was not a general history of the Romanians but, as its title indicates, an investigation of their origins and survival in Dacia up to the Magyar invasion in the tenth century. Nor was it a life's work, even though Maior's scholarship was by no means inferior to Micu's and Şincai's; it was, rather, a polemic or a reply, as Maior himself called it, to the calumnies which foreign historians had heaped upon the Romanians.[16]

Micu and his colleagues found an indispensable criterion of nation in language. Pioneers in the study of the Romanian language, they compiled the first scholarly grammars and the first etymological dictionary. They were motivated, at least in part, by a desire to refine and polish the language to enable it to serve as an efficient vehicle for the expression of new ideas and the instruction of new generations. But at the same time they recognized the political and social value of language and used the evidence it could provide to reinforce their historical arguments about the nobility of the Romanians.

Micu and Şincai laid the theoretical foundations of the study of the Romanian language in their *Elementa linguae Daco-Romanae sive Valachicae* (Vienna, 1780). Micu composed the first draft; Şincai edited it and wrote the preface. Both were eager to prove the Latinity of Romanian and, by extension, the Roman origins of the Romanians. Since they judged Romanian to have been derived from classical Latin, they sought to return it as nearly as possible to its 'original form'. Not surprisingly, therefore, they replaced the Cyrillic alphabet, which had traditionally been used for Romanian, with the Latin alphabet and used a system of Latin transcription that would demonstrate beyond any doubt the relationship between Romanian and its illustrious progenitor. The orthography they chose was etymological rather than phonetic and had been devised by Micu in 1779 for his little book of prayers, *Carte de rogacioni*.[17] A second, revised edition of the grammar, which appeared in 1805, bore only Şincai's name. In it Şincai proved to be a less rigorous Latinizer, but he yielded not at all to Micu in his insistence that Romanian was simply a corrupted form of classical Latin.

The most authoritative statement of the Latinist linguistic credo came from the pen of Petru Maior. In the preface to the *Lexicon Valachico-Latino-Hungarico-Germanicum*, the first etymological dictionary of the Romanian language, which was published in Buda in 1825, he explained the origins and nature of Romanian in the form of a conversation between an uncle and his nephew. The nephew declares that he accepts the thesis propounded in *Istoria pentru începutul Românilor în Dachia* that the Romanians are the direct descendants of the ancient Romans, but admits that the origins of the Romanian language still puzzle him. The uncle replies that there were really two Latin languages, one the classical or literary

---

[16] D. Popovici, *La Littérature roumaine à l'époque des lumières* (Sibiu, 1945), 241–3. The texts of the polemics engendered by Maior's work are to be found in P. Maior, *Scrieri*, ii (Bucharest, 1976), 198–246.
[17] BRV ii. 229–30.

language and the other the vernacular used by the common people. It was the latter, he insists, that was spoken by the colonists brought to Dacia by Trajan and that formed the basis of modern Romanian.[18]

The idea of nation espoused by Micu, Şincai, Maior and their generation differed significantly from that represented in the activities and writings of Bishop Klein and Gerontie Cotorea in the first half of the eighteenth century. The divergences are perhaps most evident in their respective treatments of history and language. Klein concerned himself with the origins of the Romanians only in passing, although he was fully conscious of their unique ethnic character and their distinctive historical evolution in Transylvania. Cotorea possessed a similar fund of information, but he conceived of Romanian historical development mainly in terms of religion. As for language, neither Klein nor Cotorea paid special attention to Romanian. They did not speculate on its origins and they composed no grammars. For serious writing they preferred Latin, which was more congenial to them than their native tongue. Micu and his colleagues, on the other hand, had, as we have seen, made history and language the marks that distinguished one nation from another and established their pedigrees.

The two generations also held divergent views on the relationship between religion and nation. To be sure, Micu, Şincai, and Maior remained Christians and served their church with devotion in various ways, but they were at the same time men of the Enlightenment. They made a clear distinction between the other-worldly pursuits of the church and the immediate, practical aspirations of human beings. Most important among the latter for them was the revival of the ethnic nation, and they viewed the assimilation of new ideas, the spread of useful knowledge, and the application of reason to social problems as indispensable for its progress. From their standpoint, then, the church as an institution could no longer provide the leadership, and religion could no longer serve as the ideology of progress, in a modern, enlightened world. All their writings make it clear that the idea of nation had outgrown the bounds of confessionalism and theocratic privilege, which had been predominant in the first half of the century.

The idea of nation espoused by Micu and his colleagues was not yet modern. Their attitude towards the mass of the common people suggests an élitist view in keeping with the prevailing tenets of the Enlightenment. They showed deep compassion for the peasantry and worked in their own ways to improve their lot. They were more directly involved in social activities than previous generations, and they took a greater, if still modest, interest in the customs and daily life of the village. Samuil Micu, for example, knew the hardships of the rural world from first-hand observation, and he urged landlords to treat their peasants in the spirit of Christian charity. He also found in peasant customs proof of the Roman origins of the Romanians, and the notes he took in the field may be taken as the

---

[18] P. Maior, 'Dialog pentru începutul limbei române între nepot şi unchiu', in *Lexicon Valachico-Latino-Hungarico-Germanicum* (Buda, 1825), 63.

first work of Romanian folklore. Şincai's contributions to village education and Petru Maior's sermons all suggest an abiding concern for the general welfare.

Despite their compassion, the intellectuals' attitude towards the mass of the population remained ambivalent. On the one hand, they used the term 'nation' in an ethnic sense and meant the people as a whole, but, on the other hand, they could not imagine the peasants as part of the political nation. Like their predecessors, they considered them ignorant and superstitious and in need of a long period of tutelage before they could participate fully and rationally in public affairs. The era of popular sovereignty had clearly not yet arrived.

The reaction of the intellectuals to peasant uprisings suggests how little regard they had for the common people as managers of their own destinies and how greatly they prized reason and knowledge as the proper levers of human affairs. Micu expressed these sentiments perfectly when he noted the stark contrast between the followers of Sofronie of Cioara and the Uniate clergy. He qualified the former as belonging to the mob and as ignorant and unconcerned with the general welfare of the nation. But he praised Uniate priests as learned, cultivated, and 'steadfast in their faith'.[19]

The massive peasant uprising led by Horea in the autumn of 1784 provoked a crisis of conscience in many intellectuals. They recognized the justice of peasant grievances, but they could not bring themselves to condone the widespread destruction of lives and property. Unlike the movements led by Visarion Sarai and Sofronie of Cioara, Horea's uprising had as its main goals relief from the burdens of serfdom, a more equitable allocation of state taxes among all classes, and a division of noble estates among the peasants. Although there were religious and national aspects to the uprising such as the forced rebaptism of Magyar Calvinist nobles in the Orthodox faith and occasional demands that Transylvania should be a Romanian land, these acts had no relation to the programme of the intellectuals. They were, rather, spontaneous expressions of the folk consciousness. Samuil Micu's condemnation of the revolt in general and of Horea in particular as an accursed man, and his advocacy of gradual, systematic reform carried out by the 'enlightened' leave little doubt about the disparity that continued to exist between popular emotion and cultivated reason.

Intellectuals thus stood in the forefront of the movement to gain rights for the Romanians equal to those enjoyed by the other nations (in the ethnic sense of the term) of Transylvania. Their strivings were but one aspect of the intense political activity in the principality initiated by the three nations after the death of Joseph II to recover their privileges. The Romanians set forth their programme in an imposing petition to the Emperor Leopold II (1790–2), the *Supplex libellus Valachorum*, the most important political document produced by the Romanians in the eighteenth century.[20] Drawn up in the winter of 1790–1, it was the work of many, including Micu, Şincai, and Maior, who wrote the

---

[19] Micu, *Istoria*, iv. 661, 663.
[20] On the nature of the petition, see Prodan, *Supplex Libellus Valachorum*, 412–34.

initial draft. The first of its two parts consisted of an elaboration of the theory of Daco-Roman continuity and an explanation of how the Romanians had been unjustly excluded from the privileged system of the three nations and four churches. The second part set forth a series of demands which reveal the triumph of ethnicity in defining nation, for the petitioners made no distinction between the élite and commoners or between Uniates and Orthodox. They urged the restoration to the Romanian nation of all rights and privileges it had enjoyed before the union of the three nations in 1437; the granting to Romanian nobles, peasants, and clergy of both the Uniate and Orthodox Churches of the same rights and immunities enjoyed by the respective social categories of the other nations; proportional representation for the Romanians in county, district, and communal administration and in the diet; the equitable sharing of taxes and other public burdens by all inhabitants of the principality in accordance with their economic and social position, but without regard to nationality or religion; and the holding of a national congress composed of nobles and clergy under the chairmanship of the Uniate and Orthodox bishops where the best means of fulfilling the demands of the Romanians could be discussed.

Neither the court of Vienna nor the Transylvanian diet was in a mood to grant the Romanians' demands at a time of general European upheaval. Their concern was to maintain the status quo by mollifying the traditional privileged orders. The only tangible Romanian success was the enactment of a law by the Transylvanian diet in August 1791 which guaranteed the Orthodox freedom of worship.

Significant Romanian political activity virtually came to an end for almost four decades. With the accession to the throne of the conservative Francis II (1792–1835) the era of the Josephinian Enlightenment flickered out. The grave crisis through which the Habsburg monarchy passed during the Revolutionary and Napoleonic Wars and the conservative reaction after 1815 made impossible the kind of political effervescence that had produced the *Supplex libellus Valachorum*.

THE GENERATION OF 1848

By the last decade of Francis's reign important changes had taken place within the Romanian élite. Lay intellectuals, mainly teachers and lawyers, now challenged the Uniate and Orthodox clergies for leadership of the nation. Eager to set their people on a new, essentially European, path of development, they were determined to accept nothing less than full political and economic emancipation, goals which they thought the clergy incapable of achieving.

The tasks they thus set themselves were formidable. Although change was in the air, the political life of Transylvania still bore the stamp of the preceding century. The diet and country government continued to be controlled by the landowning nobility or gentry, which was Magyar, and by the urban bourgeoisie, which was Saxon and, to a lesser extent, Magyar. As before, policy was shaped by the central bureaucracy in Vienna. Prospective office-holders still had to satisfy not only social but also religious criteria, since membership in one of the privileged churches—Roman Catholic, Calvinist, Lutheran, or Unitarian—was mandatory, if one hoped for advancement.

The economy of Transylvania during the period was also to a great extent rooted in the past. The great majority of the population continued to depend in one way or another on agriculture for a livelihood. But the land produced far short of its potential, since the methods used to work it had remained undisturbed by innovation. Only here and there on larger estates were new techniques or capitalist forms of organization being introduced. The majority of peasant holdings were small, the strips scattered and the tools primitive, and, because of myriad taxes and other burdens, there was little incentive to increase production.

On all counts—political, religious, and economic—the Romanians remained at the bottom of the social scale. They were not represented in the diet as a nation. Indeed, in a body dominated by the Magyars and, to a lesser extent, the Saxons, there was only one Romanian deputy—the Uniate bishop—who owed his seat not to his nationality but to his status as a large landowner. Few Romanians were members of county committees or city councils, and only a handful had positions in the provincial administration. Their Uniate or Orthodox faith continued to be as severe a liability as their 'plebeian' social origin. In sum, the Romanians were treated as a *Bauernvolk*, and thus, in accordance with tradition, were excluded from public affairs.

Nevertheless, the Transylvania of the 1830s and 1840s was hardly immobile. In economic life, the number of capitalist manufacturing enterprises (joint-stock companies) was slowly increasing, steam-driven machinery in mining and agriculture was gradually being introduced, and a few machine shops had been established. The urban population was growing steadily, if undramatically. All this activity was still modest and before 1848 did not affect the general character of Transylvania as an agricultural country. But reform had become a public matter, as a stratum of the Magyar middle nobility, which had entered the professions or had taken up politics, led an increasingly vocal and effective movement to end the feudal remnants of Transylvanian economic and political life. Inspired by the liberal ideas of István Széchenyi and other representatives of the Reform Era in Hungary, they demanded the abolition of both serfdom and the restrictive powers of the artisan guilds. They also strove to make political institutions more responsive to the will of the country at large and to accord equal rights of citizenship to all inhabitants. In their zeal to emulate the reformers in Hungary proper they paid little attention to the political boundaries between the two countries. For them, there could be only a single Hungarian problem, and as the 1840s progressed they demanded with growing vehemence the union of Transylvania with Hungary and the institution of Magyar as the language of administration and education.[21] This movement of political and economic liberalism and national self-determination was to touch Romanian intellectuals in varied and contradictory ways.

The small contingent of intellectuals who had assumed leadership of the Romanians were the spiritual heirs of the Transylvanian School, but they held to a conception of society and of social change which differed strikingly from that of their forebears. The generation which reached maturity between 1830 and 1848 strove to bring the Romanians into the broad currents of European economic and cultural life. They provided the theoretical underpinnings of the modern Romanian national movement, and in the revolutionary spring of 1848 they formulated the first comprehensive, modern national programme.

These intellectuals also drew Romanian thought into a closer communion with Western Europe than ever before. Their own ideas betrayed a distinctly Western and modern spirit. Yet, they were not Westernized. Their particular world of ideas owed much to a native tradition, which was itself a unique blend of, sometimes, contradictory traditions: the Western European, especially the Enlightenment in its Austro-German form, Romanticism, and liberalism; the Orthodox, which had combined the primal resources of a traditional rural world with the religious forms and spirituality of Byzantium; and, finally, the Transylvanian, a complex of political, social, and cultural forms to which all the peoples of the principality had contributed since the Middle Ages. Nor can contacts with the principalities of Moldavia and Wallachia be ignored. Mainly religious before the nineteenth century, they became an important reinforcement of national feeling on both sides of the Carpathians beginning in the 1830s.

Despite their diverse intellectual origins, the generation of 1848, as they are usually known, had no hesitation in proclaiming itself a part of Europe. Its members saw their own strivings as merely one aspect of a general European movement to foster political and social progress, and they sought to draw closer to the models they had discovered in French, German, and English thought. Yet at the same time they maintained a sense of balance. Although they were painfully aware of the contrast between the backwardness of their own world and the rationality and enlightenment prevailing in the West, in their eagerness to catch up they avoided the anarchy of wholesale imitation, preferring instead to shape borrowings and adapt aspirations to Transylvanian realities.

This generation belonged, on the whole, to the humbler ranks of society. With only a few exceptions, they came from the educated classes of the village and maintained a sentimental attachment to the rural world long after they had entered upon urban careers. They all received formal educations that were exceptional for Romanians of that period, although, as a rule, they did not go beyond the gymnasium. A few had specialized training in theology, philosophy, or law. In a sense, they were also self-taught. Omnivorous reading endowed

[21] *Erdély története*, iii. 1267–306.

them with a broad general culture, as is evident from the variety of problems—political, economic, social, and philosophical—they boldly undertook to solve.[22]

They earned their livings from the liberal professions—secondary school teaching, law, and journalism. It is indicative of the state of mind of this generation that as a whole they were not attracted to the priesthood. Although they had all been exposed in greater or lesser degree to theology and other religious studies and several became priests, only one made the church his career. They thus present a striking contrast to their intellectual forebears of the eighteenth century, the majority of whom had been priests. This new attitude towards organized religion in the 1830s and 1840s was a reflection of economic and social processes that had been under way in Transylvania and the Habsburg monarchy as a whole since the turn of the century. The Romanians, though economically less favoured than the other peoples of the principality, were none the less experiencing a similar breakdown of traditional patterns of behaviour and the same secularization of social life.

The intellectual interests of the Romanian generation of 1848 were wide-ranging. They were receptive to new ideas, regardless of origin, and there was hardly a discipline—history, philology, philosophy, literature, folklore, education, natural science—that failed to attract their attention. Yet, they were not satisfied merely to play with ideas, for they were committed to the resolution of immediate political and economic problems. Indeed, they felt a moral obligation to confront day-to-day realities, and, as a consequence, their writings generally bear the stamp of practicality.

They did not create works of great originality, nor, with rare exceptions, did they seek to become expert in some specialized domain of thought. Rather, they were preoccupied with the dissemination of general ideas and useful information. In their view, these were tasks better suited to the needs of Romanian society than the elaboration of abstract treatises on philosophy or learned works of history. Undoubtedly, the lingering tradition of the Enlightenment and their own didactic inclinations had much to do with the high value they placed on reason and practical knowledge. These concerns also account for their intense journalistic activity. In their hands the press became a powerful instrument for mobilizing support for political and social change.

Romanian thought in the period before the revolution of 1848 does not lend itself easily to categorization. The world-view of the intellectuals was an amalgam of Western influences and indigenous realities which can be broken down into its components only with difficulty. None the less, several trends are discernible which suggest an attachment to the major currents of Western thought of the latter part of the eighteenth century and the early decades of the nineteenth.

[22] G. Barițiu, *Părți alese din istoria Transilvaniei*, ii (Sibiu, 1890), 70–1; G. E. Marica, *Studii de istoria și sociologia culturii române ardelene din secolul al xix-lea*, i (Cluj-Napoca, 1977), 19–54; S. Dragomir, *Studii și documente privitoare la revoluția Românilor din Transilvania în anii 1848–49*, ii (Sibiu, 1944), 144–60.

The heritage of the Enlightenment was still present, but at the same time the intellectuals displayed an affinity for the sentimentality and *élan* of Romanticism and joined enthusiastically in the promotion of economic and political liberalism.

An attempt to classify the generation of 1848 as enlightened, Romantic, or liberal may profitably begin with an examination of their reception of Western philosophy. They sought in philosophy the bedrock upon which to found a new social and political order in Transylvania and to ensure the progress of the Romanian nation. As a group, they did not construct original systems. Rather, their writings took the form of translations, adaptations, and commentaries, intended, in the first instance, as teaching materials. To be sure, they wrote numerous essays containing original thoughts on such fundamental human problems as life and death, morality, and truth, but these works were not abstract excursions into the realm of ideas; they were meant to serve as elucidations of some pressing social problem and as a call to action. The dearth of abstract philosophical discourse may be explained in part by the eminently practical tasks they assigned to ideas—social reform and the awakening of the Romanian nation to a sense of its own dignity and historical mission—and in part by the absence of a native philosophical tradition. For Romanians in the eighteenth century philosophical speculation had meant theology. Then, too, Romanian intellectuals had come almost exclusively from the ranks of the clergy, and their writings reflected traditional Christian teachings about the ultimate questions of man's existence. Even Samuil Micu, Gheorghe Şincai, and Petru Maior, whose interests ranged far beyond theology, showed little inclination to follow Western patterns of metaphysical enquiry. It fell to the generation of 1848 to create a philosophical tradition separate from theology in a society which could offer little stimulus or criticism for pure adventures in ideas.

The philosophical thought of the intellectuals reveals the extent of their debt to the West. The greatest single influence was undoubtedly Kant, not so much directly as through the interpretations of his system by his successor at the chair of philosophy at Königsberg, Wilhelm Traugott Krug.[23] A measure of Krug's (and Kant's) popularity among the Romanians lies in the four translations of his works made in the 1830s and 1840s. Krug owed his popularity to the critical and anti-dogmatic attitude he had absorbed from Kant. Such a stance encouraged Romanian intellectuals to persevere in their opposition both to the political status quo in Transylvania in general and to the clerical dominance of cultural life within their own nation in particular. They were also drawn to Krug by his emphasis on the ethical content of thought, for, like most Romanians of the day, they judged the national awakening to be essentially a moral cause.

---

[23] A. Andea, 'Cultura românească şi filozofia kantiană în prima jumătate a secolului al xix-lea', *Anuarul Institutului de Istorie şi Arheologie Cluj-Napoca*, 22 (1979), 157–78; I. Petrescu, 'Un discipol paşoptist al lui W. T. Krug: Aron Pumnul', *Studia Universitatis Babeş-Bolyai*, philological ser., fasciculus 1 (1968), 89–97.

The Romanians preferred Krug to the master probably because he was less abstract, less speculative, and more concerned with the application of ideas to the solution of social problems. Practicality was a quality Romanian intellectuals greatly admired, for they understood their own function in society—the fostering of political, economic, and cultural development—in concrete terms. Like Krug, they conceived of philosophy as offering the ultimate principles upon which individuals could make their own judgements as to what was good and true and eternal. They taught that the aim of philosophy was to organize the data of experience and provide the criteria of truth. For the generation of 1848, then, it provided a guide to action, a means of evaluating the customs and institutions of their own time.

The rationalism and empiricism of Kant, as interpreted by Krug, received their most forceful expression among the Romanians of Transylvania in the writings of Simion Bărnuţiu (1808–64), who taught philosophy at the secondary schools of Blaj and was to become the chief theorist of Romanian nationhood during the revolution of 1848. He was the only one of his generation to engage in original philosophical speculation.[24] Yet he, too, displayed the same practical bent that was the hallmark of the Romanian intellectual of the time. He was less interested in working out philosophical problems than in using the indispensable perspective it afforded for the analysis and solution of political and social problems. Like other members of his generation, he saw in philosophy an instrument which, if properly used, could bring about beneficial changes in society. For him, therefore, the tasks of philosophy were the cultivation of reason and the investigation of human nature in order to reveal to man what he was and what he should become—a rational, free being endowed with inalienable rights. In this vein, Bărnuţiu argued that philosophy by its very nature had to concern itself with the aspirations of contemporary man and should, therefore, have unlimited freedom to examine all aspects of individual and social behaviour. He was particularly eager to separate philosophy from theology, which he regarded as barren and ill-attuned to the realities of modern life. For these reasons he was convinced that theology could not serve modern man as the basis of his ethical system. Instead, he equated the moral responsibility of the individual with the promotion of the general welfare.

The extent to which Romanian intellectuals in Transylvania participated in the Romantic movement is more open to question than their attachment to the ideals of the Enlightenment. They did not join in the revolt against the rationalism and materialism of the Enlightenment which occurred in Western and parts of Eastern Europe after 1790.[25] The irrational did not attract them, except,

---

[24] D. Ghişe and P. Teodor, 'Contribuţii la cunoaşterea activităţii filozofice a lui Simion Bărnuţiu', *Revista de filozofie*, 11/3 (1964), 357–69.

[25] D. Popovici, *Romantismul românesc* (Bucharest, 1969), 326–38. O. Papadima, *Ipostaze ale iluminismului românesc* (Bucharest, 1975), 324–60, contests the existence of a Romantic current among the Romanians of Transylvania.

perhaps to the extent that they took an interest in folklore. Rather, as we have seen, they prized reason as the prime instrument for bringing about social and cultural progress, and they accepted the idea of the world as essentially rational. For them, the structure of this rational world had merely been obscured by centuries of tradition and ignorance. Their task, then, as they saw it, was not to create a wholly new order of society but to reveal the beneficent principles upon which the old had been established.

An important feature of Romanticism generally was the cult of the past and of the exotic. Remote times and places offered the Romantic a refuge from reality or a source of creative inspiration. He was often driven to repeat or to try to reawaken the past to new life. Romanian intellectuals, to be sure, shared this attraction to the past; it was responsible for ethnic individuality and it supplied arguments on behalf of national rights. They took pride in their descent from the Romans and in their Latin linguistic heritage, but their commitment to the past was not uncritical. They were too acutely aware of the decline that their nation had suffered in preceding centuries to seek to resurrect the past. Moreover, they subscribed wholeheartedly to the idea of progress, and they thus turned confidently to the future expecting to fulfil all their aspirations.

Egoism of the sort cultivated by the Romantics of Western Europe who assumed an intense individualism as a manner of being and an end in itself, was muted among the Romanians. Concern for the collectivity, for the nation as a whole and a sense of responsibility to promote the general welfare overcame whatever inclination to personal self-indulgence they might have felt. Introspection was by no means absent, but it was intermittent and took second place to their concerns for society as a whole.

Scholars have attributed the flight of Western Romantics—especially the Germans—from the present at least in part to a feeling that they were superfluous men who had no useful contribution to make to existing society. They cite as the primary cause of this sense of inadequacy their virtual exclusion from the political life of the German states. Romanian intellectuals had a quite different vision of their place in society. Their commitment to a national revival focused their energies on tangible goals and saved them from the debilitating effects of inactivity and prolonged self-doubt. It is also worth remembering that the role of the Romanian intellectual in Transylvania was intrinsically different from that of his German counterpart in Prussia or most of the other German states. Although men like Bărnuţiu were effectively excluded from political life and, hence, had little, if any, influence on the shaping of public policy, they none the less enjoyed high standing within the Romanian community. As thinkers and writers in a society that was largely illiterate they were called intellectuals and were accorded positions of honour and leadership.

The Romantic spirit was not without influence among Romanian intellectuals. The enthusiasm and idealism which pervaded their sense of social mission would otherwise be inexplicable. They were clearly caught up in the spirit of the times. In Avram Iancu (1824–72), a young lawyer and later the chief Romanian military hero of the Revolution of 1848, the Romantic *élan* of the national revival perhaps achieved its most forceful expression. He shared fully the aspirations of Young Europe that were manifesting themselves throughout the continent in the decade before the revolution. Like his contemporaries in Ireland or Poland, he accepted without question the creative power of ideas, especially of those that were expressed in the rallying cry 'Liberty, Equality and Fraternity', and he did not for a moment doubt their power to transform European realities. Moreover, he possessed an abiding faith in the common sense and fundamental goodness of the peasant masses, an idea rarely encountered among Romanian intellectuals before the advent of Romanticism. Unlike the generation of the Enlightenment who saw in the peasantry a force opposed to reason and progress and one that had nothing to offer the educated, Iancu and his colleagues prized the simplicity of the rural world.

Romanticism thus had wide appeal, but it was too diffuse a current among the Romanians of Transylvania for us to be able to speak about a movement. Nevertheless, a few generalizations are possible. In a social sense, Romanian Romantics belonged to the liberal camp. Theirs was the Romanticism espoused in France by Victor Hugo, which had as its goals the creation of a sense of responsibility towards all classes and the general reform of society based upon strong ethical ideals. It was also the social Romanticism of Felicité Robert de Lamennais, of the Lamennais of the *Paroles d'un croyant* (1834), with its overwhelming concern for humanity and compassion for the sufferings of the poor and its advocacy of a practical religion that would bring about goodness and progress in this world.[26] This variety of Romanticism, not the current of sentimentalism, exoticism, and egoism, attracted the Romanians, a Romanticism which brought the educated closer to the masses in a spirit of mutual trust and understanding.

Liberalism was the third major European movement of ideas to touch Romanian intellectuals in Transylvania. Their preoccupation with national goals imbued their brand of liberalism with a collectivist character. Like liberals elsewhere in Europe, they, too, advocated individual freedom, but the long struggle to free their nation from subordination to outsiders had obliged them to put the interests of the community ahead of individual rights. This stand lies at the heart of their response to Hungarian liberalism in 1848.

The ideas of the Reform Era in Hungary of the 1830s and 1840s also had a strong leavening effect on Romanian liberal thought. The efforts of István Széchenyi to modify economic and social relations in Hungary (and Transylvania) by limiting peasant dues and labour services, by making the nobility responsible for bearing part of the tax and military service burden, and by stimulating economic development aroused much enthusiasm among Romanian

[26] I. Breazu, 'Lamennais la Românii din Transilvania în 1848', *Studii literare*, 4 (1948), 176–97.

intellectuals. They could foresee only an improvement in the condition of their people from such a thorough overhaul of the status quo. Furthermore, Széchenyi's moderation and emphasis upon legal, constitutional means satisfied their commitment to orderly change.[27]

Another current of Magyar liberalism—that represented by Lajos Kossuth and the more radical reformers of the 1840s—found little support among Romanian intellectuals. Unlike Széchenyi, who was a moderate on the nationality question, Kossuth and his followers were alarmed by the national awakenings of the Romanians and Slavs, viewing them as a threat to the territorial integrity of Hungary and the very existence of the Magyar nation. To combat their alleged centrifugal tendencies, Kossuth urged the assimilation of the non-Magyars as rapidly as possible through the introduction of Magyar as the language of public administration and as the language of instruction and an obligatory subject of study in schools. In Transylvania the advocates of assimilation in the diet enacted a language law in 1842 which mandated the use of Magyar in government and the judiciary at every level and even in the Romanian Uniate and Orthodox Churches' administrations and schools.

Romanian intellectuals were nearly unanimous in their condemnation of the law. Bărnuţiu, declaring language to be man's most precious possession, wrote that the character and nationality of a people were based upon language, and, if deprived of it, they would lose both.[28] Others denounced the law as an attempt to destroy the moral and spiritual fibre of the Romanian nation. Although the law never went into effect, the animosity it had aroused between Romanians and Magyars revealed a fundamental incompatibility between liberalism and national strivings. Yet, the commitment of the Romanians to liberal ideals remained unshaken, and a basis for cooperation with like-minded Magyars survived the language controversy.

Romanian intellectuals were by and large economic liberals. They advocated the least possible restraints on economic activity, arguing for competition among producers, the dissolution of the craft guilds, the elimination of internal and foreign tariffs, and the abolition of serfdom. In a positive vein, they favoured the rapid expansion of modern, capitalist forms of production in all branches of the economy, especially in industry.[29] George Bariţiu (1812–93), the founder in 1838 of the newspaper *Gazeta de Transilvania*, and of its literary supplement *Foaia pentru minte, inimă şi literatură* (the principal organs of Romanian intellectuals), and their editor until 1850, was convinced that economic life in the future would be dominated by large-scale manufacturing enterprises—the factory system— which would be capable of producing greater quantities of goods more efficiently

[27] FM 4/40 (1841), 313–15.

[28] S. Bărnuţiu, 'Un document pentru limba română din an 1842', FM 16/38 (1853), 285–8, and 16/39. 295–8. Because of the censorship, the article could not be printed in 1842, when Bărnuţiu submitted it.

[29] G. E. Marica et al., *Ideologia generaţiei române de la 1848 din Transilvania* (Bucharest, 1968), 237–50.

and cheaply than any previous system. He also grasped the importance of a flourishing commerce, upon which both industry and agriculture ultimately depended for markets and raw materials. Not surprisingly, he and most of his colleagues expressed unreserved admiration for the bourgeoisie of Western Europe as the most creative and modern of social classes.

The *laissez-faire* character of their economic thought is evident also in their treatment of the problem of poverty. They denounced it as an evil and displayed the most touching sympathy for those afflicted by it. They also railed against the privileges of aristocrats and landowners, whom they held responsible for the widespread misery in the countryside. But they showed little inclination to regulate individual economic activity in the interest of society as a whole. Quite the contrary. Bariţiu, for example, accepted the major tenet of modern industrialism: to produce as many goods as efficiently as possible. He urged a new dynamism, a greater intensity in economic life and the inculcation in workers and entrepreneurs alike of the spirit of gain and acquisitiveness. Thus, he and his colleagues discovered the solution to economic underdevelopment in intelligence, individualism, and enthusiasm.

The economic ideas of Romanian intellectuals undoubtedly owed much to the general tenets of liberalism they had absorbed from foreign sources. But to a greater degree their thought was moulded by prevailing conditions in Transylvania and by their own efforts to bring about a national regeneration. They were convinced that any change in the existing economic organization of Transylvania could not but benefit the Romanians. Their attitude towards the guild system is a case in point. They urged the abolition of the guilds, first, because they were anachronisms incapable of meeting the productive needs of modern society, and, second, because they were the means by which the Magyars and Saxons continued to exclude the Romanians from commerce and the crafts and thereby maintain their monopoly over economic life. They also hoped that the abolition of the guilds would hasten the creation of a prosperous Romanian middle class, the absence of which, in their view, had deprived their nation of the modern leadership Western Europe enjoyed. They had no doubt that Transylvania would follow the same path of development as Western Europe, and the notion that the Romanians could achieve progress by remaining an agrarian society was utterly foreign to them.

CHURCH AND NATION

The attitude of the intellectuals towards the Orthodox and Uniate Churches and towards religion in general reveals an interweaving of rationalist and liberal thought with the pursuit of national goals. Religion had ceased to be the dominant spiritual and ethical force in their lives. On the basis of the rationalism they had absorbed from the Enlightenment and from Krug and other Western philosophers and inspired also by the social Romanticism of Lamennais, they had arrived at a new moral code related to but distinct from traditional Christianity. It had a general human character and was based on the natural attributes of man —reason and common sense—and on faith in his innate goodness and unlimited perfectibility. Among the virtues it extolled were tolerance, a sense of justice, and a commitment to social change. Although the intellectuals seldom mentioned religious doctrine, their attitude towards the church and its teachings was not determined solely by humanitarian and rationalist theory. Social realities appear to have been decisive.

Although the majority of the generation of 1848 found the teachings of the church largely irrelevant to contemporary political and economic life, they did not seek to abolish organized religion. Nor did they embrace atheism. Rather, they continued to attend church and to observe traditional religious customs. Their attitude cannot be described as anticlerical either because they had no desire to exclude the clergy from the movement of national regeneration or from the prosperous and enlightened society that they intended to build. But they thought of the church mainly as a social institution. Recognizing the immense services it had rendered the nation in the past as the preserver of language and customs, they were eager to put its resources to use in the national cause. In the modern world, they argued, the role of the church could no longer simply be that of a repository of past treasures; it must commit itself to the solution of contemporary problems and must become a truly national institution, as responsive to the material needs as to the spiritual welfare of its faithful.

To transform the church into an instrument of social change, the intellectuals strove to gain a greater voice in its affairs. They became advocates of 'representative church government', of reforms that would grant laymen a decisive role in all matters except doctrine and ritual. The Uniates, led by Bărnuţiu and Bariţiu, demanded the restoration of the diocesan synod, a body composed of both laymen and clergy, as the supreme governing body of the church. In a newspaper article in 1843 Bărnuţiu demanded an end to one-man rule by the bishop and recognition of the principle of representative government and rule by the majority.[30] Orthodox laymen raised similar demands during the election of a new bishop in 1847. They objected to the domination of this national event by the higher clergy as contrary to both canon law and the spirit of the times.

To make the church a more effective instrument of the national revival the intellectuals strove to 'liberate' the Uniate and Orthodox Churches from Hungarian Roman Catholic and Serbian Orthodox 'domination' respectively. As we have seen, since the establishment of their church in 1700, Romanian Uniates had stubbornly resisted attempts by the court of Vienna and the Hungarian Roman Catholic hierarchy to bring them into a closer communion with the Latin rite. Now, in the decade before the revolution of 1848, Uniate intellectuals

---

[30] S. Bărnuţiu, 'Săborul cel mare al episcopiei Făgăraşului', FM 6/4 (1843), 26–9; 6/5, 33–7.

viewed with alarm the increasing use of the Magyar language in church administration and schools as evidence of continued Hungarian Catholic designs upon
the autonomy of their church. The history of the Romanian Orthodox Church
was even less encouraging for the intellectuals, for even though Joseph II and his
successors had allowed a regular church organization to function, the bishops had
exercised little freedom of action. The state closely supervised its affairs, and in
matters of both doctrine and administration the diocese of Transylvania remained
subordinate to the Serbian metropolitanate of Karlowitz. Such a situation was
intolerable for the intellectuals. They demanded an end to subservience to
foreigners, so that the Romanian churches might at last be able to fulfil their true
social mission.

A new vision of nation had thus become dominant in the thought and
aspirations of the Romanian generation of 1848. Nation was defined not by
religion but by language and history, and it embraced all Romanians, regardless
of class or confession. Although the nation absorbed their energies, Romanian
intellectuals did not feel any the less a part of Europe. Influenced by the heritage
of the Enlightenment and by the Romantic and liberal currents of their own
time, they saw no contradiction between commitment to national goals and
solidarity with all European peoples. They still thought of progress not in terms
of separate ethnic communities but as a general advance of humanity. Such
idealism was to be severely tested by revolution.

BUKOVINA, 1774–1848

The course of development taken by the Romanians in Bukovina differed
significantly from that of the Romanians in Transylvania. In Bukovina no strong
national movement arose. The Orthodox Church as an institution offered no
solid foundation for either political or cultural self-determination, and lay intellectuals were few in number and disunited. The main cause of these conditions
was the nature of the Austrian administration of the territory. It severed political,
economic, and cultural ties with Moldavia, an act which left the Romanians in
Bukovina without national institutions of their own and without the support
necessary to create and foster new institutions.[31] The psychological blow to the
Romanians was equally grave. The Austrian annexation interrupted the continuity of their historical development, rendering them stateless and merely one of
several ethnic groups competing for political and economic survival.

The province of Bukovina had been carved out of 10,000 km² of northern
Moldavia in 1774 when Austrian troops occupied the area. The pretext was to
defend imperial borders from the plague and an invasion of vagabonds and to
open up communications between Transylvania and newly acquired Galicia, but

---

[31] For an extended account of Austrian policy, see M. Iacobescu, *Din istoria Bucovinei*, i. *1774–
1862* (Bucharest, 1993), 93–304.

Austria was also anxious to obtain compensation for Russia's expanded influence in the Romanian principalities after her successful war with the Ottoman Empire. The sultan recognized Austria's possession of the territory in the convention of 7 May 1775.

The court of Vienna kept Bukovina under a military government until 1786 in order to facilitate the transition from Moldavian to Austrian administration. It intended to integrate the new province into the empire as thoroughly as possible and thus showed little interest in preserving Moldavian institutions. At first, Austrian authorities tried to bring as many *boiers* as possible into the provincial administration, but few showed the aptitude or had the necessary social standing required for high office. Here and there *boiers* opposed the new regime outright. They objected particularly to the interference of the authorities in their relations with their peasants and yearned for a revival of Moldavian administration when they were the uncontested masters of the countryside. Although the majority accommodated themselves to the new order of things, as may be seen in the corps of volunteers they organized during the campaigns against the Ottomans in 1788–9 and the French in 1809 and 1813, they continued to harbour grievances against the 'foreign' administration.[32] Perhaps no other single measure provoked such sustained opposition as the administrative subordination of Bukovina to Galicia in 1786, an arrangement that was to last until 1849, when Bukovina was finally recognized as an autonomous crown land. The *boiers* expressed their dissatisfaction in various ways, notably by refusing to attend sessions of the Galician estates, a tactic which, in the end, proved counterproductive because it deprived them of even a modest voice in the affairs of their province. In any case, they were powerless to maintain its Moldavian character. The administrative link with Galicia had opened Bukovina to unprecedented ethnic diversity, especially to Jewish and Ruthenian immigration and, for a time, strong Polish and Roman Catholic influences in education.

The population of Bukovina increased steadily, primarily through immigration, which Austrian authorities encouraged in order to develop the economy.[33] In 1774 the estimated population was 75,000; in 1810 it was 198,000, and in 1848 378,000. The changes in the province's ethnic composition were dramatic. In 1774 the Romanians constituted an overwhelming majority, roughly 64,000 to 8,000 Ruthenians and 3,000 others. By 1810 the Romanian share had fallen from 85 per cent to 75 per cent (150,000 to 48,000 non-Romanians), and in 1848 there were 209,000 Romanians (55 per cent), 109,000 Ruthenians (29 per cent), and 60,000 others (16 per cent). The Jewish population rose from 526 in 1774 to 11,600 in 1848. A few Romanian leaders publicly lamented the dilution

---

[32] E. Prokopowitsch, *Die rumänische Nationalbewegung in der Bukowina und der Dako-romanismus* (Graz, 1965), 35–7.

[33] R. F. Kaindl, *Ansiedlungswesen in der Bukowina seit der Besitzergreifung durch Österreich* (Innsbruck, 1902), 1–71. See also the report on the population, society, and economy of Bukovina by the military governor in 1786 in Hurmuzaki, *Documente*, vii (Bucharest, 1876), 452–73.

of the Romanian character of Bukovina, but they lacked the power to stem the tide of immigration.[34]

The structure of Romanian society in Bukovina in the early decades of Austrian administration was similar to that of Moldavia. But whereas Moldavia underwent significant social and economic change in the 1830s and 1840s, the Romanians of Bukovina experienced little progress. The great majority were peasants. Eighty per cent were dependent upon landlords or monasteries, while the rest were *răzeşi*. Few Romanians practised crafts as a profession. In the countryside peasant families made their own clothes, household items, and farm tools, but in the cities and towns non-Romanians came to monopolize the crafts, while commerce became the preserve of Jews and other non-Romanians. As a consequence, a Romanian middle class was practically non-existent.

No other Romanian institution suffered more acutely under Austrian rule than the Orthodox Church. It caught the full brunt of Joseph II's zeal for order and efficiency, for he was determined to put its clergy and resources at the disposal of the state, as in Transylvania. The first step was to sever its ties with the Moldavian church. In 1781 Austrian officials persuaded the metropolitan of Moldavia to renounce his jurisdiction over the Orthodox of Bukovina, where-upon the bishop of Rădăuţi assumed the title of exempt bishop of Bukovina and moved his residence to Cernăuţi, the new political centre. Since the canon law of the Orthodox Church required bishoprics to be attached to a metropolitanate, Joseph II by decrees in 1783 and 1786 placed the new diocese under the jurisdiction of the Serbian metropolitan of Karlowitz, a link that had never before existed. At the same time the government of Bukovina assumed direction of the church's finances. In 1782 it ordered the closing of fourteen monasteries and the confiscation of their properties, which were used to create the Orthodox Religious Fund, an endowment intended to support various church administrative and philanthropic activities. Only three monasteries—Putna, Suceviţa, and Dragomirna—were spared, but their governance was closely monitored by the state. Other income was added to the fund from the sale of church property in Moldavia and the cession of lands belonging to the old bishopric of Rădăuţi. Although the fund came under the control of non-Romanians and non-Orthodox, it was efficiently managed and provided the wherewithal to make the Bukovinan clergy one of the best educated and the church itself one of the best endowed in the Orthodox world. All these measures were capped by a comprehensive 'Geistlicher Regierungsplan', sanctioned by Joseph II on 29 April 1786, which governed church affairs with only minor changes until 1918.[35] It gave the state a decisive voice at all levels of church administration, effectively curtailing its role as a national institution. Henceforth, parish priests and district protopopes were appointed by the governor upon the recommendation of the bishop, and the bishop himself was appointed directly by the emperor.

---

[34] I. Nistor, *Der nationale Kampf in der Bukowina* (Bucharest, 1919), 90–106, 127–44.
[35] Id., *Istoria bisericii din Bucovina* (Bucharest, 1916), 9–12.

The connection with the Serbian metropolitanate and the steady tide of Ruthenian immigration had serious consequences for the national character of the church. During the episcopate of Daniel Vlahovici (Vlahović) (1789–1822), a Serb from Karlowitz, the Ruthenian language was introduced into the church service in areas settled by Ruthenians, especially between the Prut and Dniester Rivers, and Ruthenian priests were recruited for the new parishes. For Vlahovici, the essential problem was the welfare of Orthodoxy; the language used to propagate its teachings and the nationality of its priests were secondary. But even his Romanian successors, notably Eugen Hacman (1835–73), could not afford to subordinate the church to Romanian national interests for fear of alienating the Ruthenians and thereby weakening Orthodoxy in its struggles with the Uniate movement originating in Galicia.

As with the church, so with the schools. In fostering education, Austrian authorities in Vienna and Cernăuţi were primarily concerned with the administrative and economic needs of the province and neglected the specific interests of the Romanian and Orthodox majority. Shortly after the annexation, in 1777, a provincial school fund was created, but its resources were used to establish and maintain German and, later, Latin schools, a programme which lasted essentially unchanged until the 1840s.[36] The first such schools were the two *Hauptschule* in Cernăuţi and Suceava, in which the language of instruction was German, although courses in the Romanian language were available. The *Hauptschule* in Cernăuţi had the additional responsibility of training teachers, but few Romanians attended. Both the Orthodox clergy and the population at large showed a keen mistrust of innovations, especially when they were the work of foreigners. In 1785 of 68 pupils attending the *Hauptschule* in Cernăuţi, only 5 were Romanian. Yet, the Romanians made some progress. Their numbers at the German gymnasium in Cernăuţi, which opened in 1808, were large (10 out of 24 students in the first class), even though the language of instruction was German (except for classes in the Orthodox religion, which were taught in Romanian). Completion of studies at the gymnasium enabled Romanians to attend institutions of higher learning throughout the empire, an opportunity they had not previously enjoyed.

The administrative subordination of Bukovina to Galicia in 1786 proved detrimental to Romanian education. In 1793 the government council in Lemberg relieved communes in Bukovina of the responsibility of building and maintaining schools. The immediate result was a decline in the number of Romanian village schools, as the majority of taxpayers showed no inclination to support education voluntarily. Apparently, Roman Catholic Church authorities in Galicia, who supervised education in Bukovina, were primarily responsible for this abrupt change in educational policy. They may have sought in this way to promote Polish Roman Catholic or Ruthenian Uniate schools at the expense of

---

[36] Id., *Istoria fondului bisericesc din Bucovina* (Cernăuţi, 1921), 20–41.

the Orthodox, in which they obviously had no interest. Roman Catholic influence over the educational system continued to grow after the turn of the century. Two imperial decrees in 1815 dealt a severe blow to Romanian and other Orthodox schools by placing all didactic and administrative matters in the hands of the Roman Catholic consistory in Lemberg, which made the appointment of Roman Catholic teachers mandatory in all schools whenever a vacancy occurred. Since the few Romanian village schools then in existence were always short of teachers, the new policy meant that persons who did not know Romanian, usually Poles from Galicia, would have the responsibility of teaching Romanian children. One of the consequences was a decline in attendance.

The Catholicization and Germanization of education continued largely unimpeded until the appointment of Eugen Hacman as bishop in 1835. In 1837 he submitted a long memorial to the Emperor Ferdinand (1835–48) in which he recited the shortcomings of Romanian Orthodox education.[37] He was particularly distressed by the large number of candidates for the priesthood entering the Orthodox Theological Academy in Cernăuți, which had been established in 1826, and who were destined for Romanian parishes, but could not read Romanian because they had studied only German or Polish in elementary and secondary schools. Attributing this unfortunate situation to the neglect of Romanian interests on the part of the provincial government, he proposed that the school fund, which had been created with contributions from the Romanian clergy, be used to establish a network of schools throughout the province in which the teachers would be Orthodox who knew Romanian. To ensure success he recommended that the Orthodox bishop be given jurisdiction over the new schools. The bureaucracy in Vienna took no action on his project until 1844, when the emperor approved in principle the main points Hacman had raised. But it took the turbulence of 1848 to bring the bishop's proposals to fruition. The Orthodox Church gained the right at last to administer its own Religious Fund and to supervise the elementary and secondary schools which it financed. Romanian became the language of instruction in all rural elementary schools, except between the Prut and the Dniester, where Ruthenian was to be used. The overall effect on Romanian education was beneficial, but progress was painfully slow during the second half of the century.

Romanian intellectual life in Bukovina presents a striking contrast to that in Transylvania. Literary activity and scholarship were modest in volume and lacking in originality. *Belles-lettres* was limited to the copying of manuscripts of various popular books such as the Legend of Alexander the Great and the Trojan War. There were also school manuals, most of which were printed in Vienna, and a few practical grammars and bilingual dictionaries, but no histories of the Romanians and no original linguistic works.[38]

---

[37] I. V. Goraș, *Învățămîntul românesc în ținutul Sucevei, 1775–1918* (Bucharest, 1975), 58–61.
[38] C. Loghin, *Istoria literaturii române din Bucovina, 1775–1918* (Cernăuți, 1926), 12–22.

A Romanian national movement did not exist. National sentiment was kept alive among the small *boier* upper class through contacts with family members and, occasionally, with leading political figures in Moldavia, as in 1821, when large numbers of *boiers* fled to Bukovina to escape the consequences of the Hetairist movement. But the propagation of ideas about the common ethnic and cultural heritage of the Romanians was left to a handful of intellectuals.[39] Only one literary and cultural society existed—Societatea Literară în Eparhia Bucovinei (Literary Society in the Eparchy of Bukovina), which was founded in 1846 and whose members were priests and church administrators. It accomplished nothing worthy of note and by 1850 had disbanded. Nor were there Romanian newspapers. A modest proposal in 1817 by Teodor Racoce, a translator for the government council in Lemberg, to publish a Romanian gazette came to nothing, mainly, it seems, because of the lack of interest and financial support from his fellow Bukovinans.[40]

The absence of a vigorous intellectual life and of a strong national movement among the Romanians of Bukovina was primarily the result of their separation from their traditional cultural and religious centres in Moldavia and their absorption into a foreign, mainly German, social and cultural world. The court of Vienna and the imperial bureaucracy actively promoted this separation by severing old ecclesiastical ties between Moldavia and Bukovina, by discouraging the importation of publications from the Romanian principalities, and by promoting education in German. The one national institution which the Romanians possessed—the Orthodox Church—was dominated by a foreign bureaucracy and led by ecclesiastics who had little understanding of the new idea of nation and, hence, were unable to provide the same cultural and political leadership as the church in Transylvania. There were too few Romanian intellectuals and public-spirited *boiers* to compensate for the lack of clerical leadership and to establish and maintain other institutions capable of promoting national interests. Organized political activity had to await the Revolution of 1848.

[39] T. Bălan, *Refugiaţii moldoveni în Bucovina, 1821 şi 1848* (Bucharest, 1929), 12–16; N. Iorga, *Histoire des Roumains de Bucovine* (Jassy, 1917), 76–81.

[40] Iacobescu, *Din istoria Bucovinei*, i. 344–8.

6
1848

FOR Romanian intellectuals, 1848 signified the triumph of the idea of nation. In both the principalities and the Habsburg monarchy they justified demands for independence or political autonomy by invoking the inherent right of the ethnic community to self-determination. In Moldavia and Wallachia they sought to throw off the Russian protectorate and to restore the historical equilibrium with the Ottoman Empire, and in Transylvania, the adjoining Banat region of Hungary, and Bukovina they undertook to unite all Romanians in a single, autonomous 'duchy'. They even contemplated a union of all Romanians on both sides of the Carpathians, for they felt strongly the bonds of ethnicity, language, and culture. But such thoughts were fleeting, as political realities, notably the pragmatism of Russia and Austria, constantly intruded upon hypotheses and reveries. Yet, the idealism of the forty-eighters persisted, never more so than in the sense of solidarity they felt with the other small nations of Europe struggling to free themselves from the rule of others. This particular sense of community owed much to Western thought and example, and, thus, 1848 also serves as a measure of the Romanians' integration into Europe.

MOLDAVIA AND WALLACHIA

The Revolution of 1848 in the Romanian principalities was primarily the work of liberal intellectuals, the *paşoptişti* (forty-eighters), who had come to maturity in the 1830s and 1840s. It was they who initiated it, defined its goals, and gave it direction. Leadership was theirs almost by default. It could not come from a commercial and industrial middle class, which was small and lacked cohesion. It was, rather, the generation of 1848, committed to change in political and economic organization and animated by an optimistic vision of the future, who gave theoretical coherence to the aspirations of diverse classes.

The forty-eighters were a remarkably homogeneous group. They belonged to the *boier* class, though generally not to the highest ranks or the oldest families, and they had benefited from similar educational opportunities, which were the prerogatives of their class. After completing their formal education they could expect to pursue careers in the army, a favourite occupation of their class, or enter the middle levels of the government bureaucracy, the paths taken by previous generations of *boiers*' sons.

The generation of 1848 was set apart from its predecessors by its first-hand acquaintance with Western Europe. The majority had gone to France to complete their studies, but a few, like Mihail Kogălniceanu, had taken their degrees at a German university.[1] In any case, their spiritual second home was Paris. Here, besides attending classes, they met leading figures of French intellectual and political life and the representatives of the subject nationalities of Eastern Europe. They formed societies to promote a national culture and to discuss the great political and social issues of the day, and they drew up ambitious plans for reform at home.

The Romanian forty-eighters felt themselves to be a part of Europe. They recognized the West as a political and cultural model for their own part of Europe and had few doubts that its pattern of development was applicable to the principalities. Their ideas about political forms and economic progress were thus greatly influenced by the liberal and *laissez-faire* doctrines of the day. It is by no means coincidental that they turned to liberal rather than conservative solutions for the problems that beset their two countries. Any type of authoritarian rule, however enlightened, could have little appeal for men intent upon freeing their people from 'autocratic' Russia and 'despotic' Turkey and eager to broaden citizen participation in public affairs.

Despite their admiration for the West, the forty-eighters were not abstract thinkers who sought to impose institutions upon their people that had little relation to historical experience. On the contrary, keenly aware of conditions at home, they were highly selective in their application of Western theory and practice. But the contrasts between the principalities and the West, which became more striking as their knowledge of Europe deepened, made them impatient to begin the work of reform and to make up for lost time.

The members of the generation of 1848, like the reforming *boiers* before them, were distinguished by a critical attitude towards existing institutions and customs. Attacks on the establishment were, as we have seen, far from novel occurrences. *Boiers* of all ranks had indulged in the practice with passion and enthusiasm. But they had rarely called into question the prevailing social order and had shunned genuine innovation, preferring instead to return to an earlier era when their own rights and privileges had been inviolate. The forty-eighters, by contrast, intended to right wrongs. For them, no institution was sacrosanct.

The Wallachians were more aggressive and more uncompromising in their demands for reforms than their Moldavian colleagues. The cause seems to lie in the greater social differentiation in Wallachia, where the lower *boier* ranks and the fledgling middle class were larger and more cohesive and had become more active politically. In Moldavia, on the other hand, the landed, conservative aristocracy continued to dominate political and social life.

Characteristic of the radical thought of Wallachian intellectuals in the decade before the outbreak of the revolution was the critique of Wallachian society by Alexandru C. Golescu (1815–73). The son of the great *boier* Dinicu Golescu, he had studied at the Collège de France in Paris between 1835 and 1838. When he

[1] D. Berindei, *Cultura naţională română modernă* (Bucharest, 1986), 432–43.

returned home he had been shocked by the disparity in the economic level and the spirit of enterprise between his own country and Western Europe. The misery of the peasant moved him deeply. He pointed out in a letter from Paris to his brothers in 1835 that the peasant was not free, as they had thought, for he could not leave the landlord's estate without permission, a boon which was never granted, because of the shortage of labour. At the other end of the social scale, he found the *boier* class, as he knew it in Bucharest, undeserving of its privileges. He thought it intolerable that 90 per cent of the population should have to endure the extremes of poverty in order to provide luxury for such a lot that had given itself over to 'sensualism, vice, and egoism'. For him, the model of a true *boier* was his father, who was always ready to commit his own wealth to the general welfare. He urged a thorough overhaul of the existing social and economic system, but he acknowledged that to carry out such fundamental reforms as the granting of land in full ownership to the peasantry would require enormous amounts of money that were simply not to be had. Even the patriotic *boiers*, he lamented, were deep in debt, for while they possessed great estates, they could not cultivate them, because of the inadequate supply of labour.[2]

The forty-eighters were also distinguished from previous generations by a singular devotion to national goals. They were guided by a new conception of nation, as defined by the circle around *Dacia literară*, which encompassed all Wallachians and Moldavians, regardless of social class, who would henceforth share in all the benefits as well as bear the burdens of the community. Their thought was remarkably free of narrow class interests. Although the reforms they advocated would benefit the burgeoning middle class and the liberal *boiers*, they did not consciously place the interests of one class ahead of those of another. Sustained by a romantic idealism and, in the spring of 1848, caught up in the enthusiasm of a new world apparently in the making, they turned their attention to the rapid achievement of broad national and social objectives.

They also understood more clearly than their predecessors the need for effective organization. Since they were confronted by the same suspicion from the native princes as the reforming *boiers* had experienced under the Phanariots, they were obliged to pursue their political aims in secret or under the guise of literary societies. The arrests of Ion Cîmpineanu in 1839 and of Dumitru Filipescu in 1840 had shown them the limits of political action, but these chilling events did not deter them from the work of planning and organization.

The most important of the new societies was Frăţia (Brotherhood), which was founded in Bucharest in 1843 by Nicolae Bălcescu, who had been a member of Filpescu's conspiratorial group; Ion Ghica, a professor of geography and geology at Academia Mihăileană in Iaşi; and Christian Tell, a major in the Wallachian army. Its purpose was to maintain cohesion among the proponents of political and social reform and keep them in a state of readiness to carry out a change of

---

[2] G. Fotino, *Din vremea renaşterii naţionale a Ţării Româneşti; Boierii Goleşti*, ii (Bucharest, 1939), 14–20.

system. To avoid the fate of earlier societies its members observed strict secrecy, using the organization of the Masonic lodges as a model. The society's founders were eager to expand their membership in both principalities, and Ghica was one of the most assiduous in furthering regular contacts between leading Wallachian and Moldavian liberals. But Frăția did not flourish. Its small membership and the vigilance of the authorities in both principalities made significant political activity impossible.

The members of Frăția, including Bălcescu and Ghica, established a new society, Asociația pentru Înaintarea Literaturii Românești (Association for the Promotion of Romanian Literature), in Bucharest in 1845.[3] Its avowed purpose was to assist writers to develop their talents as a means of furthering the general welfare. The association proposed to pay them for works in all domains which would contribute to the education of young people and create a taste for reading, especially among the mass of the population. The members of the association also harboured revolutionary goals, notably the political union of all the Romanians, but they were careful not to attract the attention of the authorities. Their main accomplishment was the publication of the scholarly *Magazin istoric pentru Dacia*, mentioned earlier. The association practically ceased its activities after a number of its founders left for Paris in 1846.

Romanian intellectuals generally had found Paris a more congenial location for their activities than Bucharest or Iași. The first of their organizations had been Societatea pentru Învățătura Poporului Român (Society for the Instruction of the Romanian People), which they had established in 1839.[4] Its immediate task was to disseminate useful information in both Moldavia and Wallachia, and it was thus the first cultural society to extend its activities beyond the boundaries of a single principality. Its members' initial undertaking was to send French newspapers and other publications to Bucharest and to provide a reading-room for the public. The newspapers they selected were generally liberal and were intended to inform Romanian readers of significant social and political changes taking place in the West and thus to arouse them to action at home. They were also committed to work for the autonomy of the principalities and their eventual union, but they thought it best not to make such goals public for the time being.

The most important of all the Paris societies was undoubtedly Societatea Studenților Români de la Paris (Society of Romanian Students of Paris), which was founded in December 1845.[5] It had both Wallachian members—the brothers Dumitru and Ion C. Brătianu and C. A. Rosetti, the sons of *boiers*, and Alexandru C. Golescu—and Moldavians—Mihail Kogălniceanu and Ion Ionescu de la Brad, an agricultural economist. Bălcescu joined upon his arrival in Paris in July 1846 and soon became its leader. He was the most radical among them and the least tolerant of the status quo. To solve the problems of Romanian society

---

[3] C. Bodea, *Luptele Românilor pentru unitatea națională, 1834–1849* (Bucharest, 1967), 54–9; *Anul 1848 în Principatele Române*, i (Bucharest, 1902), 44–61.

[4] Bodea, *Luptele Românilor*, 22–7.   [5] Ibid. 78–94; *Anul 1848*, i. 16–23, 61–88.

he demanded fundamental changes in social and economic structures, not just a replacement of princes. He sensed that a whole society needed regeneration. He was also certain that the success of the coming revolution, which he thought inevitable, would depend upon how much support it could attract from all segments of the population, and to mobilize them he urged a massive propaganda effort under the banner 'Patria, Frăția, și Libertatea' (Fatherland, Brotherhood, and Liberty). In foreign policy the members of the society were more moderate. They favoured cooperation with the Ottomans in order to counter the influence of Russia, in their view, the chief obstacle to both independence and union. They decided to use the diplomatic skills of Ion Ghica and his personal acquaintance with Reshid pasha, the new Ottoman grand vizier, to persuade the Ottoman government to support political and social reform in the principalities as a weapon against Russia. Although Ghica did not make the trip to Constantinople, he did become a regular correspondent of the semi-official *Journal de Constantinople*, supplying it with information about Wallachia designed to win the sympathy of Ottoman officials.

The members of the society drew inspiration from a variety of intellectual contacts in Paris.[6] They attended lectures at the Collège de France by the historian Jules Michelet on revolution and the right of nations to develop as they chose, and by the Polish poet Adam Mickiewicz on the mission of Poland to lead the struggle of the Slavs for freedom. These were heady times. The Romanians shared the vision of still other representatives of Eastern European peoples and their French supporters of a new Europe composed of free peoples working together and guided by faith in the idea of nation. In all matters France was their model, and although they admired England's constitution, they thought her concentration on industry and commerce revealed the lack of a soul. Their idealism was, then, romantic, not economic.

In both principalities dissatisfaction with the prevailing political order was widespread. The great *boiers*, who were still a force to be reckoned with, harboured long-standing grievances. In Moldavia, as we have seen, they had come into sharp conflict with Prince Mihai Sturdza. They objected to his authoritarian ways and his failure to consult them, and some among them even coveted the throne for themselves. They denounced him to St Petersburg and Constantinople and hatched little plots in the general assembly, but, as they were divided among themselves and had no following in the population at large, Sturdza was untroubled by their occasional outbursts. These skirmishes were, in effect, a continuation of the traditional contest between the prince, as the representative of centralizing political tendencies, and the great landed aristocracy, which sought a return to the era of *boier* ascendancy. In Wallachia many

⁶ J. Breazu, *Edgar Quinet et les Roumains* (Paris, 1928), 98–112; I. Breazu, *Michelet și Românii* (Cluj, 1935), 50–2, 72–4, 101–8; O. Boitoș, *Raporturile Românilor cu Ledru-Rollin și radicali francezi în epoca revoluției dela 1848* (Bucharest, 1940); G. Zane and E. G. Zane, *N. Bălcescu la Biblioteca Poloneză din Paris* (Bucharest, 1973), 5–54.

great *boier*s espoused similar aims. But a number of the most aristocratic families—the Golescus and the Ghicas among them—supported moderate reforms. They tried, for example, to persuade Prince Gheorghe Bibescu to place himself at the head of a movement of renewal in order to prevent a violent outbreak by the restless peasants and urban lower classes. They preferred to introduce reforms from above, such as the abolition of peasant servitude and the installation of an efficient public administration, in order to preserve the existing social structure and their own places in it. They even called upon Pavel Kiselev, who had continued to advise his princely successors from afar, to help them, but Bibescu remained impervious to their advice and entreaties.

The middle class and the peasantry were also aggrieved. They chafed at high taxes to the state, and the peasants were desperate to reduce their mounting obligations to landlords. The standard of living of the peasants had deteriorated in the 1840s, because of unsettled economic conditions in Europe and a series of local natural calamities, notably a severe drought and an epidemic of animal diseases, which had sharply reduced agricultural production. Between 1846 and 1848 opposition to the Sturdza and Bibescu regimes intensified. Segments of the population that had not openly defied authority before now came forward. In Moldavia the commercial and industrial associations of Iaşi in 1846 protested against Sturdza's plan to raise taxes again; in several rural areas small and middle-size landlords also objected to the payment of additional taxes; and in a number of *judeţe* elections to the general assembly in the summer of 1847 were hotly contested by liberal *boier*s. Throughout both principalities peasants refused to perform labour services, and incidents of violence and flight abroad increased in the autumn of 1847 and the following spring.[7]

Moldavian and Wallachian intellectuals, eager for change, were roused to action by the events in Western Europe in the spring of 1848. The first overt reaction to the February revolution in Paris came from Romanian students gathered there.[8] They enthusiastically welcomed the overthrow of Louis-Philippe and sent a delegation to congratulate the new republican government. They spent long hours debating how the events they had witnessed would affect their own countries and what action they themselves should take. Outbreaks of violence in Vienna and Pest in the middle of March brought revolution closer to the principalities and gave new urgency to their discussions. At Bălcescu's quarters on 20 March they drew up a list of reforms to be introduced simultaneously in both principalities. With the exception of the article on property, it bore a remarkable similarity to the Filipescu programme of 1840 and provided the substance of a public proclamation of reform in June.

Bălcescu and his colleagues decided to return home at once in order to organize the struggle for reform. The Wallachians headed for Bucharest. Bălcescu

---

[7] On unrest in the countryside, see G. Platon, *Moldova şi începuturile revaluţei de la 1848* (Chişinău, 1993), 265–303.

[8] *Anul 1848*, i. 140–1.

and Alexandru G. Golescu, a cousin of Alexandru C. Golescu, travelled together through Germany where they discussed the possibilities of joint action with Polish and other East European revolutionaries with Prince Adam Czartoryski, the leader of the Polish emigration. Czartoryski agreed to send Polish officers to help organize the Wallachian army and wrote to Lamartine, minister of foreign affairs in the provisional French government, urging him to send 20,000 rifles to Wallachia. Bălcescu and his friends reached Bucharest at the beginning of April. The Moldavians arrived in Iaşi only after violence had broken out.

In Iaşi a few great *boiers* opposed to Sturdza, younger liberal *boiers*, and representatives of the middle class and other urban classes, perhaps a thousand in all, met at the Hotel Petersburg on 8 April to decide upon a course of action. This meeting was the culmination of several weeks of small private gatherings and several public manifestos denouncing despotism, all occasioned by news of the events in Paris, Vienna, and Berlin. Moderates prevailed and persuaded the gathering to support a petition to the prince setting forth all their grievances and proposing suitable reforms. They also agreed that as soon as their petition had been delivered their assembly and all other associations would be dissolved. The main reason for such caution seems to have been the fear that their protest movement would be pushed to extremes by the urban lower classes and the peasants.

A committee chaired by the poet Vasile Alecsandri drew up a *Petiţia-proclamaţie* (Petition-proclamation) addressed to both the population at large and the prince. Their overall objective was to install a moderate liberal political regime and to stimulate economic development.[9] They set down as a basic principle of government the strict adherence to the law by officials as well as citizens, an obvious reference to the corruption and arbitrariness of Sturdza's authoritarian regime. They then proceeded to outline the rules for electing a new, more representative assembly with enhanced powers, including the right to make proposals to the prince on all matters affecting the general welfare and to examine all ordinances of the government concerning the administration of public affairs and justice before they were put into effect. As for the economy, they urged the creation of a national bank 'to facilitate commerce' and the abolition of all tariffs 'harmful to agriculture and commerce', but for the peasants they made only a general plea for an improvement in their relations with the landlords and the state. They were obviously committed to reform and believed in the efficacy of good institutions, but they had no thought of overturning the existing political and social structures of the country, that is, of acting like revolutionaries.

Sturdza received the petition-proclamation on 9 April and agreed to thirty-three of its thirty-five points, rejecting only those concerning the dissolution of the general assembly and the formation of a national guard. He apparently also

[9] Ibid. 176–9; V. Şotropa, *Proiectele de constituţie, programele de reforme şi petiţiile drepturi din Ţările Române în secolul al XVIII-lea şi prima jumătate a secolului al XIX-lea* (Bucharest, 1976), 158–61.

objected to the abolition of censorship. The leaders of the protest movement, to
Sturdza's surprise, stood firm. They demanded acceptance of the entire petition.
Sturdza withdrew to the army barracks and that evening took steps to crush the
opposition. Several persons were killed in brief fighting, and some 300 were
arrested. Among those who fled, either to Transylvania or Bukovina, were
Alecsandri and a young officer, Alexandru Cuza, the future prince of the United
Principalities. Sturdza was now bent upon permanently stifling all dissent. Anyone even suspected of opposition was made subject to arrest; a strict censorship
was imposed; and students returning from France were stopped at the border and
interrogated before being allowed to proceed.

Moldavian liberals regrouped in Cernăuți, in Bukovina, where they formed
Comitetul Revoluționar Moldovean (the Moldavian Revolutionary Committee)
and commissioned Mihail Kogălniceanu to draw up a new statement of principles, *Dorințele Partidei Naționale în Moldova* (The Desires of the National Party
in Moldavia) which was published in August. More liberal than the petition of
9 April, it endowed an elected assembly with extensive powers, including the
right to initiate legislation, and it expanded the rights of *judeţe*, cities, and rural
communes to manage their own affairs without interference from the central
government.

Kogălniceanu also drafted a constitution for the new liberal Moldavia, *Proiectul
de Constituție*, which established the legislature as the dominant branch of government with the power to vote taxes, draw up the annual state budget, stimulate
agriculture, industry, and commerce, reform the laws of the land, elect the
prince, and even choose the metropolitan and bishops of the Orthodox Church.
Kogălniceanu proposed that all the orders of society be represented in this
all-powerful body, but he stopped short of advocating universal suffrage. He
favoured, instead, the creation of electoral colleges, which would give the upper
classes a preponderance. Like the majority of his colleagues, he felt obliged to
take into account the social and political realities of the time, and thus he
recognized the continued leading role of the *boiers* and limited the participation
of the mass of the peasants in government, because of their lack of education and
experience.[10]

A quickening of political activity had also occurred in Wallachia in March. As
in Moldavia, pamphlets circulated demanding a new political system and fundamental economic and social reforms. The most important was *Ce sînt meseriaşii?*
(Who Are the Artisans?). Inspired by the Abbé Sieyès's *What Is the Third Estate?*
of 1789, its anonymous author classed as *meseriaşi* everyone, including peasants,
who did not belong to the *boier* class and who was engaged in some form of
production or commerce. Since, in his view, they represented practically the

---

[10] V. Şotropa, 'Proiectul de constituţie al lui Mihail Kogălniceanu din 1848, în contextul
ideologiei revoluţionarilor din ţările române', *Anuarul Institutului de Istorie şi Arheologie*, 10 (1973),
229–45. On Kogălniceanu's political views and activities in general, see A. Zub, 'Din activitatea
politică a lui M. Kogălniceanu la 1848', *Revista de istorie*, 29/7 (1976), 999–1012.

whole nation, he urged that henceforth they have a preponderant political role in keeping with their economic and social contributions to the nation. He proposed in effect that they replace the *boiers*, whom he accused of being unproductive and of shirking their responsibilities, as the leading class of society.[11]

The liberal *boiers* had also been roused to action. Characteristic of their thought was a petition drawn up in late March in which they expressed disillusionment with the manner in which the country had been governed in the preceding decade. The reforms they demanded ranged widely, if unsystematically, over every area of public administration: the removal of all ministers currently holding office; the abolition of the censorship and recognition of the fundamental right of freedom of speech; the reform of judicial procedure; and the abolition of the tribute paid to the sultan as unworthy of a free nation. The lesser *boiers* (those of the fourth rank) added their own complaints, which were far more radical than those of their liberal upper-class colleagues and included the outright abolition of the social rank of *boier* and the equitable allocation of taxes among all classes of the population.

It was the liberal, Western-educated intellectuals, the majority *boiers*, who took the lead in organizing direct action against the old regime. In March C. A. Rosetti, one of the founders of Frăţia and the owner of a printing house in Bucharest, and Ion Ghica, among others, formed a revolutionary committee in Bucharest. They were joined at the beginning of April by Bălcescu and Alexandru G. Golescu, who had just arrived from Paris. The latter had already met with Christian Tell, another of the founders of Frăţia and a major in the Wallachian army, in Giurgiu, and together they had decided to begin a revolution without delay. They agreed that an armed uprising should take place simultaneously at two points—Bucharest and Oltenia—in order to divide the 'forces of repression' and spread the revolution quickly to every part of the country. Tell and his forces took responsibility for holding the five *judeţe* west of the Olt River, the starting-point of Tudor Vladimirescu's movement, as a base for future operations. They all recognized that the success of their enterprise depended upon the mass support of the peasants. Yet, they entertained no hope of a spontaneous uprising on behalf of their cause, because of the alienation they sensed among the rural population. They decided, therefore, to launch a sustained propaganda effort in the countryside in order to undo the decades of mistreatment and neglect which the peasants had suffered and thereby overcome their suspicion of outsiders, particularly from the city.

Bălcescu and Golescu discussed their plans with the committee on 20 April. Bălcescu wanted the revolution to begin at once, on 23 April, Easter Day, because he thought the element of surprise would tip the balance in their favour. But the majority, citing the lack of preparation, decided to postpone action. The next day they were joined by Ion and Dumitru Brătianu, also recent arrivals from

[11] *Anul 1848*, i. 460–7.

Paris, who brought a promise of aid from Lamartine. Their discussions continued on into May. The revolutionary committee was expanded to include moderates such as Ion Heliade Rădulescu, and an executive commission, headed by Bălcescu and Ghica, was formed to draw up a plan for the insurrection and to take responsibility for carrying it out. Rosetti replaced Ghica, who was dispatched to Constantinople as a confidential agent to seek the benevolent neutrality of the Ottoman government. The commission, using the discussions at Giurgiu between Golescu and Tell in April as a guide, decided upon a simultaneous uprising at various places and chose 21 June as the date.

In the mean time, the Russian government had been watching events unfold in the principalities with growing alarm. In late March it had informed Sturdza and Bibescu that its armies would again be sent across the Prut if any attempts were made to change the political system introduced by the Organic Statutes. Such a threat emboldened Sturdza to resist the demands of the liberals and reduced the moderate Bibescu to inaction. In April, after the scattering of the petitioners in Iaşi, Tsar Nicholas sent an aide, General Alexander Duhamel, to the principalities to investigate the situation. In Iaşi he urged Sturdza to make a few modest concessions in order to defuse the situation, but the prince would have nothing to do with 'liberalism'. Duhamel went on to Bucharest, arriving on 12 May to find the situation far more dangerous than in Iaşi. He recommended the immediate dispatch of 20,000 Russian troops to assure public order, but Bibescu rejected the offer.[12]

The Ottoman government also judged the situation in Wallachia alarming. It sent Talaat effendi, as special commissioner, to Bucharest in May to urge Bibescu to suppress the revolutionaries. But the prince took no action, and thus the initiative remained with the revolutionary committee.

The committee put its plans for a general insurrection into effect at the beginning of June. Its members fanned out from Bucharest in all directions to alert sympathizers in the *judeţe* to their plans and to coordinate local uprisings. The focus of their activity was Islaz, on the Danube west of the Olt River, where Christian Tell had assembled a small armed force. Here before a large and enthusiastic gathering on 21 June Heliade Rădulescu, on behalf of the revolutionary committee, read a proclamation setting forth the programme of the revolution.[13] It represented the culmination of two ideas which had gained wide currency among the educated since the latter half of the eighteenth century—one, a conception of nation beholden to criteria other than social rank, and the other, political autonomy for the principalities based upon the original treaties with the Ottoman Empire. The preamble made ethnicity the test of membership in the nation. It declared every Romanian—villager, artisan, merchant, priest,

---

[12] B. Jelavich, 'The Russian Intervention in Wallachia and Transylvania, Sept. 1848 to March 1849', *Rumanian Studies*, iv (Leiden, 1979), 20; G. G. Bezviconi, *Călători ruşi în Moldova şi Muntenia* (Bucharest, 1947), 385–9.

[13] *Anul 1848*, i. 490–501; Şotropa, *Proiectele*, 175–95.

boier, and prince—a son of a common fatherland and possessing the right to share in its governance. Then, referring to the treaties between the early Wallachian princes and the sultans and the later agreements between Russia and the Ottoman Empire, which guaranteed respect for the traditional political rights of the principality, it expressed the 'will of the Romanian nation' to preserve its internal sovereignty and independence. The forty-eighters thus expressed no hostility towards the sultan and even declared their intention of preserving all existing treaty obligations towards him, but they could not conceal their hostility to Russia and demanded an end to the regime instituted by the Organic Statutes, which, they claimed, had violated the very autonomy Russia had by treaty sworn to defend. They then enumerated the principles by which they intended to set the principality on a new, liberal course: equality of rights for all citizens, an equitable sharing of public burdens through a progressive income tax, broad participation in public life through an expanded franchise, freedom of the press, speech, and assembly, the abolition of *clacă* with an indemnity to landowners, an expanded educational system and equal and free instruction for everyone in accordance with his intellectual capacity, an end to all ranks and titles of nobility, and the election of the prince from any category of the population for a five-year term.

The proclamation of Islaz was a characteristic programme of the European liberal intellectuals of 1848 with its emphasis upon individual liberties, its faith in good institutions, and its provision for an increased role for the citizenry in public affairs. But these were not simply borrowings by the Romanians from Western European experience. The evolution of the principles which the revolutionary committee expressed so forcefully may be traced back through the memoranda of the reforming *boiers*, the proclamations of Tudor Vladimirescu, the Constitution of the Carbonari, the plans of the circle around *Dacia literară*, and the aspirations of the liberal *boiers* in the legislative assemblies of the two principalities. The proclamation of Islaz dealt with problems specific to Wallachia and put forward solutions arising from a long tradition of indigenous social and political thought leavened by contact with what the Wallachian forty-eighters accepted as universally valid principles.

When the reading of the declaration of principles had ended, a provisional government headed by Heliade Rădulescu, Ştefan Golescu, a leading liberal, and Tell was proclaimed. Accompanied by military units and a large number of peasants, it set out at once for Craiova, which was occupied without incident on 25 June.

Bucharest, however, was the main theatre of action throughout the summer and early autumn. Here the uprising had been planned for 22 June, but Bibescu's belated attempt to arrest the members of the revolutionary committee caused a delay. Although Rosetti and several colleagues fell into his hands, Bibescu recognized the emptiness of his success, for it was clear that he had practically no support in the country at large. His visits to the army barracks produced only expressions of sympathy for the revolutionaries, not the renewal of allegiance he had sought, while the corporation of merchants, which he had hoped to organize into a citizen guard to protect the capital from revolution, waited only for a signal from the revolutionary committee to join the insurrection.

The revolution in Bucharest began on 23 June with the ringing of church bells. The streets filled with people and copies of the proclamation of Islaz were distributed among them. The prince's guard made no attempt to intervene and allowed a delegation led by Ion Brătianu and Nicolae Golescu, members of the revolutionary committee, to enter the palace to present their demands to the prince in person. Bibescu quickly agreed to sign the new 'constitution', as they called the proclamation. He also accepted the formation of a new cabinet of ministers, which included Bălcescu as minister of foreign affairs, Rosetti as head of the police, and Heliade Rădulescu in charge of religious affairs. Then, on 25 June, Bibescu unexpectedly abdicated and fled to Braşov. It may suddenly have dawned on him how hopeless his position had become. He had no sympathy for most of the reforms he had just approved, and, then, one day after he had agreed, in effect, to become a constitutional monarch, he lost the support of Russia. The Russian consul bluntly informed him on the 24th that his government regarded the constitution as a contravention of the Organic Statutes and had instructed him to leave Bucharest.

A new, provisional, government, composed of the officials appointed at Islaz on 21 June and the cabinet of ministers accepted by Bibescu on the 23rd, took office on the 26th. One of its first acts was to abolish all censorship. By granting every citizen the right to express his views freely on all things, it sought to create a new political atmosphere conducive to the election of a truly representative general assembly. An immediate result was the burgeoning of the newspaper press.[14] On 24 June Rosetti had already begun to publish *Pruncul Român* (Romanian Infant), which was a champion of radical economic and social reform during its short existence (it ceased publication on 23 September). In its first issue he called upon the populace to form a national guard to protect the rights they had won and appealed to the Moldavians ('our brothers') to unite with the Wallachians to oppose 'any enemy of our liberty'.[15] Bălcescu, anxious to gain mass support for radical reforms, published *Învăţătorul Satului* (Village Teacher), which sought not only to inform the peasants about current issues but to make them active supporters of the new regime. Other newspapers bore such suggestive titles as *Reforma* (Reform), *Constituţionalul* (Constitutional), and *Naţionalul* (National).

The provisional government hastened to submit its programme to popular approval. At a festive gathering outside Bucharest on the 'Field of Liberty' on 27 June a large, enthusiastic crowd roared approval of the constitution. At the same time, recognizing the importance of propaganda as a means of arousing and

---

[14] N. Iorga, *Istoria presei româneşti* (Bucharest, 1922), 81–91.
[15] C. Bodea (ed.), *1848 la Români: O istorie în date şi marturii*, i (Bucharest, 1982), 547–9.

maintaining mass support, the government appointed a special commissioner in every *judeţ* to explain its policies and legislative programme to the populace.

The government also moved quickly to right what both conservatives and liberals had long condemned as a moral wrong. On 8 July it declared all gypsy slaves free as of 22 July. Many owners spontaneously freed their slaves. Others appeared before a commission, especially set up for the purpose, to claim compensation.

Of immediate concern to the revolutionaries was the establishment of a military force capable of defending the new government. They recognized the impossibility of opposing foreign intervention by conventional means and therefore shifted the emphasis from a large standing army to non-permanent forces composed of a national guard, *dorobanţi* (professional infantry), and volunteers. They based their new military system on the idea of a national reserve, which could be mobilized quickly in an emergency and was to have as its nucleus units of the national guard especially organized for the purpose in all cities and towns and at important centres in the countryside.[16] Gheorghe Magheru, who had served in the Russian army in 1828–9 and had had much subsequent military experience, was appointed commander of the new national army.

Perhaps the most pressing internal problem facing the revolutionary government was what to do about a disaffected peasantry. From the very beginning of their movement in March, the forty-eighters had recognized the need for immediate reform. The radicals among them had made their position clear in the pamphlet *Ce sînt meseriaşii?* They wanted the abolition of *clacă*, complete personal liberty for the peasants, adequate grants of land made to them for all time, and compensation for the landlords from the state, not from the peasants, on the basis of current land prices. They justified these measures as a simple act of social justice towards the workers of the land. Other pamphlets and a memorandum presented to Talaat effendi in May contained similar demands. The document that produced the greatest reaction in the countryside was the proclamation of Islaz. Article 13, which declared an end to *clacă*, had an electrifying effect. The news spread rapidly, and peasants immediately stopped performing labour services for landlords and lessees. But such action threatened the country with economic catastrophe, and on 25 June the government instructed the prefects of all the *judeţe* to make the peasants understand that they must continue to fulfil their labour obligations until the new, representative assembly had enacted the necessary legislation. Article 13, for the time being, was thus merely a promise.

The postponement of a decision on *clacă* was a sign of serious divergences within the government.[17] Heliade Rădulescu, influenced by the landowning *boiers*, represented the majority opinion which held that an immediate emancipa-

---

[16] A. Stan, 'Încercări de organizare a unei rezistenţe armate în timpul revoluţiei muntene de la 1848', *Studii: Revistă de istorie*, 16/3 (1963), 621–42; id., 'Gărzile naţionale în revoluţia din 1848 în Ţara Românească', *Studii: Revistă de istorie*, 18/4 (1965), 879–94.

[17] Id., *Le Problème agraire pendant la révolution de 1848 en Valachie* (Bucharest, 1971), 39–46.

tion of the peasants and a wholesale redistribution of land would be harmful to both the revolution and agriculture. He reasoned that such drastic action would probably lead to widespread unrest, thereby offering a pretext for foreign military intervention, and would certainly reduce the size of the harvest and perhaps bring the country to the brink of financial and social chaos. On the other side of the question stood a small group headed by Bălcescu, which demanded the immediate implementation by decree of the government's professed agrarian aims.

These differences, which were related to broader issues and persisted throughout the short life of the provisional government, made a consistent agrarian policy impossible. Government measures were, therefore, often contradictory. On 28 June it issued a proclamation to the peasants declaring that it had abolished *clacă* and that within three months all peasants would be landowners, but at the same time it required them to harvest the autumn crops of their existing landlords and lessees. Yet, neither promises nor admonitions had any effect because the peasants were in no mood to delay their emancipation. The government's reaction, uncharacteristically, was to threaten. Beset by worries over its fragile authority within the country and the imminence of foreign intervention, it yielded to the pressure of moderates to take a firm stand on the agrarian question. On 18 July it warned the peasants that it would not allow them to improve their status at the expense of landlords and would require them to pay for any damages caused by their failure to carry out stipulated labour obligations. This declaration had no more effect than earlier admonitions, except, perhaps, to increase the confusion and discontent of the peasants.

The government tried to gain support for its gradualist approach by dispatching special commissioners into the countryside to explain its policies, to administer oaths of allegiance to the proclamation of Islaz, and to enlist volunteers for the national guard. But here, too, divergences within the government led to unforeseen consequences. Bălcescu and his supporters, who counted on the peasants to be the chief defence of the revolution both at home against a conservative reaction and against an attack from outside, wanted to use the commissioners to stir revolutionary fervour in the villages. That is precisely what happened. Whether they intended it or not, the commissioners raised the level of expectation among the peasants, but failed completely to persuade them to perform labour services for their landlords.[18]

Mounting unrest in the rural areas convinced all factions in the government that a solution to *clacă* and related questions could no longer be postponed. On 21 July it established a commission on property, composed of one *boier* and one peasant from each *judeţ*, whose task would be to draft an agrarian law in the spirit of Article 13 of the proclamation of Islaz for submission to the forthcoming constituent assembly. The commission began its work on 21 August, but liberals

[18] *Anul 1848*, ii (Bucharest, 1902), 201–3; *Documente privind revoluţia de la 1848 în Ţările Române: B. Ţara Românească, 12 martie 1848–21 aprilie 1850* (Bucharest, 1983), pp. xi–xii, 94, 161.

and conservatives were so divided that they could not reach a consensus on any matter of substance. In the end, political events overtook the commission. It never completed its work, and the agrarian problem remained unresolved.

The provisional government was anxious, none the less, to carry out as rapidly as possible the many promises it had made at Islaz and on the Field of Liberty. It judged the first step to be the elaboration of a fundamental law, and, accordingly, on 28 June, barely two days after coming to power, it set down the rules for electing a constituent assembly. The primary task of the assembly would be to draft a constitution embodying the principles of the Revolution. Three categories of 'interests' were to be represented—property, that is, the *boiers*; commerce, industry, and 'intelligence', or the middle class and the forty-eighters themselves; and the villagers, the peasants—but not equally. Some 7,000 land-owners were to have 100 seats in the assembly; 50,000 merchants, artisans, and intellectuals another 100; and the overwhelming majority of the population, roughly 1,850,000 peasants, 100 seats. The government justified limiting the peasants' representation by citing their lack of political experience, a concern it expressed by instituting a system of indirect voting in rural areas. Elections were scheduled for the final two weeks of August, and the constituent assembly was to open in Bucharest on 6 September. But momentous and unforeseen political changes, which cut short the life of the provisional government, brought a suspension of the entire process on 16 August.

In early July Russian military intervention in Wallachia seemed imminent. On the 7th Russian troops entered Moldavia in order to prevent the establishment of a revolutionary government in Iași similar to that in Bucharest. On the 10th the Wallachian government, certain of a Russian invasion, fled to the mountains. But Russian troops remained in place, and the government returned to Bucharest two days later. The tsar appears to have had no intention of removing the provisional government, at least not at the moment, mainly because he lacked support from the other powers for such drastic action. He proposed, instead, to work through the Ottoman government to keep the situation in hand, but he was determined to uphold all Russia's treaty rights in the principalities.[19]

The differences between the tsar and the provisional government were fundamental and in the end proved irreconcilable. Maintenance of the Russian protectorate was contrary to the government's stated goal of reducing its dependence on foreign powers. Bălcescu had made the point clear on 25 June when as minister of foreign affairs he reminded the foreign consuls of Wallachia's 'right of independent internal administration'. To reinforce what he had said, the government dispensed with the sultan's right of investiture of a new executive and on its own authority adopted a national flag, the symbol of sovereignty. The radicals clearly intended to seek full independence, but both they and the conservatives were anxious to avoid provoking foreign intervention.

---

[19] D. A. Sturdza *et al.*, *Acte şi documente relative la istoria renaşterei României*, ii (Bucharest, 1889), 4–8: Foreign Minister Nesselrode to Russian diplomatic missions, 31 July 1848.

During the summer the government carried on relations with various foreign countries as a sovereign state. It was particularly anxious to maintain contact with the Western powers, even though they had not granted it recognition, in order to enlist their support in restraining both the Russians and the Ottomans. To present its case directly to Western leaders it dispatched special emissaries to France, Austria, and the Frankfurt Parliament. In Paris, where he arrived in July, Alexandru G. Golescu was a tireless defender of the revolution.[20] He kept French officials and public opinion informed of events in Wallachia and negotiated for the purchase of arms and for the sending of French military instructors. Dumitru Brătianu performed similar services in Vienna and Pest. Ioan Maiorescu, who was the provisional government's special envoy to the Frankfurt parliament, waited in vain for a strong German central government to emerge and a single mighty German army to be formed that would come to the aid of the Romanians and the other small nationalities of Eastern Europe. The government in Bucharest sent no representative to London, but acquainted Palmerston, the Foreign Secretary, with its aims through diplomatic dispatches.[21]

The provisional government gained little from its diplomatic initiatives. It looked to France first, but the republican government, no longer headed by Lamartine and beset by internal problems, was only perfunctorily sympathetic and made promises of guns and other support that it could not keep. In appearance Britain seemed sympathetic, too. Palmerston's policy was to prevent armed intervention in the principalities by either Russia or the Ottomans as part of his long-range strategy to impede Russia's drive for ascendancy in South-eastern Europe. Neither the Austrian government, harried on all sides by revolution, nor the new Hungarian government, born of revolution in Pest in March and intent upon creating a strong Hungarian national state, showed any inclination to come to the rescue of the Wallachian provisional government.

Through all the events of spring and early summer the provisional government had been careful to avoid alienating the sultan. Since it had never entertained more than modest hopes of gaining substantive support in the West against Russian intervention, it turned to the Ottomans as the only power receptive to a joint effort to limit Russian influence in the region. Through Ion Ghica, its representative in Constantinople, it attempted to win Ottoman recognition by promising to respect all Wallachia's obligations to the sultan. The idea of thwarting Russian designs in the principalities struck a responsive chord in Constantinople, but the Ottoman government was at the same time under heavy Russian pressure to bring the Wallachian problem under control.

Since the first outbreaks in March Russian policy towards revolution in Central

---

[20] T. Ionescu, 'Misiunea lui Al. Gh. Golescu la Paris în 1848', *Revista de istorie*, 27/12 (1974), 1727–46.

[21] *Documente privind revoluția de la 1848 în Țările Române*, 163–5. On Britain's interest in the principalities in 1848, see B. Marinescu, *Romanian-British Political Relations, 1848–1877* (Bucharest, 1983), 13–43.

Europe had been one of caution, but the tsar had made it plain that he would not tolerate drastic political changes in the principalities. He had been alarmed by the overtly anti-Russian tone of the reformers in both Iaşi and Bucharest and informed both princes that Russia was determined to maintain her protectorate and warned against any modification of the Organic Statutes. The sending of troops across the Prut on 7 July left no doubt about his intentions. Although Nicholas did not contemplate taking similar action in Wallachia, a circular letter of 31 July from Foreign Minister Nesselrode reiterated his government's determination to carry out its treaty obligations. By then consultations with the Ottoman government were already under way with a view to coordinating any action that might become necessary to prevent 'revolutionary excesses'.

The Ottomans appeared willing at first to negotiate with the provisional government, but by no means as equals. The sultan sent a special representative, Suleiman pasha, to the Danube backed by an army of 20,000. On 31 July he crossed the river at Giurgiu with part of that force and only then began discussions with a Wallachian delegation, composed of boiers and 'notables', an official Ottoman euphemism for revolutionaries, although he would have preferred to deal only with the boiers, whom he regarded as the true representatives of the country. Suleiman pasha was a relative moderate among Ottoman statesmen, but he bluntly warned the Wallachians that if the existing state of affairs continued, he would use his army to bring an end to the 'false position' into which the revolutionaries had led their country.

The negotiations went badly for the Wallachians because Suleiman pasha operated from a position of strength which they could not match. On 4 August they proposed to replace the provisional government by a princely lieutenancy (locotenenţa domnească), a governing council composed of six ministers to be chosen by themselves, but Suleiman rejected the idea on the grounds that it was simply the revolutionary government under a new name. He finally approved a princely lieutenancy shorn of radicals and consisting only of moderate liberals such as Nicolae Golescu, minister of internal affairs; Heliade Rădulescu, minister of public instruction; and Christian Tell, minister of war, but he stipulated that any changes in existing laws and practices would require the prior approval of the sultan. Despite opposition from Bălcescu, Rosetti, and other radicals, who considered such a concession an abandonment of autonomy, the moderates agreed to Suleiman's conditions, which, in effect, reaffirmed the sultan's suzerain powers over Wallachia's internal political affairs. Suleiman now recognized the new government in the name of the sultan and on 14 August invited the foreign consuls to resume contacts with it. For the moment it appeared that the new regime, brought to power by the revolution, had, at least in a modified form, surmounted its gravest crisis.[22]

[22] On the negotiations with Suleiman pasha, see the reports of the British consul in Bucharest, Robert Colquhoun, to Palmerston: Documente privind revoluţia de la 1848 în Ţările Române, 98–100, 105–7, 122–5, 137–9.

Ottoman authorities by no means considered matters settled. Suleiman required the princely lieutenancy to send a delegation to Constantinople to submit the reform programme adopted at Islaz to the sultan for his formal approval. Suleiman had given the delegation to understand that its trip was a mere formality and that the proclamation of Islaz would be sanctioned with only insignificant changes. But the delegation, which arrived in Constantinople on 22 August received an unusually cool reception. It appears that conservative *boiers*, using their traditional contacts among Ottoman officials, had succeeded in discrediting both the revolutionary government and Suleiman, but strong representations by Russian diplomats in Constantinople, who made plain the tsar's displeasure with events in Wallachia, were probably decisive. In any case, Ottoman officials refused to recognize the delegation as legal and recalled Suleiman, informing the delegation that none of his assurances could be considered binding.[23] The delegation had no choice but to return home on 16 September. The sultan appointed Fuad pasha, chief secretary of the imperial council and an opponent of reform, to take Suleiman's place as commissioner to Wallachia and instructed him to cooperate with Russian authorities in re-establishing the old regime in Wallachia.

Cooperation between Russians and Ottomans meant the end of the Wallachian forty-eighters' hopes of survival by playing one power off against the other. In desperation they turned again to the West. On 3 September the new minister of foreign affairs, Ion Voinescu, dispatched an urgent note to Palmerston explaining why neither Russia nor the Ottoman Empire had the legal right to occupy the principality. Drawing upon historical tradition, he pointed out that the 'capitulations' creating the political relationship between Wallachia and the Ottoman Empire at the end of the fourteenth century specified that in return for an annual tribute Wallachia would retain the right to manage her internal affairs without outside interference. He insisted that the capitulations had been regularly renewed and were still in force. Noting, disingenuously, that Russia's protectorate had been created in the eighteenth century for the sole purpose of defending the autonomy of the principality, he concluded that intervention now would be a flagrant violation of her treaty obligations towards both the Ottoman Empire and Wallachia. He expected a sympathetic hearing in London because throughout the crisis the British government had sought to prevent military intervention by any party, and to that end the British consul in Bucharest, Robert Colquhoun, had served as a mediator in the negotiations between the provisional government and Suleiman pasha in Giurgiu. But now Palmerston made no move to support the beleaguered princely lieutenancy.

Fuad pasha arrived at Galaţi with a large army on 8 September. A few days later he moved to Giurgiu to join other Turkish troops, and on the 25th he entered Bucharest at the head of a force of some 20,000. They met fierce

<hr />

[23] On the negotiations with Suleiman pasha, see the reports of the British consul in Bucharest, Robert Colquhoun, to Palmerston: *Documente privind revoluţia de la 1848 în Ţările Române*, 167–70.

resistance, which was led by the fire brigade of the city and an infantry battalion, but the numerically superior Ottoman forces prevailed. Looting and pillaging by the occupying army followed the cessation of organized resistance. When a measure of calm had been restored Fuad called together leading *boiers* and read a *firman* from the sultan dissolving the princely lieutenancy and appointing Constantin Cantacuzino, a *boier* who had served in the government of Prince Alexandru Ghica, as *caimacam*, or temporary administrator.

Although the Russians had approved the occupation of Bucharest and the dismissal of the princely lieutenancy, they were disappointed by the lack of vigour on the part of Ottoman authorities in pursuing the revolutionaries. The tsar was now intent upon combating revolution everywhere in Central Europe, and Wallachia had acquired particular strategic importance, because of the startling progress of the Hungarian revolution to the north. He and his advisers therefore decided to occupy Wallachia and simply notified Fuad of the fact. On 27 September a Russian army under General Alexander Lüders crossed the Milcov River, which separated Wallachia from Moldavia, and on the next day it entered Bucharest.

From this time on the Russians were in control of Wallachia, and Fuad and other Ottoman officials were relegated to observer status. The leaders of the revolution scattered, many choosing exile, some in Constantinople and Brusa, others in the West, the majority making Paris their base. During the rest of the year Russian occupation authorities were preoccupied with purging the administrative apparatus of 'revolutionaries' and their sympathizers. They also tried to seal off Wallachia from Transylvania, where the Romanian revolution was gaining momentum in the autumn of 1848.[24] Their military administration lasted until the signing of the Convention of Balta Liman with the Ottoman government on 1 May 1849.

THE HABSBURG MONARCHY

Romanian intellectuals in the Habsburg monarchy also responded quickly and enthusiastically to events in Western and Central Europe in the spring of 1848. As the old order collapsed they were stirred to action by expectations of achieving long-sought national goals. They were liberals, but they saw in civil liberties and representative institutions, first of all, guarantees of national political autonomy. The course which their revolution took in the regions of the monarchy they inhabited was determined by historical tradition and prevailing social and political circumstances. The most important movement for self-determination occurred in Transylvania, where the Romanian population was the most numerous and where, as we have seen, Romanian intellectuals and clergy had

---

[24] A. Stan, *Revoluţia română de la 1848* (Bucharest, 1987), 250–62.

achieved a high level of national consciousness. It was in Transylvania also that the clash of nationalities was the most bitter, as Magyars and Romanians competed for dominance. In Hungary (the Banat and the adjoining area of Crişana, or Bihor, to the north) the antagonism between Magyars and Romanians was less acute, but Romanian opposition to Serbian control of the Orthodox Church administration and schools there was unyielding. In Bukovina Romanian leaders were determined to preserve the Romanian ethnic character of the province, but they could rally neither the Orthodox Church hierarchy nor the mass of the population to support their political goals.

The Romanian revolution of 1848 in Transylvania was, as in the principalities, a revolution of the intellectuals. It was they who formulated its goals and devised a strategy to achieve them. The objectives they pursued were grounded in the world of ideas specific to the evolution of Romanian society in Transylvania, and, thus, they gave priority to national emancipation. But they were also idealists. They believed wholeheartedly in human progress, in the unlimited ability of men to improve their condition through the reform of their institutions. Like their counterparts elsewhere in Europe, they professed faith in the swift and glorious transformation of society. Unfortunately, as events were to show, they misjudged the rhythm of change in history and foresaw the collapse of the old regime before they had any right to expect it.

The Romanian movement was affected in various ways by the events in Vienna and Buda-Pest,[25] especially by manifestations of liberalism. The proclamation of a democratic government in Pest on 15 March by a group of young radicals and idealists led by the poet Sándor Petőfi had the most telling effect on Romanian intellectuals. By democratic Magyar liberals meant a ministry responsible to the electorate, universal suffrage, equal treatment before the law, freedom of association and of expression, and taxation based upon the ability to pay, and they established a committee of public order to make abstract principle a reality. Although the committee was soon superseded by a more moderate government headed by Count Lajos Batthyány as prime minister, its programme lost none of its attractive force. The Batthyány ministry itself solemnly pledged to be responsive to the 'national will' and to protect the constitutional rights of all the citizens of Hungary regardless of nationality or religion.

Yet, liberal political ideas represented only one facet of Magyar aspirations. Even stronger, because of their irresistible emotional appeal, were the claims of nationality. Since the last decades of the eighteenth century Magyar intellectuals had been increasingly attracted to the idea of nation and after nearly half a century their consciousness of themselves as the heirs of a great cultural and historical tradition had reached its height. Like their counterparts elsewhere in Europe during the spring of 1848 they, too, sought fulfilment in the creation of a national state. When, therefore, the Committee of Public Order proclaimed

---

[25] Buda and Pest were separate cities until their unification in 1873.

Hungary's full constitutional autonomy *vis-à-vis* German Austria it was carrying out an unwritten but none the less imperative mandate. The Battyány ministry went further; it declared its intention to restore the boundaries of historical Hungary through the incorporation of Transylvania, Croatia, and other territories it claimed as dependencies of the Crown of Saint Stephen, an act that would transform the medieval kingdom into a Magyar nation-state. The leading exponent of these policies was Lajos Kossuth, the minister of finance, who had won a large popular following because of his liberal political views and his opposition to Habsburg rule. But his attempts to carry out Magyar national goals ran counter to the aspirations of the other peoples of Hungary to achieve their own national ambitions and led to what has aptly been called the central tragedy of 1848.[26]

Romanian intellectuals were also roused to action by the imminence of far-reaching political and social change. Throughout Transylvania they enthusiastically joined in public meetings and issued spirited declarations of principle. The programme enunciated by the Magyar liberals in Pest held a particular attraction for them. Although they were intent upon protecting their nationality, they also looked forward to building a new Transylvania in accordance with the enlightened principles of the day. Since they shared the liberal aspirations of many Magyar political leaders and intellectuals, a firm basis existed for cooperation between the two nationalities.

In the latter half of March and the beginning of April the majority of Romanian leaders were certain that a new era in the relations of the peoples of Transylvania had arrived. At this point they were little concerned about the union of Transylvania with Hungary. Timotei Cipariu (1805–87), a noted philologist and the editor of the newspaper *Organul Luminării* (Organ of Enlightenment), predicted that the constitution of the new Hungary, because of the March events in Pest, would be based upon principles completely different from those that had characterized public life in the past. The new constitution would, he was certain, guarantee to all citizens, regardless of class, religion, or nationality, full equality before the law and the unfettered right to develop their individual talents. On the delicate question of language rights Cipariu was even willing to grant an exception: in the interest of efficiency and because of the political and cultural pre-eminence which the Magyars enjoyed, Magyar should be accepted as the primary language of public administration.[27]

Cipariu saw little reason for the Romanians and the other non-Magyar nationalities to fear the union of Transylvania with Hungary. He professed complete faith in the attachment of Magyar liberals to the ideals of liberty, equality, and fraternity, and he predicted that the new diet would be elected in accordance with these enlightened principles and would, therefore, guarantee the right of all peoples to develop freely as distinct national entities. It was inconceiv-

---

[26] R. W. Seton-Watson, 'The Era of Reform in Hungary', *Slavonic and East European Review*, 21/2 (1943), 166.

[27] *Organul Luminării*, 1/65 (1848), 368.

able to him that men who had proclaimed themselves liberals could act otherwise. Furthermore, he saw positive benefits for the Romanians in the union. In the first place, it would hasten economic and social progress by abolishing outmoded structures that had kept the mass of the population in subjection. The union would also strengthen the Romanian nation by bringing together the 1,300,000 Romanians of Hungary and the 1,500,000 of Transylvania, thereby thwarting any attempt to deprive them of their nationality. On the other hand, he warned, if the Romanians rejected the union and Transylvania remained independent under its archaic constitution, they could not hope to achieve equality for decades to come.

George Barițiu, the editor of *Gazeta de Transilvania*, admitted to having been overcome with emotion upon receiving reports of events in Paris and Vienna. He thought the key to the future development of Transylvania lay in the union of the principality with Hungary, which he called the 'reform of reforms'. Yet, his acceptance of the union was not unconditional. Although willing to accept Magyar as the general administrative language of the new Hungary, he insisted that the other nationalities be guaranteed the full use of their own languages in education, the church, and local government. In his view, the main task confronting Romanian intellectuals was to fortify their nationality by establishing schools and cultural organizations and by cultivating national consciousness among the people through works of history and literature. If successful, he argued, their nationality would rest on solid foundations, and they would not have to fear present or future political changes. He also reminded his compatriots that they did not stand alone, for all Romanians, including those in Moldavia and Wallachia, were united by 'genetic, literary, and religious relationships'.[28]

The main reason for Barițiu's optimism was his sympathy for the programme of the Magyar liberals and his belief that civil liberties and equality of rights for all citizens were a prerequisite and a guarantee for social progress. For him, freedom of speech and of assembly were as natural as eating and drinking. He envisioned the swift establishment of liberal political institutions, especially an annual parliament chosen on the basis of universal manhood suffrage. Together with a responsible ministry and freedom of the press he was certain that it would curtail any tendency towards arbitrary government and would allow the Romanians the same opportunity as their neighbour to defend their national interests.

The first important public manifestation of concern for the consequences of the union of Transylvania with Hungary was a proclamation drawn up by Simion Bărnuțiu on 24 March. He was attending the Saxon Law Academy in Sibiu when the crisis broke, and he watched with increasing dismay the indecision of his compatriots over the question of the union. His suspicions concerning the ultimate goals of Magyar leaders, both liberals and conservatives, towards the Romanians had not diminished in the years following the dispute over the

---

[28] FM 11/16 (1848), 121.

Magyar language law of 1842. Now thoroughly alarmed by the course of events, he sought to awaken Romanian intellectuals throughout Transylvania to the danger that threatened their nation.

Bărnuţiu made the preservation of Romanian nationality the paramount issue of the day. He argued that the Romanians, 'the descendants of the Romans', had for too long been denied their rightful place among the nations of Transylvania. Now, they had an opportunity to recover all that had once been theirs, but they had to proceed 'with their eyes open', lest they lose their most precious possession—their nationality. They must, he admonished, reject the union until their rights had been fully assured and their representatives had taken seats in the diet. The immediate task of all patriots, he argued, was to ascertain the will of the nation and to draw up a programme to carry it out, and to these ends he urged the convocation of a national congress as soon as possible.[29]

In the month following the circulation of Bărnuţiu's appeal Romanian leaders gathered in various centres to exchange ideas. Out of these discussions emerged the outline of a national programme and the decision to convoke a representative assembly to debate it.

Despite the opposition of the governor of Transylvania, József Teleki, the organization of a national congress proceeded at a feverish pace. Intellectuals and clergy from all over Transylvania were drawn into these labours, and plans were made to invite Romanians from Hungary and Transylvania who were living in Moldavia and Wallachia to participate. Bărnuţiu and his colleagues were also eager to draw the peasants into their movement and dispatched emissaries in all directions to urge them to attend the congress.

At a preliminary congress attended by intellectuals and some 6,000 peasants at Blaj on 30 April Bărnuţiu, who delivered the principal address, declared that the time had come at last for the Romanian nation to recover its ancient rights, and for serfdom, which had held them in bondage for centuries, to be swept away. His audience responded enthusiastically, but what he said next proved sobering. He admonished them not to behave like revolutionaries who tried to achieve their ends by violence and thereby showed themselves unworthy of liberty, but rather to respect the law and give the landlords their due until matters could be set right by constitutional means. Bărnuţiu's attitude was shared by most of the forty-eighters. In spite of a romantic belief in the inevitability of progress and a solemn acceptance of their responsibilities towards the common people, they had preserved their faith in reason. Considering themselves the most reasonable of men, they thought it their prerogative to dictate the means of achieving social justice and national equality. They had an equally strong faith in the efficacy of just laws and good institutions, and once they had secured both, they had no doubt that the grievances of the masses could be quickly settled. For these reasons Bărnuţiu and his colleagues urged the peasants to be patient and not to upset the

---

[29] S. Dragomir, *Studii şi documente privitoare la revoluţia Românilor din Transilvania în anii 1848–1849*, v (Cluj, 1946), 108–10; *Revoluţia de la 1848–1849 din Transilvania*, i (Bucharest, 1977), 90–2.

'normal' process of change by acts of violence.[30] The peasants at Blaj heeded this advice and returned peacefully to their villages. Bărnuţiu and the other intellectuals judged the meeting a success and hastened their preparations for the great assembly scheduled for 15 May.

By the beginning of May Bărnuţiu had gained the support of all Romanian leaders for his programme, except George Bariţiu and Andrei Şaguna (1809–73), the newly elected bishop of the Orthodox Church. Bariţiu was pursuing a distinctly personal set of goals. He dismissed the union as being of little importance and thought it inopportune to take an anti-unionist stand. Convinced that the entire Habsburg monarchy was in the throes of a radical transformation, he saw no connection between the union and the achievement of equality and civil liberties by the Romanians. True to his liberal principles, he proposed a federalization of Transylvania as a solution to the intractable nationality problem. He advocated the creation of Magyar, Saxon, and Romanian cantons based on the Swiss model, each with extensive political and cultural autonomy, but united in matters common to all through a federal diet. This body was to be representative, 'as in North America', and all three languages were to be official.[31] Though no less committed to the welfare of the nation than Bărnuţiu, Bariţiu offered a programme that was devoid of the emotionalism inherent in Bărnuţiu's pronouncements. Their close cooperation did not begin until the autumn of 1848, after the outbreak of civil war.

As for Andrei Şaguna, Bărnuţiu and other intellectuals treated him with reserve, for, in spite of his energetic church reforms, they doubted the strength of his commitment to the national cause. Şaguna had in fact concerned himself almost exclusively with church affairs during his first two years in Transylvania. None the less, experience had taught him to appreciate the dynamism of national feeling, and he recognized both its destructive and its creative potential. In Pest in the 1820s he had witnessed the breakup of the Greek-Macedo-Romanian community, and in Karlowitz in the 1830s and 1840s he himself had become involved in the strife between Serbs and Romanians. Consequently, the problems of nationality in Transylvania were hardly foreign to him. He sympathized with the aspirations of Romanian intellectuals for some form of autonomy as a means of improving the material and cultural existence of their people. But he could never become one of them because he could never make the idea of nationality his master, as they had done. He viewed the national movement both in 1848 and later on as only one aspect of the complex process of social change. Although he recognized the idea of nationality as the dominant motive force in contemporary Europe, he consistently measured its aspirations and accomplishments against what were for him eternal values—the teachings of Christianity and those secular ideas that had proved their validity in the long course of human history. He was certain, therefore, that whatever progress the Romanian nation

[30] A. Papiu-Ilarian, *Istoria Românilor din Dacia Superioară*, ii (Vienna, 1852), 145–7.
[31] G. Bariţ, 'Unirea Transilvaniei cu Ungaria', FM 11/12 (1848), 95–6.

might make would depend upon the welfare of the Orthodox Church and loyalty to the Habsburg dynasty. Yet, he and Bărnuţiu quickly reached a compromise on fundamental issues: he accepted Bărnuţiu's idea of Romanian nationhood, and Bărnuţiu agreed to add to it an oath of loyalty to the imperial house.[32]

On 14 May, the day before the congress at Blaj, Romanian leaders met to draft the final text of a national programme. The initiative still lay with Bărnuţiu. In a forceful speech, which epitomized the thinking of many of his generation, he again warned against the acceptance of the union, characterizing it as an instrument to maintain Magyar predominance and stifle the development of the Romanian nation. He urged his colleagues not to be misled by Magyar promises of universal suffrage, a responsible ministry, and other freedoms, for the price would be their nationality; these benefits were offered to the Romanians only as individual citizens of Greater Hungary, not as a corporate entity, a nation, with its own destiny to fulfil. Thus, he concluded, liberty had no meaning unless it was national, and only in an autonomous Transylvania, where they formed a majority of the population, could the Romanians hope to preserve their most precious possession—their nationality.[33]

In the lengthy discussions that followed, three issues were paramount: political autonomy, religious divisions, and the status of the peasantry. On the first Bărnuţiu was obliged to modify his stand concerning the primacy of nationality and agreed to accept limitations on the Romanians' right of self-determination. Moderates, led by Şaguna and Bariţiu, persuaded the conference to couple the proclamation of Romanian nationhood with an oath of loyalty to the House of Habsburg and to place the protest against the union of Transylvania with Hungary at the end rather than at the beginning of the programme. Şaguna and his associates were guided by what seemed to them the practical realities of their situation. On the one hand, they considered their nation too weak to pursue a wholly independent policy, and thus they looked to the court of Vienna for the protection they needed. But, on the other hand, experience had taught them that Austria might eventually come to terms with the Magyars and that, as a result, they would be left to their own devices. For the time being, therefore, they urged a middle course that would maintain 'correct' relations with both Vienna and Buda-Pest.

Bărnuţiu and the younger intellectuals, who were his most ardent followers, also had to yield to the moderates on the question of a reunion of the Orthodox and Uniate Churches. They condemned the competition between them as antinational and eagerly sought a formula for ending the rivalry between Orthodox and Uniates. But it was clear that a forced reconciliation would cause an even wider split and seriously undermine national unity at this critical moment. The

---

[32] Dragomir, *Studii şi documente*, v. 185.
[33] S. Bărnuţiu, *Românii şi Ungurii; Discurs rostit în catedrala Blajului 2/14 mai 1848*, ed. G. Bogdan-Duică (Cluj, 1924), 9, 31.

matter was dropped, and the article in the national programme dealing with the religious issue merely expressed the general desire for religious harmony and the independence of the Romanian church.

The peasant question was also debated at some length. There was unanimous agreement that serfdom, which encompassed the great majority of the peasantry, was an inhuman institution and ought to be abolished without delay. But no one —neither Bărnuțiu and his supporters nor Şaguna and the moderates—thought that the peasants should be allowed to carry out their own emancipation. Instead, they recommended that it be done through legislation and be accompanied by expanded opportunities for education. A majority argued against giving the landlords any indemnity for services lost, and everyone agreed that the peasants should not be made to pay for their own emancipation. But no one seems to have thought very much about how the new freeholder was going remain economically independent on an inadequate plot of land.

At the national congress on 15–17 May some 40,000 persons who had gathered on the Field of Liberty outside Blaj approved a sixteen-point programme. It was a characteristic manifesto of the intellectuals of 1848 in Central Europe and represented the most comprehensive and forceful statement of Romanian aspirations made up to that time. Bărnuțiu and his colleagues, who were mainly responsible for its final form, no longer justified their demands on the basis of historical right or imperial patent, as their predecessors in the eighteenth century had done, but rather relied on a principle they believed to be universally valid: the natural rights of man. They now extended these rights, subsumed under the slogan 'liberty, equality, and fraternity', from individuals to entire nations. Their preoccupation with nation is nowhere more evident than in the sixteen points themselves.

They proclaimed the independence of the Romanian nation and its full equality with the other nations of Transylvania and declared their intention to protect its rights by creating a new political system based on liberal principles. For the first time in such a public document they stressed the connection between economic development and national progress and thus demanded both an end to serfdom and recognition of equality of opportunity in commerce and the artisan trades. They also stressed the need for a well-informed, literate citizenry, if liberal political institutions were to prosper, and therefore they made provision for a modern school system. Unlike their more cosmopolitan forebears of the period of the Enlightenment, who fostered learning for its own sake, they insisted that education was a task that could be performed successfully only in national schools and in the national language. Religion, too, was subordinated to nationality, and Christianity as such appears largely irrelevant. The intellectuals gave expression to the widespread desire of Orthodox and Uniates to be rid of Serbian Orthodox and Hungarian Roman Catholic interference respectively in their affairs, but their main objective was political and cultural rather than canonical—to enable the churches to serve the national cause more effectively.

At its final session on 17 May the congress elected a permanent committee of twenty-five members, with Şaguna as president and Bărnuţiu as vice-president, to provide the national movement with continuity and leadership. It also chose two delegations, one, headed by Şaguna, to bring the national programme before the court of Vienna, and the other, under Bishop Ioan Lemeni of the Uniate Church, to represent the congress at the forthcoming diet of Transylvania in Cluj.

Relations between the Permanent Committee and the Transylvanian government rapidly deteriorated. Governor Teleki, supported by the majority of Transylvanian Magyar leaders, refused to recognize the existence of a separate Romanian nation. Because of the committee's opposition to the union of Transylvania with Hungary, he accused it of subversion and ordered it to disband. He also suspected its members of irredentism, of promoting a pan-Romanian movement, whose alleged goal was the creation of a Daco-Romanian state stretching from the Black Sea to the western boundaries of Transylvania. There was little substance to the change. Romanian intellectuals on both sides of the Carpathians certainly speculated on the possibility of a united Romania, but the Transylvanians, in particular, were cautious.

The initiative for some sort of pan-Romanian action seems to have come mainly from the Wallachians, especially the representatives of the provisional government in Bucharest. Alexandru G. Golescu and Ioan Maiorescu both of whom passed through Transylvania on diplomatic missions to the West, suggested a united Romania under either Austrian or Russian auspices.[34] In more lyrical terms, Alecu Russo, an exile from the abortive revolution in Moldavia in April, spoke of 'one powerful nation, with the sea and two rivers as barricades and with Roman blood in our veins, . . . no longer Moldavia, nor Transylvania, nor the Banat, but only Romania, with its capital to be named Rome'.[35] In Transylvania such ideas were expressed in strictest confidence, for the members of the Permanent Committee were anxious to avoid the taint of disloyalty towards Austria, which might irreparably damage their own cause. They showed little enthusiasm for political union as an attainable goal in the foreseeable future. First of all, they recognized that the two Romanian principalities were weak, and second, they were conscious of their own precarious situation and were certain that Austrian aid would be necessary if they were to surmount the challenge of Magyar nationalism.

In the mean time, the delegation chosen to bring the national programme to Vienna encountered little understanding at the imperial court. On 23 June, Şaguna and a small group presented the Emperor Ferdinand with a revised version of the sixteen points which stressed the right of the Romanians to

---

[34] *Anul 1848*, iii (Bucharest, 1902), 731, and iv (Bucharest, 1903), 224, 229. Persuasive arguments that union was a serious goal of the forty-eighters are made by Cornelia Bodea, *Lupta Românilor*, 131–58. See also Stan, *Revoluţia română*, 110–30.

[35] I. Breazu, 'Alecu Russo în Ardealul revoluţionar la 1848', *Transilvania*, 72/2 (1941), 127.

equality with the other nations of Transylvania and protested against the union of Transylvania with Hungary as destructive of their nationality. The emperor received them graciously, but he suggested that the major problems that concerned them had already been resolved by the Hungarian diet and recommended that they negotiate directly with the Hungarian government on matters of detail.

Beset by similar petitions from all sides, the court with some relief shifted responsibility for the Romanians on to the Magyars. The Romanians had traditionally counted for little in the calculations of Austrian policy-makers, who viewed them as a mass of peasants incapable of contributing anything of substance to the governance of the empire. But in the spring of 1848, threatened with the collapse of the world they knew, these officials discovered uses to which even outcasts could be put. At the beginning of June the council of ministers discussed ways of mobilizing the Romanians and Slavs to combat the 'aggressive' policies of the Magyars. The minister of finance, Karl von Krauss, feared that the latter might, if unchecked, become the dominant element in the empire, and the minister of war, Count Theodor von Latour, raised the possibility of an alliance between the German provinces and those peoples of Hungary who saw their own advantage in the maintenance of a unitary empire. He suggested that the Romanians could well serve as the core of this alliance, which might ultimately even enable Austria to extend her influence into the Danubian principalities. Most of Latour's colleagues approved such a policy in principle, but, because of the dangerous situation in which the empire found itself, they recommended caution and concessions to the Magyars.[36]

Bishop Lemeni fared no better at the diet of Cluj. Enthusiasm for the union of Transylvania with Hungary was overwhelming among the Magyar majority, and on 30 May they approved it. Only on 20 June did the diet take up the issues raised in the Romanian programme. It decided that most of their grievances had already been satisfied, since the union had made them full citizens of the new Hungary, and recommended that the Romanians take up any unresolved questions in the Hungarian diet in Pest. It also established a commission on the union to work out the final details of the union with the Hungarian government.

At the end of June Şaguna and several members of his delegation travelled from Vienna to Buda-Pest to take part in the work of the Commission on the Union. Only after hard bargaining among its members, and bowing to the urgings of Prime Minister Batthyány and Minister of the Interior Bertalan Szemere, did the Magyar majority on 27 September approve a bill granting significant concessions to the Romanians. It formally recognized the Romanian nationality and the autonomy of the Orthodox and Uniate Churches; allowed the free use of the Romanian language in village affairs, the church, and elementary and secondary schools; and provided for the appointment of Ro-

---

[36] Á. Károlyi, *Az 1848-iki pozsonyi törvénycikkek az udvar előtt* (Budapest, 1936), 344–5.

manians to public office in proportion to their numbers.[37] But because of the deteriorating situation in Transylvania and the increasingly strained relations between the court and the Hungarian government, the project was not submitted to the Hungarian diet until May 1849.

In Transylvania, in the mean time, the battle lines had become more sharply drawn. A special Hungarian government commissioner ordered the dissolution of the Romanian Permanent Committee on the grounds that it was obstructing the lawful union of Transylvania with Hungary. This act and the attempted arrest of committee members pushed Romanian leaders further towards an alliance with the court against the Hungarian government. The Austrians, for their part, had taken heart after successes against revolutionaries in Bohemia and northern Italy during the summer. They found willing allies for a counterstroke against the Magyars in the non-Magyar peoples of Hungary, who had come to see their own existence jeopardized by Magyar national aspirations.

In Transylvania the Austrian military commander, General Anton von Puchner, gave his blessing to a second Romanian national congress at Blaj at the end of September. The delegates reaffirmed their opposition to the union of Transylvania with Hungary, repudiated the authority of the Hungarian government in Transylvania, and pledged again their loyalty to the imperial house. On 30 September Bărnuţiu, as the president of a new national committee, worked out a plan for cooperation with Puchner, but, significantly, the latter avoided any reference to a Romanian nation or any commitment to support its political aspirations. Nevertheless, when he publicly denounced the Hungarian government and assumed the powers of civil governor of the principality on 18 October the National Committee responded at once with a call to arms. Romanian intellectuals did not regard their alliance with Puchner as inconsistent with their principles. In the face of Magyar nationalism, Austrian aid seemed the sole means by which they could achieve their national goals. They still clung to the idea that the Habsburg monarchy would somehow be transformed into a federalized constitutional monarchy.

Puchner's army and his Romanian allies proved no match for the Hungarian forces under General József Bem, which by the middle of December controlled most of Transylvania, except for the strongholds of Sibiu and Braşov. In desperation, Puchner prevailed upon the Romanian National Committee to send Şaguna, who had returned home in October, to Bucharest to seek the intervention of the Russian army.

At a hastily assembled national congress, Bărnuţiu and his colleagues reluctantly agreed to Puchner's request, but used the occasion to restate their attachment to liberal principles and the idea of nationality in a new thirteen-point programme. What distinguished it from earlier documents was the assumption that an autonomous Romanian duchy, although without fixed boundaries, had

---

[37] S. Márki, 'Az erdélyi unió-bizottság', *Budapesti Szemle*, 95 (1898), 332–7; J. Béer, *Az 1848—49 évi népképviseleti Országgyűlés* (Budapest, 1954), 583–5.

already come into being. The National Committee intended to seek recognition of this fact and of itself as a provisional Romanian government from the new Emperor Francis Joseph, who had ascended the throne on 2 December. It chose Şaguna to head a small delegation to explain to Austrian officials in Vienna the new idea of self-determination.[38]

Şaguna made his way to Vienna via Bucharest and Cernăuţi, in Bukovina. On 6 January 1849 he met General Lüders, the commander of the Russian army of occupation, who declined to become involved in Transylvanian affairs without specific instructions from St Petersburg. A few days later Şaguna resumed his journey, reaching Olmütz, in Bohemia, where the court had established itself after a new revolutionary outbreak in Vienna, on 4 February. His delegation was joined by Romanians from the Banat and Bukovina. Lengthy consultations persuaded them to go beyond seeking national rights separately within each of the three provinces and to work together to obtain the court's sanction of a political union of all the Romanians of the monarchy.

Romanians in the Banat and Bukovina had responded quickly to the revolutionary events taking place in Vienna and Buda-Pest. The course which their movements took was largely determined by social and political conditions specific to their regions, but, as in Transylvania, the defence of national rights overshadowed other issues. Here, too, leadership came from intellectuals and the clergy, joined by a few large landowners.

In the Banat, an area of mixed Romanian, Serbian, and German population in southern Hungary, the immediate objective of Romanian leaders was to obtain recognition of a Romanian Orthodox church separate from the Serbian metropolitanate of Karlowitz. They were thus carrying on a struggle that had erupted in the 1830s when the Romanians had sought to elect one of their own as bishop of Arad.[39] They had felt themselves on the defensive in a province where the governance of the Orthodox Church was in the hands mainly of Serbs and where they were, consequently, underrepresented, despite the fact that they outnumbered the Serbs in the Banat approximately two to one (of the 813,000 persons living in the Banat at the beginning of the nineteenth century, 173,653 were Serbs and 394,228 Romanians). Since the Romanians had no other institution of similar importance except the church, they were convinced that national emancipation had naturally to begin here. In response to dramatic political events throughout the Habsburg Monarchy in the spring of 1848 laymen and clergy met for the first time on 16–17 May in Lugoj to plan a course of action. They refused to attend the national church congress convoked by Metropolitan Joseph Rajačić in Karlowitz on 27 May. Instead, they decided to petition the new Hungarian government to allow the Romanians to hold their own church congress where they could elect a metropolitan, organize

[38] N. Popea, *Memorialul Archiepiscopului şi Mitropolitului Andreiu baron de Şaguna, sau luptele naţionale-politice ale Românilor, 1846–1873*, i (Sibiu, 1889), 230–2; FM 12/3 (1849), 17–19.
[39] G. Ciuhandu, *Episcopii Samuil Vulcan şi Gherasim Raţ* (Arad, 1935), 355–69.

their church, and discuss other important matters affecting the Romanian nation.[40]

The decisions taken at this and similar small gatherings elsewhere were superseded by a national congress held in Lugoj on 27 June. It was primarily the work of laymen led by Eftimie Murgu, who represented a major current of Romanian aspirations in the Banat. While according a national church due importance, they none the less gave priority to a political solution to the problem of national rights in the Banat and in the Habsburg monarchy in general. Murgu (1805–70) had obtained degrees in philosophy (1827) and law (1830) from the University of Pest, and, besides a law career, he had taken part in the scholarly polemics in the Banat over the origins of the Romanians and the nature of their language.[41] In *Widerlegung der Abhandlung* (1830) he sustained the thesis of the Transylvanian School that the Romanians were descended from the Roman colonists settled in Dacia by Trajan, that Romanian was an evolved form of Latin, and that the Romanians of the Banat, Transylvania, Moldavia, and Wallachia formed one nation and were the oldest people of the region. In 1834 he was hired by Gheorghe Asachi to teach philosophy at Academia Mihăileană in Iaşi, and three years later he moved to Bucharest to teach philosophy at the Academy of St Sava. Here he met a number of young radicals, Nicolae Bălcescu and Dumitru Filipescu among them, and became one of the organizers of Filipescu's unsuccessful conspiracy in 1840. Murgu was expelled from Wallachia in 1841 and then ran afoul of the authorities in his native Banat, being imprisoned from 1846 until the spring of 1848 in Pest on charges of conspiring to undermine the territorial integrity of Hungary. Released in May 1848 in the general spirit of conciliation of the period, he hastened back to the Banat. With the approval of the Hungarian minister of the interior he and several colleagues organized the national congress at Lugoj on 27 June in order to draw up a programme of reforms for submission to the Batthyány government.

Murgu faced a dilemma common to liberals everywhere in Eastern Europe in 1848. He was committed to bringing about the emancipation of his nation, but at the same time he recognized the need for all the nationalities to stand together against the conservative great powers of the region. He was enthusiastic about the liberal legislation of the Hungarian government and was certain that the age of liberty for all peoples had finally arrived. As a guarantee against a resurgence of the old regime he advocated an alliance between the Romanians and the Magyars, an idea to which he remained faithful until the collapse of the Hungarian revolution in August 1849. But he took a sterner view of relations with the Serbs, and in his letter convoking the congress at Lugoj he declared that its main objective was to give the Romanians an opportunity to decide their own fate and to demonstrate publicly that the Banat was not a Serbian land. At Lugoj the some 10,000 persons who attended the congress approved a programme which

---

[40] I. D. Suciu, *Revoluţia de la 1848–1849 în Banat* (Bucharest, 1968), 58–61.
[41] On his career during the revolution of 1848, see E. Murgu, *Scrieri* (Bucharest, 1969), 12–59.

forcefully asserted Romanian nationhood, but refrained from criticizing the Hungarian government. It demanded the creation of a Romanian national guard with Murgu as its commander, the recognition of Romanian as an official language throughout the Banat, and the establishment of an independent Romanian Orthodox church in the Banat.[42]

The course of events during the rest of 1848 left Romanian aspirations in the Banat unfulfilled. Within the Romanian movement itself the two main currents drifted apart. Although the adherents of each demanded national emancipation, they differed in the means to their ends. Murgu and his supporters sought an alliance with the Magyars and participated in the governance of the new Hungary as deputies in the Hungarian parliament. But more conservative elements looked to Vienna for the support of nationality, since they were as wary of the Magyar liberals as they were of the Serbian Orthodox clergy. Led by the large landowners Petru and Andrei Mocioni, the Romanian committee in Timişoara, which had been formed in October 1848, entered into regular contact with the National Committee in Sibiu in order to bring about the political union of the Romanians of the Habsburg monarchy and to make certain that in the Banat the Romanians were not placed under Serbian ecclesiastical or civil administration.[43] They were spurred to action by Emperor Francis Joseph's confirmation on 15 December of Joseph Rajačić as patriarch of the Orthodox Church in the Habsburg monarchy and other acts which they interpreted as recognition of the Voivodina region of southern Hungary, including the Banat, as a Serbian Crown land. It was thus with mixed feelings of expectation and apprehension that Romanian representatives from the Banat arrived in Vienna in January 1849.

In Bukovina Romanian intellectuals and clergy had also been roused to activity in the spring of 1848 by the general wave of unrest sweeping the Habsburg monarchy and, especially, by the arrival of political refugees from Moldavia. The activists, few in number but dedicated to bringing about a political revival of the Romanians of the province, were led by the three Hurmuzaki brothers. Descendants of a Moldavian *boier* family and possessing law degrees from the University of Vienna, they established a small committee composed of themselves and a few moderate *boiers* and professors from the Orthodox Theological Academy in Cernăuţi to coordinate Romanian political activities.

The influence of the liberal and national ideas of the day was evident in the twelve-point petition to the emperor drawn up in June by Eudoxiu Hurmuzaki (1812–74).[44] On behalf of the 'Romanian nation' of Bukovina he requested, first of all, the recognition of Bukovina as an autonomous province with its own parliament, a body that would represent equally all the orders of the country—clergy, landlords, intellectuals, bourgeoisie, and peasants—without regard to

---

[42] Suciu, *Revoluţia*, 98–113.   [43] Ibid. 206–20.
[44] Bodea, *1848 la Români*, i. 608–13; Iacobescu, *Din istoria Bucovinei*, i. 375–82.

religion. Hurmuzaki clearly had in mind an essentially Romanian Crown land, since the intent of the petition was to strengthen the Romanian character of the province. In order to 'preserve nationality' he urged the establishment of a network of Romanian elementary schools and the appointment of professors of Romanian language and literature in the secondary schools, and he insisted that all official bodies accept petitions in Romanian. He also called attention to the numerous social and commercial links between Bukovina and the 'kindred' states of Moldavia and Wallachia and by implication suggested that they be strengthened, adding somewhat disingenuously that such action would have a beneficial effect on the economy of the whole monarchy. Hurmuzaki recognized the importance of the Orthodox Church in Romanian cultural life and, like his colleagues in Transylvania and the Banat, sought to enhance its role as a national institution by securing its right to self-government and by increasing the role of laymen in its cultural and economic affairs. To do this he requested the election of the bishop by a national synod, representing all the orders of society, and proposed that the Orthodox Religious Fund be administered by a national committee. He thought of both church and fund as Romanian institutions and simply ignored the growing number of Ruthenians in the church. Evident, too, was his commitment to economic liberalism as he recommended the creation of a provincial credit institution, the regulation of the situation of the peasants, and the abolition of customs barriers within the province and at its frontiers.

Despite their national and liberal zeal, the Hurmuzakis and their colleagues lacked both the organization and the mass support to influence the course of events in the province. They made no effort to mobilize Romanian peasants behind the national programme (there was little in it to arouse their enthusiasm, in any case), and the Orthodox Church hierarchy remained aloof from the national struggle. Bishop Eugen Hacman had always been wary of involving the church in politics and was now particularly anxious to prevent an irreparable schism between Romanians and Ruthenians. Nor did he welcome the efforts of the Hurmuzakis and other liberal laymen to increase their role in church governing bodies.[45]

In the absence of specifically Romanian political institutions, the Hurmuzakis, like Romanian intellectuals in Transylvania a decade earlier, founded a newspaper to disseminate their ideas and mobilize public opinion. *Bucovina* began publication on 4 October 1848 as a weekly under the editorship of George Hurmuzaki. Besides defending national interests in Bukovina, its founders intended to use their paper as a 'bridge' between Romanians everywhere.[46] They thus gave extensive coverage to the struggles in the principalities and Transylvania to defend the rights of nationality and bring about economic and

---

[45] I. Nistor, *Istoria bisericii din Bucovina* (Bucharest, 1916), 64–71: T. Bălan, 'Conflictul Episcopului Eugen Hacman cu preoţii din Bucovina, în anul 1848', *Revista arhivelor*, 4/2 (1941), 314–34.

[46] T. Bălan, *Activitatea refugiaţilor moldoveni în Bucovina, 1848* (Sibiu, 1944), 27–34, 45–6; Iacobescu, *Din istoria Bucovinei*, i. 417–24.

social reforms. They were especially concerned about the fate of Moldavia and Wallachia. They contrasted the 'enlightened regime' under which the Romanians of Bukovina lived with the conditions created by the 'terrible Turco-Russian' army of occupation in the principalities and were convinced that progress towards liberty and happiness there depended upon close relations with Austria and Germany.

The intellectuals and a few churchmen (but not Bishop Hacman) demonstrated their pan-Romanian sentiments during Bishop Şaguna's brief stopover in Cernăuţi in January 1849 on his way from Bucharest to Olmütz. They enthusiastically embraced the idea of a single Romanian duchy in the Habsburg monarchy and agreed to cooperate with the Transylvanians to obtain the emperor's approval.[47]

At Olmütz the Romanians of Transylvania, the Banat, and Bukovina formed a single delegation and drafted a new national programme, which had as its primary goal Romanian political unity and autonomy. Presented to Francis Joseph on 25 February 1849, it called for the holding of a national congress immediately after the cessation of hostilities for the purpose of establishing political and ecclesiastical institutions and electing a national political leader and an archbishop to whom all Romanian bishops would be subordinate. The delegation also requested an annual Romanian national assembly, the introduction of Romanian as the official language, proportional representation for the Romanian nation in the imperial parliament in Vienna, a special commission to advise the court and the council of ministers on Romanian affairs, and the assumption by the emperor of the title 'Grand Duke of the Romanians'.[48] No previous document had expressed so clearly the ideal of Romanian unity within the Habsburg monarchy. It also signified the acceptance by the Romanians of federalism as the only feasible solution to the monarchy's nationality problems.

The calculations of the Romanians were undone by the promulgation of the new imperial constitution of 4 March, which re-established the historical Crown lands and made no mention of federalism or the creation of new political entities. Attempts by the Romanian delegation to have their proposals reconsidered were curtly dismissed with the admonition that the best course for them to follow would be loyalty to the emperor.[49] From this time on the Romanian political movement gradually lost momentum as German centralists gained the ascendancy in Vienna.

In Transylvania the fighting intensified. In early March Hungarian armies captured Sibiu and Braşov and drove Puchner's forces across the border into Wallachia. The Romanian National Committee fled Sibiu on 11 March and

[47] Bodea, *1848 la Români*, ii (Bucharest, 1982), 966–70; C. Burac, 'Hurmuzacheştii şi problema unităţii româneşti', *Revista arhivelor*, 69/4 (1992), 390–9.

[48] Bodea, *1848 la Români*, ii. 960–5.

[49] M. Popescu, *Documente inedite privitoare la istoria Transilvaniei între 1848–1859* (Bucharest, 1929), 32–6, 61–2.

effectively ceased to function. The main centre of resistance shifted to Munții Apuseni in western Transylvania, where Avram Iancu, one of the organizers of the national congress in May 1848, at the head of a peasant militia held out until the end of the war in August.

A desperate effort to mediate between the Hungarian government and Avram Iancu was undertaken by Nicolae Bălcescu in the spring of 1849.[50] In May he met Lajos Kossuth, who had become governor of an independent Hungary after the Hungarian parliament had deposed the Habsburgs on 14 April, to try to persuade him to join with the Romanians on both sides of the Carpathians in a united campaign to save the revolutionary ideals of the previous spring from being overwhelmed by Habsburg and Russian armies. Bălcescu and other leaders of the Wallachian Revolution were chagrined that the Romanians of Transylvania had allied themselves with the Habsburgs, whom they considered the embodiment of tyranny and reaction. But Bălcescu found himself in a difficult position. He sympathized with their efforts to preserve their nationality, but he thought that the peril which confronted all the small nations of Eastern Europe required support for the Magyars, the only nation 'still fighting against Russia and her despotic allies'. His immediate objective in meeting Kossuth was to obtain help in expelling Russian armies from Wallachia and restoring the independent liberal government of the previous year. Eftimie Murgu, who continued to represent his Banat district in the Hungarian parliament and who had voted in favour of dethroning the Habsburgs, warmly supported his friend's initiative.

Bălcescu's hopes for a *rapprochement* between the Romanians and the Hungarian government rose as the tide of battle turned against the Magyars after the intervention of Russian armies in May. Kossuth became more receptive to the idea and encouraged Bălcescu to negotiate with Iancu. But he still refused to make any concessions on administrative autonomy or language rights, which would, he was certain, compromise the political integrity of Hungary. Bălcescu's meetings with Iancu at the latter's headquarters in Munții Apuseni in the latter half of July went well, but events on the battlefield overtook him. On 28 July the Hungarian parliament finally enacted into law the bill proposed by the Commission on the Union the previous September. But it was now too late. Within two weeks a series of defeats inflicted by superior Austrian and Russian forces brought the surrender of the main Hungarian field army at Világos on 13 August, and by the end of the month all organized resistance had ceased.

The suppression of independent Hungary dashed Romanian hopes of a united, autonomous duchy. The fragile alliance of necessity between the Romanians and the court of Vienna, already strained by aspirations to national self-determination, on the one side, and an imperial restoration, on the other, disintegrated. In Transylvania a host of Austrian officials, led by the new military and civil

---

[50] S. Dragomir, 'N. Bălcescu în Ardeal', *Anuarul Institutului de Istorie Națională din Cluj*, 5 (1928–30), 1–34.

governor, General Ludwig Wohlgemuth, descended upon the principality with instructions to restore it to the status of an imperial province as quickly as possible. The Banat and Bukovina underwent a similar process. Everywhere the new bureaucracy expected the Romanians to resume their places as loyal, and anonymous, subjects of the emperor.

AFTERMATH IN TRANSYLVANIA

The hallmark of the restoration in Transylvania in the fall of 1849 and the spring of 1850 was centralism. The primary goal of Austrian officials was to bind the principality as tightly as possible to Vienna. They redrew local administrative boundaries, maintained martial law, and introduced new legislation in order to discourage all manifestations of nationalism and liberalism, especially among the Magyars.

The decade of absolutism, as the period has been aptly called, represented a low point in Romanian fortunes. In a sense, the new regime granted them equality with the Magyars and Saxons, but it was an equality of deprivation. Austrian officials in both Vienna and Transylvania continued to treat the Romanians as a peasant people incapable of taking part in the complex processes of provincial government or even of managing their own affairs. These officials were particularly wary of the peasant masses as a volatile threat to good order, and they held their priests suspect because of the spiritual and political leadership they exercised in the villages. But most of all they feared the intellectuals as the carriers of revolution and the agents of a pan-Romanian movement which aimed at bringing about the political union of the Romanians on both sides of the Carpathians.[51]

The authorities' wariness of the forty-eighters was justified, not, in the first instance, because they were revolutionaries or pan-Romanians, but because their experiences during the revolution had shattered their illusions about 'alliances' with Austria. These Romanians attributed their failure to gain recognition as a separate nation with a territory and an administration of its own to Austrian ingratitude for the services their nation had rendered the dynasty in its hour of need. Some among them, such as Simion Bărnuţiu, went into exile, while others, like Avram Iancu, simply withdrew from public life. But their national feeling remained undiminished, and the idea of nation survived as their spiritual guide. It was evident throughout the 1850s as they wrote and spoke about self-determination and liberal government that they could no longer be satisfied with a passive role in public affairs.

Romanians (and the other peoples of Transylvania) resumed political activity in 1860, as the court of Vienna tested new constitutional formulas in order to

[51] Ş. Manciulea, 'Atestate de purificaţiune', *Cultura creştină*, 18 (1938), 473–83; Popescu, *Documente*, 176, 245, 255–9, 275–6.

restore the monarchy's international standing and maintain its cohesion at home after defeat in war with France and Sardinia in 1859. Anton von Schmerling assumed these daunting tasks as minister of state in December 1860. A centralist, he had little sympathy for the Diploma of 20 October 1860, which made concessions, however modest, to a type of federalism promoted by the Magyar and Bohemian aristocracies, who sought to restore the historical rights of their respective countries. More to his liking was the Patent of 26 February 1861, which concentrated the direction of the monarchy's affairs in Vienna and reduced Hungary and the historical crown lands to the status of provinces. Nevertheless, he was ready to grant the 'loyal' nationalities a measure of autonomy in managing the affairs of their respective provinces. In Transylvania the Romanians and Saxons fell into this category, but the court continued to treat the Magyars as a threat to the monarchy's integrity and rejected their demands on behalf of historical Hungary. The majority of Magyars in both Hungary and Transylvania repaid the court by boycotting Schmerling's constitutional experiment.

Schmerling was thus obliged to rely on the non-Magyars of Hungary and Transylvania to carry out his designs. For a time he and the Romanians discovered mutual advantages in supporting each other's goals, and, as a result, the Romanians briefly achieved the national equality they had sought since the eighteenth century. But the new alliance with Austria, as in 1848, struck no deep roots of principle: the court was intent upon strengthening the Monarchy at all costs, while the Romanians were beholden to the idea of nation. The cooperation between them was based upon a mutual, but fleeting, interest in containing Magyar nationalism. In a sense, it was the Magyars who brought them together and, in the end, it was they who forced them apart. When the court realized that only a compromise with the Magyars could solve the constitutional impasse in which it eventually found itself, it showed no hesitation in abandoning its flirtation with Romanian self-determination.

For the time being, Romanian leaders held national conferences, one in 1861 and another in 1863, where they engaged in spirited debate about the course they should take and drafted plans of action. They had done these things before, in 1848, but their exertions now were the more heady because their partnership with Vienna seemed the more genuine. Such optimism was reinforced by wide-ranging public discussion of critical issues. The Romanian newspaper press under a lightened censorship revived as a forum for ideas. Its editors and correspondents joined enthusiastically in what had become a national debate and contributed no little to the creation of an informed, activist public opinion.

As the debate intensified, two main currents of opinion about the future constitutional organization of Transylvania and the place of the Romanians in it emerged. One was represented by Andrei Şaguna, the bishop of the Orthodox Church, who urged that changes in political structures indeed take into account the spirit of the times, but also respect tradition and the historical continuity of institutions. At the Verstärkter Reichsrat, a consultative assembly of prominent public figures from all parts of the monarchy which met in Vienna between March and September 1860, he offered a solution that was neither centralist nor federalist. His formula combined recognition of the monarchy's unity and the maintenance of the emperor's prerogatives with respect for local custom and the principle of national equality. He thus intended to preserve and strengthen the autonomy of existing Crown lands such as Transylvania, but would at the same time have new constitutions drawn up in each incorporating general principles such as national equality and adapting imperial legal codes and administrative practices to local circumstances.[52] Yet, he was eager to maintain the connection with Vienna because experience had taught him that Austria could serve as a counterweight to the Magyars in Transylvania and because he thought a united monarchy more likely to prosper economically and culturally than provinces and crown lands isolated from one another. Perhaps his vision of the future organization of Transylvania is summed up best by his advocacy of a 'Transylvanian consciousness', a plea to all its peoples to embrace the principle of national equality while at the same time pursuing national distinctiveness.[53]

Not all Romanian leaders were as willing as Şaguna to enroll in a united monarchy. Instead, they proclaimed the primacy of the ethnic nation and demanded a leading role for the Romanians in the new Transylvania. To be sure, they still looked to Vienna to tip the scales in their favour against the Magyars and Saxons, but for them the rights of nation were paramount. They acted as though the nation were a law unto itself and knew no bounds to its own fruition. For them, the connection with the Habsburg dynasty and the monarchy was not an organic one, as it was for Şaguna, but, rather, offered a means to an end. Their advocacy of federalism, for example, was intended to further the aims of nationhood, not to strengthen the monarchy.

This current of opinion reflected the thought of the forty-eighters and a new generation of intellectuals. George Bariţiu, the journalist and founder of the Romanian newspaper press in Transylvania, represented the former, and Ioan Raţiu (1828–1902), a young lawyer and later in the century the president of the Romanian National party, the latter. They and their colleagues were unwilling to leave the initiative to Vienna. Instead, they were determined to create their own political institutions and to have Romanians assume responsibility for Romanian affairs.[54] They also objected to Şaguna's emphasis on a Transylvanian consciousness and his tacit renunciation of a separate Romanian territory. Although they themselves endorsed the principle of national equality, they insisted that the Romanians play the leading, if not the dominant, role in Transylvania's affairs

---

[52] *Verhandlungen des verstärkten Reichsrats* (Vienna, 1860), 42–3, 431.

[53] Haus-, Hof- und Staatsarchiv (Vienna), Kabinettsarchiv, Nachlass Reichenstein: Minutes of the Diet of Sibiu, Şaguna's speeches of 27 July and 16 Sept. 1863.

[54] K. Hitchins and L. Maior, *Corespondenţa lui Ioan Raţiu cu George Bariţiu, 1861–1892* (Cluj, 1970), 47–8, 53.

because it was their ancestral home and because they formed a majority of its population.

A confrontation between Şaguna and the intellectuals took place at the national conference of some 150 delegates held in Sibiu on 13–16 January 1861. As they formulated the tasks of a newly created national committee, Bariţiu and Raţiu and their supporters demanded that it establish a political party on the Western European model to serve as the primary instrument for mobilizing public opinion and achieving national goals. But Şaguna was reluctant to pursue a course too independent of Vienna, lest the Romanians alienate what was certain to be a decisive element in their future. For their part, the intellectuals criticized his inactivity, and privately they expressed disappointment at how unreceptive Austrian officials had been to their plans. For a time they even contemplated a boycott of the court's reorganization of Transylvanian affairs, abandoning the idea only because it seemed premature. Although the matter receded into the background for the next few years, the fleeting suggestion of passive resistance was a sign of growing irritation with the court's tutelage.

The divergences between Şaguna and his supporters and the intellectuals went beyond matters of tactics and organization. They were symptomatic of a sea change in thought about community taking place generally in Eastern Europe. For Bariţiu and Raţiu and their colleagues the ethnic nation had galvanized their energies and had become the centre of their preoccupations. They made all other institutions subordinate to it. Şaguna, by contrast, continued to think in terms of distinct categories such as dynasty, church, and nation and did not grasp the all-embracing nature of the modern idea of nation. In an age of nationalism he was not a nationalist. Rather, he fitted the mould of the bishop-national leader in the tradition of Ion Inochentie Klein.

The Romanians seemed about to achieve national fulfilment at the Transylvanian diet, which was convened at Sibiu in 1863. Since the court was relying on the provincial diets to become the instruments of its new constitutional order, it made substantial concessions to all those who would support it. In Transylvania, to counteract a determined boycott of the diet by Magyars, who demanded the restoration of Hungary's historical rights and the union of Transylvania with Hungary, the court assured the Romanians and Saxons of a majority in the diet and recognized the validity of Romanian claims to national equality.[55] Thus, the diet enacted laws raising the Romanian nation and its two churches to the status of the other nations of Transylvania and their churches and recognizing Romanian as an official language alongside Magyar and German. Approval of these laws by the emperor followed in due course, but before they could come into force they required a second reading in the diet and final sanction by the emperor, a procedure that appeared a mere formality. When the

[55] Ibid. 62–3, 69–70; S. Retegan, *Dieta românească a Transilvaniei* (Cluj-Napoca, 1979), 57–79.

diet adjourned in October 1863 Romanian leaders were satisfied that they had set Transylvania on a new course.

When the diet reconvened in May 1864 a number of Romanian deputies were absent. They had been alarmed by signs that the court was prepared to abandon an autonomous Transylvania. Şaguna, in particular, sensed a general shift in Austrian policy away from cooperation with the Romanians and Slavs and towards an accommodation with the Magyars. When asked to return to the diet, he refused, reportedly saying that he did not wish to be a party to the death sentence of his nation. His premonition of disaster was well founded. Although the diet gave a second reading to the laws on Romanian nationhood and language, they remained unsanctioned, and bills dealing with the organization of public administration and justice became bogged down in committee. The diet adjourned on 29 October with little to show for its five months' work. When it met again, a year later, its sole task would be to proclaim the union of Transylvania with Hungary.

Although the political gains of the Romanians in the 1860s proved illusory, the religious and cultural foundations they laid endured. In these matters the Orthodox and Uniate Churches remained the bulwarks of the ethnic community. As a consequence of Şaguna's persistence, an Orthodox metropolitanate for Transylvania was established in 1864, which, together with the Uniate metropolitanate created in 1853, provided a legal framework and shield for cultural self-determination. Both churches operated networks of elementary and secondary schools, which offered Romanian pupils an education in their own language. Although lay leaders objected to the confessional character of these schools and would have preferred national schools, they welcomed the protection these institutions provided young Romanians against state schools, where the curriculum and the language of instruction aimed at furthering Magyar nation-building. The clergy of both churches contributed substantially to the functioning of a vigorous newspaper press: *Telegraful Român*, founded in 1853 for the Orthodox, and *Gazeta de Transilvania*, founded in 1838, which often represented Uniate opinion. These and other newspapers provided direction on crucial issues of the day in the absence of political parties. Clergy and lay leaders joined forces in 1861 to establish Asociaţia Transilvană pentru Literatura Română şi Cultura Poporului Român (the Transylvanian Association for Romanian Literature and the Culture of the Romanian People, generally known as ASTRA). Although it failed to live up fully to the expectations of its founders, it none the less represented a significant attempt to bridge confessional differences by mobilizing national cultural resources.

In both Vienna and Transylvania by the spring of 1865 it had become clear to many that Schmerling, far from assuring the strength and prosperity of the empire, was, in fact, presiding over the breakdown of government administration and a rising tide of opposition from the very elements that he had counted on for support. By August the court had decided to come to an understanding with the

Magyars which would require, among other concessions, the abandonment of both Transylvania's autonomy and the guarantees of national equality to the Romanians. Events moved swiftly. The Transylvanian diet reassembled in Cluj in November, this time with a Magyar majority, and voted without delay in favour of the union of Transylvania with Hungary. Emperor Francis Joseph replied on 25 December, accepting the idea of union, but making it conditional upon the settlement of outstanding constitutional issues between the imperial government and Hungary and the enactment of legislation guaranteeing the existence of the Romanian and Saxon nations. Yet, there was to be no turning back. On 6 January 1866 Francis Joseph prorogued the Transylvanian diet *sine die*. Since he never reconvened it, this act marked the end of the principality's constitutional history which had begun with the Diploma Leopoldinum in 1691; it had ceased in fact to exist as an autonomous principality.

The fall of Schmerling and the *rapprochement* with the Magyars led to bitter divisions among the Romanians. Strained relations between Şaguna and Bariţiu and Raţiu widened into open conflict over how to meet the new threat to national interests. Şaguna was the leading proponent of activism, urging his compatriots to work within the new system as the most effective way of defending the achievements of the diet of Sibiu and restoring the autonomy of Transylvania. But Bariţiu and Raţiu, embittered by the court's cavalier abandonment of the Romanians, rejected further cooperation with Vienna. They adopted a course of action which gained wide acceptance among Romanian intellectuals and came to be known as passivism. It required the Romanians to rely solely on their own resources and to avoid any act, such as participation in elections for the Hungarian parliament, that would signify acceptance of the new order of things in Transylvania. Yet, despite their best efforts, neither activists nor passivists had the power to change the course of events, and, as in 1849, they were relegated to the status of bystanders.

The compromise between Austria and Hungary moved forward inexorably. On 17 February 1867 the restoration of the Hungarian constitution was officially proclaimed, and three days later the emperor appointed the ministers of a new government headed by Count Gyula Andrássy, which immediately began to carry out the administrative fusion of Transylvania with Hungary. Francis Joseph's coronation as king of Hungary, the ceremonial ratification of the new partnership, took place in Buda on 8 June, and on the 20th he sanctioned the fundamental law that made the new order of things a legal reality. Almost as an afterthought he also dissolved the prorogued diets of Sibiu and Cluj and declared the legislation of the former, including the laws on Romanian nationhood and language, null and void.

The inauguration of the so-called dual system had profound consequences for the Romanian national movement. The widely perceived failure of the traditional policy of reliance on Austria, represented by Şaguna and the activists, brought laymen such as Ioan Raţiu and other proponents of passivism to the fore after a century and a half of clerical leadership. They were adamant in their opposition to dualism and demanded the restoration of an autonomous Transylvania as the only constitutional structure capable of assuring the development of the Romanian nation. The enactment of Law 44 (also known as the Law of Nationalities) by the Hungarian parliament in 1868 failed to satisfy them. Although it promised full civil and political rights to Romanians, they could exercise them only as individual citizens of Hungary, not as members of a separate ethnic community. This reinforcement of a unitary Hungary flew in the face of the new idea of nation as a corporate body possessing the inherent right of self-determination. As time passed and positions hardened, all attempts at compromise between Magyars and Romanians became unthinkable.

7

The United Principalities

BETWEEN the revolution of 1848 and 1866 the contours of modern Romania sharpened. Romanian political leaders, taking advantage of conflicting ambitions among the great powers, achieved the union of the principalities and ensured their independence. They gained these objectives in the way foreseen by an earlier generation—through a collective international guarantee in place of single-power protection. At home political institutions assumed European forms and political thought reached new levels of complexity in confrontations between liberals and conservatives. Ideological divergences increasingly centred on Europe. To the liberals it was a source of inspiration, to the conservatives a cause of anxiety, as both sides warmed to the debate over national identity and paths of development. The role of the state in both public and private life expanded relentlessly, as ministries and bureaucracies assumed primary responsibility for education, took over civil functions long exercised by the Orthodox Church, and became active promoters of economic development. The state also undertook gradually to integrate the majority of the population, the peasants, into the new nation as reliable contributors to its cohesiveness and prosperity. But agrarian reform and the democratization of the political process—the centrepieces of this grand design—proved intractable.

THE RESTORATION

The Convention of Balta Liman between Russia and the Ottoman Empire laid the constitutional foundation for a restoration of the old order in the principalities. Signed on 1 May 1849, it re-established the Russo-Turkish condominium. Thus, the princes were once again treated as high Ottoman functionaries and were no longer to be elected for life but rather appointed by the sultan for a period of seven years. The authority and independence of the legislatures were severely curtailed. The general assemblies were replaced by councils or *divanuri ad-hoc*, composed of the most important (and reliable) *boiers*. None the less, the revolutions of the previous year had made a strong impression in St Petersburg and Constantinople. Both the Russian and Ottoman courts recognized that the Organic Statutes could not be revived in their original form, and they therefore decided to appoint special commissions to revise them in accordance with the present needs of the principalities. But they had no intention of making concessions to the national and liberal spirit of the revolutions. To defend the new order they stipulated that a joint occupation army of 25,000 to 35,000 men would remain in the principalities until calm had been restored in Eastern Europe (the war in Hungary was at its height). To ensure that their will would prevail both powers appointed Extraordinary Commissioners to observe the course of events and 'supervise' the policies of the princes during the seven years the convention was to remain in force.

The two powers chose Barbu Ştirbei (1799–1869), the brother of Gheorghe Bibescu, as prince of Wallachia. A student of history and political science in Paris between 1817 and 1821, he had occupied a series of important offices during the Russian protectorate between 1829 and 1848: secretary of the drafting commission of the Organic Statutes and then successively minister of the interior, of religious affairs, and of justice. He undoubtedly owed his accession to the throne to his obvious willingness to serve a regime instituted by Russia. As prince he was a prudent and efficient administrator, but remained a convinced conservative in his political and social views.

Throughout his reign, which lasted until 1856, with a year's interruption at the beginning of the Crimean War, Ştirbei faced constant opposition from both the forty-eighters abroad, who by and large had remained faithful to the programme enunciated at Islaz, and conservatives at home, who sought to limit his powers. His attitude towards the forty-eighters was unbending.[1] He stubbornly refused the 'radicals' permission to return home, a denial he justified by the need to prevent new outbreaks of social agitation, which, he argued, would merely prolong the foreign military occupation. This reasoning was undoubtedly correct, but his hostility towards the exiles went deeper. Unable to conceal his aversion to the liberal spirit, he intended to rule as an absolute, though enlightened, prince in the tradition of his predecessors. His relations with the conservative great *boiers* were no better. Certain that they wished to replace him by an oligarchy of their own, he chose his ministers from among his friends and the members of his court. Unlike his predecessors under the Organic Statutes, he was spared the inconvenience of having to manage an elected assembly, and he rarely consulted even his own divan, a pale revival of the old princely council which served merely as a consultative body and whose president he himself appointed.

Ştirbei felt a keen sense of responsibility to promote the general welfare and took an active part in every phase of administration. The absence of a representative body prevented him from accurately gauging the mood of the country, but he none the less kept himself informed by making regular tours of inspection. These were not ceremonial visits but occasions for the gathering of information and for the detailed examination of the local administration to discover how faithfully instructions from the central authorities were being carried out. Many of the laws he promulgated had their origins in these encounters with the officials of the *judeţe*.

Ştirbei devoted much attention to economic matters, especially in the countryside. Convinced that the welfare of the country depended primarily upon an

---

[1] C. I. Scafeş and V. Zodian, *Barbu Ştirbei (1849–1856)* (Bucharest, 1981), 78–85.

efficient and prosperous agriculture, he introduced a new law regulating land-lord–peasant relations in April 1851, which remained in force until the great reform act of 1864. Ştirbei and the *boiers* were anxious to remove the causes of peasant unrest, which had threatened social upheaval in 1848. The law which they finally agreed upon represented a compromise between those *boiers* who wanted to relieve landlord property completely of all customary obligations to the village and, in effect, transform the peasants into tenants and renters, and those who preferred to maintain the system that had been introduced by the Organic Statutes. Ştirbei had the final word, and the law reflected his view that the peasant should be allowed to make free contracts with his landlord valid for a period of five years, or, if he chose, to leave the estate upon fulfilling all his obligations to the landlord.[2] Thus, the overall effect of the law was to loosen the peasant's legal, but not his economic, dependence on his landlord. Although these dispositions eased somewhat the condition of the peasants, they also reinforced the long-standing private property claims of the landlords. Ştirbei's attention to agriculture was responsible, at least in part, for a quadrupling of the value of grain and animal exports between 1850 and 1855.

Ştirbei proved to be a careful manager of the state's finances. By 1853 he had restored the country's credit and reduced its foreign debt from 14 million to 1 million *lei*. But his attempts to create a new institutional base for the country's finances were unsuccessful. Both his negotiations with Austrian bankers in 1850 to establish a national bank and his search for new permanent sources of revenue failed. The outbreak of the Crimean War and the burdens first of a Russian and then of an Austrian army of occupation undid most of his work.

Ştirbei grasped the importance of modern communications and pressed for-ward with the construction in 1854 of a network of telegraph lines, which drew the country closer together administratively and economically and linked Wallachia with Moldavia. He was also eager to begin the construction of railways in order to accelerate the economic development of the country, but discussions with entrepreneurs in Munich in 1855 were broken off because the economic concessions they demanded were, in his view, excessive.

The prince thought of himself as an enlightened monarch and put great store by education as an instrument of social progress.[3] Like his predecessor, Gheorghe Bibescu, he admired the French system of secondary and higher education and recognized the value of establishing a French college in Bucharest. But he also insisted that education not be merely an adornment of the privileged few, and therefore he had plans drafted to establish a network of primary and secondary schools throughout the country with Romanian as the language of instruction and with the curricula fitted to the needs of the general population. Progress was

---

[2] G. Penelea, 'Date privind legiuirea agrară a Moldovei din 1851', *Studii: Revistă de istorie*, 17/5 (1964), 1077–96; I. Corfus, *Agricultura în Ţările Române, 1848–1864* (Bucharest, 1982), 157–80.

[3] N. Iorga, 'Viaţa şi domnia lui Barbu Dimitrie Ştirbei', *Analele Academiei Române, Memoriile Secţiunii Istorice*, 2nd ser. 28 (1905), 7–25.

slow. By 1853 there were only twenty-four primary schools and one gymnasium, a number limited by the modest sums available in the state budget for education. At the same time Ştirbei encouraged specialized training, and his reign saw the beginnings of regular technical education in the school of Bridges and Highways (1850) and the School of Artisan Crafts (1851) and of medical training with the founding in 1856 of the National School of Surgery and Pharmacology, the precursor of the Faculty of Medicine at the University of Bucharest.

As prince of Moldavia (1849–56) the powers installed Grigore Ghica (1807–57), who belonged to one of the preimer *boier* families of the principality. He himself had gained valuable administrative experience during the reign of his uncle, Mihai Sturdza, as secretary of state (in effect, minister of foreign affairs) and minister of finance. But he remained close to the reformers and in 1848 he broke with his uncle and supported their liberal programme. He owed his selection as prince chiefly to the Ottoman grand vizier Reshid pasha, who was impressed by Ghica's moderate liberalism, which he thought augured well for a stable administration after the turbulence of the preceding year.

Ghica's liberalism survived the defeat of the revolution. As prince he was more sympathetic to the liberal agenda than Ştirbei and not only allowed a number of forty-eighters to return home, but brought many of them, including Mihail Kogălniceanu, Vasile Alecsandri, and Ion Ionescu de la Brad, into his administration. He introduced important administrative reforms, which prepared the way for the subsequent large-scale overhaul of governmental institutions, and, like Ştirbei, he showed himself to be an enlightened promoter of economic development and education.[4] Yet, he never forgot who he was. He shared the attitude of the great *boiers* on agrarian questions and recognized their right to share with him the political direction of the country. Consequently, he introduced no significant changes in landlord–peasant relations, nor did he broaden participation in political life to include the middle and lower classes. Such policies cost him the sympathy of the forty-eighters.

UNIONISTS AND GREAT POWERS

In the early 1850s major centres of Romanian political activity lay outside the principalities. From their places of exile *émigrés* kept alive their liberal and national ideals and sought to influence the course of events at home by cooperating with other forty-eighters from Eastern and Central Europe and by drawing the attention of sympathetic Western Europeans to the plight of the principalities.[5] Theirs was not, however, a unified movement, for the ideological differences that had emerged between radicals and moderates in 1848 had not been

---

[4] L. Boicu, *Adevărul despre un destin politic* (Iaşi, 1973), 98–114.
[5] N. Corivan, *Din activitatea emigranţilor români în Apus, 1853–1857* (Bucharest, 1931), 31–52; A. Iordache, *Pe urmele lui Dumitru Brătianu* (Bucharest, 1984), 135–63.

reconciled. One of the main *émigré* centres was Constantinople, where Ion Ghica formed a committee to represent Romanian interests before the Ottoman government and tried (unsuccessfully) to unite all *émigrés* in a single organization. Another centre was Paris. Here, in June 1849, C. A. Rosetti and Dumitru Brătianu established Comitetul Democratic Român (the Romanian Democratic Committee) for the purpose of keeping foreign governments and the press informed about the Romanian cause. In December it was superseded by a new, larger organization, Asociaţia Română pentru Conducerea Emigraţiei (the Romanian Association for the Leadership of the Emigration), formed mainly through the efforts of Nicolae Bălcescu. Its most ambitious undertaking was Bălcescu's mission to London in January 1850 to re-establish contact with Foreign Secretary Palmerston. Bălcescu requested British aid in bringing about the evacuation of Russian and Ottoman troops from the principalities and in convoking a national assembly, which would allow the Romanians themselves to determine their political development. Palmerston offered little encouragement, but promised none the less to see if something could be done to end the military occupation of the two countries.[6]

Bălcescu and his more radical colleagues were convinced that the outbreak of a new revolution was inevitable and, indeed, close at hand—they predicted 1852—and they eagerly took part in various organizations founded to hasten the event. During his stay in London Bălcescu joined Hungarian, Polish, Czech, and Russian exiles in forming a secret committee to bring about a 'democratic federation of Eastern Europe'. In April 1851 the Romanians in Paris adhered to the European Central Democratic Committee, which had been founded by the Italian revolutionary Giuseppe Mazzini in London the previous summer, and were represented by Dumitru Brătianu.[7] They also negotiated with Hungarian exiles over the establishment of a federation of nationalities in Central Europe, but the enterprise foundered on Kossuth's refusal to accept any infringement on the political unity and territorial integrity of historical Hungary.[8] None of these initiatives by Romanian *émigrés* significantly affected the course of events in the principalities.

In the mean time, a new international crisis, which led to the outbreak of war between Russia and Turkey in 1853 and the involvement of France and Britain the following year, brought nearer the two major goals which the forty-eighters were now intent upon achieving: the union and independence of the principalities. The diplomatic manœuvring to end the Crimean War and to resolve the 'Romanian question' was conducted, as in the past, by the great powers in accordance with their own objectives, but now for the first time the Romanians themselves played a crucial role in determining their own future.

---

[6] N. Bălcescu, *Opere*, iv (3rd edn., Bucharest, 1990), 193–200.

[7] A. Cretzianu, *Din arhiva lui Dumitru Brătianu*, i (Bucharest, 1933), 265–71.

[8] A. Marcu, *Conspiratori şi conspiraţii în epoca renaşterii politice a României, 1848–1877* (Bucharest, 1930), 27–67.

Deteriorating relations between Russia and the Ottoman Empire, caused in part by disputes over Russia's right to intervene on behalf of the sultan's Orthodox Christian subjects, had made the principalities the focus of great-power attention. When the Ottoman government, backed by Britain and France, rejected a Russian ultimatum on 16 June 1853 the Russian army, which had evacuated the principalities only two years earlier, recrossed the Prut River on 3 July and occupied Bucharest on the 6th. Ştirbei and Ghica left their respective capitals for Austria in October and were replaced by a military government headed by General Andrei Budberg, the Russian commander-in-chief who became president of the two divans, as Pavel Kiselev had done two decades earlier. Budberg entrusted the day-to-day administration to Extraordinary Administrative Councils, with a Russian as vice-president of each. Budberg himself held the real power and exercised it arbitrarily.[9] The principalities thus had to endure a new Russian occupation, but they escaped the ravages of war, as the major campaigns took place elsewhere.

Austria's reaction to these events was crucial. Throughout the mounting crisis Tsar Nicholas had counted upon Austria's gratitude for Russian aid in suppressing the Hungarian revolution in 1849 and continued assistance in maintaining the conservative predominance in Eastern Europe. Yet the Austrian foreign minister, Karl von Buol, gave Russia scant support in her diplomatic contest with the Ottomans and went so far as to urge the tsar to make the occupation of the principalities as brief as possible. Russia's crossing of the Prut was viewed in Vienna as a threat to Austria's own interests in the region, particularly her commerce on the lower Danube and in the Black Sea.[10] Efforts by Buol in the summer to mediate failed. In October 1853, after Russia had rejected an ultimatum to evacuate the principalities, Turkish troops briefly crossed the Danube, and serious fighting broke out in the Caucasus. Further international efforts to settle the conflict came to naught. Britain and France stood by Turkey and formally declared war on Russia on 28 March 1854.

Buol's demand for the evacuation of the principalities, presented to Russia on 3 June 1854, revealed the importance Austria attached to them. She overcame the last obstacle to her own ambitions there by signing the Convention of Boyadji Köy with Turkey on 14 June. It was a stunning diplomatic success, for Austria gained an almost free hand in the principalities. Under its terms she undertook to obtain by negotiation and other means Russia's evacuation of the principalities, which she recognized as an essential condition for the maintenance of the integrity of the Ottoman Empire. Austria was allowed to occupy the principalities as the mandatory of the Ottoman suzerain, but in fact she was to have complete freedom of action. The convention set no time-limit to the

[9] I. Nistor, 'Principatele Române sub ocupaţia rusească 1 iulie 1853–17 septembrie 1854', Academia Română, *Memoriile Secţiunii Istorice*, 3rd ser. 20 (1938), 232–5.

[10] L. Boicu, *Austria şi principatele române în vremea războiului Crimeii, 1853–1856* (Bucharest, 1972), 73–96.

occupation; Austria and the Ottoman Empire were to settle the matter later. The tsar was furious at Austria's 'disloyalty', but had no choice but to yield. In July and August Russian armies evacuated Wallachia, and by September they had completed their withdrawal from Moldavia.

The Ottomans, not the Austrians, were the first to take advantage of the Russians' departure. Omer pasha, the commander of Ottoman forces on the Danube, thought that by reaching Bucharest before the Austrians he could become the master of the principalities and stave off an Austrian occupation, despite previous agreements. He crossed the Danube on 27 July, and a vanguard of 2,000 troops reached Bucharest on 7 August. He himself entered the city on the 22nd and began at once to organize a civil administration from among sympathetic *boiers*. His haste and the size of his occupation army—80,000 men— reveal the supreme importance which his government attached to Wallachia as the guardian of the empire's northern frontier. Omer pasha and other Ottoman officials had no doubt that Russia, not Austria, posed the chief threat to the empire's territorial integrity.

A number of Romanian *émigrés*, among them Ion Heliade Rădulescu, returned to Bucharest with the Turkish army. Heliade received an enthusiastic welcome from the younger intellectuals of the capital as the father of modern Romanian literature and the chief architect of the revolution of 1848 (the first title was deserved, the second was not). The Austrian council of ministers immediately took note of the exiles' return and demanded the expulsion of all members of the 'Wallachian revolutionary party', but Omer pasha refused. He saw in the *émigrés* the only element among the native population he could trust, since they had not 'compromised themselves' during the Russian occupation.

The apparent Ottoman intention to ignore the provisions of the Convention of Boyadji Köy and the spectre of renewed agitation by revolutionaries in Bucharest hastened the Austrian advance into the principalities. On 30 June 1854 Count Johann Coronini, the commander of Austria's intervention forces, re- ceived instructions from Vienna to begin his own occupation and to re-establish the legal order in the principalities, but he delayed his advance until the Russians had completed their withdrawal. The first Austrian troops entered Wallachia on 19 August, the vanguard of a force of 40,000. Coronini himself arrived in Bucharest on 6 September, and on the 16th his troops crossed the border into Moldavia.

Romanian intellectuals both at home and abroad condemned the Austrian occupation. In Bucharest and other cities they expressed their defiance openly, and no party favourable to Austria formed among any category of the population. The subsequent experiences of the occupation between 1854 and 1857 cemented the hostility towards Austria, which was to become a potent force in Romanian politics down to the First World War.

The manner in which the Austrians set about organizing their administration suggests that they were preparing for a long stay. They seemed intent upon replacing the Russo-Turkish condominium with an Austro-Turkish one in which they would be the senior partner.[11] It was obvious that they interpreted the Convention of Boyadji Köy as having transferred essential control over the principalities to themselves. To strengthen their position they engineered the transfer of Omer pasha and the bulk of his army to the Crimea, which had become the main theatre of war between Russia and Britain and France. When he left Bucharest in December 1854 only a token Ottoman force of 1,500 remained behind. Austrian military commanders took over administrative functions from local civil authorities, assumed control of hydrographic projects at the Iron Gates on the Danube, and placed the mouths of the Danube under Austrian protection.

The Austrians moved methodically and cautiously. They supported the return of Barbu Ştirbei and Grigore Ghica to their thrones, not because they were Austrophiles (they were not), but because they were eager to re-establish the legal order mentioned in the Convention of Boyadji Köy. The main objective of the Austrians was to avoid 'innovations', that is, renewed activities by the forty-eighters, which might create 'disorder' and offer other interested powers a pretext for intervention in the affairs of the principalities.[12] Ştirbei returned to Bucharest on 5 October 1854 and formed a government favourable to Austria. Ghica, who returned to Iaşi on 9 November, displayed more independence. His cabinet contained only one Austrophile. But the restoration in the principalities was by no means complete. Austria, in effect, had interposed herself between Constantinople, on the one hand, and Bucharest and Iaşi, on the other, by requiring the princes to obtain Coronini's prior approval for any contact they might have with Ottoman authorities. The Austrians themselves took over responsibility for numerous aspects of Romanian–Ottoman relations—the quarantines along the Danube, the activities of the princes' agents in Constantinople, and the allocation of income from the dedicated monasteries assigned to the principalities.

Despite vigorous intervention, Austrian officials failed to subordinate either the central or the local administrative apparatus of the principalities to the monarchy's interests. The princes themselves were far from docile. Ştirbei was the more compliant, but when he acceded to Austrian demands, as in his tightening of the censorship and his exclusion of the exiles, he did so mainly because such measures fitted in with his own aims. Ghica's behaviour was more disturbing to the Austrians. Like Ştirbei, he was sympathetic to France, but, unlike him, he made no attempt to hide his feelings. He surrounded himself with Francophiles and looked to Napoleon III for aid in restoring the autonomy of the country. In domestic politics, he favoured the union of the principalities, allowed the liberal émigrés wide scope for their activities, and, by easing the restrictions on the press,

---

[11] Ibid. 211–27.

[12] I. Nistor, 'Ocupaţia austriacă în Principate (1854–1857) după rapoartele lui Coronini', Academia Română, *Memoriile Secţiunii Istorice*, 3rd ser. 20 (1938), 150–91.

he enabled the liberals to publish two influential unionist newspapers in 1855—
România literară (Literary Romania) and *Steaua Dunării* (Star of the Danube).

Many Austrian officials thought of the occupation of the principalities
as simply a prelude to their integration into the economic and political structure
of the monarchy. The most elaborate theoretical formulation of such a plan came
from Karl von Bruck, the minister of finance and a staunch advocate of
Mitteleuropa, the idea of a union of Austria and the German states to dominate
Central and Eastern Europe. He reserved an important place in his system for
the principalities as a market for Austrian manufactures and an almost inexhaustible source of raw materials.[13] Such ideas harked back to the eighteenth century,
but now Bruck and his allies pressed them with greater vigour. One influential
disciple was Coronini, who eagerly carried out Bruck's injunction to develop
the economic resources of the principalities as the 'true way' of binding them
to Austria. Although many persons in high places, notably Buol and Alexander
Bach, the minister of the interior, did not share Bruck's enthusiasm for
Mitteleuropa, they none the less sought to strengthen Austria's position along the
lower Danube through intense economic activities. Their common objectives
led in 1855 and 1856 to a systematic attempt to achieve economic dominance
over the principalities by controlling banks, railways, river navigation, and telegraph lines. Yet, this grand design failed because Austria lacked the financial
resources to carry out such an ambitious investment strategy and could never
convince private investors that a stable political regime, essential for safe
economic development, could take root in the principalities in the foreseeable
future.

War-weariness, caused by the wasting and indecisive campaign in the Crimea,
brought the belligerents to the conference table. The death of Tsar Nicholas on
2 March 1855 and the accession of Alexander II, who was more inclined than his
father to reach a peaceful settlement, raised hopes that the war might soon end.
Although negotiations for peace in Vienna between March and June 1855 were
inconclusive, they offered the first opportunity for a general airing of views on
the future of the principalities. In particular, their union into a single state came
under serious discussion. Baron François Bourquenay, the French minister to
Austria, who had raised the issue, argued that union would remove Moldavia and
Wallachia from the exclusive influence of any one power and would establish a
natural barrier to any threat to the Ottoman Empire (he obviously had Russia in
mind).[14] Unionists in Moldavia and Wallachia, however, could take little comfort
from Bourquenay's advocacy, for as the discussion proceeded it became evident

[13] L. Boicu, 'Les Principautés roumaines dans les projets de Karl von Bruck et Lorenz von Stein
pour la constitution de la "Mitteleuropa" à l'époque de la guerre de Crimée', *Revue roumaine d'histoire*,
6/2 (1967), 233–56.

[14] D. Sturdza *et al.*, *Acte și documente relative la istoria renașterii României*, ii (Bucharest, 1889), 638–
9, 641–3: Protocol 6, 26 Mar. 1855, and annex; M. A. Ubicini, *La Question des Principautés devant
l'Europe* (Paris, 1858), 6–10.

that the powers thought of union in terms of their own foreign policy objectives and were prepared, as in the past, to use the principalities as territorial compensation to achieve broad international agreements. In 1854, for example, Napoleon III, impatient for a solution to the 'Italian question', had proposed that Austria cede Lombardy and Venetia to Sardinia and take the principalities in exchange.[15] After the Crimean War had broken out France and Prussia had considered punishing Russia by reconstituting an independent Poland and then giving Austria a protectorate over Moldavia and Wallachia as compensation for the loss of Galicia.

In Iaşi and Bucharest the princes and the leaders of various conservative and liberal groups strove to influence the deliberations of the powers before and during the Vienna Conference. Grigore Ghica sent an observer, a convinced unionist and a forty-eighter, Costache Negri, to the conference, and Barbu Ştirbei drew up a memorandum which set forth the arguments on behalf of autonomy and disputed the usual Ottoman claims that the principalities were an integral part of the empire. Politicians and intellectuals stood squarely for union and independence, but they were not yet well enough organized to mount an effective campaign of their own. The conference ignored both them and the princes.

The Vienna Conference broke up without reaching an agreement on ending the war. Nor did it accept union as a solution to the Romanian question. Rather, it left the principalities as they were, dependent upon the Ottoman Empire as their suzerain. Yet, the allies made far-reaching decisions about their future. They abolished Russia's protectorate, dismissed Ottoman claims to sovereignty, and reasserted the autonomy of Moldavia and Wallachia, stipulating that a new charter of rights for the principalities be drawn up.[16]

France and Austria acted in concert to break the diplomatic stalemate following the failure of the Vienna Conference. On 14 November 1855 Bourquenay and Buol signed a protocol setting forth the peace terms which Austria would convey to St Petersburg in the form of an ultimatum. Two matters were crucial: first, Russia must agree to the neutralization of the Black Sea, which would require her to remove her fleet and demolish her fortresses along its shore, and second, she must cede to Moldavia territory in southern Bessarabia bordering the Danube delta. Delivered to St Petersburg on 28 December these terms were grudgingly accepted by the Russian government on 16 January 1856. The general peace conference opened in Paris on 25 February.

The powers were divided into two camps on the question of the union of the principalities. France, Russia, and, initially, Britain favoured it; Turkey and Austria were opposed. Napoleon III's support of union was based in part upon his attachment to the principle of nationality as the basis for the future political

[15] T. W. Riker, *The Making of Roumania* (London, 1931), 39–40.
[16] Sturdza *et al.*, *Acte şi documente*, ii. 620: protocol 1, 15 Mar. 1855, annex.

organization of Europe. His concern for the principalities accorded with his thinking about Italy and Poland. But, as with the Italians and Poles, his support of Romanian aspirations was meant also to serve the broader objectives of French foreign policy. He sought to enhance French influence in the East by supporting newly independent or autonomous states in the region. Thus, a united Romania would become one of the pillars of a new political configuration in Eastern Europe that would look gratefully to France for leadership. For her part, Russia could hardly promote the principle of self-determination of peoples and tended to regard a united Romanian state as a barrier to her influence in South-eastern Europe. But Russian diplomats perceived in the growing controversy over the union an opportunity to draw France away from her allies and, consequently, they came over to the side of union.[17] British representatives did not oppose union, seeing it as an added reinforcement against Russian penetration into the Balkan provinces of the Ottoman Empire. Only after the peace conference did they revert to an anti-unionist stand when they concluded that the strengthening of the principalities would serve French rather than British interests in the region. Ottoman officials remained adamantly opposed to union on the grounds that the principalities were an integral part of the empire and that union was simply a prelude to independence. Austria was also four-square against union because it would interfere with her own efforts to dominate the principalities. Austrian officials were also concerned about the Romanians in Transylvania, whose strivings for political autonomy in 1848 had raised the possibility that a united Romanian principality beyond the Carpathians would have an irresistible attraction for them and, in time, would threaten the territorial integrity of the monarchy.[18]

Count Walewski, the French foreign minister, raised the question of union officially on 8 March urging his colleagues to resolve it in a positive manner. Clarendon, the British foreign secretary, and Alexei Orlov, the head of the Russian delegation, concurred. Ali pasha, the sultan's representative, rejected the idea on the grounds that the principalities had always been separate and insisted (without offering any evidence) that their respective populations had no wish to unite. Buol refused even to discuss the merits of the case, citing a lack of instructions from Vienna, but, taking his cue from Ali pasha, he argued that the great emphasis which the Moldavians and Wallachians had placed on their autonomy proved that they wanted to remain separate. When Walewski countered that the desire of the Romanians for union had its roots in their common origins, language, and religion, Buol retorted that nationality was not a sufficient reason to alter the 'existing political configuration' of a state. Another of Buol's favourite arguments was immediately turned against him. In urging

[17] V. N. Vinogradov, *Rossiia i ob'edinenie rumynskikh kniazhestv* (Moscow, 1961), 87–100.
[18] L. Boicu, *Diplomația europeană și triumful cauzei române, 1856–1859* (Iași, 1978), 80–3; I. Nistor, *Corespondența lui Coronini din Principate: Acte și rapoarte din iunie 1854–martie 1857* (Cernăuți, 1938), 905, 1038.

rejection of the union, he pointed out that the populations of the principalities had not been consulted, whereupon Clarendon is reported to have exclaimed: 'All right, let's consult them.'

The Treaty of Paris ending the Crimean War, signed on 30 March 1856, decisively affected the political development of Moldavia and Wallachia. Although they remained under Ottoman suzerainty, they now benefited from the collective protection of the powers, who forbade any single power to interfere in their internal affairs. All the signatories, including the Ottoman Empire, recognized the administrative independence of the principalities, the right of each to maintain a national army, to legislate, and to engage freely in commerce with other countries. The powers also established the procedures for revising the fundamental law (the Organic Statutes) of each principality. They created a special commission of inquiry and instructed it to go to Bucharest to gather information and draw up recommendations on the future form of government of the principalities. In a striking departure from their usual treatment of the principalities the powers provided for the election of a special advisory assembly, a so-called *adunare ad-hoc*, in each principality, which should serve to make known public opinion on all important matters before the commission. All the information thus gathered was to be presented to a conference of the powers in Paris, where final decisions would be made and communicated to the principalities in the form of a *hatti-sherif* promulgated by the sultan. Finally, the powers stipulated that all foreign troops should be withdrawn from the principalities as soon as the Ottoman Empire and Austria could make the necessary arrangements.

The treaty left unresolved the two most critical constitutional questions for Romanian political leaders—union and independence. Yet, it marked significant progress towards both. It redefined the relationship between the principalities and the Ottoman Empire by treating Romanian matters as distinct from other aspects of the Eastern Question, acts that undermined claims that the principalities were integral parts of the Ottoman Empire.

The Treaty of Paris affected the principalities in yet another way—through the regulation of navigation on the Danube. The powers established a permanent commission, composed of riparian states, including the representatives of Moldavia, Wallachia, and Serbia, to draw up statutes governing the use of the river and to oversee their implementation. A provisional 'European Commission', consisting of France, Austria, Britain, Prussia, Russia, Sardinia, and the Ottoman Empire, was to function for two years and to concern itself with purely technical matters such as dredging the channel between Isaccea and the Black Sea. But its life had to be extended beyond 1858 because the permanent commission could not be formed, owing to Austria's refusal to recognize its jurisdiction over the upper course of the river. The principalities were allowed only a modest role in all these undertakings, even though their section of the Danube was the longest, on the grounds that they were not sovereign states. In any case, Austria, intent upon securing a privileged position on the lower Danube, adamantly opposed a greater role for the principalities.[19]

Fateful for the future course of Romanian–Russian relations was the cession by Russia of parts of three southern districts of Bessarabia to Moldavia. The area which was lost amounted to only 5,000 km² and was of modest economic importance. But now Russia no longer bordered the Danube, and, most serious of all, the tsar felt the loss of this territory as a personal humiliation and was determined to recover it.

Russia's cession of southern Bessarabia to Moldavia added to the existing strains in Russo-Romanian relations. Although Russia's protectorate of the 1830s and 1840s and role in the suppression of liberal movements in 1848 were the most immediate causes of hostility towards Russia in the principalities, neither Moldavians nor Wallachians had reconciled themselves to the annexation of Bessarabia in 1812. *Boiers* and intellectuals were painfully aware of the relentless Russification to which an authoritarian, centralizing regime had subjected the Orthodox Church, education, and cultural life, but they lacked the means to reverse the integration of the province into the Russian Empire. After the principalities achieved union and independence Bessarabia was to be the chief obstacle to friendly relations between the new Romania and Russia.

Shortly after the signing of the Treaty of Paris the powers had to resolve two important questions concerning the principalities: the reappointment of the princes and the evacuation of Austrian troops. The first was pressing. The seven-year reigns of the princes, who had been appointed under the terms of the Convention of Balta Liman in 1849, were about to end. The anti-unionist powers—Austria and Turkey—prevented the reappointment of Ştirbei and Ghica and had them replaced by *caimacami* (regents) installed by the sultan in July 1856. In Moldavia the anti-unionist *boier* Teodor Balş proved to be a faithful instrument of Austrian policy. His counterpart in Wallachia, Alexandru Ghica, the former prince, owed his appointment in part to the influence of Stratford de Redcliffe, the British ambassador in Constantinople, who was impressed by Ghica's hostility to Russia and independence of Austria.[20]

The evacuation of the Austrian army from the principalities gave rise to serious international complications. The whole matter became entangled in the elections of the *adunări ad-hoc*. Austria was anxious to maintain a strong presence in the principalities until after the elections as a means of influencing their outcome. Her intransigence led the international commission of inquiry on the principalities provided for in the Treaty of Paris to delay its work, a device used by Russia to put pressure on Austria to yield. Austria retaliated by making withdrawal contingent upon a satisfactory delimitation of the new boundary between Russia and Moldavia in southern Bessarabia. The dispute quickly turned into a

[19] S. G. Fócas, *The Lower Danube River* (Boulder, Colo., 1987), 256–61; M. Kogălniceanu, *Cestiunea Dunării* (rev. edn., Bucharest, 1882), 15–37.

[20] Boicu, *Austria şi principatele române*, 386.

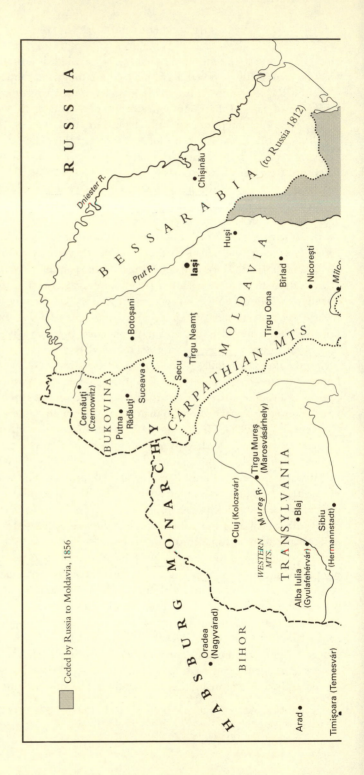

Ceded by Russia to Moldavia, 1856

RUSSIA

Dniester R.

BESSARABIA (to Russia 1812)

Chişinău

Prut R.

Huşi

Iaşi

Botoşani

MOLDAVIA

Bîrlad

Nicoreşti

Milc

Tîrgu Neamt

Tîrgu Ocna

Secu

Suceava

CARPATHIAN MTS

Cernăuţi
(Czernowitz)

Putna

Rădăuţi

BUKOVINA

HABSBURG MONARCHY

Tîrgu Mureş
(Marosvásárhely)

Cluj (Kolozsvár)

Mureş R.

TRANSYLVANIA

WESTERN
MTS.

Blaj

Sibiu
(Hermannstadt)

Alba Iulia
(Gyulafehérvár)

Oradea
(Nagyvárad)

BIHOR

Arad

Timişoara (Temesvár)

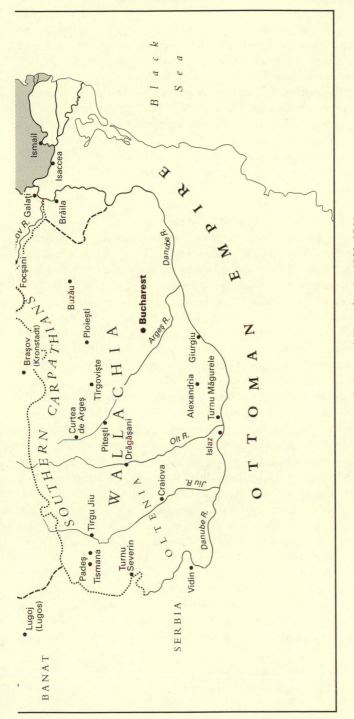

MAP 2. Moldavia, Wallachia, and Transylvania, 1829–1866

general contest among the powers for predominance in the region. France
backed Russia in order to gain support for her own objectives, especially her
efforts to diminish British influence in South-eastern Europe. Britain, on the
other hand, conceded nothing to Russia and urged the Austrians to prolong their
occupation of the principalities. Before matters deteriorated further, a settlement
was reached at a meeting in Paris on 6 January 1857 of all the signatories of the
peace treaty. The powers called upon Austria to withdraw her troops from
the principalities by 30 March, a summons she acceded to, and they settled the
disputed boundary in southern Bessarabia in favour of Austria and Britain and,
almost as an afterthought, Moldavia, by awarding the town of Bolgrad to the
latter. But they reversed the decision taken at the peace conference of Paris to
grant the Danube delta to Moldavia as a means of separating Russia and Turkey,
and, instead, assigned it to Turkey, thereby cutting Moldavia off from the sea and
preventing her (and Wallachia) from becoming maritime powers.

In the principalities, meanwhile, the supporters of union and independence
had become increasingly bold. They had greeted the Treaty of Paris coolly as an
instrument designed to postpone as long as possible the resolution of the two
issues that might undo all the calculations of the powers in South-eastern Europe.
But they were determined to press ahead, and in May and June 1856 they began
to marshal their forces in anticipation of the elections of the *adunări ad-hoc*. In
Moldavia the unionists could count on the backing of Prince Grigore Ghica, and
on 11 June they established a legal organization, 'Societatea Uniunii' (Society of
the Union), to coordinate their burgeoning campaign.[21] Their main objective
was the immediate union of the principalities under a foreign prince, 'preferably
of the Latin race', from among the ruling families of Europe. The membership
of the society was heterogeneous, being composed of conservative great *boiers* as
well as middle-class and *boier* liberals, but all its members were at least temporarily
united in their support of the union. They avoided discussion of the future
political organization of the united principalities because disagreements among
them were so sharp that they feared for the success of the union movement.
Official support for the unionists ended abruptly in July when Prince Grigore
Ghica was replaced by the *caimacam* Balş. Encouraged by Austria, he initiated a
vigorous anti-unionist campaign which included dismissals of unionists from the
civil service, a few arrests, and the suppression of the unionist press.

In Wallachia, too, the unionists were feverishly organizing themselves. In the
summer of 1856 they formed a central committee to coordinate their work in
Bucharest with the activities of their supporters in the provinces. The *caimacam*
Alexandru Ghica tolerated the committee, although he was himself a conservative, and even permitted a unionist press to flourish, notably *Concordia*, the main
organ of the unionists, which began publication on 18 February 1857 with C. A.
Rosetti as the *de facto* director.

[21] Sturdza, *Acte şi documente*, iii (Bucharest, 1889), 531–3, and ix (Bucharest, 1901), 449–52.

The unionist movement in both principalities gained momentum in the early months of 1857 as the commission of inquiry arrived in Bucharest and elections of the *adunări ad-hoc* drew near. In Iaşi in February unionists formed the Electoral Committee on Union to mobilize wider support for their cause and to draw up a comprehensive political programme. Despite the mixed character of the committee, in which conservative *boiers* and liberal intellectuals again sat side by side, its objectives were consistently liberal. The programme which it published on 13 March repeated earlier calls for union under a foreign prince and for the autonomy and neutrality of the new state to be guaranteed collectively by the powers. But now the unionists went further. They elaborated the principles that would guide the political organization of their new country.[22] They warmly endorsed the election of a general assembly that would represent the interests of the entire nation and enact all the reforms necessary to strengthen the Romanians as a nation and to raise them to a European level of civilization. They also committed themselves to equality before the law and to an impartial system of justice, but they felt obliged to add 'respect for property' to their list of principles in order to retain the confidence of the *boiers*. In Bucharest on 15 March the National party, as the proponents of the union now called themselves, agreed on a programme similar to that of the Moldavians, and through its umbrella organization—the Central Committee of the Union—it proposed to coordinate its activities with those of the unionists in Iaşi. Unionists in both principalities were heartened by the return of the forty-eighters from exile in 1856 and 1857, notably C. A. Rosetti and the Brătianu brothers. Bălcescu was not among them, for he had died of tuberculosis in Italy in 1852 at the age of 33.

The convocation of the *adunări ad-hoc*, in which the unionists placed great hopes, had to be postponed because the commission of inquiry did not arrive in Bucharest until March 1857, that is, not until the disputes over Austria's evacuation of the principalities and the new Russian–Moldavian frontier had been settled. These matters, in turn, had complicated negotiations between the powers and Turkey over the contents of a *firman* from the sultan convoking the *adunări ad-hoc* and outlining the procedures for their election. It took five months of bargaining, from September 1856 to January 1857, before the text of the *firman* had been approved by all the powers.[23] Promulgated by the sultan on 26 January 1857, it provided for the representation of all social categories in the assemblies, but, in effect, it ensured the predominance of the possessing classes, especially the great landowning *boiers*. They were to have two delegates from each *judeţ*, whereas the lesser *boiers*, the *răzeşi*, and the majority of city-dwellers received only one (the inhabitants of Bucharest and two other cities from each principality had two delegates each). The metropolitans and bishops were members by right. The franchise accorded the cities was a recognition of the growing importance of

[22] Ibid. iii. 1107–8, and iv (Bucharest, 1889), 40–5.

[23] A. I. Gonţa, 'Firmanul pentru convocarea divanurilor ad-hoc şi problema unirii Principatelor Romîne', in *Studii privind unirea Principatelor* (Bucharest, 1960), 281–96.

the middle class in economic life, but the most important departure from previous methods of representation was the granting of voting rights to the *clăcaşi*, who were allowed to elect one delegate from each *judeţ* and thus would have about one-fifth of the seats in each assembly.

Austria and Turkey had by no means renounced their opposition to union. Their plan was to hold the election for the assembly in Moldavia as soon as possible, since unionist sentiment appeared weaker there than in Wallachia, and to draw up voting lists before the National party had had time to organize its supporters. During the ensuing electoral campaign the new *caimacam*, Nicolae Vogoride, a Greek who had obtained Moldavian citizenship in 1846 and who had been appointed to the position upon the death of Balş in March 1857, used every means at his disposal—bribery, falsification of the voting lists, rigid control of the press, and the wholesale replacement of unionists in the militia and civil service with men certain to do his bidding—in order to ensure victory for the opponents of union. Hoping to be appointed prince himself with the support of Austria and Turkey, he rejected out of hand protests from the unionists and the commissioners of the pro-union powers. The corruption of the electoral process was so blatant that the National party decided to abstain, and, as a result, anti-unionists won the election on 19 July.

Their success, however, was short-lived. France demanded that the sultan annul the elections. When he refused, and was backed by Austria and Britain, a major crisis erupted, as the pro-union powers—France, Russia, Prussia, and Sardinia—broke off relations with Turkey on 6 August. The Anglo-French alliance, on which the implementation of the Treaty of Paris depended, appeared on the verge of collapse. But neither party was prepared to accept the consequences of such an event. Napoleon III valued the alliance with Britain as an indispensable means of achieving his foreign policy goals on the continent, notably the settlement of the Italian question, which was more important to him than the union of the principalities. Nor did Clarendon think the fate of Moldavia, 'a barbarous little province at the end of Europe', was worth risking a break with France. At a meeting between Napoleon III and Queen Victoria and their principal advisers at Osborne on the Isle of Wight on 6–10 August a compromise was worked out by which the French renounced the idea of a complete union of the principalities in favour of an administrative union to be accomplished by the creation in each principality of similar institutions. For their part, the British agreed to advise the sultan to annul the Moldavian elections and hold new ones. The effect of the so-called Pact of Osborne was to render superfluous the whole machinery for dealing with the union created by the Treaty of Paris.[24] In Constantinople the consequences of the electoral crisis, especially the break in relations with the four pro-unionist powers, had brought

[24] Riker, *The Making of Roumania*, 130–40; A. Oţetea, 'L'Accord d'Osborne (9 août 1857)', *Revue roumaine d'histoire*, 3/4 (1964), 677–96.

the Francophiles to power, led by the foreign minister Ali pasha and the grand vizier Mustafa pasha, who readily acceded to the terms of the Pact of Osborne. New elections were held in Moldavia beginning on 10 September and in Wallachia beginning on 19 September. In both the unionists carried the day.

The Moldavian *adunare ad-hoc* began its work on 4 October 1857, the Wallachian on 12 October. Unionists dominated the proceedings—Mihail Kogălniceanu and Alexandru Cuza in Iaşi; C. A. Rosetti, the Golescu brothers, and Dumitru Brătianu in Bucharest. But the assemblies were far from homogeneous socially or politically. As for social composition, great *boier* landlords formed the majority, which was reinforced by the clergy. Liberals and radicals, who in general represented the middle class and the peasants, found themselves on the defensive. Nevertheless, as the deputies sought out ideologically compatible colleagues four recognizable political groupings began to coalesce—conservatives, moderate conservatives, and moderate and radical liberals. The two liberal groupings and the moderate conservatives operated within the National party, but it was little more than a loose coalition, since the union and enhanced autonomy were the only issues upon which they could agree. Both assemblies, the Moldavian on 19 October and the Wallachian on 21 October, immediately passed resolutions calling for union, autonomy, neutrality, and a collective guarantee of the new order by the powers.

The deputies were also anxious to take up other pressing issues without delay. In Moldavia they plunged into a spirited debate about the future political and economic organization of the country. No aspect escaped their scrutiny: fundamental rights (equality before the law, individual liberty, the inviolability of the home, freedom of religion); a further weakening of ties with the Ottoman suzerain (a reduction in financial obligations, freedom of commerce); and political reform (the complete separation of the legislative power from the executive, a responsible ministry, and the irremovability of judges). The moderate liberal stand won surprisingly large majorities on all these matters, except for the principle that the future legislature should be broadly representative of 'all the great interests of the nation'. The vote was indeed 41 to 4 in favour, but there were 23 abstentions, mainly from the centre and the right, which opposed any expansion of the franchise to include the mass of the population.

The debate on the agrarian question revealed a major split within the ranks of the unionists. Peasant deputies had come to the assembly with the expectation of acquiring full property rights to the land they worked and of abolishing *clacă*. They warmly supported union, but, as Kogălniceanu remarked, they understood it to mean more than just a combining of the principalities. On 21 November they presented a petition to the assembly recounting in moving terms the hardships of rural existence and demanding both an end to the *boieresc* (the common term in the village for labour services) and the allotment to them as their own property of up to two-thirds of the landlord's estate. Although large landowners were prepared to give up labour services, they were adamant in opposing any limitations on their property rights, and they spoke ominously about the 'communistic tendencies' of the peasants. They suggested that the best way for peasants to acquire land was through 'voluntary understandings' with landlords. The majority of the deputies were little inclined to engage in social experiments, and when the vote came on the peasant deputies' proposal, it lost 44 to 25.[25]

These issues were curiously muted in the Wallachian assembly. The moderate and liberal deputies, who favoured social progress and broader citizen participation in political life, decided to postpone consideration of fundamental changes in political institutions until a later assembly when they would no longer be a minority and could thus shape those institutions to fit their reform agenda. Almost all the unionists, liberals and conservatives, were anxious to avoid serious debate on social and economic problems because they were painfully aware of the strong differences among them over the agrarian question and the democratization of political life and were afraid that divisiveness at this stage would impede the achievement of union. Peasant deputies followed their lead. They chose not to press their grievances at this time, but demanded the right to be adequately represented when a future assembly took up agrarian problems.

The centre of attention shifted to Paris with the closing of the Wallachian assembly on 22 December 1857 and the Moldavian assembly on 2 January 1858. The powers' commission of inquiry issued its report on 7 April 1858 about conditions in the principalities and the wishes of the Romanians as expressed in the *adunări ad-hoc*, and the seven guarantor states met in Paris on 22 May to discuss its findings. At its first session Walewski, the president, urged approval of the union of the principalities. He was supported by Pavel Kiselev, now the Russian ambassador to France, and the representatives of Prussia and Sardinia. Speaking for Turkey, Fuad pasha raised familiar arguments in favour of continued separation, while the Austrian minister to France, Count Joseph Hübner, claimed that the granting of union would merely encourage other states to impinge upon the integrity of the Ottoman Empire. The Earl of Cowley, British ambassador to France, urged his colleagues to concentrate on matters that would reconcile the wishes of the Romanians with those of their suzerain. Subsequent deliberations revealed the willingness of the powers to compromise, but Hübner continued to oppose any measure that seemed unionist. He objected strenuously to the new designation of Moldavia and Wallachia as the United Principalities and to the establishment of a central commission to deal with matters common to both countries. But in the end Austria settled for the continued administrative separation of the principalities, even though all present recognized that they were simply postponing the inevitable.

The decisions of the conference were embodied in the Convention of Paris, signed by the seven powers on 19 August. Its main purpose was to endow the

[25] N. Adăniloaie and D. Berindei, *Reforma agrară din 1864* (Bucharest, 1967), 83–100.

principalities with a definitive organization. Although the powers stopped short of granting union and left them under Ottoman suzerainty, they agreed that the United Principalities of Moldavia and Wallachia should henceforth administer themselves freely and 'without interference from the Ottoman government'. They had still to pay the tribute, and the princes were still to be invested by the sultan, but all the parties to the agreement knew that these obligations were now mere formalities, as they themselves reaffirmed their collective guarantee of the principalities' autonomy. Yet the convention was much more than a treaty regulating the international status of the principalities. In setting forth the fundamental rights of citizens and the qualifications and duties of political leaders, it took on the attributes of a constitution, and those who drafted it were clearly sympathetic to the liberal ideas they had encountered in Bucharest. Thus, it provided for: a legislative assembly for each principality elected for a seven-year term, with a central commission meeting periodically at Focşani, on the Moldavian–Wallachian border, to consider laws of common concern; a prince, either a Moldavian or Wallachian for either principality, to be elected by the assembly for life; a council of ministers responsible to the assembly; separate national armies, but with a single commander-in-chief appointed alternately by the two princes; the irremovability of judges and their independence of the executive power; and a common Court of Cassation at Focşani. The convention also abolished the *boier* ranks and privileges, proclaiming equality before the law and the principle of public office open to every citizen on the basis of merit. But it set such a high property qualification for voting that the number of electors was limited to a few thousand persons, mainly large landowners and the upper middle class. The restricted franchise was a major contradiction; it was certain to impede the passage of liberal political and economic reforms, particularly the new law governing landlord–peasant relations which the convention itself had recommended as urgent. Finally, the powers placed the government of each principality in the hands of a provisional commission of three *caimacami* until the election of the princes.

The main function of the provisional commissions was to oversee the election of new legislative assemblies, which were to choose the princes. In Wallachia the three *caimacami*, who were installed on 30 October 1858, were conservatives. They used every means at their disposal—suppression of the liberal press, restrictions on public meetings, and the manipulation of voter lists—to ensure a conservative assembly. In Moldavia, however, two of the *caimacami* belonged to the National party. They appointed liberal civil servants, lifted the press restrictions imposed by Teodor Balş, and, in general, supported the liberal unionist programme. Yet, regardless of the political preferences of the *caimacami*, the narrow franchise gave the advantage to conservatives.

The spirited election campaign in Moldavia at the end of December 1858 resulted in an assembly favourable to union. Of the 55 delegates, 33 belonged to the National party. They sought a candidate for prince who supported union and shared their political and social philosophy. Yet, when the assembly opened on 9 January 1859, the majority was deeply divided on the choice of a candidate, and at one point there were 38 candidates in the running, a competition which many unionists feared might allow one of the conservative candidates—the former prince Mihai Sturdza or his son Grigore—to carry the day. But finally the liberals agreed on Alexandru Cuza, a forty-eighter and a well-known supporter of union, whom they elected prince on 17 January with 48 out of 55 votes.

The election for the assembly in Wallachia, held between 20 and 24 January was a disappointment for the liberal unionists. Although the majority of the voters in the cities supported the candidates of the National party, the direct electors in the *judeţe*, where *boier* landowners were strong, voted conservative. As a result, when the assembly began its work on 3 February, two-thirds of the 72 delegates were conservatives. Both they and the National party were divided into numerous factions. When it became apparent that neither side could elect its candidate, Dimitrie Ghica, the son of Prince Grigore Ghica, proposed that they proclaim their support for union by electing Alexandru Cuza, as their colleagues in Moldavia had already done. The vote for Cuza, on 5 February, was unanimous. The Romanians by themselves had thus achieved *de facto* union by adhering to the letter of the Convention of Paris.

ALEXANDRU CUZA

The new prince of the United Principalities was descended from a well-to-do family of service nobles. They had held important positions in the central and district administration of Moldavia since the seventeenth century, but they were not among the great *boier* families. Alexandru Cuza was born on 20 March 1820 and, like many boys of his class in the period before the revolution of 1848, he received his schooling at a French pension in Iaşi and was then sent to Paris. He took his baccalaureate in letters in 1835 and enrolled in the Faculty of Law, but did not complete his studies.

Upon his return home he served for a time as a cadet in the army, but resigned in 1840 and became a member of the court of the *judeţ* of Covurlui, in the south, serving as its president between 1842 and 1845. During this period he was associated with the radical societies being formed in Bucharest, and in 1846 he joined some of his friends on a trip to Paris. For his part in the turbulence in Iaşi in 1848 he was forced into exile, but returned in July of the following year shortly before the arrival of the new prince, Grigore Ghica, whom he served in various administrative posts. He also rose steadily in rank in the army. Under the *caimacam* Nicolae Vogoride in 1857 he served briefly as prefect of Covurlui at Galaţi, but resigned in protest over the fraudulent registration of voters for the election of the *adunare ad-hoc*. Under the provisional commission of the three *caimacami* in 1858 he became acting commander of the Moldavian militia, the position he held at the time of his election as prince. Cuza undoubtedly owed his election to his long patriotic service, his consistent unionist position, and his liberal, though not radical, political and social ideas.

The double election of Cuza met with a mixed response from the guarantor powers, for it raised again the same issues that had clouded the drafting of the Convention of Paris. In Vienna the actions of the Moldavian and Wallachian assemblies were denounced as revolutionary, for Austrian officials continued to view any form of union as an obstacle to political and economic penetration of the lower Danube and as encouragement to the alleged centrifugal tendencies among the Romanians of Transylvania and Bukovina. They even contemplated military intervention. France, on the other hand, remained steadfast in support of union. Napoleon III's goal was to expand French influence in a country of Romance culture which could serve to cut off Russia's access to the Mediterranean and keep Austria distracted. Russia favoured union as a means of weakening Austria and Turkey, but especially as a device to forge closer relations with France.[27] Sardinia and Prussia were ready to approve union if only to further their own ambitions in Italy and Germany respectively. Britain vacillated. For a time her statesmen seem to have thought that a united state on the lower Danube could not but be a client state of Russia, but they gradually became resigned to *de facto* union. All the powers finally agreed to meet in Paris on 7 April to consider a response to the Romanian *fait accompli*.

Cuza decided not to wait for events to take their course, but initiated a vigorous diplomatic campaign of his own to gain recognition of his election. He dispatched Moldavian and Wallachian delegations to Constantinople in the middle of February 1859 to obtain investiture by the sultan as quickly as possible, but Turkish officials were in no mood to act until after the conference of the powers had rendered a verdict. It was with the conference in mind that Cuza sent special emissaries to Western Europe and Russia. The first, and most successful, mission was that of Vasile Alecsandri to Paris, London, and Turin.[28] Napoleon III and Walewski received him warmly and promised to send a military mission to the principalities, to reorganize the militia, and to establish an arms manufacturing industry. In London Alecsandri received assurances from Foreign Secretary Malmesbury and others that they wished his country well, but little else. In Turin he and his party were treated as brothers. Although he had no illusions about the nature of these sentiments, he was buoyed by the sympathy and understanding he had encountered on all sides. But Cuza's emissary to Vienna, Ludovic Steege, a financier and an old friend, had a quite different

[26] D. Berindei and E. Cojocaru, 'La Reconnaissance de la double élection d'Alexandru Ioan Cuza, vue à la lumière de la correspondence diplomatique autrichienne', *Revue roumaine d'histoire*, 8/1 (1969), 15–16, 19.

[27] E. E. Chertan, *Russko-rumynskie otnosheniia v 1859–1863 godakh* (Kishinev, 1968), 68–102.

[28] D. Vitcu, *Diplomaţii unirii* (Bucharest, 1979), 60–8.

reception. Buol agreed to see him only as an old acquaintance and refused to accept a letter from Cuza explaining the nature of the double election.

In the mean time, the conference of Paris had opened on 7 April. At the first session France, Britain, Russia, Prussia, and Sardinia recognized Cuza as the elected prince of both principalities. They complained that the double election did not conform to the Convention of Paris, but to avoid incidents and to facilitate the smooth functioning of a regular administration they proposed that the sultan, as an exception, grant Cuza investiture as prince of both Moldavia and Wallachia. The Ottoman and Austrian representatives, as usual, objected, but in the face of the united front of the other powers they yielded, though they continued to seek some formal means of protecting their interests in the principalities.

The conference proved incapable of reaching a speedy resolution of any matter, in part because of Turkey's determination to postpone action for as long as possible, and in part because of the deteriorating relations between Austria and Sardinia. The delegates finally had to suspend their deliberations when war broke out between Austria and Sardinia and her ally France on 29 April. Austria's defeat on the battlefields of northern Italy in June and the armistice arranged by Napoleon III and Francis Joseph followed by their preliminary peace at Villafranca on 11 July, allowed the powers to turn their attention once again to the lower Danube. At the third and final session of the conference on 7 September all the guaranteeing powers, including Austria and Turkey, accepted the double election.

Final recognition of the union of the principalities required further negotiations between Turkey and the powers. But the course of events in the principalities themselves made the outcome all but certain. There the momentum for union proved irreversible as institutions and public services in the two countries merged. Their armies had, in effect, already been unified under a single command. Now the currency, the telegraph lines, and the customs services were fused into one; officials in the two capitals maintained contact with one another directly without going through their respective foreign ministries; and the Central Commission at Focşani worked feverishly to unify laws and administrative procedures.

Cuza decided in June 1860 to press ahead with negotiations with Turkey and the powers to effect complete union and prepared a memorandum modifying the Convention of Paris to serve as a focus of discussion.[29] After his visit to Constantinople in September, which was undertaken to mollify Ottoman officials and was a great personal success, the Ottoman government moved slowly but inexorably towards approval of the memorandum. Finally, on 1 May 1861 it circulated a note to the powers inviting them to a conference to sanction the

---

[29] N. Corivan, *Relaţiile diplomatice ale României de la 1859 la 1877* (Bucharest, 1984), 64–102; B. Jelavich, 'The Ottoman Empire, the Great Powers and the Legislative and Administrative Union of the Principalities', *Rumanian Studies*, ii (Leiden, 1973), 48–83.

'expressed desires of the Romanian people'. For all intents and purposes it had accepted union. Cuza now regarded Moldavia and Wallachia as constituting a single Romania.

The Conference of Constantinople, which opened on 25 September 1861, brushed aside the remaining obstacles to union raised by Ottoman negotiators and persuaded the sultan to issue a *firman* on 4 December recognizing union. One final impediment remained: a single administration and a single legislature meeting in Bucharest could exist only for the duration of Cuza's reign; afterwards the government of the principality would revert to the old system of separate administrations and assemblies together with a revived central commission at Focşani. Few participants took this provision for anything more than a device to allow the Ottomans to exit gracefully from the principalities. Cuza offered the correct interpretation of events when on 23 December he proclaimed the union fulfilled and 'the Romanian nationality established'.

Cuza moved swiftly to complete the administrative union of the principalities. He convoked the first joint session of the legislatures of Moldavia and Wallachia for 24 January 1862 in Bucharest, which was now the capital. Two days before they assembled he appointed the conservative leader Barbu Catargiu prime minister to head the first government of the United Principalities. The final act in the creation of the new unified state was the law of 21 February 1862, which abolished the Central Commission at Focşani. The term 'România' (Romania), which had been frequently, if unofficially, used in the 1850s to refer to a unified state between the Black Sea and the Carpathians, now became the common name for the United Principalities and beginning in 1862 it was used in the country's official acts.

LIBERALS AND CONSERVATIVES

During the critical period before and after the administrative union a modern political system gradually assumed tangible form. The institutions of a national state were created, replacing a superstructure founded upon a monopoly of power by a single class, the *boiers*. Political parties became indispensable machinery for the functioning of these institutions, and the free flow of ideas served as a powerful catalyst of change. Political thought, previously repressed or censored, rose to the surface of public life in all its vitality as individuals and groups openly expressed their preferences. The clash of ideas, in turn, encouraged the like-minded to unite to defend high principles and achieve specific social and economic goals. Their conviction that success would depend upon consistency and cohesion led eventually to the formation of political parties and the emergence of the party system. The groupings that came together in the 1860s lay somewhere between the coteries of *boiers* of the Phanariot period and a modern party. On the one hand, they were no longer composed of dissatisfied aristocrats who had sought power to further narrow class interests and who usually had acted in a conspiratorial manner, relying for support on foreign governments or a random gathering of malcontents at home. But, on the other hand, the new groupings lacked unity and discipline.

Political groupings of this sort had begun to take shape during the period of the Organic Statutes in the assemblies. The best example was the National party led by Ion Cîmpineanu. The pressures of the revolution of 1848, particularly the need to define principles and elaborate programmes of action, accelerated the division of the National party into separate conservative, moderate, and radical factions, even though the boundaries between them remained blurred. The scattering of the forty-eighters and foreign intervention after the revolution interrupted the process of coalescence, but it resumed with greater momentum than ever during the campaign to elect the *adunări ad-hoc* in 1857 and to gain control of the electoral assemblies in the following year. Like-minded individuals joined forces to win seats and promote shared principles. A newspaper, which made possible the wide dissemination of ideas and programmes, was often the magnet that drew men together. During the desperate struggle for union the various factions temporarily set aside their political differences to reconstitute the National party as a coalition. But once union had been achieved and the work of endowing the new state with institutions had begun old enmities reappeared, now more acute than before.

The two main political tendencies of Cuza's reign were, broadly speaking, liberalism and conservatism. The former represented a synthesis of the ideas of the reforming *boiers* during the period of the Organic Statutes, the ideology of 1848, and the more radical aspirations of the latter 1850s and early 1860s. The majority of liberal leaders had been intensely active in 1848 and favoured steady social and political change. Conservatism, on the other hand, was the heir to the traditions and privileges of the pre-1848 era. Its representatives were anxious to preserve existing social and economic structures and to restrict the franchise and reserve public office to the propertied classes.

Romanian liberalism had its origins in the critical spirit manifested in the writings of certain *boiers* and intellectuals at the turn of the century. As we have seen, some called into question the very structures upon which the political and social life of the principalities rested and urged reform, especially of political institutions. Various projects of reform were inspired by the example of France and England or drew upon the Romanian constitutional tradition. The Constitution of the Carbonari of 1822 in Moldavia is noteworthy because it reflected many facets of the liberal spirit: respect for private property with due recognition of the right of expropriation for the public good, individual civil liberties, equality before the law, and freedom of commerce.

The economic changes which the principalities had begun to experience in the latter decades of the eighteenth century and, then, more rapidly in the 1830s and 1840s increased the political importance of the middle class and provided a solid social base for the flourishing of liberalism. Liberal ideas benefited from the support of the business and certain elements of the landowning classes, who were eager to profit from the growing commerce in grain and sought to refashion economic and political institutions to suit their own interests. The middle and lesser *boiers* (rarely the great *boiers*, who were wedded to the traditions of the past) and part of the free peasantry were swept along by the new opportunities for private enterprise and profit. In the rural areas the main category of the lesser *boiers*, the so-called *boiernaşi*, who consisted of such diverse fiscal categories as the *neamuri*, *mazili*, and *ruptaşi*, also supported liberal ideas, out of self-interest. They found middle-class values congenial and disdained as anachronistic the privileges of the old *boier* class, which stood in the way of their economic and social advancement.

Liberalism as a political movement achieved greater cohesion in the period of the Organic Statutes. Liberals were the most intransigent opponents of the existing political system, which they themselves had helped to institute, but which, in effect, had reserved power to the prince and the narrow stratum of the great *boiers*. Behind the conspiratorial movement led by Dimitrie Filipescu in 1840 was a set of assumptions about individual liberty and constitutional government which pushed liberal thought to its furthest point before the revolution of 1848, for Filipescu and his colleagues wanted to abolish privileges of class and extend the political process to the mass of the population. Not only ideas but also the functioning of representative institutions helped to propagate the liberal spirit. The work of the general assemblies between 1834 and 1848, despite their conservative majorities and the intransigence of the princes, gave those deputies who believed in the free exchange of ideas and in the ability of citizens to manage their own affairs a taste at last of the parliamentary experience. The revolution of 1848 in Wallachia was, as we have seen, the culmination of a half-century of radical liberal theory and moderate practice.

After the administrative union of the principalities in 1862 a division of forces within liberalism occurred. It was deeper in Wallachia than in Moldavia. In Wallachia a radical group, dubbed 'the reds' by their opponents, broke away from the moderates. They had been the most revolutionary of the forty-eighters and the most committed of the unionists and were led by C. A. Rosetti, Ion C. Brătianu, and several of the Golescu brothers. They were well organized. They had a central 'club', or committee, in Bucharest, which served as the headquarters for a network of similar clubs in cities and towns throughout Wallachia, and they used their newspaper *Românul* (Romanian) effectively to spread their ideas and maintain party cohesion. They introduced a number of innovations into Romanian politics by mobilizing the masses in the cities as a means of overcoming the political advantages of the conservatives. Large public gatherings and street demonstrations were among their favourite weapons, which, moreover, became a regular feature of election campaigns.[30]

---

[30] A. Stan, *Grupări şi curente politice în România între unire şi independenţă* (Bucharest, 1979), 55–62.

Occupying the centre of the political spectrum were the moderate liberals. In Wallachia many who had participated in the revolution were anxious to ensure steady economic and social progress through enlightened political institutions, but drew back from radical solutions. Nicolae Kretzulescu (1812–1900), a moderate forty-eighter, favoured the abolition of all privileges and the assurance of equality before the law, which he thought indispensable for the creation of a modern society. But he denounced his radical colleagues as 'imitators' who sought to 'implant' Western institutions in Romanian society without regard for the 'true needs of Romania'. Ion Ghica was another moderate. He had stood with Nicolae Bălcescu during the revolution, but in the years of exile he had become estranged from the radicals. After the union of the principalities he tried to establish a strong 'moderate liberal party' as a means of combating 'extreme' solutions to the country's problems from both the radicals and conservatives, but he had to be satisfied with a small personal following. Representative of many younger moderates was Vasile Boerescu (1830–83), who, in his eagerness 'to wipe away the backwardness of the past', advocated a more dynamic pace of change than his older colleagues. But a strong centrist party eluded him as it had Ghica.

The majority of Moldavian liberals were moderates. Liberalism itself was weak, mainly, it appears, because of the relatively few members of the middle class who took part in political activity (much of the commerce and banking was in the hands of foreigners, especially Jews, who were not citizens and, hence, could not vote or run for public office). In these circumstances the peasants represented the potential social foundation of liberalism, but they could not offer strong political support as long as the franchise was limited to the wealthy. In any case, Moldavian liberals, unlike the Wallachian radicals, could not conceive of using the masses to achieve their ends. The leading figure was Mihail Kogălniceanu, whose ideas and personality provided cohesion for Moldavian liberalism during its formative period.

The majority of liberal leaders, both radicals and moderates, owed their wealth and social position mainly to agriculture. With a few exceptions, like Ion Ghica, they were not large landowners. Ion Brătianu was typical. A middle-sized landowner, he had commercialized his estates, concentrating on wine-making, orchards, and animal husbandry, and he sold the bulk of his produce on the market in Bucharest. The Golescu brothers fell into the same category. Kogălniceanu's economic interests revealed a synthesis of agricultural and business pursuits that was to become characteristic of liberals later in the century. He possessed extensive estates, which he exploited intensively with machinery and hired labour, but he was also engaged in industry (he owned a cloth factory in Tîrgu Neamţ) and in commerce (his barges carried grain on the Prut River to ports on the Danube). One of the few liberal leaders not engaged in agriculture was C. A. Rosetti. He bought and sold foreign wines, but the bulk of his income came from his printing house, the most famous product of which was the newspaper *Românul*, long the voice of radical liberalism in Wallachia.

Both moderates and radicals were conscious of an imbalance in the Romanian social structure, specifically the absence of a strong bourgeoisie. With their eye on Western Europe, they were convinced that modern society must be based upon its industrial and commercial classes, not the landed aristocracy, as in the 'feudal order', which they viewed as in irreparable decline. Accordingly, they assigned to a dynamic and innovative bourgeoisie the leading role in the development of Romania, and they strove to attract to their party merchants and artisans, who, they thought, had a natural democratic vocation.[31] But many liberals also looked to the peasantry for support, although not at once. Ion Brătianu expressed the prevailing view when he suggested that the peasants could in time become a bulwark of Romanian liberties and nationality after a careful upbringing supervised by a liberal government.

The attempt to form a united liberal party during Cuza's reign foundered on the inability of the Wallachian radicals and the Moldavian moderates to compose their differences. The radicals took the initiative in the belief that a broad liberal front was necessary to overcome the traditional conservative predominance. C. A. Rosetti had conceived the idea of creating a strong coalition with the Moldavians and uniting around Cuza to help the prince carry out his reform programme. When he broached the matter with Kogălniceanu in December 1861, the latter refused to go along. He objected to both the reform agenda of the radicals and the manner in which they intended to carry it out. He thought that their 'advanced ideas' were 'compromising the affairs of the country', and he was repelled by their efforts to involve the 'crowd' in government. Instead of cooperating with the radicals, he drew closer to Cuza.

Romanian conservatism perpetuated a view of society inspired by earlier centuries. Mihai Sturdza had used the term 'conservative' for the first time in 1823 in a memorandum attacking the reformist activities of liberal *boiers*. He had applied it approvingly to those great *boiers* who wanted to maintain the existing social and political order.[32] This brand of conservatism expressed itself most consistently in the *boiers'* attitude towards property and landlord–peasant relations between the latter decades of the eighteenth century and Cuza's reign. It is also discernible in their ideas on culture and foreign influence. In the 1830s and 1840s Prince Mihai Sturdza and his supporters had been alarmed by mounting French political influence in Moldavia. Fearing the spread of ideas hostile to the established order, they had tried to discourage the sending of *boier* sons to Paris for study and recommended Austria, Prussia, and even Russia as alternatives. When such admonitions fell on deaf ears, Sturdza contemplated depriving those who

---

[31] Ibid. 44–5; I. C. Brătianu, *Acte şi cuvântări*, i/1 (Bucharest, 1938), 269: Brătianu's memorandum to Prince Alexandru Cuza, Feb. 1859.

[32] Hurmuzaki, *Documente*, suppl. 1, pt. 4 (Bucharest, 1891), 6.

had studied in France of their civil and political rights. Wariness of Europe expressed itself in other ways as well. Characteristic was the condemnation of radical liberalism by conservatives as the essence of extravagant Western theories of development totally incompatible with the character and needs of Romanian society.

The social and economic base of conservatism in the 1850s remained several hundred *boier* families who were united by blood and by the need to defend their remaining privileges. The majority of conservative leaders possessed extensive estates, which were generally leased and farmed in traditional ways. They were stronger politically in Moldavia than in Wallachia because their chief opponent, the native urban middle class, was considerably weaker in Moldavia. Yet, conservatives were conscious of how limited their base of support was and how tenuous their hold on power was becoming as political life slowly but inexorably opened up to other classes. They tried, rather half-heartedly, to attract to their side the free peasantry and a part of the commercial middle class, who shared with the large landowners an interest in expanding the export of grain, but it became clear to them that conservatism would have to depend for political success on devices other than mass support.

Conservatism was the predominant political current after the union of the principalities in 1859, in part at least because of the limitations on the right to vote stipulated in the Convention of Paris of 1858. In both Moldavia and Wallachia conservatives controlled the assemblies and were thus in a position to direct the reorganization of Romanian society in accordance with their own vision of it. Initially, they enjoyed greater cohesion than the liberals because they could all accept a simple, clear-cut programme—the defence of large landholdings, the creation of a political system based upon order and stability, and rule by the propertied classes rather than by the 'mob'. To some extent their cohesion was based upon a negative approach to the problems confronting the new state, and they expended more energy combating liberal initiatives than in drawing up a dynamic, positive programme of their own. The electoral advantages they enjoyed seem also to have discouraged systematic political organization. They were persuaded that such activities at the local level and even at the centre were unnecessary.

Despite agreement on principles, the conservatives failed to create a united political party. Individuals and small groups were reluctant to submit completely to a central authority. Under such circumstances party discipline depended mainly upon the skill and forcefulness of the party leader. At the beginning of Cuza's reign the conservatives had found their man in Barbu Catargiu (1807–62), an implacable defender of the great estates who advocated a political system resting upon the will of landowners.[33] His conception of government resembled

---

[33] A. Iordache, *Originile conservatorismului politic din România şi rezistenţa sa contra procesului de democratizare, 1821–1882* (Bucharest, 1987), 236–8, 248–58.

the aristocratic republic advocated by some of the reforming *boiers* of the late Phanariot period. Like them, he opposed arbitrary rule by the prince, or despotism, and like others of his class, he thought that evolution rather than an accelerated pace of change suited Romania, which, in his view, was just emerging from medieval structures. Any attempt to exceed certain natural limits, such as the greater participation of the masses in government would, he was certain, lead to anarchy. Catargiu did little to organize the conservatives as a party, depending rather upon his own energy and determination to give them direction. An authoritarian, he operated from his home in Bucharest with the help of a small coordinating committee of friends. Such methods were perhaps efficient, but they exacerbated personal and group rivalries. The most important dissident group was headed by a moderate conservative, Dimitrie Ghica, the son of Prince Grigore Ghica, who criticized Catargiu for his intolerance of differences even on minor questions and his insistence that the decisions of the leader must prevail over the opinions of other individuals and groups. He thought that party policy ought to be determined by a consensus of prominent members and that differences of opinion ought to be encouraged, and while he did not expect a perfect community of ideas, let alone ultimate truth, to emerge, he (and his colleagues) had no doubt that open discussion lay at the heart of constitutional government. He also wanted to expand the base of support of the party to include the middle and petty bourgeoisie of the cities, thereby removing them from the exclusive influence of the radicals. Such ideas, however, ran counter to the prevailing direction of conservative thought.

The conservatives in Moldavia were in a stronger position than their colleagues in Wallachia. Because of the weakness of the native middle class, they had no serious rivals for power, and in the assembly they overwhelmed the six liberal deputies. As in Wallachia, the conservatives lacked organizational unity, and, instead, formed a number of small groups led by powerful individuals. These, in turn, achieved a certain degree of cohesion through their opposition to Cuza, which became more uncompromising as he turned increasingly to the liberals for support.

The administrative union of the principalities, especially the fusion of the two legislatures, strengthened the position of the conservatives. Yet, even now, despite their power, or perhaps because of it, they did not come together in a formal party. They lacked an organizational structure, a formal programme setting forth immediate and long-term goals, and even a newspaper. When Catargiu was assassinated in June 1862 there was no one to take his place, and they temporarily fell into disarray.

The factionalism within the conservative and liberal parties proved harmful to the development of democratic political institutions. The legislature possessed considerable authority on paper, but it required strong leadership from within to ensure its status as a coequal with an ambitious prince.

FOUNDATIONS

Relations between Cuza and the assembly were tense almost from the beginning of the new national administration. The causes were complex, partly ideological, involving differing agendas for reform, and partly political, arising from Cuza's determination to lead and unwillingness to tolerate opposition to his projects.

Cuza had much in common with the liberals. Like them, he wished to bring about fundamental changes in the social, economic, and political organization of the country. He was closer to the moderates on political reform and somewhat more radical than they when it came to social innovation. Nevertheless, he preferred to work with the moderates rather than the radicals, and in the early years of his reign he hoped to create a strong centre party to serve as the instrument to push his programme quickly through the legislature. He was suspicious of the radicals, because of their past secret revolutionary activity and their avowed intention to democratize the political system by, among other ways, diminishing the powers of the prince. In particular, he objected to their efforts to arouse the masses, the kind of ferment he thought harmful to a new state that was undergoing a fundamental transformation and was continually threatened by foreign intervention.

Whatever Cuza's preferences among the liberals may have been, he was confronted in 1862 with the immediate problem of having to deal with a legislature dominated by conservatives, whose views on every important issue ran counter to his own. Yet, he could not act without the cooperation of the assembly, for he himself advocated the participation of representative institutions in the building of a modern society. As we have seen, he was obliged to turn to Barbu Catargiu to form the first government after the administrative union. But there could be no genuine cooperation between them. The conservatives were opposed to electoral and agrarian reform, which were high on Cuza's agenda, and the prince continually showed his disdain for the conservatives by ignoring their parliamentary majorities.

Cuza was, in fact, unable to cooperate for long with any of the existing parties or major groupings. One reason was undoubtedly their own factionalism and competition for political advantage, which impeded the development of a stable working relationship with the executive branch. The abolition of the Central Commission at Focşani may also have exacerbated the situation because that body had served as a buffer between the prince and the legislature. Yet, the main cause of Cuza's deteriorating relations with the politicians was his resolve to bring his ambitious reform programme to fruition in his own way without alterations imposed by a refractory assembly. At first, he played one party off against the other in the hope that they would neutralize each other, but eventually he was forced to rely on influential individuals in the assembly to carry out his programme.

The opposition to Cuza gradually coalesced into what came to be known as the 'monstrous coalition'.[34] It was composed of the right and the left, which normally differed on every important political and social question, but now found common ground in their hostility to the prince. Each had its own reasons: the conservatives feared the electoral and agrarian reforms which Cuza was intent upon introducing, and the radicals were angered at having been denied the opportunity to form a government. But both were united in their defence of the existing constitutional system, which Cuza, frustrated by his inability to work with the assembly, increasingly ignored. The conflict between him and the coalition, then, became one of parliamentary power versus personal rule.

The conflict broke out into the open in debates in the assembly in February 1863 over the address to the throne. A majority, including the radical liberals C. A. Rosetti and Ion Brătianu and the moderates Dimitrie and Ion Ghica, accused Cuza of having violated the constitution by instituting arbitrary government and by interfering in the election of deputies. The conservatives went even further, demanding that Cuza abdicate in favour of a foreign prince. But neither they nor their allies pressed the issue because they feared that the overthrow of Cuza might jeopardize the union, which the powers had recognized only for the duration of his reign. Moreover, as Ion Brătianu put it, a foreign prince under the prevailing circumstances would have meant a 'Muscovite or Austrian prince or a Turkish pasha', none of whom, he was certain, would have had any sympathy for the liberal reform agenda. On 18 February 1863 the assembly finally approved an address to the throne which, in effect, constituted a vote of censure against the prince. Inconclusive for the moment, these disputes were the beginning of a process that culminated three years later in Cuza's forced abdication.

Cuza himself was more determined than ever to assume full power, or, as he put it, the 'direction of the government', and pressed forward with his plans to overhaul the political system. His advisers set to work drafting a new constitution which provided for: a limitation on the powers of the assembly (the prince would have the authority to convoke and dissolve the legislature, and ministers would not be responsible to it and would not be obliged to respond to interpolations unless instructed to do so by the prince); the creation of a senate, which would decide on the constitutionality of all legislation before it was enacted into law and whose members would be appointed by the prince; and the establishment of a council of state, composed of three senators and three deputies, also appointed by the prince, whose main task would be to draw up legislation. Cuza's model was the French constitution of 1852, and he submitted his draft to the French ambassador in Constantinople for comment.

Cuza found in Mihail Kogălniceanu a liberal leader uniquely suited by commitment to reform and political skill to carry out his programme. For his part,

[34] C. C. Giurescu, *Viaţa şi opera lui Cuza Vodă* (Bucharest, 1966), 159–71; V. Russu, 'Monstruosa coaliţie şi detronarea lui Al. I. Cuza', in *Cuza Vodă in memoriam* (Iaşi, 1973), 503–38.

Kogălniceanu, discouraged by the political rivalries in the assembly, had reluctantly concluded that an authoritarian regime was necessary to effect a comprehensive overhaul of agrarian relations, which, in his view, was indispensable for
all economic and social progress. He formed a government on 23 October 1863
and began at once to bring political institutions and social relations into conform-
ity with Cuza's master plan. His tenure as prime minister, which lasted until 7
February 1865, proved to be the most productive of Cuza's reign.

The controversy over two fundamental issues of political and economic development—electoral reform and a new agrarian law—came to a head during this
period. Electoral reform had been a high priority of both moderate and radical
liberals since the election of Cuza in 1859. They were convinced that genuine
national integration, which, in their view, depended upon the representation of
all classes in the political process and significant social and economic reforms,
could take place only if the power of the conservatives was diluted by a
broadening of the franchise. But all attempts before the installation of the
Kogălniceanu government had foundered on the stubborn resistance to change of
the conservative landlord majority in the assembly. Cuza and Kogălniceanu
decided to challenge their opponents directly. On 15 April 1864 Kogălniceanu
introduced a bill in the assembly which increased the size of the electorate
significantly by lowering the annual tax requirement for indirect and direct
voters. He had no doubt what the conservative reaction would be, but he could
not overcome the persistent doubts of moderate liberals about the capacity of the
common people to take part in government. They demonstrated their concern
by sponsoring amendments which limited the right to vote directly for candidates
and to run for office to those persons who could read and write, a requirement
that would greatly reduce peasant representation in the assemblies, because of
widespread illiteracy in the countryside. Nevertheless, even the amended bill
promised to increase the number of voters significantly over what the electoral
articles attached to the Convention of Paris had allowed. For that very reason the
bill did not become law. The conservatives in the assembly refused even to
discuss it, for its threat to the existing political order was all too apparent: if it had
been passed, it would not only have ended their domination of the assembly, but
would also have made possible the passage of an agrarian law that would, they
were certain, have destroyed their control of the land and its inhabitants.

Kogălniceanu had in fact already begun his campaign on behalf of agrarian
reform. On 16 March 1864 he had introduced legislation in the assembly which
abolished *clacă* and other peasant dues and services and granted peasants land,
'which they possessed or were supposed to possess in accordance with existing
laws'. As compensation for the loss of dues and services from their *clăcaşi*,
landlords were to receive a 'suitable indemnity' to be paid by the peasants
themselves over a twenty-year period and guaranteed by the state. Thus,
Kogălniceanu (and Cuza) recognized the right of the *clăcaşi* to the land they held
in usufruct. The legislators of reform were not, then, really giving land to the

peasants, but were, instead, substituting private ownership for 'feudal control' of the land. The indemnities they offered the landlords represented the capitalized value of dues and services owed them by the *clăcaşi,* not compensation for the land. Kogălniceanu and other liberals made this idea plain when they declared that to take away one *prajină* (180–210 m²) of land from the *boier* or the *clăcaş* would be a gross injustice. They thus reaffirmed the inviolability of private property as the social foundation of the nation. The new law, moreover, offered peasants who were not entitled to grants of land from their landlords the right to buy land from the state.[35]

The ensuing debates in the assembly revealed a significant change in the attitude of the conservatives since Cuza's refusal to sanction their own bill in June 1862, which had offered an inadequate one and a half hectares to every peasant family. They now accepted the principle of emancipation with land, but they sought to maintain the economic integrity of their estates by limiting their own contribution to small, marginal plots of land and by making the state primarily responsible for satisfying the peasants' needs through the sale of its own lands. Since neither they nor Kogălniceanu would compromise on the question of granting land to the peasants from private estates, they reached an impasse, which led the centre and the right to pass a motion of censure against the government, 63 to 36, on 25 April. As a result, the government offered its resignation, but Cuza refused to accept it. Now convinced more than ever that agrarian reform could not be carried out by parliamentary means, he decided to dispense with the assembly, but retained Kogălniceanu as his principal collaborator. On 27 April he prorogued the assembly until 14 May. Although the leaders of the opposition sensed what was about to happen, they were unable to mount a defence, largely because the bitter divisions over the agrarian question had thoroughly undone the cohesion they had achieved in 1863.

On 14 May the assembly gathered in extraordinary session, summoned by Cuza to consider the earlier bill on electoral reform. The majority ignored his message and declared their intention not to hold public sessions until the outstanding issues in dispute between the assembly and the prince had been resolved in a constitutional manner. As they were about to lay their proposal before the house, Kogălniceanu rose and read a decree from Cuza dissolving the assembly. When the opposition deputies protested and refused to leave the chamber, Kogălniceanu had them forcibly removed by soldiers.

On the same day Cuza addressed a proclamation to the country explaining that the drastic action just taken had been forced upon him by the 'implacable opposition' of a 'turbulent oligarchy', which had continually thwarted all his efforts to improve the general welfare. He also announced that he would submit for the approval of the people a new electoral law and the draft of a new

---

[35] V. I. Ionescu, *Opera lui Mihail Kogălniceanu sub raportul faptei şi gîndirii social-economice* (Craiova, 1979), 161–4.

constitution (*Statut*). Cuza and Kogălniceanu moved swiftly to consolidate their position. A plebiscite was hastily organized between 22 and 26 May and resulted in overwhelming approval of the reforms: 682,621 votes in favour, 1,307 opposed, and 70,220 abstaining.

Since the new electoral law and the *Statut* were at variance with certain provisions of the Convention of Paris, Cuza felt obliged to obtain approval of his constitutional reforms by the guaranteeing powers.[36] Assured of the support of France and Britain, he travelled to Constantinople on 5 June to meet Ottoman officials. After several weeks of hard bargaining, during which he had to resist heavy Ottoman and Austrian pressure to introduce substantial changes in both the electoral law and the *Statut*, all the powers signed an agreement on 28 June recognizing the need for changes in the Convention of Paris, thereby, in effect, ratifying the coup of 14 May. In return for accepting a few minor changes in his reforms, Cuza had won a major prize—the powers' recognition of the right of the United Principalities to modify all laws relating to their internal administration without foreign approval, except in matters affecting relations with their Ottoman suzerain.

The new electoral law and constitution were, in Cuza's view, inextricably linked. Despite liberal provisions in both, they were not primarily liberal documents. The electoral law, to be sure, increased the number of voters substantially, from a few thousand under the Convention of Paris to some 570,000. The taxpaying and property qualifications kept only a relatively few persons from voting, but the system of electoral colleges and the indirect election of deputies significantly diluted the voting strength of the majority, who fell into the category of primary, or indirect, electors. Fifty of them chose a single elector (who had to have a substantial annual income) to cast a ballot directly for a candidate. The functioning of the electoral colleges particularly disadvantaged peasants (and other rural inhabitants), since their college could send 66 deputies to the assembly, whereas the one for urban residents sent 94, despite the fact that the rural population was far larger than that of the cities. Although on the surface electoral rights approached the level of universal male suffrage, the new law was not a profession of faith by Cuza in the democratic process. It was, rather, an attempt to reconcile the democratic spirit, representing his ideal, with an authoritarian executive power, a reluctant concession on his part to the demands of practical politics.

The liberal provisions of the electoral law were further vitiated by the *Statut*, which turned the legislature into a simple office for registering and confirming the decisions of the prince. Cuza's experiences with the assembly in the first years of his reign seem to have destroyed his confidence in a broadly representative legislature. The *Statut* thus brought about a fundamental change in the relation-

---

[36] A. Lăpedatu, 'Austria și lovitura de stat de la 2/14 mai 1864', Academia Română, *Memoriile Secțiunii Istorice*, 3rd ser. 28 (1946), 68–113; R. V. Bossy, *L'Autriche et les Principautés-Unies* (Bucharest, 1938), 367–86.

ship between the executive and legislative branches of government.[37] It granted
the prince such powers as to render his will almost absolute. In the enactment of
laws, for example, he alone could initiate legislation; he had an absolute veto
over bills passed by the assembly; and he could legislate by decree when the
legislature was not in session, although he was obliged to explain the reasons for
his actions when it reconvened.

The legislative branch was thus subordinate to the prince and exercised only
limited powers. The elected assembly, composed of 160 deputies, could debate
bills presented to it, but could only delay those which it opposed. It had the right
to approve the state budget, but if it did not do so in time, the government could
continue to spend money on the basis of the previous budget. A senate, the
majority of whose members were appointed by the prince, had to approve all the
bills passed by the assembly before they could become law, except the budget,
and had the right to judge the constitutionality of laws. A council of state,
consisting of appointees of the prince and presided over by him, had the
responsibility of drawing up all legislation to be presented to the assembly. Its
members also participated in the assembly's debates on proposed legislation as
delegates of the prince, but could not vote.

The influence of the French constitution of 1852 was manifest throughout the
Statut, especially in those articles limiting the powers of representative bodies and
establishing the preponderance of the executive. The *Statut* thus maintained
parliamentary forms, but henceforth the substance of Romanian constitutionalism
lay in the personal rule of the prince.

The swiftness and decisiveness with which Cuza had imposed his new political
order had left the opposition in disarray. But their confusion proved to be only
temporary. The coup of 14 May revived the monstrous coalition and reinforced
the determination of its leaders to replace Cuza with a foreign prince, who
would be forced to respect the powers of the assembly and, of course, their own.
The radicals, led by Rosetti and Ion Brătianu, became the most formidable
opponents of the new political system.

The coup had, none the less, cleared the way for Cuza to move briskly ahead
with his economic and social reforms. The centrepiece was the agrarian law. On
14 July 1864 he instructed the new Council of State to draw up a bill that would
abolish *clacă* and other labour services and dues owed by peasants to their
landlords and would assure the peasants the possession of the land to which they
were legally entitled, while guaranteeing a fair indemnity to the estate owners.
Using Kogălniceanu's earlier bill as a guide, the drafting committee had a text
ready by 23 August which the full council, with Cuza himself presiding, quickly
approved.

The so-called 'rural law' sanctioned by Cuza on 26 August dealt extensively
with the redistribution of land. It recognized the full property rights of the *clăcaşi*

---

[37] P. Negulescu and G. Alexianu, *Tratat de drept public*, i (Bucharest, 1942), 212–19.

to the land they already possessed in accordance with previous laws, which had made allotments on the basis of the number of draught animals, that is, the productive capacity, of the individual peasant. Those peasants who did not already possess the specified amount of land to which they were entitled would receive a supplement, but widows without children, minors, and those whose occupations on the estate were not agricultural and who had not performed *clacă* received only a house and a garden. The law also limited the amount of land made available to peasants to two-thirds of the landlord's estate. But forests, which were essential for the economic well-being of many households, did not enter into these calculations. Peasants were allowed to use the forests in accordance with tradition for fifteen years, after which the landlord could reclaim his property rights to them. Peasants who did not come under the provisions of the law, including young married couples, were permitted to settle on lands near their village owned by the state, if they wished. The new peasant proprietor was forbidden to sell or mortgage his land for a period of thirty years; afterwards, if he wished to sell, the village commune could exercise its right of pre-emption. The law also abolished for all time *clacă* and the tithe and other dues and services which the peasants had owed the landlord for centuries. But the peasants had to assume the lion's share of the compensation payments due landlords. Each new peasant proprietor had to pay a considerable sum—between 51 and 133 *lei* anually for fifteen years—into an indemnity fund, which in turn issued rural communal bonds to the landlords to be redeemed in instalments during a fifteen-year period.

Implementation of the law began immediately, but the process was slowed because of the absence of comprehensive regulations concerning both general procedures and special cases. Kogălniceanu tried to remedy the situation by issuing a stream of circulars to prefects, a procedure which proved confusing, as instructions were continually modified to deal with new situations. The lack of impartial surveyors to carry out the delicate task of delimiting the new peasant holdings from the rest of the estate caused constant friction between landlords and peasants, who had no confidence in private surveyors hired by the landlords. Disputes also arose over the provision of the law calling for the consolidation of scattered pastures, hayfields, and arable plots wherever possible. This was a laudable attempt to counteract the steady fragmentation of peasant holdings caused by successive inheritances, but in practice all too often the landlords used the exchanges of land simply as a device to push poor quality land off on to the peasants. In all these encounters the peasants usually came out second best, and many who were entitled to land received none or too little to cover their needs.[38]

Of the immediate consequences of the rural law, the most obvious was the granting of 1,810,311 hectares of land to 463,554 peasant families, or roughly an average of 4 hectares per family. Some 60,000 of these families, however,

[38] Adăniloaie and Berindei, *Reforma agrară din 1864*, 245–300.

received only land enough for a house and garden. Later, 48,342 additional families of newlyweds received 228,329 hectares. Although a substantial amount of land thus changed hands, large landholding had by no means ceased. After the reform landlords together with the state still held about 70 per cent of the arable land and pastures, while peasant property (that belonging to the former *clăcaşi* and to *răzeşi*) represented about 30 per cent. Nor did the agrarian reform lead to peasant prosperity. The compensation payments were a heavy burden for the majority of peasant families and brought ruin to the poorest among them. Agricultural production in the year following the reform stagnated and in some regions even declined, in part because many landlords had done nothing to make up for the loss of *clacă* and, hence, lacked both labour and draught animals to carry on the operations of their estates. Production also suffered because many peasants did not know precisely which lands would be theirs and were, consequently, reluctant to raise a crop that might in fact belong to someone else. But by the spring of 1866 the crisis had been surmounted, and production once again was on the increase.

Cuza was eager to develop other branches of the economy as rapidly as possible through the creation of new institutions and the reorganization of old ones, and he showed no hesitation in using all the powers of the executive to accomplish his ends. But he lacked the necessary financial resources. The income from various state taxes, most of which dated from the period of the Organic Statutes and continued to fall most heavily on those least able to pay—the peasantry and the lower classes of towns and cities—proved inadequate for ordinary needs let alone an ambitious plan of economic expansion.

Cuza was thus forced to turn to foreign capital, but he was quickly disabused of the notion that the Western powers, because they had placed Romania under their collective protection, would feel an obligation to provide economic and financial help.[39] Both governments and private investors were wary of committing large amounts of capital to enterprises they judged risky in a country they perceived as politically unstable and economically backward. They preferred to use local resources, a strategy manifest in the manœuvring of British and French investors to establish a bank in Bucharest with the exclusive right to issue banknotes. In 1865 Cuza granted such a concession to an Anglo-French consortium to establish Banca României (Bank of Romania), undoubtedly the most important banking act of his reign. Although he was reluctant to subordinate an important share of the Romanian economy to foreign interests, he was persuaded that the new bank would funnel massive amounts of capital into the country and that a strengthening of financial ties to Britain and France would ensure their support for his foreign policy. But he was disappointed on both counts.

In carrying out his grand design to endow the United Principalities with modern institutions, Cuza gave particular attention to the judicial system, which

---

[39] G. Zane, *Studii* (Bucharest, 1980), 176–203.

he was anxious to reshape in accordance with the needs of a European state. In a series of laws promulgated in 1864 and 1865 he placed the administration of justice on essentially Western European foundations. In so doing, he annulled venerable codes that had been in place since the beginning of the century, such as the Caragea Code of 1818 and the Suțu code of penal procedure of 1820. A new civil code, which he sanctioned on 16 December 1864 and had as its model the French Civil Code of 1804, took the individual as the foundation of law, assuring him of personal freedoms, guaranteeing equality of all citizens before the law, and safeguarding private property. A code of civil procedure (21 September 1865) was based on a corresponding code of the Swiss canton of Geneva of 1819, and codes of penal law (30 October 1864) and criminal procedure (14 December 1864) had French codes of 1810 and 1808 respectively as models. Another law (18 December 1864), regulating the admission of candidates to judicial office, proclaimed merit as the primary criterion of selection and promotion.

To assure the country of an orderly administration of public affairs and a capable and well-informed citizenry Cuza proposed to bring public education 'within reach of all classes' and to make certain that it met the true needs of Romanian society. As the centrepiece of his plan he promulgated the comprehensive education law of 1864, which regulated instruction at all levels: it put forward the principle that primary education should be obligatory and free and that every village should have its own school; it mandated the building of secondary schools in urban centres, especially școli reale (*Realschule*), which would prepare students for careers in agriculture, commerce, and industry; and it expanded the curricula of the two universities—Iași, founded in 1860, and Bucharest, in 1864—to include medicine, the physical and natural sciences, and mathematics, in addition to the humanities and law. Although the number of schools and students increased and the universities offered superior instruction, Cuza realized only a small part of his ambitious project. The main obstacle was the lack of funds to provide the teachers, the buildings, and even the books necessary for primary and secondary education. Nor could he overcome the prejudice of society at large in favour of classical and humane studies at the expense of agronomy, commerce, and economics, and, thus, he did not live to see the day when, as he put it in 1859, a doctor of agricultural sciences would enjoy the same respect and advantages as a doctor of literature.

Manifest in the *Statut* and other major legislation was the tendency to increase the authority of the central government over autonomous institutions. New laws concerning the Orthodox Church are a case in point. From the very beginning of his reign Cuza had shown himself a zealous partisan of the secular state. He was determined to bring the Orthodox Church fully under the supervision of the state in all but strictly theological matters, a goal he in large measure accomplished. During his reign no elections of metropolitans or bishops took place. Whenever a vacancy occurred it was filled by a temporary administrator. Cuza also took drastic measures to bring the income of monasteries under state control.

He dissolved by decree a number of large and small monasteries in both principalities in 1860 in order to make better use of their buildings and resources for the public good, especially education. In the same year he had the training of priests reorganized and the seminaries themselves brought under the direction of the ministry of cults and public instruction.[40]

The most important of Cuza's church laws, from an economic standpoint, had to do with the secularization of monastery lands. He was eager to bring the roughly quarter of the country's territory which they controlled under state direction in order to rationalize their management and increase their productivity. Especially delicate was the question of the properties belonging to the dedicated monasteries. The government proposed in August 1863 to pay the Orthodox holy places in the Ottoman Empire a sizeable indemnity, but the patriarch of Constantinople rejected the offer. The Ottoman government, which supported him, circulated a note to the guanteeing powers on 23 December requesting their intervention to uphold the Convention of Paris, which had stipulated the procedures for settling the matter. Kogălniceanu, as prime minister, decided to proceed with secularization without waiting for action from the powers. The measure was enormously popular in the legislature among both conservatives and liberals and had the support of public opinion, which regarded the measure as a further affirmation of national sovereignty. When Kogălniceanu introduced his bill secularizing monastery properties in the assembly on 25 December 1863 it was immediately approved by a vote of 93 to 3. It made all the lands and other possessions of the monasteries the property of the state and provided for the payment of an indemnity to the holy places for their loss of revenues from the dedicated monasteries. After the hostile reaction of several powers, notably Russia and Austria, a compromise was reached in May 1864 which brought recognition by the powers of secularization in return for an increased indemnity to the holy places. Thus, the long-standing dispute over the dedicated monasteries, largely a product of the Phanariot regime, was laid to rest.[41] The law also ended the substantial role of all monasteries in the economic life of the country as their extensive agricultural lands now fell under state supervision.

Other laws curtailed the role of the church in civil affairs and completed state domination of its administrative structure. The new civil code removed divorce cases from the jurisdiction of church courts and made civil marriage obligatory. The law on the organization of communes of 31 March 1864 took the recording of births, marriages, and deaths out of the hands of the clergy, making this task the responsibility of the mayors of communes. Still other laws regulated monastic life and administration, instituted new procedures for the appointment of metropolitans and bishops, which reserved a decisive role for the prince, and

---

[40] M. Păcurariu, *Istoria Bisericii Ortodoxe Române*, iii (Bucharest, 1981), 113–28.
[41] M. Popescu-Spineni, *Procesul mânăstirilor închinate* (Bucharest, 1936), 71–114.

established a unified, autocephalous Romanian church, with its own synod presided over by the metropolitan of Ungrovlachia, who now bore the title 'primate of Romania'. All this legislation was part of a general secularization of Romanian society. This process was the logical outcome of liberal thought about the role of the church in society, as manifested in the programmes of the generation of 1848, and represented the culmination of social and economic changes under way since the latter decades of the eighteenth century.

Cuza encountered no serious opposition from politicians as he laid the institutional foundations of a modern state. Kogălniceanu was in part responsible, for he had conducted the elections of the autumn of 1864 with great skill. Relying at the local level on the administrators of the *judeţe*, the *prefecţi* (prefects) and *subprefecţi* (subprefects), who were accountable to the central government, he ensured the government's complete dominance of the assembly and of local elected bodies. The tasks facing the government were eased also by the presence of a majority of newcomers in the assembly; they had had little or no experience in public life and were docile instruments in the hands of government managers. Consequently, even the most complicated pieces of legislation, such as the budget for 1865, could be rushed through the assembly in a single day. Occasional attempts by a few courageous deputies to amend a bill were brushed aside at a mere sign from the prime minister. Yet, despite the subservience of the legislature, Cuza and his ministers preferred to legislate by decree. For them, democratic procedures were less important than the swift achievement of institutional reform.

Cuza's main objectives in foreign policy were international recognition of the union and the strengthening of the country's autonomy. He was anxious to establish regular diplomatic relations with foreign countries, particularly the West, in order to eliminate one more of the sultan's few remaining prerogatives and to promote economic development. Although the powers were unreceptive to formal arrangements, they did not hesitate to deal directly with the principalities when it suited their purpose. In the autumn of 1860 Cuza succeeded in opening a diplomatic agency in Paris, which had as its primary mission the cementing of close relations with the United Principalities' chief sponsor in Western Europe. He also sought to conclude economic conventions with other states, particularly of the sort that would allow the principalities to set tariffs and take other measures to foster their own economic development. As it was, their commerce continued to be governed by treaties between foreign states and the Ottoman Empire. The first such international agreement between the principalities and a foreign state was the telegraph convention with Russia of 15 December 1860.

Besides France, Cuza paid particular attention to Austria, because of her key role in international affairs and her large Romanian population in Transylvania, Bukovina, and the Banat. He desired friendly relations and proposed establishing permanent diplomatic representation in Vienna, but Austrian officials remained cool to all his overtures. The main reason was their uneasiness about Cuza's intentions in Transylvania, an attitude which they thought justified both by the close relations maintained by prominent political figures in the principalities with Transylvanian Romanians and Cuza's intermittent negotiations with Hungarian émigrés.[42]

In the spring of 1859 Cuza sought to take advantage of Magyar and Romanian discontent in Hungary and Transylvania to gain political and economic concessions from Austria and, in case of war between her and France and Sardinia, to secure autonomy for the Romanians of Transylvania. France and Sardinia offered him strong encouragement. At the end of March Cuza met with General György Klapka, representing the Hungarian émigrés. On the 28th he agreed in principle to supply arms from France to the Hungarians for an anti-Austrian insurrection, but as a condition he insisted that the nationality conflicts of 1848–9 be avoided. After nearly two months of negotiations an agreement was reached which met Cuza's terms. It promised equality of rights to all the inhabitants of Hungary without regard to nationality or religion, guaranteed extensive local autonomy, recognized all languages as official, and held out the possibility that Transylvania would regain its separate political administration, if a majority of the inhabitants so desired.[43] But the war which had broken out between Austria and France and Sardinia in April was over so quickly that the Hungarian–Romanian agreement could not be put into effect. None the less, discussions about an alliance continued off and on over the next four years. In May 1863 Cuza and General István Türr, on behalf of Hungarian émigrés, revived the idea of a Hungarian insurrection aided by Romania and coordinated with an attack on Austria by Italy.[44] Cuza was willing, but asked to see evidence of an understanding between the Hungarians and the Romanians of Transylvania. Nothing came of these negotiations mainly because Napoleon III, upon whom the success of the enterprise depended, was not at the moment inclined to take action against Austria. Yet, a precedent had been set; as time passed the status of the Romanians of Transylvania became a cardinal point of Romania's foreign policy.

Despite his success in carrying out an ambitious legislative programme, his overwhelming majority in the assembly, and his tight control of the bureaucracy, Cuza's position was gradually undermined. He himself was partly responsible. He forced Kogălniceanu, whom he suspected (unjustly) of wanting to be prince, to resign as prime minister in February 1865, thereby depriving himself of one of his most effective allies. Then, he tried to assuage the hostility in the assembly over his authoritarian methods by concessions. In December 1865, for example, he

---

[42] Stan, *Grupări și curente politice*, 147–58; G. Chiriță, 'Periodicul bucureștean "Naționalul" (1857–1861) și probleme Transilvaniei', *Studii: Revistă de istorie*, 25/1 (1972), 81–96.

[43] D. Berindei, 'Mihail Kogălniceanu, prim-ministru al Moldovei, și emigrația maghiară (1860–1861)', in *Studii și materiale de istorie modernă*, ii (Bucharest, 1960), 223–44; E. Kovács, *A Kossuth-emigráció és az európai szabadságmozgalmak* (Budapest, 1967), 335–56.

[44] Kovács, *A Kossuth-emigráció*, 246–54.

announced that the deputies would once again have the right to question ministers, but when the new president of the assembly in his first speech expressed regret that many of those who had played a prominent role in the country's affairs could find no place for themselves in the legislature (a clear reference to the prince's heavy-handed treatment of the opposition), Cuza took offence and forced him to resign. This and similar episodes were taken as evidence of both Cuza's weakness and his unwillingness to move towards representative government. As a result, support for the parliamentary system grew on all sides.[45]

The prince's enemies on both the right and the left were encouraged to regroup. In the summer of 1865 the monstrous coalition was reconstituted, bringing together such otherwise incompatible elements as conservatives and radical liberals, who temporarily put aside differences in their determination to remove Cuza from the throne and replace him with a foreign prince. The conservatives condemned him as too liberal and could not forgive him for his agrarian and electoral reforms; the radicals abandoned him because he was not liberal enough. Both groups resented his abuses of power and feared outright dictatorship and sought a return to pre-*Statut* constitutionalism. Cuza was thus largely isolated politically and, tired and ill, was himself contemplating abdication, as he intimated in his message to the legislature at the beginning of its session in December 1865. Such signs of lassitude encouraged the plotters to proceed.[46] Led by the radicals with Ion Brătianu and Rosetti at their head, they decided to carry out their coup swiftly in order to avoid public disorders and the foreign intervention that had often accompanied them. They won over key elements of the army, who arrested Cuza on the night of 23 February 1866. The prince offered no resistance and signed the abdication papers immediately. Shortly afterwards he was allowed to leave the country for Austria, where he lived until his death in 1873. His departure into exile symbolized the end of one era and marked the beginning of another in the evolution of modern Romania.

The year 1866 is a convenient date at which to pause in order to measure the distance the Romanians had travelled since the final decades of the eighteenth century. The union of the principalities had been accomplished, and the independence of 'Romania', as Romanians themselves now called their country, had for all practical purposes been assured. Significant progress in rationalizing government had been made, and both Romanian citizens and foreign governments could expect it to act predictably and to abide by its commitments. The new state had also acquired the instruments necessary to carry out its responsibilities— a strong executive to provide direction, a parliament to represent a diversity of

[45] T. Drăganu, *Începuturile şi dezvoltarea regimului parlamentar în România pînă la 1916* (Cluj, 1991), 165–83.

[46] P. Henry, *L'Abdication du Prince Cuza* (Paris, 1930), 1–28; G. Chiriță, 'Preludiile şi cauzele detronării lui Cuza Vodă', *Revista de istorie*, 29/3 (1976), 347–71.

opinion, political parties to serve as the machinery of change, and up-to-date codes of law to foster social stability and economic progress. Broad principles— liberalism and conservatism—were also in place to guide politicians and intellectuals as they shaped the national agenda. Most important of all, the élite had crossed the threshold into Europe, accepting membership in its community of nations as permanent, if not always beneficial.

The general path of development that Romania was to follow down to the Second World War had thus been laid out.[47] In domestic affairs the strong executive and the near monopoly of power at the centre, in Bucharest, were the hallmarks of government. A two-party system contributed significantly to the stability and democratization of political life, even though the popular will was sometimes thwarted by the mechanisms of privilege and by public apathy. As for the economy, industrialization made steady progress, but agriculture remained the foundation of the country's well-being, and those who sought agrarian reform encountered a formidable obstacle in tradition. The most dramatic change in social structure was the continued advance of the middle class. No other class could match its dynamism in economic and political enterprise, for the large landowners disappeared and the peasantry and urban workers lacked experience and leadership.

Romania's international relations, political, economic, and cultural, continued to be shaped by the process of integration into Europe. In a sense, integration meant dependence, and all members of the élite recognized that the country's security and prosperity could be achieved only in concert with the great powers, never in isolation from them. Yet, they could not agree on how fast and how complete integration should be, and thus the controversy over national identity and models of development intensified. The Europeanists argued for continued urbanization and industrialization, while diverse groups of traditionalists sought spiritual well-being in the village and material progress in agriculture. Although their differences could not be reconciled even as a new world war approached in 1939, all sides to this great debate agreed on one critical point: that the Romanians stood as always at the crossroads between East and West.

[47] I have described this period in *Rumania 1866–1947* (Oxford, 1994).

BIBLIOGRAPHICAL ESSAY

BIBLIOGRAPHIES

The main bibliography of Romanian history is *Bibliografia istorică a României*, i. *1944–1969*, iv. *1969–1974*, v. *1974–1979*, vi. *1979–1984*, vii. *1984–1989* (Bucharest, 1970–90); ii and iii (Bucharest, 1972–4) cover the nineteenth century. The historian will find *Bibliografia românească veche*, 4 vols. (Bucharest, 1910–44) indispensable for the study of intellectual and cultural life. It lists books printed in the Romanian principalities or in Romanian elsewhere between 1508 and 1830 and reproduces excerpts from the prefaces of many. A useful update is Daniela Poenaru, *Contribuții la bibliografia românească veche* (Tîrgoviște, 1973). The continuation of the 'old bibliography' is *Bibliografia românească modernă, 1831–1918*, 3 vols. (Bucharest, 1984–9), which has reached the letter 'Q'. *Publicațiile periodice românești*, i. *1820–1906* and ii. *1907–18*, and suppl. *1790–1906* (Bucharest, 1913–69), contains an exhaustive annotated listing of periodicals and newspapers published in Romania and in foreign countries in Romanian. Equally exhaustive and a unique source of information is *Bibliografia analitică a periodicelor românești*, i/1–3. *1790–1850* (Bucharest, 1966–7), ii/1–3. *1851–8* (Bucharest, 1970–2), which lists and often provides summaries of individual articles from Romanian-language periodicals.

GENERAL WORKS

A stimulating introduction to the eighteenth and early nineteenth century is Nicolae Iorga, *Histoire des Roumains et de la romanité orientale*, viii–ix (Bucharest, 1944), one of the classics of modern Romanian historiography. Constantin C. Giurescu, *Istoria Românilor*, iii/1–2 (Bucharest, 1944–6), a product of the 'new school' of history, is systematically organized and based on a careful reading of the sources. The major synthesis of the Communist era, *Istoria României*, iii–iv (Bucharest, 1964), analyses the origins of modern Romania from a Marxist perspective.

The course of development taken by Romania since the beginning of the nineteenth century has been the subject of spirited debate among historians and social theorists. Eugen Lovinescu, *Istoria civilizației române moderne,* 3 vols. (Bucharest, 1924–5), develops the theory of 'synchronism', which holds that modern Romania was steadily being integrated into Western European civilization. On the Marxist side, Lucrețiu Pătrășcanu, *Un veac de frămîntări sociale, 1821–1907* (Bucharest, 1945), emphasizes economic development and class struggle as the motive forces of change, but, like Lovinescu, accepts the need for Westernization. Ilie Bădescu, *Sincronism european și cultura critică românească* (Bucharest, 1984), a response to the 'Communist nationalism' promoted by the regime in the 1970s and 1980s, insists upon the originality of the Romanians' historical development and is reserved towards the West.

1. MOLDAVIA AND WALLACHIA, 1774–1821

Essential background to Ottoman–Romanian relations in the eighteenth century is Tahsin Gemil, *Românii şi otomanii în secolele XIV–XVI* (Bucharest, 1991). Erol Urunga, *Osmanli devleti idaresinde Eflâk-Boğdan (1774–1812)* (Istanbul, 1966), is a short legal history of Ottoman attempts to assert sovereignty over the principalities. There are ample collections of official Ottoman documents on the principalities: Mustafa A. Mehmet (ed.), *Documente turceşti privind istoria României*, ii. *1774–1791*, iii. *1791–1812* (Bucharest, 1983–6), in Romanian trans., and Valeriu Veliman (ed.), *Relaţiile româno-otomane (1711–1821); Documente turceşti* (Bucharest, 1984), in Turkish, accompanied by Romanian trans. Mihail Guboglu, *Catalogul documentelor turceşti*, 2 vols. (Bucharest, 1960–5), lists over 5,000 Turkish documents and provides summaries of many.

On government and the judicial system *Istoria dreptului românesc*, ii/1 (Bucharest, 1984), provides a useful overview. Scholarly and detailed are Valentin A. Georgescu and Emanuela Popescu-Mihuţ, *Organizarea de stat a Ţării Româneşti (1765–1782)* (Bucharest, 1989), on the structure of government, and Valentin A. Georgescu and Petre Strihan, *Judecata domnească în Ţara Românească şi Moldova 1611–1831*, pt. 1. *Organizarea judecătoreasca*, vol. ii. *1740–1831* (Bucharest, 1981), on the organization of justice. Vladimir Hanga, *Les Institutions du droit coutumier roumain* (Bucharest, 1988), is a solid introduction to the nature of customary law and its decline. The decisive role of the prince in the judicial process and the alternating application of written and customary law during the reign of Alexandru Ipsilanti are evident in a massive collection of legal sources, *Acte judiciare din Ţara Românească, 1775–1781* (Bucharest, 1973). On the political and social role of the Orthodox Church the account in Mircea Păcurariu, *Istoria Bisericii Ortodoxe Române*, ii and iii (Bucharest, 1981) is comprehensive and accompanied by extensive bibliographies. D. Furtună, *Preoţimea românească în secolul al XVIII-lea* (Vălenii de Munte, 1915), examines the cultural and material condition of the Orthodox clergy.

The international status of the principalities has been the subject of numerous monographs. A stimulating overview is Leonid Boicu, *Geneza 'Chestiunii Române' ca problema internaţională* (Iaşi, 1975). On the principalities' relations with Russia, Galina S. Grosul, *Dunaiskie kniazhestva v politike Rossii, 1774–1806* (Kishinev, 1975), analyses the question from the perspective of the Russo-Ottoman rivalry in South-eastern Europe, and Irina S. Dostian, *Rossiia i balkanskii vopros* (Moscow, 1972), places the principalities within the general context of great-power ambitions in the Ottoman Empire. Austria's political objectives in the principalities are ably described by Harald Heppner, *Österreich und die Donaufürstentümer, 1774–1812* (Graz, 1984), and her economic penetration of the lower Danube by Gheron Netta, *Expansiunea economică a Austriei şi explorările ei orientale* (Bucharest, 1931). Germaine Lebel's detailed account of French political and economic interest in the principalities, *La France et les principautés danubiennes* (Paris, 1955), is unsurpassed. Equally comprehensive on Great Britain is Paul Cernovodeanu, *Relaţiile comerciale româno-engleze în contextul politicii orientale a Marii Britanii 1803–1878* (Cluj-Napoca, 1986).

Indispensable sources for an understanding of the policies of the great powers towards the principalities are the diplomatic and consular reports of their representatives in Constantinople and the principalities published in many vols. of Eudoxiu de Hurmuzaki, *Documente privitoare la istoria Românilor*, 44 vols. (Bucharest, 1876–1942), and the NS, *Documente privind istoria Românilor*, 4 vols. (Bucharest, 1962–74). For Russia, see NS i.

Rapoarte consulare ruse (1770–1796) (Bucharest, 1962) and NS iv. *Rapoarte diplomatice ruse (1797–1806)* (Bucharest, 1974); for Austria: xix/1. *Corespondenţa diplomatică şi rapoarte consulare austriace* (Bucharest, 1922); xix/2. *Corespondenţa şi rapoarte consulare austriace (1798–1812)* (Cernăuţi, 1938); and NS ii. *Rapoarte consulare austriece (1812–1823)* (Bucharest, 1967); and for France: xvi. *Corespondenţa diplomatică şi rapoarte consulare franceze (1603–1824)* (Bucharest, 1912); suppl. 1. *Documente culese din arhivele Ministeriului Afacerilor Străine din Paris*, pts. 2. *1781–1814* and 3. *1709–1812* (Bucharest, 1885–9).

2. SOCIETY AND THE ECONOMY, 1774–1829

On population and social structure Pavel G. Dmitriev, *Narodonaselenie Moldavii* (Kishinev, 1973), analyses demographic trends on the basis of censuses between 1772 and 1803. The village has received more attention than cities and towns. Ecaterina Negruţi, *Satul moldovenesc în prima jumătate a secolului al XIX-lea; Contribuţii demografice* (Iaşi, 1984), is comprehensive. Standing on the boundary of sociology and history is Henri H. Stahl's massive incursion into the economic and social structure of the communal village, *Contribuţii la studiul satelor devălmaşe româneşti,* 3 vols. (Bucharest, 1958–65). There is a shortened version in French: *Les Anciennes Communautés villageoises roumaines* (Paris, 1969). On the urban middle class Constantin C. Giurescu, *Contribuţiuni la studiul originilor şi dezvoltării burgheziei române pînă la 1848* (Bucharest, 1972), carefully charts its emergence in the first half of the nineteenth century, and Stela Mărieş, *Supuşii străini din Moldova în perioada 1781–1862* (Iaşi, 1985), investigates the impact of privileged foreigners on urban society.

Historians of agriculture have given particular attention to the control of land and the relations between landlords and peasants. Notable surveys are V. Mihordea, *Maîtres du sol et paysans dans les Principautés Roumaines au xviiie siècle* (Bucharest, 1971), and Florin Constantiniu, *Relaţiile agrare din Ţara Românească în secolul al xviii-lea* (Bucharest, 1972). Sergiu Columbeanu, *Grandes exploitations domaniales en Valachie au xviiie siècle* (Bucharest, 1974), is a pioneering investigation of the organization of great estates, and Vasile Neamţu, *La Technique de la production céréalière en Valachie et en Moldavie jusqu'au xviiie siècle* (Bucharest, 1975), is concerned with tools, methods, and crops. The nature and effects of the leasing of land on agricultural production are examined in Ioana Constantinescu, *Arendăşia în agricultura Ţării Româneşti şi a Moldovei pînă la Regulamentul Organic* (Bucharest, 1985). Of numerous collections of documents on agriculture, especially valuable on tithes, clacă, and the control of land is *Documente privind relaţiile agrare în veacul al xviii-lea,* i. *Ţara Romînească* (Bucharest, 1961), and ii. *Moldova* (Bucharest, 1966).

Cities and urbanization have been relatively neglected. Valuable for economic and social life are Dan Berindei, *Oraşul Bucureşti: Reşedintă şi capitală a Ţării Romîneşti, 1459–1862* (Bucharest, 1963); *Istoria oraşului Iaşi,* i (Iaşi, 1980); and Constantin C. Giurescu, *Istoricul oraşului Brăila* (Bucharest, 1968). Two selections of documents, George Potra (ed.), *Documente privitoare la istoria oraşului Bucureşti (1594–1821)* (Bucharest, 1961) and *(1634–1800)* (Bucharest, 1982), illuminate the economic concerns of the well-to-do of Bucharest.

On economic activity outside agriculture two comprehensive studies reveal the complexity of the guild system: Eugen Pavlescu, *Economia breslelor în Moldova* (Bucharest, 1939), analyses the organization and religious, moral, and economic character of the guilds, and Şefan Olteanu and Constantin Şerban, *Meşteşugurile din Ţara Românească şi Moldova în evul mediu* (Bucharest, 1969), extend these concerns to both principalities and the countryside. Studies of Romanian commerce have focused particularly on its integration into the Western European network of international trade. Nicolae Iorga, *Istoria comerţului românesc; epoca mai nouă* (Bucharest, 1925), is an early attempt at synthesis that emphasizes the revolutionizing effect of the growing trade with the West. Andrei Oţetea, *Pătrunderea comerţului românesc în circuitul internaţional* (Bucharest, 1977), makes th same point and brings a rigorous analytic approach to the problem. The fullest account of fairs is Georgeta Penelea, *Les Foires de la Valachie pendant la période 1774–1848* (Bucharest, 1973). Dumitru Z. Furnică, *Din istoria comerţului la Români* (Bucharest, 1908), is a collection of documents which reveals the importance of the wholesale trade in foodstuffs. Essential for an understanding of both the mechanisms of moneylending and the growth of a credit mentality is G. Zane, *Economia de schimb în Principatele Române* (Bucharest, 1930).

3. THE SPIRIT OF THE TIMES, 1774–1829

Fundamental for the political and social thought of the *boiers* is Vlad Georgescu, *Ideile politice şi iluminismul în Principatele Române, 1750–1831* (Bucharest, 1972) (English edn. *Political Ideas and the Enlightenment in the Romanian Principalities, 1750–1831* (Boulder, Colo., 1971)). Georgescu has also published *Mémoires et projets de réforme dans les Principautés Roumaines, 1769–1830* (Bucharest, 1970), a selection of texts revealing the aims of the *boiers* in domestic and international affairs. Equally valuable for the prevailing mental climate are the sensitive readings of literary texts by Alexandru Duţu, *Coordonate ale culturii româneşti în secolul XVIII (1700–1821)* (Bucharest, 1968). Numerous authors emphasize the enduring influence of the Enlightenment. Ovidiu Papadima, *Ipostaze ale iluminismului românesc* (Bucharest, 1975), investigates the reception of the Enlightenment in the principalities and Transylvania. D. Popovici, *La Littérature roumaine à l'époque des lumières* (Sibiu, 1945), focuses on the expression of the ideas and spirit of the Enlightenment in a variety of literary genres on both sides of the Carpathians. The essays in Pompiliu Teodor (ed.), *Enlightenment and Romanian Society* (Cluj-Napoca, 1980), make plain the diversity of Romanian responses to the Enlightenment. Other scholars, such as Mircea Anghelescu, *Preromantismul românesc* (Bucharest, 1971), have discerned the strivings of Romanticism even as the Enlightenment held sway. The role of the Greek language and learning as conduits for the Enlightenment in the principalities is assessed by Ariadna Camariano-Cioran, *Academiile domneşti din Bucureşti şi Iaşi* (Bucharest, 1971) (expanded French edn. *Les Académies princières de Bucarest et de Jassy et leurs professeurs* (Thessaloniki, 1974)), and by Cornelia Papacostea-Danielopolu, *Literatura în limba greacă din Principatele Române (1774–1830)* (Bucharest, 1982).

All the above authors deal with the influence of the West, and it is evident that French literature and thought enjoyed pride of place. The classic account, Pompiliu Eliade, *De l'influence française sur l'esprit public en Roumanie* (Paris, 1898) (in Rumanian: *Influenţa franceză asupra spiritului public în România* (Bucharest, 1982)), leaves little doubt as to their effect. The studies in Alexandru Zub (ed.), *La Révolution française et les Roumains* (Iaşi, 1989), show how the ideas of the French Revolution in diluted form filtered into intellectual life and aroused expectations of emancipation from foreign domination. At the same time movements for renewal occurred within traditional, Orthodox society, one of which Sergii Chetverikov, *Starets Paisii Velichkovskii* (Belmont, Mass., 1980), eloquently describes.

4. THE BEGINNINGS OF A MODERN STATE

The uprising led by Tudor Vladimirescu has been subject to diverse interpretations. The standard accounts by Andrei Oţetea, *Tudor Vladimirescu şi revoluţia din 1821* (Bucharest, 1971), and Dan Berindei, *L'Année révolutionnaire 1821 dans les Pays roumains* (Bucharest, 1973) (updated edn. *Revoluţia română din 1821* (Bucharest, 1991)), have been challenged by Mircea T. Radu, *1821; Tudor Vladimirescu şi revoluţia din Ţara Românească* (Craiova, 1978), who takes a fresh look at widely held assumptions. The most extensive collection of sources is *Documente privind istoria Romîniei: Răscoala din 1821*, 5 vols. (Bucharest, 1959–62). On political developments following the suppression of the uprising Ioan C. Filitti, *Frământările politice şi sociale în Principatele Române de la 1821 la 1828* (Bucharest, 1932), remains the fullest account.

Two comprehensive surveys cover the crucial political, economic, and social questions of the 1830s and 1840s: Gheorghe Platon, *Geneza revoluţiei române de la 1848* (Iaşi, 1980) and Gheorghe Platon, *Moldova şi începuturile revoluţiei de la 1848* (Chişinău, 1993). Vladimir Diculescu, *Bresle, negustori şi meseriaşi în Ţara Românească (1830–1848)* (Bucharest, 1973), describes the economic conditions which promoted the growth of the middle class. On the period of the Russian occupation Ioan C. Filitii, *Principatele Române de la 1828 la 1834* (Bucharest, 1934), analyses the drafting and contents of the Organic Statutes, and Vladislav I. Grosul, *Reformy v Dunaiskikh kniazhestvakh i Rossiia* (Moscow, 1966), explains Russia's aims and evaluates Paul Kiselev's activities. A mine of information on the reigns of the princes after the Russian occupation is Ioan C. Filitti, *Domniile române sub Regulamentul Organic, 1834–1848* (Bucharest, 1915). D. Ciurea, *Moldova sub domnia lui M. Sturza* (Iaşi, 1947), is the most extensive account of Mihai Sturdza's reign. G. Zane, *Le Mouvement révolutionnaire de 1840* (Bucharest, 1964), investigates the origins and character of the Filipescu 'conspiracy' and of secret societies in general. Broad currents of political thought in the first half of the nineteenth century are covered in Valeriu Şotropa, *Proiectele de constituţie, programele de reforme şi petiţiile de drepturi din Ţările Române* (Bucharest, 1976). The following volumes in the Hurmuzaki collection of documents, which was mentioned earlier, provide valuable information about political events in the principalities and Russian involvement: xvii. *Corespondenţa diplomatică şi rapoarte consulare franceze, 1825–1846* (Bucharest, 1913), and xxi. *Corespondenţa diplomatică şi rapoarte consulare austriace, 1828–1836* (Bucharest, 1942).

Romanticism has received more attention than other intellectual currents of the period. Paul Cornea, *Originile romantismului românesc* (Bucharest, 1972), is a many-sided investigation of the beginnings and early manifestations of the Romantic spirit in literature and society generally. D. Popovici, *Romantismul românesc* (Bucharest, 1969), surveys key trends and evaluates major and minor practitioners, and Elena Tacciu, *Romantismul românesc; un studiu al arhetipurilor*, i (Bucharest, 1982), presents the unique features of Romanian Romanticism within a broad European context. N. I. Apostolescu, *L'Influence des romantiques français sur la poésie roumaine* (Paris, 1909) is a study of French inspiration and models. On the great literary entrepreneur of the period Mircea Anghelescu, *Ion Heliade*

Rădulescu (Bucharest, 1986), offers a sensitive intellectual portrait, and D. Popovici, *Ideologia literară a lui I. Heliade Rădulescu* (Bucharest, 1935), examines his aesthetic theory and practice. Maria Platon, *Dacia literară* (Iaşi, 1974), describes the foundations of literary *paşoptism*, and Alexandru Zub, *Mihail Kogălniceanu istoric* (Iaşi, 1974), the intellectual journey of the current's principal animator. Mihail Kogălniceanu, *Opere*, i (Bucharest, 1974) and ii (Bucharest, 1976), contain his literary and historical writings of the period.

5. THE ROMANIANS OF THE HABSBURG MONARCHY

The growing national consciousness of the Romanians of Transylvania in the eighteenth century is the subject of two penetrating studies: David Prodan, *Supplex Libellus Valachorum: Din istoria formării naţiunii române* (Bucharest, 1984) (English edn. *Supplex Libellus Valachorum* (Bucharest, 1971)), which places Romanian thought and aspirations in a European context, and Zoltán I. Tóth, *Az erdélyi román nacionalizmus első százada, 1697– 1792* (Budapest, 1946), the product of intensive researches in Transylvanian administrative archives. Ladislau Gyémánt, *Mişcarea naţională a Românilor din Transilvania între anii 1790– 1848* (Bucharest, 1986), is the standard work on Romanian political activity after the Supplex Libellus Valachorum. Keith Hitchins, *The Idea of Nation; the Romanians of Transylvania, 1691–1849* (Bucharest, 1985 and 1988), takes a long view of the develop-ment of national consciousness.

Serfdom, the main fact of life for the majority of peasants, is analysed in all its variety in David Prodan, *Problema iobăgiei în Transilvania, 1700–1848* (Bucharest, 1989), the product of a lifetime of fundamental research. Essential, too, is Zsolt Trócsányi, *Az erdélyi parasztság története, 1790–1849* (Budapest, 1956). David Prodan, *Răscoala lui Horea*, 2 vols. (rev. edn. Bucharest, 1984), an investigation of the origins and nature of the great peasant uprising in 1784–5, is a masterpiece of historical reconstruction and interpretation. Emanuel Turczynski, *Konfession und Nation* (Düsseldorf, 1976), makes valuable compari-sons between Romanian and Serbian cultural aspirations.

Historical writing on the two Rumanian churches is often partisan. Fundamental for understanding the condition of the Orthodox Church after the Union with Rome, especially the movements of resistance led by Visarion Sarai and Sofronie of Cioara, is Silviu Dragomir, *Istoria desrobirei religioase a Românilor din Ardeal în secolul XVIII*, 2 vols. (Sibiu, 1920–30). Ioan N. Beju and Keith Hitchins, *Biserica Ortodoxă Română în secolul XVIII: Conscripţii. Statistici* (Urbana, Ill., 1991), adduces new information about the admin-istrative structure of the Orthodox Church and the condition of its clergy. On the Uniate Church Augustin Bunea, *Din istoria Românilor: Episcopul Ioan Inocenţiu Klein (1728–1751)* (Blaj, 1900), remains the only full-length study of Bishop Klein's life and career. It may be supplemented by Francisc Pall, *Ein Siebenbürgischer Bischof im Römischen Exil: Inochentie Micu-Klein (1745–1768)* (Cologne, 1991), which shows how Klein continued to promote his ideas after his departure into exile. Augustin Bunea, *Episcopii Petru Paul Aron şi Dionisiu Novacovici* (Blaj, 1902), describes the efforts of Klein's successors to defend and strengthen the Uniate Church.

Studies on the historians and philologists of the latter eighteenth and early nineteenth century emphasize their links to the Enlightenment. Besides Popovici, *La Littérature roumaine à l'époque des lumières*, mentioned earlier, Dumitru Ghişe and Pompiliu Teodor, *Fragmentarium iluminist* (Cluj, 1972), contains perceptive essays on Micu, Şincai, and Maior and is essential reading. The same authors provide insight into the spirit of the age in their introduction to Samuil Micu, *Scrieri filozofice* (Bucharest, 1966). The principal biographies of Micu's colleagues are Mircea Tomuş, *Gheorghe Şincai; viaţa şi opera* (Bucharest, 1965), and Maria Protase, *Petru Maior: un ctitor de conştiinţe* (Bucharest, 1973).

The most thorough social and intellectual portrait of the generation of 1848 is George E. Marica *et al., Ideologia generaţiei române de la 1848 în Transilvania* (Bucharest, 1968). Marica has also written a series of essays on intellectual life, *Studii de istoria şi sociologia culturii române ardelene din secolul al xix-lea*, i (Cluj-Napoca, 1977), and has analysed and compiled a bibliography of one of the generation's leading organs, *Foaie pentru minte, inimă şi literatură* (Bucharest, 1969). Of several biographies of George Bariţiu, the fullest is Vasile Netea, *George Bariţiu. Viaţa şi activitatea sa* (Bucharest, 1966). The essays in George E. Marica, *Studii de istoria şi sociologia culturii române ardelene din secolul al xix-lea*, ii (Cluj-Napoca, 1978), form a many-sided intellectual portrait of Bariţiu. An indispensable source of information about the political activities and aspirations of Romanian intellectuals is their correspondence with Bariţiu between 1836 and 1893: Ştefan Pascu *et al.*, (eds.), *George Bariţ şi contemporanii săi*, 7 vols. (Bucharest, 1973–85). There is no up-to-date biography of Simion Bărnuţiu. G. Bogda-Duică, *Viaţa şi ideile lui Simion Bărnuţiu* (Bucharest, 1924), contains a wealth of information, and Petre Pandrea, *Filosofia politico-juridică a lui Simion Bărnuţiu* (Bucharest, 1935), analyses the sources of his thought about nation and state.

The history of Bukovina has been sorely neglected, because of the political conditions prevailing after the Second World War until 1989. The following works provide a useful introduction to the history of the region under Austrian administration, but are marked by strong national feeling. Ion Nistor, *Istoria Bucovinei* (Bucharest, 1991), completed before 1950, covers cultural and economic as well as political matters. The same author's *Der Nationale Kampf in der Bukowina* (Bucharest, 1919) describes the struggle between Romanians and Ruthenians, and his *Istoria bisericii din Bucovina* (Bucharest, 1916) focuses on the Orthodox Church as a national institution. Mihai Iacobescu, *Din istoria Bucovinei*, i (Bucharest, 1993), detailed and well documented, is evidence of renewed scholarly interest in the history of the region.

6. 1848

Several works cover the revolution of 1848 in all the lands inhabited by Romanians. Cornelia Bodea, *Lupta Românilor pentru unitatea naţională, 1834–1849* (Bucharest, 1967) (English edn. *The Romanians' Struggle for Unification, 1834–1849* (Bucharest, 1970)), is concerned especially with the organizations of the generation of 1848 and their aim to bring about the political union of all Romanians. Similar in subject-matter, but more detailed on the revolution itself is Apostol Stan, *Revoluţia română de la 1848* (Bucharest, 1987). Of individual intellectuals, Nicolae Bălcescu has received the most attention. The best starting place is probably G. Zane, *N. Bălcescu: Opera, omul, epoca* (Bucharest, 1975), a comprehensive examination of Bălcescu's thought and of his role in the events of the period. G. Zane and Elena G. Zane have edited Bălcescu's works: *Opere*, 4 vols. (Bucharest, 1974–90), which contain his historical, political, and economic writings and correspondence. George Fotino, *Din vremea renaşterii naţionale a Ţării Româneşti; boierii Goleşti*, i–ii (Bucharest, 1939), assesses the contribution of the Golescu brothers to the national revival largely through their correspondence, and Anastasie Iordache, *Goleştii; locul şi rolul lor în istoria României* (Bucharest, 1979), brings an up-to-date interpretation to the subject. On Dumitru Brătianu, Alexandru Cretzianu, *Din arhiva lui Dumitru Brătianu,* i (Bucharest, 1933), contains a short, authoritative biography and a selection of correspondence. Historians have judged the sojourn of Romanian forty-eighters in Paris and their contacts with French intellectuals to have been decisive on their thought. Aspects of this fruitful relationship are discussed in Jean Breazu, *Edgar Quinet et les Roumains* (Paris, 1928); Ion Breazu, *Michelet şi Românii* (Cluj, 1935); and Olimpiu Boitoş, *Raporturile Românilor cu Ledru-Rollin şi radicali francezi în epoca revoluţiei dela 1848* (Bucharest, 1940). Apostol Stan, *Le Problème agraire pendant la révolution de 1848 en Valachie* (Bucharest, 1971), evaluates the role of intellectuals in agrarian reform.

There are numerous collections of documents. Fundamental are: *Anul 1848 în Principatele Române,* 6 vols. (Bucharest, 1902–10), which contains official and private correspondence, government documents, and excerpts from the press; Cornelia Bodea, *1848 la Români,* 2 vols. (Bucharest, 1982), which offers a similar and well-edited variety of materials; and *Documente privind revoluţia de la 1848 în Ţările Române: B. Ţara Românească (12 martie 1848–21 aprilie 1850)* (Bucharest, 1983), which includes the official correspondence of the British consul in Bucharest.

On the Romanian movement in the Habsburg monarchy two works describe the aims and organization of the intellectuals in Transylvania: Silviu Dragomir, *Studii şi documente privitoare la revoluţia Românilor din Transilvania în anii 1848–49,* v (Cluj, 1946), which takes events up to the autumn of 1848, and Victor Chereşteşiu, *Adunarea naţională de la Blaj* (Bucharest, 1966), which describes the mobilization of the Romanians in the spring of 1848. A contemporary account of the period between the spring of 1848 and the summer of 1849 is Alexandru Papiu-Ilarian, *Istoria Românilor din Dacia Superioară,* ii (Vienna, 1852), and iii (Sibiu, 1943). On Romanian leaders, besides the studies of Bariţiu and Bărnuţiu already mentioned, Silviu Dragomir, *Avram Iancu* (Bucharest, 1965), draws a comprehensive portrait of an idealist and the chief Romanian military hero of the revolution, and Nicolae Popea, *Memorialul Archiepiscopului şi Metropolitului Andreiu baron de Şaguna, sau luptele politice-naţionale ale Românilor, 1846–1873,* i (Sibiu, 1889), allows a rich variety of sources to explain the motives and actions of the official leader of the Romanian nation. There are two extensive collections of sources: Dragomir, *Studii şi documente,* i–iii (Sibiu-Cluj, 1944–6), which includes materials from archives in Transylvania and Budapest, and *Documente privind revoluţia de la 1848 în Ţările Române. C. Transilvania,* i–v (Bucharest, 1977–92), which has reached June 1848 and when completed will undoubtedly be the most comprehensive corpus available. On the Banat the best survey is I. D. Suciu, *Revoluţia de la 1848–1849 în Banat* (Bucharest, 1968). In the absence of a comparable monograph on Bukovina, the general works cited above need to be consulted.

The political aspirations and institution building of the Romanians of Transylvania after the revolution of 1848 are described in Keith Hitchins, *Orthodoxy and Nationality* (Cambridge, Mass., 1977). Simion Retegan, *Dieta românească a Transilvaniei* (Cluj-Napoca, 1979), analyses the Romanians' participation in the constitutional experiments of the 1860s. Of the few collections of sources, Mihail Popescu, *Documente inedite privitoare la istoria Transilvaniei între 1848–1859* (Bucharest, 1929), is indispensable for the decade of absolutism, and Teodor V. Păcăţian, *Cartea de aur, sau luptele politice-naţionale ale Românilor de sub coroana ungară*, ii–iii (Sibiu, 1904–5), covers the political activities of the Romanians between 1860 and 1865.

7. THE UNITED PRINCIPALITIES

The central theme of historiography on the 1850s and 1860s is the struggle by the Romanian élite to achieve the union of the principalities and independence. Dan Berindei, *Epoca Unirii* (Bucharest, 1979), provides a general survey of the period, emphasizing domestic political and economic developments. The standard account of the diplomatic manœuvrings of the great powers remains T. W. Riker, *The Making of Roumania* (London, 1931). It should be read in conjunction with Leonid Boicu, *Diplomaţia europeană şi triumful cauzei române 1856–1859* (Iaşi, 1978), a well-documented study of the intertwining of Romanian aspirations and great-power rivalries. Austria's economic and political interests in the principalities and opposition to their union are explained in L. Boicu, *Austria şi Principatele Române în vremea războiului Crimeii 1853–1856* (Bucharest, 1972), and R. V. Bossy, *L'Autriche et les Principautés-Unies* (Bucharest, 1938). On Russia's role both V. N. Vinogradov, *Rossiia i ob'edinenie rumynskikh kniazhestv* (Moscow, 1961), which discusses official policy up to the election of Cuza as prince, and E. E. Chertan, *Russko-rumynskie otnosheniia v 1859–1863 godakh* (Kishinev, 1968), which traces the development of relations with the United Principalities, draw extensively on Russian archival sources. Barbara Jelavich, *Russia and the Rumanian National Cause, 1858–1859* (Hamden, Conn., 1974), brings to light new information from the papers of the Russian consul-general in Bucharest. Her balanced account of Russo-Romanian relations, *Russia and the Formation of the Romanian National State, 1821–1878* (Cambridge, 1984), provides historical perspective on the union of the principalities.

The contributions of the Romanians themselves to the cause of union are evaluated in Dumitru Vitcu, *Diplomaţii Unirii* (Bucharest, 1979). The work of Romanian exiles in Western Europe was important, too, as is evident in N. Corivan, *Din activitatea emigranţilor români în Apus (1853–1857)* (Bucharest, 1931), and the correspondence of Dumitru Brătianu in Cretzianu, *Din arhiva lui Dumitru Brătianu*, ii (Bucharest, 1934). The most authoritative biography of the chief architect of the United Principalities is Constantin C. Giurescu, *Viaţa şi pera lui Cuza Vodă* (Bucharest, 1966). The essays in *Cuza Vodă in memoriam* (Iaşi, 1973) provide a comprehensive overview of the prince's aims and accomplishments. The importance of economic cooperation between the principalities in preparing the way for their administrative union is assessed by Adrian Macovei, *Moldova şi Ţara Românească de la unificarea economică la unirea politică din 1859* (Iaşi, 1989). Two collections of sources are indispensable: Dimitrie A. Sturdza et al., *Documente relative la istoria renaşterei României*, ii–x (Bucharest, 1889–1909), which contains materials of every kind on the 1850s, and *Documente privind unirea Principatelor*. i, iii (Bucharest, 1961–3), on domestic politics, and ii, vi–vii (Bucharest, 1959–84), on international relations, notably Austrian consular reports and French and British diplomatic correspondence, 1856–9.

On political parties Apostol Stan, *Grupări şi curente politice în România între unire şi independenţă 1859–1877*, is a valuable introduction to liberal and conservative currents. Anastasie Iordache, *Originile conservatorismului politic din România şi rezistenţa sa contra procesului de democratizare, 1821–1882* (Bucharest, 1987), traces the rise of conservatism as a coherent political force. No such study of liberalism exists, but Marin Bucur, *C. A.*

Rosetti: Mesianism și donquijotism revoluționar (Bucharest, 1970), delineates the features of its radical variant. Ion C. Brătianu has been badly neglected. For the decade before the union recourse must be had to his own writings in Ion C. Brătianu, *Acte și cuvântări*, i/1 (Bucharest, 1938).

Works on the economy have focused on agriculture. Ilie Corfus, *Agricultura în Țările Române, 1848–1864* (Bucharest, 1982), covers all aspects of its development, and N. Adăniloae and Dan Berindei, *Reforma agrară din 1864* (Bucharest, 1967), describes the enactment and application of reforms. Other branches of the economy have received less attention. A valuable survey, covering industry, commerce, credit, and transportation as well as agriculture is *Dezvoltarea economiei Moldovei, 1848–1864* (Bucharest, 1963).

INDEX